The Private Government of Public Money

Also by Hugh Heclo

MODERN SOCIAL POLITICS IN BRITAIN AND SWEDEN: FROM RELIEF TO INCOME MAINTENANCE

EUROPEAN PROGRAMMES FOR ONE-PARENT FAMILIES (*with Christine Cockburn*)

GOVERNING EUROPE: NEW POLITICS IN THE OLD WORLD (*editor*)

Also by Aaron Wildavsky

IMPLEMENTATION (*with Jeffrey L. Pressman*)

PLANNING AND BUDGETING IN POOR COUNTRIES (*with Naomi Caiden*)

BUDGETING AND EVALUATION IN RECREATION POLICY, OR MONEY DOESN'T GROW ON TREES (*with Jeanne Nienaber*)

THE REVOLT AGAINST THE MASSES AND OTHER ESSAYS ON POLITICS AND PUBLIC POLICY

THE POLITICS OF THE BUDGETARY PROCESS

The Private Government of Public Money

Community and Policy inside British Politics

Hugh Heclo and Aaron Wildavsky

University of California Press
Berkeley and Los Angeles

0679921

67851

University of California Press
Berkeley and Los Angeles

© Hugh Heclo and Aaron Wildavsky 1974

Library of Congress Catalog Card Number : 73-79474
ISBN : 0-520-02497-4

Printed in Great Britain

For Beverley and Mary

Contents

Acknowledgments   ix

List of Abbreviations   x

Introduction   xi

1   *Kinship and Culture: The Expenditure Community*   1

   The Government Community   3

   Mutual Confidence   14

   Common Calculations   21

   Climate   29

2   *The Nuclear Family: The Treasury*   37

   An Introduction to Treasury Norms   40

   The Good Treasury Man   50

   On Making the Impossible Seem Effortless   61

   Forming 'The Treasury View'   68

3   *Village Life in Civil Service Society: Department–Treasury Bargaining*   76

   The Ambience of Collaboration   78

   Strategies and Deals   88

   Underspending, Transfers and Delegation   103

   Role Conflict : The Principal Finance Officer   118

4   *The Earthly City: Cabinets, Politicians and Other Worldly Men*   129

   The Spending Ministers : Fighting your Corner   134

   The Minister's Briefing   138

   The Minister as Combatant   142

   Chief Secretaries : Unsung Makers of Major Choices   151

Chancellor of the Exchequer : Victim or Victimizer
of the Spending Ministers? 159

The Cabinet Carveup – Getting What There is to Give 169

The Treasury and Chancellor Prepare 171

Cabinet Committees 181

The Cabinet Meeting 188

5 PESC *and Parliament: New Machines for Old Problems* 198

The Coming of PESC 202

The Politics of Projection, or Rashomon Revisited 216

Trial by Technique 217

Payoffs and Punishments 226

Incrementalism to the nth Power 238

Parliament : Who Cares? 242

6 *There Must Be a Better Way:* PAR *and the New
Rationalism* 264

Government Reform, British Style 266

PAR Meets the Machine: Or, the Fine Art of
Obtaining Pearls from Clams 276

PAR in Action : What Good Is It? 288

7 *The Politics of Advice:* CPRS *and the Government Centre* 304

The Grit in the Machine 309

Who is Your Client? Who is Your Advocate? 321

Access – The Loneliness of the Long-Distance Thinker 326

The Uneasy Conscience 333

8 *Idylls of the Constitution* 340

Chestnuts We Have Known 341

So What? Expenditure Decisions and Policy Choices 343

Thought and Action : The Philosopher's Stone 360

Government and Action : The Power Complex 373

A Last Word 381

Bibliography 390

Index 393

Acknowledgements

AARON WILDAVSKY wishes to thank the Warden and Fellows of Nuffield College for their hospitality during a year in England when much of the research for this book was completed. Hugh Heclo wishes to thank his wife Beverley for allowing their London home to be turned into an outpost on Whitehall. Both of us also wish to thank the devoted secretaries – Cecilia Dohrmann, Elizabeth Gerring, Beverley Heclo and Mark McLeod – who transcribed innumerable tapes and typed more drafts of each chapter than anyone now cares to remember. We were fortunate in having diligent research assistants who unearthed useful data and helped correct many of our errors: James Boskey, Brian Kettell, Brian Neve, David Smith, and Barbara Wendorf.

We are grateful for the helpful comments on our manuscript from David Donnison, Neville Johnson, Anthony King, Richard Rose, and certain political administrators who must, as always, remain anonymous. Mappie Seabury performed her usual distinguished job of editing portions of manuscript. And last but never least in a book about expenditures, we express our gratitude to various benefactors for indispensable financial support. The Guggenheim Foundation generously supplemented a sabbatical year from the University of California at Berkeley for Aaron Wildavsky. The Warden of Nuffield College, Oxford, D. N. Chester, and the Director of the Institute of Urban and Regional Development of the University of California at Berkeley, Melvin Webber, provided funds for research assistance. The Social Science Research Council in Britain enabled us to conduct a second round of interviews, to supplement our findings with additional research assistance, and to complete the final manuscript.

H.H.
A.W.

List of Abbreviations

CPRS   Central Policy Review Staff

PAR   Programme Analysis and Review

PARC Programme Analysis and Review Committee

PESC Public Expenditure Survey Committee, now also used to refer generally to the yearly Public Expenditure Survey

PFO   Principal Finance Officer, sometimes also identified as a department's Accountant-General

Introduction

No Government has so far yet been prepared to display
to Parliament or to the public the actual processes by
which it reaches decisions in this field....

Sir Samuel Goldman, *Second*
Permanent Secretary of the
Treasury, Public Sector,
23 March 1791 [1]

MONEY TALKS. It speaks to the purposes of men and nations.
Government spending decisions not only affect the public's standard of living but also reflect the standards by which public men
live.

Our first aim is to describe the expenditure process as it actually
operates in British central government. British government is
about many things, but if anything, it is about the process of allocating up to half the nation's resources through public spending.
During 1972/3, British public expenditures were estimated at
approximately £28,000 million, or over £500 per year for every
man, woman, and child on the island. To help pay the bill, Britons
paid about one-fifth of their total personal income into the income
tax and national insurance coffers; no one can be sure how much
they paid through indirect taxation. Surely little the State does,
short of war, is more important than constantly using so much
of the nation's work and wealth. Few other governmental activities
so consistently affect the everyday life of citizens.

Our second aim is to use the expenditure process as a spotlight
for illuminating the characteristic practices of British central
government. Not all public policy resolves into questions of money
and not all questions of money elucidate the political process.

1. H.C. 549 (1970-1), para. 116. All citations in our text use the official
title of the witness at the time of his testimony.

Nevertheless the task of allocating money is the most pervasive and informative operation of government. It tells us how politicians and civil servants co-operate, bargain and fight – both among themselves and between each other. It tells us much about cabinet government, professional administration, parliamentary democracy and a host of other traditionally, and usually formally, understood doctrines. In short, the expenditure process is an immense window into the reality of British political administration.

A peek through that window reveals a fascinating glimpse of how our governors actually govern. How do civil servants use their ministers and get used in turn? What makes some ministers better than others at getting more money from Treasury and Cabinet? Why, when the prizes supposedly go to the swift and the clever, does the slow and plodding minister, impervious to the discomfort of his colleagues, often get his way? Why do Treasury and department officials trade secret information and what do they get in return? If well over 95 per cent of current expenditures are determined by past commitments, what then is the significance of Cabinet decisions? What does 'collective government' mean when it comes to putting public money where the Cabinet's mouth is?

While politicians occupy the headlines and journalists speculate on the hidden significance of Mr X replacing Y, seemingly routine expenditure decisions exciting no visible comment can already have determined the course of substantive policy for years to come. What makes some spending departments, regardless of minister, more successful than others? Why, in the midst of immense money flows, are some policies left in the backwater whilst others bob merrily along on the crest of the wave? Why are certain policies chopped and changed with little apparent regard for the real costs of doing so? When will departments and the Treasury make deals about permissible limits of future spending and when will they fight it out to the last memorandum? What mysterious ingredient enables some common sense reforms to succeed and others to crumble in the Whitehall community? Why are vital public issues seldom decided on their merits? By learning about the politics of public money and of British central government, we shall also have learned something about the interrelation between spending decisions and the public policies that effect all citizens' lives.

Little has been written that would tell anyone how the spending departments, Treasury officials and Cabinet members actually interact with each other and with the world outside to produce the mammoth pattern of public spending. Admirable historical work has given us some knowledge about the control of public monies during former centuries, but evidence on current practices is almost non-existent.[2] This neglect by students of contemporary British government is particularly curious given the preoccupation with the expenditure process among scholars interested in the politics of earlier eras. For generations the fundamental changes in British government, indeed the entire saga of the nation's constitutional history, have been interpreted largely in terms of the struggle for money. Every schoolboy hears the stories of successive struggles between King and nobles, King and Parliament, Commons and Lords.

The struggle for money continues today and remains as politically informative as ever. Its neglect is probably not because 'insiders' will not tell but because 'outsiders' assume they already know. We have preferred to begin by assuming our own ignorance. It is at least one assumption with which few are likely to argue. The cure for ignorance about how something gets done is to talk with those who do it; the cure for the confusion which then replaces the ignorance is to think about what you are told. Almost all the information for this book has been garnered from those who are or have been participants in the expenditure process. But the interpretation and arrangement of the answers are our own.

Our interpretation has been expressed by recasting not simply the answers but many of the questions found in traditional British political analysis. While writing about real-world political ad-

2. Sir Ivor Jennings' *Cabinet Government*, 1st ed. (Cambridge: Cambridge University Press, 1936) still provides one of the best accounts of the expenditure process, particularly for the 1930s. The second (1951) and third editions (1959) do not add materially to the earlier study. Samuel Beer's *Treasury Control*, 2nd ed. (Oxford: Clarendon Press, 1957) contains information about the organisation of the Treasury as a whole in the 1950s and a useful one volume history of the Treasury is Henry Roseveare's *The Treasury* (London: Allen Lane, Penguin Press, 1969). A review of the Treasury's post-war role in managing the economy is Samuel Brittan, *Steering the Economy*, 3rd ed. (London: Penguin Books, 1971). Its formal structure is described in Lord Bridges' book, *The Treasury*, 2nd ed. (London: Allen and Unwin, 1969).

ministration has been notably sparse, there has been no shortage of criticism. The Civil Service has been castigated alternatively for usurping its political masters' power and for being too cautious and unimaginative. Superman and supermouse make odd bedfellows. Worldly ex-ministers declaim that each incoming minister must demonstrate his '*machismo*' to officials as an initiation test of political virility; the more bemused will note that there is always a tendency to blame past errors on malfunctioning in the structure of advice. The hoary problem of whether the civil servant or the minister shall prevail, which we had thought was a subject reserved for professors who could not think of better questions for their introductory students, is very much alive. We want to show why the question as usually put – who has more power over policy – is badly stated along all its dimensions. Policy is not a constant but a variable, and power is not a finite sum but expandable on all sides.

We have also chosen to reinterpret the timeworn debate as to whether the Treasury is too powerful, not powerful enough or, like Baby Bear's porridge, just right. Even inside some parts of government there is a great deal of misunderstanding. The Treasury sometimes is rumoured to be run by cold and humourless men who, like the heartless child genius keeping the insect alive for the pleasure of sticking pins in it longer, delight in protracting the agony of would-be spenders so as to be better able to turn them down more often. Praise of Treasury men, when it suits, comes in terms of logical brains and merciless minds. Being bright and knowingly negative are not characteristics, however, that distinguish Treasury men from those who play similar roles elsewhere in the world. They are all 'no' men, abominable or otherwise.

However quaint and faintly ridiculous the idea may seem at first, the distinguishing feature of Treasury men who deal with public spending is not their intellect or their ideas but their emotions. Their supreme skill lies in personal relations. When they succeed where others fail, it is because they recognise the overriding importance of giving and getting a personal commitment. Bringing colleagues along with you makes sense when, according to the official head of the Civil Service, 'The first thing to be noted about the central government of this country is that it is a federation of departments.'[3] Though political administrators in many countries face a federation of departments, not all have the social sense to make use of that fact. Ultimately, British Treasury men know that their desires cannot prevail unless they maintain a community to support them. That is their central truth.

Anyone can issue a ukase that is ignored when possible, out-flanked when necessary, and, if all else fails, crushed and crumbled between the layers of bureaucracy. People may co-operate when they have no choice; coercion has its uses and is not to be despised. Far better, however, to create a nexus of interest so that co-operation flows from a sense of mutual advantage; better still to undergird the dictates of reason with the ties of emotion, to make community the handmaiden of policy. You go along with the Treasury, then, because you must, because you expect to gain, and, ultimately, because you are part of a civil service society that wants to do so.

We have therefore interpreted our subject matter, not in the usual terms of relative power and divisions of responsibility, but in terms of community and policy. Community refers to the personal relationships between major political and administrative actors – sometimes in conflict, often in agreement, but always in touch and operating within a shared framework. Community is the cohesive and orienting bond underlying any particular issue. Policy is governmental action directed toward and affecting some end outside itself. There is no escaping the tension between policy and community, between adapting actions and maintaining relationships, between decision and cohesion, between governing now and preserving the possibility of governing later. To cope with the world outside without destroying the understandings their common life requires – this is the underlying dilemma facing the community of political administrators.

From the emphasis on community flow many well-known

3. Sir William Armstrong; 'The Civil Service Department and its Tasks', *O and M Bulletin*, vol. 25, no. 2 (May 1970) pp. 63–79 HMSO. Reprinted in *Style in Administration*, Readings in British Public Administration, ed. Richard A. Chapman and A. Dunsire (George Allen & Unwin for Royal Institute of Public Administration, London 1971), p. 318. An additional insightful interpretation is Norman Macrae's 'The People We Have Become,' *The Economist*, April 28 1973, pp. 8ff.

evils – delay, ambiguity, contradiction, self-absorption. Delay arises because of the time-consuming efforts to bring along other officials and departments. Ambiguity helps paper over the cracks of disagreement so that officials can co-operate a while longer. Contradiction emerges out of efforts to appease contending forces, often giving each a little and neither enough. Self-absorption comes from the close proximity of small groups of powerful men who depend on each others' good opinion. They know, if others do not, that today's passionate concern will give way to tomorrow's irrepressible cause and that the gain involved in one current issue must be balanced against the cost of souring relationships for many future concerns. The price of community may be bid too high : the citizens who are to be served and problems that must be met may slowly recede from view until they appear as if viewed from the small end of the telescope, distant, blurry and easily blinked away.

But policy pursued at the expense of community also proves counter-productive. A machine which can meet its first challenge only at the price of self-destructing with the second, third or nth challenge farther down the road is not of much use to anyone. British policy-makers like to be around to fight another day and shrink from any machine that only reminds them of past carnage. This, as we shall see, is what befell certain well-intentioned Cabinet reforms of the 1960s. In 1970, the Central Policy Review Staff was created ostensibly to help the Cabinet look collectively into important issues that used to be the special preserve of individual ministers or of no one at all. Yet political administrators may easily come to resent and fear a man or organisation whose business it is to take the 'larger' view on their departmental business, to do so with the Prime Minister's special favour, and without the hard responsibility of executing policy. Policy may need better intelligence, but community demands that it not be acquired at others' expense.

Like all social scientists, we face the dual task of trying to account for continuity and change. A study of the contemporary expenditure process provides a splendid opportunity to do both. While seeking to describe current procedures in Great Britain, we have also given attention to the past, since many believe that there is little similarity at all between former days and this. Most of what happens must reflect continuity. Spontaneous generation is rare. Old problems – how to apportion cuts, distribute increases – continually reappear; new people continually replay old roles – Ministers gain by doing more in their area, Chancellors of the Exchequer by keeping spending (and hence taxation) down.

Of course there is also change. In British expenditure practice, innovation appears in new machinery: in particular the Public Expenditure Survey Committee, which we believe to be the most important innovation in its field in any western nation. By elucidating the conditions that made this reform possible and contrasting it with others that failed (notably the Cabinet committees of non-spending ministers) we can try to understand the requirements for successful change. So, too, we can contrast American failures to institute programme budgeting with British efforts to avoid these errors through the nascent Programme Analysis and Review Committee. Accumulated experience on how the Cabinet works can be laid against efforts of the new Central Policy Review Staff to improve decision-making at the top.

How can we penetrate the work-a-day world of these political men? The rules by which they live, the customs they observe, the incentives they perceive and act upon are important, not only to them, but to the people they govern. To understand how political administrators behave we must begin by seeing the world through their eyes. The world does look different depending on whether the participant is in Parliament or Government, spending Department or Treasury. Observe a principal finance officer supporting the Public Expenditure Survey, a device which limits his department's spending; we might easily assume irrationality, unless we also knew that the Survey protects otherwise vulnerable programmes. Another man, a minister, might accept in Cabinet a huge cut in his departmental funds without visible protest; others, observing his unhappy fate, learn to go down fighting in full view of Cabinet colleagues and thus of the hundred critical others who will soon know of his (mis)deeds. It is much easier to get a House of Commons Select Committee on Expenditure established than to get Members of Parliament interested in something which they themselves do not see fitting into their career prospects. We tell our tale largely from the viewpoint of participants, then, not to signify our agreement, but to explain their actions. The participant is the expert on what he does; the observer's task is to make himself expert on why he does it.

A happy byproduct of watching how people work together is that you, too, can learn how to work with them. It became obvious at a very early stage that mutual trust was the leitmotif of all working relationships and that in order to be accepted into our chosen political community we had to show ourselves trustworthy. The researcher can begin with letters of introduction from people already so regarded, but this will not take him far. While a letter may get him in the door, its authority will not last beyond introductory civilities. The moment the interviewer shows unfamiliarity with the subject (though why else would he be there?), he will begin to feel himself on the smooth slipway to the outer office. Ministers and officials need to be reassured that they are talking to fellow insiders who will understand what is being said. They also want a return on their investment of time in the form of an exchange of information. Economisers at heart, these political administrators are not used to giving something for nothing. Hence the researcher's dilemma: to learn more he must already know much; he cannot get information without at least a small fund to begin with and he has trouble obtaining that without prior knowledge. No loan without good credit – no job without experience. What to do?

The observer can start accumulating capital by talking to 'ex's', the important men who are no longer active community members but who once participated in Cabinet meetings and negotiations between spending departments and Treasury. Today's details are different, but yesterday's spirit is likely to be very much alive. With a little luck and much perseverance it should be possible to locate others who are not interviewed too often and who will trade a bit of the old for something of the new. From there on it is a matter of nursing your hoard of information carefully so that it will, as the old financial phrase goes, fructify. Once this initial trust exists, officials are anything but faceless men. They are likely to be alert, aggressive, eager to exchange opinions, savouring a good argument with fellow _aficionados_ of their craft.

There were obvious limitations on what we could ask politicians and senior civil servants. We suggested that interviews be granted on the understanding that we would not ask about current cases or personalities, a restriction that widened our entry and avoided the temptation to compete with journalists for current news, which would have been hopelessly out of date by the time this book was published (almost three years after we started work in the winter of 1970) or a pale recollection of the more lurid hypotheses that excite the imagination when real news is temporarily in short supply. Respondents were asked to describe, not who did whom in last week, but how people generally go about doing each other in; not who personally helped them, but where and how they normally look for support. If we did our work well, it should be as nearly relevant in a decade as it is now. Personalities and issues will change, headlines will surely be different, but the main features of the expenditure process, and of the political-administrative culture it reflects, should have longer staying power.

At present, the public can scarcely be said to perceive these features, not even 'through a glass darkly'. The political-administrative culture of British central government is a shadowy realm usually left to chance observations in politicians' memoirs or civil servants' valedictories. For this reason we devote our first chapter to setting out some basic concepts for appreciating the underlying unity behind the expenditure process and British central government. Probably less is known about the characteristic behaviour of civil servants and their political masters than about fertility cults of ancient tribes. We certainly know less about the customs and mores of finance officers and Treasury principals than about witch doctors and faith healers, though each shares a bit of the others' function. Thus Chapter 2 begins at the core of the British expenditure process: the official Treasury and the special culture within which its work on expenditures takes place. From there we branch out (Chapter 3) to explore bargaining between the official Treasury and departments, and between (Chapter 4) ministers and the Cabinet as a whole.

Politics proceeds not only by powerful men bargaining but also by puzzled men learning to adapt their minds and operations to emerging problems. Chapters 5, 6 and 7 examine four important contemporary adaptations in British government – PESC (Public Expenditure Survey Committee), PAR (Programme Analysis and Review), CPRS (Central Policy Review Staff), and Parliamentary Select Committees. We conclude (Chapter 8) by trying to apply what we have learned about public spending to some broader questions of government: what does the expenditure process teach us about political administration and the classic problems of British government? How do expenditure practices affect the substance of public policy? How should advice on public policy be organised at the centre?

Our own view is that the overriding importance of apportioning up to half the nation's income each year throws current arrangements for resource allocation into serious question. The subordination of spending policies to economic policy is now unwise and will, we think, become increasingly unacceptable with the passage of time. The operation of the Treasury, neither moving toward substantive analysis of policies itself nor facilitating the use of outside analysts will, we expect, be still more unsatisfactory tomorrow than it is today. We doubt whether a Treasury that works for the Chancellor of the Exchequer and a Cabinet Office that works for ministers and their departments can provide satisfactory advice to Prime Minister. But it is not Prime Ministers especially who need more fresh air. The entire community is under-ventilated. The need, in short, is less attention to community and more to policy.

Though few readers are likely to come away with the impression that this book is too short, the topics it does cover are vastly exceeded by those it does not. We are not directly concerned with the management of the economy or with such macroeconomic subjects as money supply, interest rates, full employment, and so on. Little is said about the Bank of England, which is not to say we consider it an unimportant institution, but rather that much silence is better than a few ignorant words. This book is about expenditures in the context of British political administration; it is appropriate for us to discuss how various economic formulas are used in the struggle for money, but not whether the economic formula itself was wise or whether the methods by which it was selected are appropriate. Similarly, within the compass of one volume we cannot adequately discuss the intricacies of local authority or nationalised industries' financing.

From some of our language or evidence, a few readers may imagine that we intend to suggest that British political administration is little more than a game played out by insiders in close physical, mental and professional proximity. Those who read more closely will see that, far from thinking ministers and officials are unconcerned with subject matter, we are at pains to show how hard they work at it. But, unlike some people, we do not believe that subject matter is self evident. The issues, substance, content, policy alternatives or whatever one calls it, does not speak for itself inside government. Men must take policy content in their hands and use it, with craftsmanship or clumsiness, sensitivity or dullness, for good or ill. It is precisely because we feel that the subject matter of policies is so important that we consider improvements in the workings of the British executive to be necessary. Our respect for dealing intelligently with the content of particular public policies is, in fact, so great that we have forsworn the temptation to suggest we are treating them in depth, when neither space nor time nor knowledge will permit.

We especially recall the comment of a permanent secretary that our manuscript did not pay sufficient attention to the 'purpose of public expenditure, the considered – if sometimes hard-fought – decisions on the substance of public policy'. But we also recall that he, like most other officials, found even the most general mention of department policy-making to be too sensitive for public consumption. Because our work has concentrated on the interaction between policy and expenditure, we have not been able to give as much attention to the content of policy as we should have liked. Anyone disappointed by our neglect of this and a host of other important subjects is encouraged to bring his labours to the task, recognising that others' precepts for a more adequate account and their practice in providing the information to write it are likely to be several light years apart.

Our extensive and intensive use of interviews means that we cannot relegate our expression of gratitude to the usual genuflection at the end of a preface. The foremost obligation is to thank our two hundred or so 'co-authors' – officials, retired officials, ministers, ex-ministers in almost all departments, and Members of Parliament, past and present. We owe a special and obvious debt to officials of the Treasury. All our co-authors were gracious; many were more helpful than they imagined; a few were more helpful than they meant to be. It was touching how often they took pains to make sure that we appreciated the deeper, as opposed to surface, operations of British government. Although we were never inclined to do anything else, their entreaties did indicate how misunderstood they feel their work to be. It is impossible not to come away with deep admiration for the general calibre of British political administrators. They deserve better than they have received at the hands of academics. While many may disagree with our interpretation, we hope most will agree that we have captured something of their world.

This is not to say that our study has been all sweetness and light. To understand, even to admire, is not necessarily to applaud. We are, as we were rightfully reminded on several occasions, not inside Whitehall or Westminster or Downing Street. Some respondents doubted that an outsider could ever understand 'what it is really like'; a few seemed to think that a little access, more sherry, and much charm would yield a neat public relations return. Naturally we prefer to play our own game. The chief defence of the social scientist is to subsume his subject matter, competitors and/or critics under a larger category of his own choosing. Like good Treasury men we have tried to get inside the situation without being captured. (A person can study zoology without becoming a monkey, as is well known, though the uncharitable may observe that we have put the null hypothesis under severe strain.) Like good Treasury men, we have listened carefully to each viewpoint but remained presumptuous enough to think that we see the larger picture. Being inside holds no greater monopoly on (mis) understanding than does being outside. Our hope has been that by listening to those inside we might end by knowing as much about some aspects of the process (and more about how the parts relate to the whole) than do participants, if only because these busy men lack the time to meander around, asking colleagues to reflect on their work, writing down the answers and brooding about what it all means.

A final word of warning. From what we know of British political administrators, this book is likely to occasion a new game for insiders, a game concerned with pinning names on the many quotations given in the text. We would warn anyone tempted to play with attributions that we have gone to some trouble to maintain anonymity; sources are seldom what they seem. Knowing how important embarrassment-avoidance is in the close-knit Whitehall village, we have tried to protect our neighbourly co-authors as best we can, disguising where we could not safely confound.

In this, as in other ways, we hope to have merited the trust put in us by many excellent public servants. Just as political administrators value their anonymity and secrecy, so scholars prize different virtues. We have spread our opinions everywhere, from obvious declarations to the slightly more subtle arrangement of material and choice of emphasis. Not merely the last chapter but the entire book is suffused with our values and judgements. In the end we should be judged by the same rules as our political administrators : credit invariably must be shared; the blame is all ours.

1 Kinship and Culture: The Expenditure Community

There is an establishment – or maybe it's more accurate to say a series of somewhat distinct and somewhat overlapping networks.

Cabinet Office official

The trouble is the Civil Service's obsession with the smooth working of the machine.

A minister

It's a question of knowing how to deal with members of one's own group.

Permanent secretary

THE PART of society that interests us is government. Within that sphere we ask: Who matters most? How are they related? Who owes what to whom and how are these obligations repaid? This is kinship. Culture comprises the standards through which these relationships are regulated. How do participants structure competition and facilitate co-operation? What are the ties that bind and the feuds that divide? How is the new accommodated to the old?

British government is an idiom; the usages, manners and deportment of British government are much more than a summed set of rules or powers. Contextual knowledge shades into each particular feature and, if stared at long enough, each specific activity merges into its background. The unfortunate observer is likely to be left facing only the grin of the Cheshire cat, or its British government equivalent – abstract concepts of ministerial responsibility, Cabinet government, civil service anonymity and so on.

Political life at the centre of British government seems a highly interrelated whole, yet words can be written and read only one at a time in strict sequential order. Analysis must subdivide reality to make it manageable. One way of allaying this difficulty is to use concepts which retain at least some flavour of the essential unity amid diversity. Rather than set ministers against civil servants or weigh divided chunks of power among institutions we prefer to speak of political administrators and their community relationships. When we speak of family life in the Treasury or village life in Whitehall we are talking about people united by coherent patterns of praxis, the shared experiences that facilitate learning.

But we are also speaking of people whose common kinship and culture separates them from outsiders. Coherence among British political administrators is expressed through exclusiveness. Their interactions are sequestered within the executive. Apart from the final decisions reached, their behaviour is neither known nor intended to be known beyond government circles. Insiders are overwhelming; outsiders are overwhelmed. In a word, governing public money is a private affair.

This privacy at the political centre can best be introduced in terms of four central features in British government. None is absolutely unique to Britain, but there are probably few nations where all four can be found to the same extent or in such powerful combination. The structure of government community sets the basic outline for distinguishing insiders from outsiders. Mutual trust is a pervasive bond expressing an awareness of how to deal with members of one's own group and, by extension, strangers. Common calculations help political administrators deal with a complex world but also separate them from the layman, who finds it difficult to see why government cannot simply decide on the right policy and execute it. Political climate often gathers force outside government but blows this way and that largely through insiders' concentration on their own reactions and assessments. Community, confidence, calculations and climate are variations on the theme of a shared, exclusive group life in British government.

Because much is shared, much is disputable. Men of common kinship know they can continually bargain and fight for what they want from each other, not in a once-and-for-all massacre, but in the marketplace exchange of an agreed culture, day after day and year after year. The market is political. The medium of exchange is repute. The bargaining counters are public monies. The signals are bids to allocate more to this and less to that governmental programme. Channels of communication are opened by the willingness of participants to listen and to take part in the market : both activities require trust. The kinsmen must speak in common idioms or they will have difficulty in communicating. They must refine the technical apparatus or they will not be able to distinguish their own messages from the confusion of a world filled with static. To interpret messages properly, they need to know who are the senders and receivers, how they relate to one another and what the rules of broadcasting allow them to do. The medium is government and the message is public money. To know who gets what, we must begin with the communal relationships that structure the process of expenditure.

The Government Community

Few people are directly involved. When we speak of political administrators in British central government, we mean the assemblage of ministers and senior civil servants who preside over the work of Cabinets and departments. At the margins of government are a number of important backbench M.P.s, journalists, and interest group leaders, altogether only a few hundred people. The following figure gives some idea of the small numbers at the heart

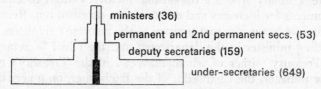

ministers (36)
permanent and 2nd permanent secs. (53)
deputy secretaries (159)
under-secretaries (649)

(Source: Sir Richard Clarke, 'The Number and Size of Government Departments', *The Political Quarterly*, vol. 43, no. 2, April–June 1972, table II).

of British political administration and the tiny corps of Treasury representatives (shaded area). If the figure were extended to cover all civil servants engaged in central administration, the next layer would measure 118 yards; the remaining staff of central government departments would extend almost two-thirds of a mile.[1] Looked at in the round, and with no disparagement intended, political administrators are a pinhead on the body of British central government.

Schematically, these men are arrayed in a maze of departments, ministries, boards, councils, offices, and committees that defy all but the most psychedelic imagination. Disregarding a number of detailed embellishments, we can divide British political administration into three parts: 1) a Cabinet of ministers, subdivided into ministerial committees which are mirrored by comparable committees of civil servants; 2) three central groups – the Treasury, dealing with economic and financial affairs; Civil Service Department, responsible for personnel and management affairs; and Cabinet Office, servicing the Cabinet as a whole and Prime Minister; and 3) nine to ten operating departments, some of which (such as Department of Health and Social Security) spend ten or more times the amount spent by smaller ministries.

The diagram opposite sets out a skeletal picture of one round in the spending process within the Executive. In effect, the starting point is the end of the last round: Treasury and spending departments begin from a series of ongoing discussions about the spending and control of money already allocated by the Cabinet and approved by Parliament. While the department, with the special attention of its Principle Finance Officer, develops its new spending plans, the Treasury is at work assessing the prospects of the economy and the room for new public expenditure. The department's bid for new money goes to the group of officials in the Treasury who are responsible for overseeing expenditure. Arguments for increases and decreases are thrashed out. Remaining disagreements are sent upward to the respective ministers, the spending minister in the department and the Chief Secretary in the Treasury (either of whom may call in the Treasury's most senior minister, the Chancellor of the Exchequer, on a very diffi-

1. The figures are, as of 1 October 1971 (1 August for the Treasury), 684,000 and 6,286,000, respectively and are taken from Clarke's Table II. Staff figures exclude military and overseas locally-engaged staff. In an independent estimate, F. M. G. Willson has put the policy-making centre of British government at 3500 with a nucleus of 350 'of whom not more than 50 – and probably nearer 30 – are "party political",' F. M. G. Willson, 'Policy-Making and the Policy-Makers', in Richard Rose (ed.), *Policy Making in Britain*, (London: Macmillan, 1969), pp. 360-1.

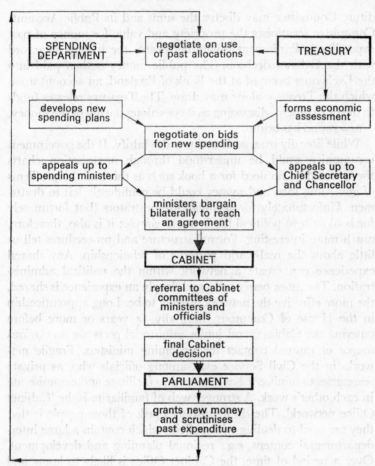

cult matter). The spending bids, containing areas of agreement and disagreement between department and Treasury, then go to the Cabinet for decision by ministers as a group. Treasury ministers will also present their view of the spending total as proposed and suggest whether cuts or increases are necessary to meet the needs of the economy. Discussion is likely to be referred down to Cabinet committees of ministers, which are in turn serviced by groups of civil servants from the departments and Cabinet Office. The resulting settlements and disagreements are then taken back to the entire Cabinet for final decision. While its Expenditure Committee may discuss the sums and its Public Accounts Committee scrutinises the propriety and value for money of past expenditure, Parliament invariably grants the money in accord with the Cabinet decision. The public money is then paid into the Exchequer account at the Bank of England, an account upon which the Treasury alone may draw. The Treasury releases funds to the department, discussing as it goes along the use of the money. A new round has begun.

While literally true, such outlines also falsify. If the government community could be understood through organisation charts there would be no need for a book such as this and the problems of governing men and money could be confidently left to draftsmen. Unfortunately for political administrators (but fortunately for bookwriters) political life is not so simple; it is also, therefore, much more interesting. Formal structure and proceedures tell us little about the real-world patterns of relationship. Any shared experience can create a network within the political administration. The more persistently and deeply an experience is shared, the more effective the network is likely to be. Long apprenticeship in the House of Commons (normally 14 years or more before entering the Cabinet) and junior ministerial posts are an obvious source of mutual contact for upcoming ministers. Fragile networks in the Civil Service exist among officials who, as private secretaries to ministers, have learned to facilitate and commiserate in each other's work. A stronger web of familiarity is the 'Cabinet Office network'. The distinguishing mark of these people is that they are used to dealing with policies which contain a large interdepartmental content, e.g., regional planning and development. Over a period of time, the Cabinet Office is likely to know and call upon these officials when interdepartmental issues arise and people in several departments need to be squared. Probably the most persistent and deeply felt experiences concern the struggle for money. This concern is manifested, as we shall see, in the Treasury network people. The three dozen or so Treasury supply division officials and departmental finance officers naturally are at the heart of the network. Added to these are those permanent secretaries interested in finance and some of the policy people in areas (e.g., housing, local government) intimately connected with financial issues.

A number of the most important features underlying British

political administration can best be appreciated in contrast with the United States. It is, for instance, hardly possible to overestimate the difference in size between central political-administrative establishments in the two nations. There is no such thing in Britain as the equivalent of 40 men with doctorates carrying out research or staffing an office to advise the Treasury or Cabinet, as can be the case in the Executive Office of the President. Four or five would be more like it, two or three not unlikely, and 15 or 20 reserved for only the most strategic purposes. This is not to say, of course, that the effective intellectual weight brought to bear on a question is any different in the two countries.

The small numbers at the centre in Britain mean (apart from the obvious overwork) that the co-operation of operating departments is essential. 'There are so few people that there's no chance of the Treasury taking things over,' a high official explained. 'It is utterly dependent on the departments to do most of what has to be done.' The task of the Treasury, regular Cabinet Office and now also of the Central Policy Review Staff is to work with, through, and around departments. Participants may disagree or be disagreeable, but the system will not work unless they get together. The Treasury itself might do a study here or there, but for most things it must co-opt or coerce or contract with departments. Small size, if nothing else, explains why a member of the Central Policy Review Staff spoke of the need for co-operation in the midst of conflict. 'Sixteen men,' he observed, 'cannot make up a counter-Whitehall'. The smallness at the centre also explains why the Cabinet Office, a handful of top calibre civil servants, is crucial to the conduct of government business. To survive, the Cabinet – like any committee or elementary sea creature – requires a constant and manageable circulation of material through its body. Without the Cabinet Office to direct the mass of department requests, highlight major issues and pace the flow of papers, the Cabinet works would become irretrievably clogged.

British political administration is concentrated spatially as well as numerically. The labels underneath the two slots in the capital's letterboxes capture the spirit perfectly – 'London' and 'All Other Places'. Basically, if you are not in (or within easy reach of) London, you are politically nowhere. Success in political administration depends on the judgements of your fellows and to be judged you must get to London. In a hundred different ways, the provincial can reveal that he is not intimately acquainted with current wisdom. He is likely to be written off, for an important part of merit in the eyes of the judges is an awareness of current modes, even phrases of thought that are the special preserve of those 'in the know'.

Within London itself, the vital political living space is highly compact. Government departments may be huge but their top political and civil service leadership is likely to be concentrated within a thousand yards of Whitehall. No wide Washingtonian avenues string out the leadership of the great departments of State. The office of one's opposite number is probably only a few minutes' walk away. Lunch can be taken within five hundred yards at one of the clubs in Pall Mall or, more convenient still, at the Cabinet Office mess, where Ministers do not come, membership is by invitation only, and attendance is a sign of acceptance into the upper reaches of the Civil Service.

Our study necessarily shares this London-oriented prejudice. Of course, there is much more to political life in Britain than Whitehall talking to Westminster talking to Fleet Street. But the fact remains that to study the actual disposition of public money in British national government, no one need venture very far outside London.

He must, however, listen carefully. Conversation is a quiet code; it is meant to be private. No one has to raise his voice or strain to hear because all who need to know are but a whisper away. Differences are expressed in the absence as well as the presence of sound. Walking the corridors of British departments is quite unlike doing the same thing in Washington. The halls in Britain are virtually deserted except for the tea porters and elderly men and women who guide you and your legitimising slip of paper to the appointed place; in the United States the halls are likely to be crowded, though most in the crowd are strangers and few can give you directions on the mysterious placement of offices. Interest groups in America create more noise because they have to make a fuss to be heard. The hush does not mean that, in British departments, interest groups are negligible. They are not outside the corridors of power, merely difficult to hear as they glide effortlessly into their places as an unofficial appendage of government. British interest groups may have to accommodate themselves to strong ministries, but they can be more confident of getting a good part of what they most want. The current (1973) strained relations between trade unions and government are only an exception substantiating the rule, a cautionary tale to suggest why the usual ways are regarded as the best ways. When community breaks down, the search for intelligent policy may also suffer.

The crucial fact about all this is that British political administrators invariably know or know about each other. Life at the top in Britain may not be warm-hearted chumminess, but it does demonstrate a coherence and continuity unknown in the United States. If co-ordination means the degree to which different participants take each other into account (if only to disagree), then British political administration is extraordinarily well co-ordinated. Whereas in Washington the men who know each other are likely to be connected through common concern with a single area of policy, in London they know each other, period. Just as it would be unthinkable for a Prime Minister not to know personally his cabinet appointees, so everyone who is anyone has got to have extensive personal contacts. Only recently, with the creation of the great conglomerate departments (Trade and Industry, Environment, etc.), has personal acquaintance tended to become more noticeably circumscribed.[2]

Self-awareness easily shades into self-preoccupation. Political administration in Great Britain is profoundly narcissistic because each participant must and does care greatly about what his fellows are doing and thinking. To be more precise, it is not so much the individuals who are self-absorbed, as the governmental apparatus of which they are a part and to which they must necessarily respond. To say that British political administrators care more about themselves than about the country would be wrong; to say that more of their time and attention is devoted to themselves than to outsiders would be closer to the truth. Comparison with a government, such as the United States, at the other extreme of community makes this point clearer.

The politician in the United States is far more of an outsider, even when his party is in power, than his British counterpart even when in Opposition. The American finds government less a re-

2. 'In a small department you know everyone,' an Assistant Secretary told a *Times* reporter, 'but now I only know people of my rank and above. That is a loss for the junior staff because it brings you on if you have personal contact with the people above you.' *The Times*, 8 May 1972.

pository of authority, to be drawn on so long as a few colleagues do not object, than a long obstacle course where the last hurdle is rarely in sight or, better still, a Chinese puzzle in which each solution is merely the prelude to a more ingeniously contrived secret. In the United States the government is elected and the political administrator trying to make policy must then form and reform coalitions within the executive, legislature and interested publics. In Britain the important interactions occur within the government once it has been formed by the Prime Minister. The parliamentary parties are an extension of this fact, in that their opinions of individual capabilities are fed into the forever twisting grapevine of politicians, civil servants and 'lobby' correspondents through which reputations are made and unmade. Even when speaking of what public opinion will stand, the British political administrator, whose career is heavily contingent on the judgement of his fellows, is likely to be referring to his strong sense of opinion within government. His American counterpart tries hardest to infer opinion in society. Each knows where his fortunes must ultimately be made.

If the surface of expenditure politics appears placid within the British executive, this illusion is created because it is manifestly in the interests of political administrators that it should remain so. The fear of creating political embarrassment for ministers is a huge motivating force in Britain. The minister's private secretary, his top officials, the people they deal with in the Treasury, the Cabinet Secretariat, the men in party headquarters – all are incessantly engaged in avoiding the ridicule which the parliamentary Opposition tries to heap upon the Government at every opportunity. It is not only doing well, but not appearing to one's fellows to be doing poorly that is important.

The most publicly visible manifestation of the self-centred, interior perspective in British political administration occurs within the House of Commons. To observe Members of Parliament in the lobbies rating the performance of the day, exchanging (seemingly) revealing titbits about ministers, discussing the latest coup or gaffe; to see how reluctant they are to part from the company of their fellows is to sense that the source of sustenance in their lives comes from within government. Potential ministers' behaviour is tested by scoring points in discussion at the House of Commons. An extraordinary amount of care is lavished on framing and answering questions, not necessarily because they have any intrinsic importance, but because of fear of embarrassment on one side and the hope of inducing it on the other. Where the U.S. political administrator should be able, he need not be clever. His opposite number in Britain, in order to keep up his standing, must show that he is more intelligent than others, or at least that he knows his business in a quick and seemingly spontaneous way.

The House of Commons is a tough league. Everyone knows and talks about everyone else. Egos are always at stake. Men make and lose reputations by the measure of their ability to think on their feet. It is not profundity (though that is not ruled out) so much as facility that matters. M.P.s, and the lobby correspondents who observe them, live a cloistered life in which the points scored in their own arena are the ones that count most. Consider this recent dramatic report in *The Times*:

> Late or soon, the moment comes when a Prime Minister shows that he is master of the House, and it came for Mr. Heath yesterday between 3.15 and 3.35 p.m.... As his gladiatorial performance developed, Mr. Heath brutally savaged Mr. Roy Jenkins, the former Chancellor, with personal insult; left Mr. Michael Foot for once fuming in silence; dominated the Opposition benches; and drew cheers and laughter from his own rank and file at will.... It all provided a notable sign of Mr. Heath's increasing assurance and command, for performances like yesterday's have an influence on Westminster politics that eventually spreads out into the country beyond. The rank and file of governing parties warm to an invincible gladiator, and Opposition parties begin to grow critical of front-benchers who lose every skirmish.

The only thing wrong with the account is the statement that the debate necessarily had implications in the country at large.

The question period in the House of Commons may falsely appear as trivial to an outsider, because a single question or two or three could be so easily evaded. So facile a conclusion would neglect the profound impact of this cockpit on the kinds of men who come forth to govern in Great Britain. Participation in a Congressional Committee, where hours (possibly days) of informed questioning may bring forth far more information useful for legislation, is important as an apprenticeship for making policy, but far less so for impressing colleagues. If human talents were perfectly correlated with a capacity for making the instant and telling jibe, the parliamentary arena might be a superb training ground for ministerial leadership.

Our concern is the Executive; it is an equally if not more exacting arena than the House of Commons, although in a different way. It requires less oratory and more action. Blunders come easy. Where the American seeks to create the power he needs to use, the British leader by contrast must use the power he has. The American political administrator is so preoccupied piecing together *ad hoc* majorities – in committees, the Houses of Congress, the Executive Office, bureaux, departments, commissions, interest groups – that he has little energy or time to worry about the execution of his grand design which, in any event, may bear scant resemblance to the initial proposal. The great American weakness, therefore, lies in implementation. The danger in Britain is just the opposite : the government may agree all too quickly, before the major implications of the policy are understood or the affected interests realise what is about to happen to them, leaving all concerned agape and aghast as the machine implements the policy with its usual splendid impartiality, that is, with equal harm all round. If the time for the American to worry is before his policy is approved, the day of reckoning for the Briton is after. 'My God, we have to be careful here,' a worried minister told us. 'Before you know what is happening the thing is being carried out everywhere, in the most remote corners, and you are responsible!'

Perhaps we are saying no more than that the sense of sovereignty in Britain is immeasurably stronger than in the United States. British political administration is both inclusive and exclusive. It is exclusive in that the Cabinet and national government accept no rivals; it is inclusive in that all necessary authority is generally perceived to be at the centre. Though discrete concessions may be made to all, neither Opposition, nor Parliamentary committees, nor dissident backbenchers, nor local authorities normally are allowed to destroy the main thrust of national policy. One ex-minister summed up what we have been trying to convey when he said that 'the most important distinction in British politics is between the government and everybody else. The government performs, the rest of us just talk. That is why it is so crucial for a minister to defend his department and to seek more for it. What he does matters to a great many other people.'[3] The British political system is organised to produce majorities that can act out their will, provided only that they know what their will is. It is no small proviso.

The two concepts traditionally used to describe British politics at the centre – Cabinet government within a Unitary State – tend to posit the political will of the executive as self-evident; British government is taken as, somehow, always knowing its own mind. Both concepts are still useful primers, as long as we do not try to force them into taking us too far down the road. To speak of a Cabinet government and unitary state does give us a preliminary, general appreciation for the predominance of national over local, executive over legislative perspectives in British political administration. Once pushed on our way, however, we cannot get much mileage out of these formal concepts. When we start using them to account for continuity they splutter badly; when we try to explain change, the knock develops in earnest; and when we turn uphill toward actual practice, it is time to get out and walk. A second volume would be required to study the meaning of unitary state as expressed in relations between national government and local authorities. Here we limit our attention to relations at the centre and to the operation of Cabinet government. But exactly who or what the 'centre' is and how it works, is a nice question. Cabinet government is only the insignia on the coach; we wish to know what goes on inside.

Inside, political administrators are at the wheel, or more accurately, scrambling over the seats to find maps, brakes, and steering devices to help them organise policy advice and make

3. The same thought has been expressed in similar words by another ex-minister, Lord Boyle:

. . . I do not think it takes many Ministers very long to make what is the most important discovery one ever makes in politics; this is that the most important distinction in our whole national political system is the distinction between the Government and the non-Government. . . . As soon as one becomes a member of the Government one has to measure one's words and actions and think in terms of reality, in a way that one does not have to do when the executive machine is not at one's disposal.

Sir Edward (now Lord) Boyle, 'Who Are the Policy Makers?' *Public Administration*, vol. 43, autumn 1965, p. 255.

decisions about spending public money. Kinship tells participants who is who; culture tells them how to act toward each other. But both are abstract concepts. We can begin putting flesh and blood into the subject by turning to the single most pervasive feature of the expenditure process: the relationships of mutual trust among participants.

Mutual Confidence

You grow up together over the years and you know each other; you and the Treasury get used to each other.
Principal Finance Officer

The whole system is largely based on trust in the person.
Permanent secretary

Most see that it pays to be frank with the Treasury.
Treasury undersecretary

Imagine the top layers of the executive arm of British government as a system of reputations. The elements of the system are the holders of top official positions. The counters by which reputations are measured and traded are units of esteem. These counters can be used to help obtain faster promotion or better positions or quicker action or indulgence of policy preferences. Esteem is measured in terms of intellect (is he bright?), influence (can he carry along his colleagues and masters?), and especially in terms of trust (is he reliable?). All three factors combine to affect the participants' sense of mutual confidence.

The number of people involved is at most a few hundred, and they change but slowly. They all know or have heard about each other, and they all enjoy rating one another. Ministers are likely to be aware of, not only each others' political performance, but the exact university degree (first, second or third) that colleagues won and where. There is no permanent secretary who is not prepared to rate the leadership abilities of ministers under whom he has served. No Treasury official of any experience hesitates to judge the incisiveness and reliability of his opposite numbers in the departments. No departmental finance officer worth considering is unaware of the extent to which Treasury supply officials know the substantive merits of the proposals he sends them. The ratings work by slow accretion. It is difficult to get a high rating and equally difficult to lose one. But over the years events reveal to colleagues that some men are bright and others dull; some strong, others weak; some trustworthy and others not.

The one inescapable theme in virtually every interview we conducted is the vital importance participants place on personal trust for each other. By trust one is speaking of personal dependability, 'soundness', a feeling that here is a person in whom one can reliably place confidence and confidences. Mutual trust is considered paramount by officials who know they will have to continue doing business with each other year after year on issue after issue; they believe that, if professionalism means anything, it means knowing how to treat members of one's own group. Trust is vital between ministers and civil servants, each of whom must fight the other's battles, one behind Cabinet doors and in the public arena, the other among the mass of departmental expertise and official encounters. Mutual reliance is important, though as we shall see less operational, among ministers of the government who survive by hanging together against the other party's crowd and an intractable world. Since everyone's prospects for power over policy and authority over decisions depend on the judgement of colleagues, reputation in general is always likely to be more important to participants than is any issue in particular.

From this central place of personal trust, much else follows. The desire to create and maintain trust explains the great dread of being caught by surprise that prevails among both ministers and civil servants. To be surprised is no sin, but to be seen to be surprised decreases confidence and nurtures distrust among colleagues. Avoiding embarrassment to ministers in public, and particularly in the House of Commons, is one of the driving forces throughout British government. Many failings of a minister may be overlooked, but misjudgement and error is far less damaging than to be seen as unsure, surprised, and out of touch with important events. The same motive force operates even more forcefully within the executive itself; ministerial embarrassment and civil servant loss of face are two sides of the same coin. Avoiding a decline in reputation among their peers is a matter of utmost concern to officials who still hope to go further and do more than they have done. Ministers and civil servants who refuse information to Parliament are not dissembling when they lay great stress on the 'embarrassment' that this would cause.[4] Sharing information widely is thought to reduce the scope for ministers and officials to deal with each other in mutual confidence. For those with eyes to see, it is clear which personal working relationships count to these men.

British central government recognises mutual dependance even, indeed especially, in the midst of conflict. Treasury–spending department relations are a superb expression of the networks of reciprocal trust. The top men in the Treasury insist that 'we encourage an almost symbiotic relationship with the departments'.

What is at stake goes well beyond mutual pleasantness. It is a question of building and using personal working relationships. One must do more than simply not mislead others. 'I try to create an atmosphere so they'll tell me things they shouldn't,' a Treasury supply officer observed. 'And I do the same, sometimes sending [the department finance officer] a copy of a paper I have done for my masters. You can't expect to get something for nothing.' Men know they are assessed on their ability to establish confidential relationships. Another Treasury man put it bluntly : 'I think you're judged on how far you manage to get inside the other department. I should have enough contacts to know how things are going. Even if the department's minister wouldn't agree and his civil servants shouldn't say, you should know it.'

The same imperatives apply from the department's side. Civil servants there unanimously agreed that when they had the confidence of Treasury people, they could do things that would otherwise be difficult if not impossible. 'For example,' a finance officer declared, 'you can then simply ring up on the phone and say "I cannot justify this up to the hilt but it has merit. Can I do it?" If there is this confidence the answer will be yes, because he trusts you.' The major task of the departmental finance officer is to obtain support from the Treasury, and without a good personal reputation he is useless to his department. Permanent secretaries have long drawn the necessary conclusions. They will tell you that 'finance officers who lack respect inside the Treasury have got to go'. Another permanent secretary concluded that 'If the Treasury does not have this confidence in you, it will create all

4. See, for example, H. C. 549 (1970–1), pp. 34, 36, 46.

kinds of road blocks and go out of its way to find the cons in your argument.'

The reputations that accrue to individuals carry over to their departments as a whole. After a time departments come to be known as loose or strict, careful or sloppy, sound or wild, or however you put it in relation to expenditures. A Treasury minister observed that the reputations of departments were common currency. 'I knew which departments were very responsible about their spending and meticulous in scrutinising their own expenditures. If the minister from one of these departments said he could not cut any more I would believe him. In other departments I wouldn't. I would raise with my officials my feelings about which departments were hard workers and which weren't, and they generally agreed with me, although they pointed out that in some circumstances I had misjudged one or another department.' Whoever helps one department gain the reputation (deserved or not) of being careful with money and another of being loose, helps or harms their respective organisations a great deal.

How is trust established? The shortest answer by a department finance officer was 'I must be honest'. Another added that 'apart from being frank with the Treasury you must be seen to be frank'. This means, according to a third, that 'you must set out the weaknesses of your case as well as the strengths. The minister, of course, often says he does not want all the arguments put to the Treasury but you do it anyway and argue that your strengths outweigh the weaknesses.' Why, we asked, is it necessary to be so frank? 'Because just as I tell the minister, they [the Treasury] will find out anyway; they are no fools. And if the Treasury have to find out for themselves they will think, without any question, that the weaknesses they have found are more important than any strengths you have presented in isolation.' The idea, as a permanent secretary put it, that 'the Treasury will always catch up with you in the end' is well entrenched. Quite apart from and overriding any of the financial and personnel sanctions at the Treasury's command, there is the sense that such frankness is the way of dealing with someone in one's own group.

Trust is established also by showing the Treasury that the department is well able to look after itself. A permanent secretary, who had come from the Treasury, 'knew you had to show the Treasury that you had a rigorous internal expenditure control system in your own department'. Demonstrating good internal controls fosters confidence and makes the department's life easier. 'Conversely,' observed a Treasury under-secretary, 'if the department has blotted its copybook, the Treasury is suspicious, awkward, and, failing to persuade us, the department has no alternative but to go to the minister'.

Departments are tempted to increase Treasury confidence by overconsulting them so as to avoid any suggestion that things might be going on they did not know about. The Treasury may be brought in at the very first stages and made aware of the pressures 'so they can see we are doing the best we can right from the very outset. This shows them that you are not bullying or rushing your way through the project.' Occasionally, a Treasury man even will be invited to visit field sites and installations 'so that when later we say we have to replace a boiler house they'll have some idea what it's all about'.

But confidence is more than a question of frankness, consultation and internal controls. Treasury people do not like to trust men who are not able. Getting competent work done in departments is one way they have to protect their reputation and learn who to trust. Since they cannot observe the work directly they must take the department official's ability to discuss and defend it as a surrogate of his competence. 'You know that if the person can't answer questions or probes,' said a Treasury Assistant Secretary, 'then he is not a person with whom you can deal on a confidential basis.' A man who can cope with Treasury scepticism earns – and deserves – respect. There is, however, one way a finance officer can still maintain Treasury respect for a poor case. First he must acknowledge that it does not make a great deal of sense; after that password it is permissable for him to say that 'there may be holes, I know, but the Minister wants it and thinks it is politically important'. Then both civil servants can address the question like the insiders they are.

Mutual confidence, particularly at higher levels, is created not only by talk but by action. When a Treasury man speaks of trust, one thing he wants to know is whether the department official can keep his side of the bargain. When they agree that 'as between ourselves, this is the line we will take with our ministers', the Treasury man expects that the minister will be briefed accordingly, with a straight face and with noticeable impact. Or as one

Treasury undersecretary put it, 'Can my opposite number deliver his master or not?'

Up till now we have made it too easy : honesty is the best policy and virtue is rewarded. But aside from the usual temptations to 'try one on', real conflicts of interest exist and cannot be avoided. There are multiple allegiances and hence multiple confidences to be kept or broken. The department finance officer cannot always please his permanent secretary, his minister and his Treasury counterpart. The Treasury principal cannot always please his departmental counterpart and his organisational superior. Trust in one context may appear to be betrayal in another.

How much do departmental and Treasury civil servants tell each other? There are hard choices to be made and responses vary. The most typical is that 'you are still not playing double dummy' and do not say all. 'I share as much with the Treasury as I can in order to establish trust,' a department finance officer said. 'But that last bit of information you don't share. This is where you have to consider your loyalty to the minister.' Common interests in expediting work, making a knowledgeable appearance, and building confidence normally suggest that a two-way traffic would be mutually advantageous.

Let us take two views of the same situation : first the finance officer. How much, we asked, do you share? 'The extent of sharing depends on how much I am trusted and I trust the man who works on this in the Treasury. I may write a letter to him and then call up and say I haven't said it all and there is additional information of which he ought to be aware. This is background. He may brief his minister and send me a personal copy of the brief he put forward. This is the essence of the British system.' A high Treasury official did not disagree at all. 'It's very common to have the department's finance officer dictating over the phone to us the points to be made against his own case – things he can't say to his own department for fear of making his life there impossible. The reverse also often happens. Treasury people will tell the Finance Officer that 'the case is good but don't say it that way, say it this way instead'.

But by no means need interchanges always be so overt. The norm of frankness, as many noted, is particularly difficult to apply when a department official disagrees with his minister's clear wishes to do something. 'You can usually sense these things,' a retired ex-official from high in the Treasury reflected, 'though nothing's said in so many words.' A current Treasury man of equal prominence confirmed this : 'If a minister wants to do something that isn't sensible, it will be perfectly clear that he has instructed his officials to come along to us. We know they're under orders and it conditions our reactions. So when we're awkward, the department people go back and tell their master he'll have to take over. There's a feeling that if a minister wants something silly, let him fight for it himself.' None would characterise this behaviour as ' "sneaking" to the Treasury'. Nor, with the trained sensitivities of these men, is there any need to do so.

Civil service coziness is reined by their need for ministerial support. Personal trust between officials is unlikely to produce significant results without a complementary confidence between officials and their ministers. Ministers are expected, in the British phrase, to defend their corner. Extracting money from the Exchequer to support the great interests of his department is one of the prime ways in which the reputation and career of a minister is built. Ministers know that colleagues in the Cabinet and officials within the department are watching their behaviour and will tell others whether they are considered competent people. Here are a series of ministers as portrayed by a high official :

> When you had a good minister like —— you were fine. He was first class, intelligent, ruthless, progressive. He knew where he stood. He was tough in negotiation with the department and with his colleagues. —— was also good. He was extremely intelligent and highly articulate though not as decisive as —— yet he worked like a Trojan. Money rained in on us when he was minister. There was respect in the department for him. Later everything was different. Confidence was lacking. Our ministers were not frightfully bright or determined. We had less income and more headaches.

The weak minister is scrutinised unmercifully by his officials. When we asked how they knew if a minister were strong the answer was that he was sometimes able to persuade them and, what is more important, his colleagues in Cabinet. The weak minister, by contrast, never knows his own position and cannot obtain funds for his officials. Of him it is said contemptuously, 'When he takes the question to his colleagues he loses. The more he says the worse we do. I almost had to ask him to keep quiet because if he said nothing we would not lose as much.'

Similarly, the minister knows that his fortunes depend to some extent on how his officials are regarded by others. When we asked experienced observers how to account for the success of certain ministers in gaining funds, they would often reply, 'In fighting for his corner the success of a minister depends first on personality, second on his reputation among his colleagues, third, what is very important, the reputation of his department at the Treasury.' The better its reputation with the Treasury, the more a department will get and the better its minister will look. He will not have to use his stock of political resources in moving officialdom if his own people can do it for him. Just as officials may have to suffer despairingly with a man who 'is hopeless as an advocate in the Cabinet and with the Prime Minister', ministers may occasionally have to make do with a permanent secretary whose relations with the Treasury are unsatisfactory.

Justification by faith alone is not a Treasury doctrine; good works are required. Trust depends in part on competence – or at least the appearance thereof – and yet spending issues are vast in number, complex in their interrelationships and uncertain in their ramifications. How, then, can anyone make competent decisions about what should be spent on the vast range of government activities?

Common Calculations

> Every government learns pretty quickly that it is easier to talk about restraining public expenditure . . . than to make cuts which can have any immediate impact.
> *Harold Wilson*, The Labour
> Government 1964–1970, *pp. 34–5*

> This is not a *tabula rasa* on which they can write whatever story they wish.
> *Sir Samuel Goldman*, First
> Report from the Select Committee on Procedure, 1968–9, *p. 2*

0679921

Ninety-eight per cent of the expenditures are committed.
All we did is mess about at the margins.

Permanent secretary

No single mind can comprehend the full complexity of all public spending issues. A few of the difficulties involved can be paraphrased from a recent Treasury memorandum by the terms incomparability, uncontrollability and uncertainty. There is no objective criterion for comparing different programmes; many expenditures depend on external events and are thus largely beyond government control; changing economic, political and social circumstances often can have unpredictable consequences for expenditures.[5] All political administrators face these problems and search for ways to simplify the decisions they must take.

Even if one man or group could accomplish the intellectual feat for a single spending decision, it would still be physically impossible to find time to analyse the past commitments, present choices, and future probabilities of all issues. The small size of upper political and administrative levels, a feature which makes personal relationships of trust possible, also makes intellectual shortcuts and labour-saving routines indispensable. For ministers and top officials, the one commodity in shorter supply than money is time. The three dozen or so ministers are occupied by work in Cabinet and its committees, in the House of Commons and their constituencies, as well as contacts with the major interests affected by what they do. The substantive business of their departments probably occupies less than half the working week of ministers. Cabinet government British-style also means that opportunities for collective decision-making are rare and the time for doing so, brief. Since the Second World War the Cabinet at its maximum has averaged 23 members and 90 meetings a year. Thus Sir Richard Clarke, in talking about limits on the size of superdepartments, takes as one outer boundary the amounts of business that a single minister can be expected to handle in Cabinet.[6]

5. Memorandum by the Treasury, 'The Determinants and Objectives of Public Expenditure', H.C. 549 (1970–1), pp. 53 ff.

6. Sir Richard Clarke, *New Trends in Government* (Civil Service College Studies, HMSO, 1971), p. 33.

Treasury people are better off in one respect; men busy with the public sector spend almost all their time on expenditures. But they are worse off in another regard; since their work spans several departments, demands on Treasury men for consistency of decision are heavy. The entire Treasury sector overseeing public spending comprises only 28 people above the level of principal. This terribly small size makes it easy for Treasury people to get to know each other but difficult to probe all bids for spending. If a certain Treasury undersecretary devoted every minute of every working day for a full year simply to reviewing existing government expenditure, he would be able to give perhaps 35 seconds to every £100,000 spent.

'Look here,' retorted a Treasury man in response to an innocent question about the amazing breadth of his knowledge, 'nobody can know all this. It's a bit of a put-on. Most things I just leave alone. I am lucky if I can pick out three or four issues during the year on which to put in some serious time and attention. My job is to figure out where it's worth spending my time and to poke around just enough to know that nothing terrible is happening elsewhere. I capitalise on things I know best and the information I pick up to create the impression that I know more than I do because they won't attempt to bounce one past me if they think I am on to them.'

To make their jobs manageable, the men responsible for making public expenditure decisions use certain short-cuts or rules-of-thumb. Personal trust, which we have mentioned and will repeatedly emphasise, is one invaluable aid to calculation. With such trust, every sum need not be redone, many details can be confidently overlooked, advance warnings can reduce uncertainty, informal chats will distinguish the real fire from smoke-screen issues, and political administrators can more confidently bypass most that goes on.

Probably the most widespread and frequently used aid to calculation is to concentrate on expenditure changes at the margins. Nowhere do the constraints imposed by the past on the future stand out more starkly than in the annual allocation of government spending. The following figure, showing the share of public expenditure going for various purposes, suggests something of this immense inertial weight.

Percentage of total public expenditure (including debt interest)

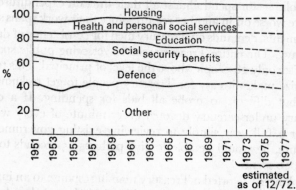

estimated as of 12/72.

(Adapted from *Social Trends*, no. 3, 1972, table 147; and Cmnd. 5178, table 2A)

A Financial Secretary to the Treasury wanted to make sure we understood that 'the margin for real ministerial power in expenditure decisions is seriously limited because most of the total sum is predisposed. There are statutory commitments that are unquestioned as ongoing policies, and there is the natural growth of existing policies which expand in line with the population of beneficiaries or consequent decisions that had to be made by virtue of already existing decisions.' The degree of manoeuverability varies somewhat from programme to programme, but all political administrators would agree with Sir Samuel Goldman that 'the public sector is something that exists. It is the end product of a long process of development and the changes that can be made are subject to pretty severe restraints and limitations.'[7]

How much leeway, then, do departments and their ministers actually have in altering expenditures during a single year? Saying he was giving an informed guess, Sir William Armstrong (formerly Permanent Secretary of the Treasury and later official head of the Civil Service Department), asserted that 'the highest figure I have ever heard anybody put on it is about $2\frac{1}{2}$ per cent . . .' of total public spending.[8] That Sir William was citing a figure toward the high side is indicated by a Treasury memorandum concluding that 'even the important post-[1967] devaluation decisions in-

7. H.C. 410 (1968–9), p. 2.   8. Ibid., p. 33.

volved reducing projected rates of increase over the next two years and affected levels only by $1\frac{3}{4}$ and $2\frac{1}{2}$ per cent'.[9] In view of the strenuous efforts made to decrease expenditures in 1967/8, the scope for major reductions in more normal times appears to be almost minute, more useful for psychological than for any other reason.

The marginality of Labour's post-devaluation cuts were not a function of party but of the reality of government. In June 1970, an efficiency-minded Conservative government came into office pledged to economy; every department was instructed to examine its whole range of activities with a view to eliminating items except those which 'can most appropriately or conveniently be done in the public sector'. The resulting changes announced by the Chancellor simply reduced the projected annual rate of increase in total public expenditure from $3\cdot5$ per cent to $2\cdot8$ per cent. These laboriously-won changes in the course – or rather acceleration – of expenditures are in fact scarcely more than the notional allowance for underspending (shortfall) which the Treasury includes in its expenditure projections.[10]

Our argument is not merely that some expenditures are so committed as to permit only marginal change; it is that virtually all expenditure decision-making instinctively concentrates at these margins. Incrementalism in expenditure is understood and taken for granted by all British political administrators. They know it, live with it, and employ it in their daily work.

Expenditures that have remained unchanged for a long time are likely to be impervious to assault. Examining them is probably administratively difficult and certainly politically unrewarding; opportunities for success are few and the chances of disturbing previously useful relations are many. No one wants to reopen endless series of old quarrels or to fight expenditure battles simultaneously on a hundred fronts. For those who wish to keep expenditures from rising too fast, the appearance of proposed new programmes, or large increases in old ones, offers their best opportunity for seeking restraint before it is too late. Men who wish to do more than has been done before necessarily devote their atten-

9. Treasury memorandum: 'The Planning and Control of Public Expenditure', ibid., para. 28, p. 21.

10. *House of Commons Debates* H.C. 812 (1970–1) col. 117; Cmnd. 4515 (1970) para. 3; H.C. 549 (1970–1), pp. 79 ff.

tion to new proposals with large expenditure implications. The world over, examination of expenditure deals with increase–decrease analysis from an existing base made up of the pattern of past decisions.[11]

There is no reason to believe that the method in Britain has changed since the turn of the century. 'The procedure,' as explained to the Committee on National Expenditure (1922) by experienced Treasury officials, 'was broadly that the estimates of the previous year were taken to form a base line, and that the deviations from that line were arrived at by consultation between the Chancellor of the Exchequer and the minister at the head of the department. . . . The essence of this system was to take the previous year's normal expenditure from which to measure departures.'[12] A statement by a contemporary department finance office could be generalised throughout the entire governmental apparatus : 'We find that a good starting point in our work is to look at the past trends and find out what happened last year. Then essentially what we do is question any new item.'

The current situation was publicly summarised by John Hunt, then Treasury Deputy Secretary overseeing much of the public expenditure sector : 'One must remember in all this that in looking at percentage increases and decreases one is looking at changes at the margin. You have got very big programmes here with commitments which are quite inescapable. . . the adjustments – whether

11. See Naomi Caiden and Aaron Wildavsky, *Planning and Budgeting in Poor Countries* (New York: John Wiley and Sons, 1973); Guy Lord, *The French Budgetary Process* (Berkeley and Los Angeles: University of California Press, 1973); Aaron Wildavsky, *The Politics of the Budgetary Process* (Boston: Little Brown, 1964); John Campbell, 'How Powerful is the Japanese Ministry of Finance?' (Columbia University, mimeographed, 1971).

12. Jennings, *Cabinet Government*, p. 157. Such increase–decrease analysis has always been used to make the Chancellor's case for holding back public spending, though it is of course given little publicity when unfavourable to that case. The Chancellor in 1934, for example, accepted the advice of a senior Treasury official to speak of expenditure restraint only in general terms since, this official observed, 'the facts are all wrong. This year's Supply Services are 1·25 million less than last year's original estimates. . . . There is, therefore, no real basis for quoting effective figures. Moreover, a similar difficulty arises if an attempt is made to compare this year's expenditure with the expenditure of 1931. . . .' T. 171/315 (1934).

the adjustment can be upwards or downwards... are changes at the margin....' [13]

To say that everything cannot be changed at once is not to say that nothing can be altered at all. A few per cent a year add up to substantial changes over a period of time. A total aggregate change of 2 per cent may conceal the fact that several programmes have increased by 6 or 8 per cent while others have gone up only by 1 per cent or have even shown a decrease. The following table shows that while spending changes are marginal, they are by no means equal, either among programmes or within the same programme at different times. But as we shall see at length in chapter five, such statistics tell us little about government priorities and what is happening inside the expenditure community. The numbers are not the story. What they do suggest is that, given we are talking about anywhere from one-third to one-half of total national output (depending on how the sums are done), no one need apologise for devoting his time and attention to marginal changes. No one dealing with the allocation of public money need feel that the area within which he works, though more restricted than many would like to believe, is of less than immense importance.

By observing whether expenditure items have shown stability over time, and by scanning the political environment to see if any change is likely, participants learn by elimination what they can ignore. If they have no reason to propose a change and if others do not, they can let stable numbers lie. Their most objective clues about what is important to others are the percentage increases and decreases in proposed expenditure from the base established the previous year. These are the items others want to change. Reputations are self-assessments drawn on the same type of analysis. A political system in which people know and rate one another creates incentives for the development of comparative measures enabling key individuals to see how well they are doing. After one minister had said in regard to spending that he had gotten his share and perhaps a bit more, we asked how he knew what his proper share was. 'There were,' he replied, 'two and only two objective criteria. One, what had happened before. What was our share of total government expenditure last year? Are we doing as well this year? Two, what is the rate of growth of the department compared with the rate shown by others?'

13. H.C. 549 (1970–1), p. 65.

TABLE I. – *Percentage change in Public Expenditure over previous Year*
(expenditure in cost terms and at 1972–73 outturn prices: absolute amounts shown in parentheses for 1969–70)

Programme	1969–70*	1970–71*	1971–72*	1972–73†	1973–74†	1974–75†	1975–76†	1976–77†
Defence and External Relations	− 8·9% ($£3,324$ m)	+ 1·0%	+ 3·6%	+ 2·0%	+ 7·1%	− 0·7%	+ 5·8%	+ 2·5%
Trade, Industry, Employment, Investment grants	+ 3·5 ($£1,435$ m)	− 3·3	− 5·8	+ 27·9	+ 10·8	− 9·9	− 15·8	− 23·8
Nationalised Industries (capital expenditure)	− 11·3 ($£1,738$ m)	+ 9·7	− 9·7	+ 5·2	+ 9·9	+ 8·8	− 0·3	+ 1·1
Roads and Surface Transport	+ 2·6 ($£1,107$ m)	+ 5·6	− 4·1	+ 16·0	+ 3·7	+ 4·5	+ 3·0	+ 3·0
Housing	− 3·1 ($£1,364$ m)	0·0	− 7·4	+ 12·0	− 7·7	− 3·3	− 1·6
Law and Order	+ 5·6 ($£660$ m)	+ 11·5	+ 7·5	+ 7·1	+ 5·9	+ 6·8	+ 6·6	+ 5·7
Education	+ 2·6 ($£3,027$ m)	+ 5·7	+ 5·8	+ 5·5	+ 5·4	+ 4·1	+ 5·4	+ 5·1
Health and personal Social Services	+ 2·7 ($£2,467$ m)	+ 8·1	+ 3·9	+ 5·2	+ 5·4	+ 4·6	+ 4·7	+ 4·7
Social Security	+ 6·8 ($£3,572$ m)	+ 6·9	+ 16·0	+ 14·1	+ 3·3	+ 0·8	+ 1·0	+ 0·3
Total of above and all other programmes	+ 0·1 ($£21,414$)	+ 5·0	+ 4·0	+ 10·0	+ 4·8	+ 1·1	+ 1·6	+ 1·2

*outturn (provisional outturn for 1972)   †estimate as of December, 1972
Source: calculated from *Public Expenditure to 1976–77*, Cmnd. 5178, table 2A

Comparisons with the past might be sufficient to determine whether you are doing as well as others, but it cannot help you improve your situation. These figures might start you thinking but they cannot tell you if your department is particularly vulnerable to large cuts or whether you have opportunities to make substantial gains. For the twin purposes of protecting against cuts or making substantial additions to expenditure, an analysis of the political climate is required.

Climate

> If the climate is right we will try; if the climate is wrong we wait; if the climate is positively bad, we batten down the hatches until the squall is over.
> *Finance officer*

> The question is, is there something people are prepared to pay for rather than something else? The minister has to put it in hard cost terms, not so much economic as political. What is too much? Is it wanted on the terms in which it can be presented? Can we get away with it?
> *High official*

> Departments see every ministerial decision for reflation as the signal to put in all their bright ideas.
> *Ex-Treasury undersecretary*

Despite the networks of trust and aids to calculation, the operating environment of expenditure decision-making is ambiguity. Political administrators learn to assess the climate before determining expenditure strategy. To misjudge the climate may mean to suffer a surprising reverse, perhaps to be embarrassed, possibly to lose reputation and trustworthiness itself. Yet normally climate can be judged only on an intuitive basis. Ministers and officials grow up in a political environment and learn to be sensitive to the expenditure implications of events; such sensitivity is one aspect of that vague but vital factor that political administrators invariably refer to as 'experience'. As the permanent secretary at a major spending department put it, 'Having been at the Treasury you can read the signs; you can tell when the screws are really on and when they aren't.' A principal in a Treasury supply division expressed the same feeling. 'During last year I had the feeling things weren't that tight. Last summer things seemed to get tighter and now the pressure is getting harder still.' Rather than leave the matter entirely at the level of intuition, however, we pressed our respondents to be sufficiently precise so that something specific could be said about determining the expenditure climate.

One vital climatic factor is so prevalent as to be almost a constant: Britain, unlike the United States and some other industrial nations, does not have a thick cushion of economic plenty from which to draw and, if necessary, fall back upon when the international payments accounts turn sour. Economic wealth (gross domestic product) per person in Britain is less than one-half that of the United States and less than three-fourths that of France; Britain's postwar rate of economic growth has typically hovered at about half the rate enjoyed by many other industrialised nations. Despite its substantially higher tax rates, it would be inconceivable for Britain simultaneously to undertake a foreign war, a major anti-poverty programme, and exploration of outer space as did the United States in the mid-sixties. Although Britain historically has survived on narrow margins, exporting and investing abroad to pay its import bill, the precariousness of its economic position has been borne home with a vengeance in a series of postwar balance of payments and currency crises.

Economic crises and emergency cuts in government spending have recurred so often as to be a normal part of the contemporary British expenditure process. At least a dozen major cutting exercises punctuated the years 1950–70.[14] In most cases, these exercises have followed a deteriorating balance of payments' situation, speculation against the pound, and international creditor pressure to 'hold back' public expenditures. Typically, such 'cuts' have concerned slowing down the rate of increase in expenditures rather than reducing absolute levels of government spending. But a cutting exercise does at least make gestures toward restrictiveness regardless of what, if anything, ever shows up in the final outturn

14. Jan 1952; July 1955; Feb 1956; Sep 1957; July 1961; Oct 1964; July 1965; July 1966; July 1967; Nov 1967; Jan 1968; Oct 1970.

figures. If nothing else, the post-war economic crises have given a periodic jolt of clarity to the British expenditure climate.

Treasury officials know and Chancellors of the Exchequer soon come to see that it is far easier to hold down the rise in expenditures in a time of national economic crisis. The more severe the emergency is, or appears, the greater the Chancellor's ability to impose sacrifices on his recalcitrant ministerial colleagues. 'As long as England has her back to the wall,' an ex-Chancellor told us, 'the hawks win. As soon as the sun comes out the doves win, especially if an election is in the offing.'

Similarly when for purposes of economic management the government deliberately embarks upon policies of reflation or deflation, the changing mood is picked up quickly by officials who have spent years developing a fine sensitivity to ministerial nuances. Listen to the former head of one Treasury supply division :

In 1960–1 the Treasury was on top of things. The 1960 balance of payments crisis, for example, was good ammunition. In the division we were told to cut everything we could and for once we had a Cabinet decision behind us to make it stick. Then in 1962–3 we were on the defensive, with reflation the order of the day. It was much more difficult for the division to be tough because we knew that if we refused a request and the Minister went to Cabinet, in the current reflationary mood he'd be likely to get it.

Sometimes a change of (or within) government can give expenditure signals as clearly as any economic crisis. In January 1958, for example, Chancellor Peter Thorneycroft and two other Treasury ministers resigned. 'The Thorneycroft resignation,' agreed all our respondents who served during that period, 'had the effect of the government saying "if people want expenditure they can have it". It was a tremendous shift of attitude.' By the same token, the arrival of the Conservative government in June 1970 indicated a new and more stringent climate, however temporary it turned out to be. 'After the 1970 Conservative victory,' a Treasury official recalled, 'we found the departments had already internally got the message on economy. We found that some battles [for cuts] the Treasury had given up long ago were suddenly won.' Two years later, during prolonged unemployment in 1971/2, the same Government eagerly sought to create jobs through increased spending, and the message went out 'how much more can you spend right away?' By May 1973 signals were again reversed, producing £500 million in public spending cuts to facilitate faster economic growth.

Such circumstances, however, are exceptional. Economic climate shades into political climate, and the spending implications of most events are not self-evident; men have to give them meaning. Take, for example, the Suez crisis. A good case might have been made for sharply increasing the amount of air–sea lift capacity as well as generally enhancing the state of readiness of the armed forces. But this is not what happened. The observer in the early 1970s can still sense the powerful impact of the Suez trauma on thinking about defence and foreign policy. Instead of convincing political leaders that the nation had not done enough, the humiliation of 1956 apparently demonstrated to their satisfaction that it had tried to do far too much. Suez thus began a process of disengagement that led to still further cuts in defence expenditure. Regardless of whether the post-Suez minister of defence was Conservative or Socialist, he knew what he was up against. 'I could not raise the ceiling on defence,' recollected one ex-minister, 'because the climate was against raising it. Therefore I was left with the choice of priorities within existing totals.' For a time, a minister of defence may have been able to make a name for himself by cutting more than his predecessors, a semi-miraculous phenomenon in the world of public spending.

There are seemingly mysterious events that combine to make some proposals for expenditure more desirable than they otherwise might have been. While a lifetime of experience has not revealed to officials how these specific events work their magic, they discover that suddenly some things are 'in'; others are not respectable and lead to criticism. 'Almost like the length of skirts,' a department finance officer mused, 'it changes from year to year. When the issue you are interested in is on the ascendant one can present a reasoned case to which the government will be receptive.' Pressed to specify how he knew what was 'practical', another top civil servant could only say, 'There are changes in public fashion. Building [X] right now is out of favour. On the other hand there is a feeling we ought to spend more on environment, so these kinds of proposals tend to look more practical than others.' In the 1950s, we are told, public indignation about the state of roads was growing and 'we in the Treasury knew cutting here was not on so we did not try it'. Much the same could be said about hospital building. It is commonly believed that the Concorde airplane project, once opposed by Labour, eventually won favour when the Wilson government became interested in entering the Common Market and thought this project would help. So also today one may guess that the Conservative government's interest in economy may go by the board where the pre-eminent goal of maintaining good relationships within the Common Market is involved, or where the increase of employment in Northern Ireland might be thought likely to lessen the need for military force. From the confidential talks between Prime Minister and Chancellor before a full Cabinet meeting to the ruminations of assistant principals, political administrators throughout government can be found cocking a weather eye to the spending climate.

Unfortunately for those who like clear directives, ministers, as well as events, are uncertain agents in creating an expenditure climate. When officials mention instances of clear ministerial directives they almost invariably refer to a well-known economic crisis and modify the statement with a phrase such as 'for once', 'at last', or 'exceptionally'. Often there is no formal decision to cut or increase spending 'but a series of decisions shows you that ministers are taking a different attitude – almost unconsciously'. Climate emerges gradually, as officials turn on their well-trained sensors. The messages and moods gradually filter down, especially among the finely tuned listening posts inside the Treasury. 'You're always hearing from your elders and betters,' a supply division principal informed us, 'what they've picked up at meetings.' Most senior officials also are in a position to read in the official minutes the points made during Cabinet debate. In these rough and ready ways, the principle of control by elected officials is being upheld. Whether or not they know it – and often they do not – ministers are creating the atmosphere which colours understandings and calculations among officials.

Most difficult are the occasions where ministerial decisions are clear enough, but clear in contradictory directions from one week to the next. 'Very often there is uncertainty as to what the general policy is,' said a Treasury official. 'Maybe you don't know the ministers' view or maybe they've made inconsistent decisions, calling for economy this week and approving £X million more the following week.' Since government is not a perfect cybernetic machine, with commands going down and obedience going up, men must judge and act. And this is what they are paid to do.

Skill in coping with an ambiguous climate is particularly important in the Treasury. If the spending department misjudges, they can always blame the Treasury; if the Treasury official gets it wrong and is overruled, he can blame only himself. There are usually one or two horror stories current of the most recent principal who got the Government's mood wrong, to some dramatic effect. For those engaged in the day-to-day control of public spending, the most important way of assessing climate is deceptively simple: they watch the run of decisions. 'I'll know when ministers are taking a favourable view of [X programme] when I send up something dubious and it gets through,' commented an experienced Treasury principal. Another Treasury man put it this way: 'My superiors may say that a proposal is not particularly meritorious but not absurd either and possibly will help with unemployment, so let it through. Or the reverse happens; they'll say that something has merits but is not in line with general government policy, so we'll recommend that ministers reject it. You get to know the general feeling by whether or not they're being hard on things you recommend.' In addition to this somewhat formal guidance through observed decision, there are the innumerable chats, notes, and informal contacts which, as we shall see, characterise the Treasury as an organisation.

In all corners of British central government, climate is assessed also by that pervasive aid to calculation: marginal rates of change. Everyone knows that everyone else plays this game, and anticipated reactions are a vital climatic barometer. Percentage changes in individual expenditure blocs are typical signals for opportunity or vulnerability. Political administrators know that as their 'proportion of the total goes up, the rest are going to start watching and wondering about us. This can go on only so long before someone else's turn comes.' Perhaps one issue occupies the centre of the stage, and there is a fear that older activities will lose support. Word may come down from the Treasury that certain activities are due for special scrutiny for no other reason than that they haven't been looked at for a while. Or during one of the periodic economy drives someone will say that a particular activity has not borne its share of past reductions and it is high time that it did so.

By the same token, an area with a lagging record of increases eventually arouses claims for compensatory fair play.[15] The neglected boulder often becomes the cornerstone of the house, as classes of expenditures suddenly move ahead when it becomes apparent they have been overlooked. 'One argument that can really produce a radical change,' a minister asserted, 'is if something has been held back a long time. That is what happened with the road programme which was held back in the 1950s and in the early 1960s strong arguments could be made that it was time to spend. By the time others came into the government Ernie Marples' road programme had such a momentum no one could get it disestablished.'

There is, of course, some unreality in trying to compartmentalise climate of opinion by discrete categories. A concluding look at two general assessments by political administrators in the field of education may convey a more lifelike impression.

I

We never got an overall ceiling but did everything on an *ad hoc* basis considering the general climate. Is the government generally relaxed in attitude or restrictive or tense in expenditure terms? The personality of one's own minister is more important than his party. Is he a good minister, aggressive and determined? Are the departments up against certain imperatives which they must meet such as the consequences of a rising birthrate in the field of primary education? What is the attitude about education in the country? This varies over periods of time. From 55 to 65 it was all for expansion. During the years 51 to 55 there was tough economy drives for two or three years. After Suez Macmillan was genial. The political climate made a difference.

II

At a place like the Education Ministry cost effectiveness takes

15. This strategy was semi-formalised in the mid-thirties when the defence ministers distinguished a portion of their claims for money as 'deficiency' payments, that is, amounts needed to make good the ten years of restraint in defence spending. Arguments of the Secretaries of State for War and for Air were models of their genre. Cab. 23/77 (1933).

you a little way but not very far. Your sense of what's possible is constituted by three or four calculations. First, what per cent of GNP is your ministry's programme currently getting in relation to others? Second, and related to this, you look at the percentage increase and see whether or not what you want means doing others out of their share. Third, you look at educational politics, that is, the thinking of institutions and conferences as to whether or not we are going too fast or too slow, and you look at variants in professional opinion. Finally you look at the parliamentary system and what, as expressed there, public opinion will take.

If the preceding quotations suggest that there is more art than science to the expenditure process, they are not far wrong. There is no neat formula for assessing climate, any more than there is for distributing trust or making calculations. But there are regularities and norms; political administrators' behaviour is ruleful, not random. In this chapter we have sought to introduce a few of the most prominent regularities underlying the expenditure process. British political administration demonstrates a compactness, coherence, in short, a community united by ties of kinship and culture. If not precisely closed, the community is not exactly open either. The outsider has a chance, but a chance only to learn and operate within the existing framework of mutual understandings. He cannot carve out his own niche in his own terms.

Life would be cozy indeed if this community had no more to do than revel in its own self-identity. But it is paid also to do a job: to adjust public spending to the outside world and its problems. At the vortex of all the confidences, calculations and climatic assessments involved in doing this job stands the Treasury. It is the great communication net (some would say knot) of the expenditure process, the vantage point from which to observe all that happens elsewhere. As political administrators know, and academics learn, understanding the expenditure process begins at the Treasury.

2 The Nuclear Family: The Treasury

Really, you know, it's the most British of British institutions.

A Minister

...This thing is certain; that we have not got it [direct power over other departments]; that the Treasury has never possessed it, and that we have gone on very well without it.

George Hamilton, first permanent secretary of the Treasury, 1873

The highest skill at the Exchequer does not lie in calculations, but in judgements of all kinds.

Richard Fitz Nigel, Dialogus de Scaccario, c. *1178*

No ONE doubts that H.M. Treasury plays the central role in the expenditure process. But beyond this simple and important statement lie vast, uncharted realms of political life. One way to begin coming to grips with this 'most British institution' might be to list the Treasury's formal powers. However, as one zealous Parliamentary committee discovered, definitions of these powers are scarcely to be found in documents, much less statutes. 'What is called "Treasury control" is better described as a complex of administrative practice...empiric rather than theoretical.'[1]

Another approach is to dissect the Treasury organisationally, as in the figure on page 38.

1. H.C. 347 (1957–8), p. xxxvi.

H.M. Treasury Organisation Chart, 1971

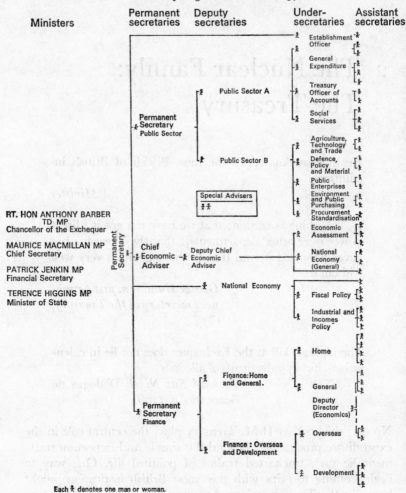

Each ℟ denotes one man or woman.

(by permission of the Controller of H.M. Stationery Office)

Though the Treasury is obviously a small organisation, the men in it cover (in some sense of that word) virtually the entire range of governmental activity. They are concerned not only with government expenditure (Public Sector group at top of the figure) but also with managing the nation's economy (National Economy groups in the middle) and with financial policy (Home and Overseas finance groups at the bottom). But expenditure control is clearly the Treasury's biggest job in terms of organisational effort, occupying as it does about half of the total top manpower. The key locus of control over spending are the Treasury supply divisions (which we shall speak of together as the Public Spending Group). These seven subunits (Social Services; Agriculture, Trade and Technology; Defence; Public Enterprise; Environment; a finance group dealing with overseas expenditure; and a General Expenditure division handling the Public Expenditure Survey) are headed by seven undersecretaries, each with several assistant secretaries and a handful of principals. Together these few dozen men oversee all national government expenditure. They constitute a set of listening posts and action stations, braced by day-to-day contacts which penetrate deep into all other Whitehall departments.

The Treasury is, as its ex-permanent secretary Lord Bridges put it in 1961, 'the most political of departments.'[2] Bridges offered three justifications for this view. Though playing a declining role, detailed, day-to-day expenditure control allows the Treasury 'to pull departments up in those fields where the department is rather losing touch with reality or is deceiving itself'. Second, there is the question of creating new policies: 'since nearly all policies involve some expenditure, the Treasury gets an opportunity to know about the principles and has some hand in the shaping of nearly all departmental policies'. Finally, in its job of managing the economy 'much of the [Treasury officials'] advice [to ministers] is the personal judgement of a layman – one experienced in examining affairs – a judgement as to how much it is right to allot to a particular kind of expenditure, as compared with other claimants'. As Lord Bridges realised, no clear line exists 'between the objective study of facts and political considerations in a sense which implies the views of a Party politician.' Whatever myths may exist concerning the institution's partisan orientation, there is no escaping the essentially political nature of much of the Treasury's work.

Treasury officials are at the heart of political life within the British executive, but formal powers and organisational charts offer little understanding of their real behaviour. To breathe life

2. Lord Bridges, 'The Treasury as the Most Political of Departments', Pollak Lecture, Harvard University, Cambridge, Mass., 1961.

into the subject, we must look at the Treasury men themselves and the way they work. What are considered norms of desirable behaviour? How do they learn what they are supposed to do? How do Treasury officials divide necessary tasks among themselves and relate to one another so that the work gets done? How do they face up to demands imposed on them from without, and those they impose on themselves from within? In the end, how and why do they recommend that this expenditure be made, and that not? To the extent we can begin to answer these questions we shall have learned something about the culture of the Treasury.

An Introduction to Treasury Norms

> Naturally we are not enthusiasts for spending schemes. It is not our role in life to be enthusiastic about expenditure.
>
> *Leo Pliatzky, Treasury under-secretary*, Evidence to Trade and Industry Subcommittee, Expenditure Committee (1970–1), *p. 64*

> We have got a certain expertness of our own, because we have got special advantages in our central position, and in the apparatus of experience and comparative knowledge which we wield.
>
> *Treasury spokesman*, Sixth Report of the Select Committee on Estimates, *(1957–8), Q. 1050*

> We see it all; they [the departments] don't.
>
> *High Treasury official*

Although Treasury men are supposed to be able, to be 'in the know', no one ever tells them directly how or what to know. 'I was flung in,' was a typical comment, 'without an introduction or any preparation whatsoever.' At best there may be a change-over period of several weeks with the retiring official. Some technical information will be written down but there is nothing about the job itself. Old files will relate what has been done in the past;

current files contain information on pending issues and the Treasury position. But all respondents agreed that reading them was not much help. The new recruit is likely to find it less difficult to sense the substance of his job than to understand the Treasury itself – who to see and where to go. The new Treasury official reads what he can and plunges in. Perhaps he will meet a colleague in the corridor who will inquire if everything is going along all right. Small wonder that Treasury men at all levels described their first few months as 'bewildering' and 'traumatic'.[3]

Treasury men at all levels agreed also that, in the words of one undersecretary, 'I learned by starting to make decisions, by dealing with the issues of the job as they arise.' From permanent secretary to assistant principal, Treasury officials learn what is expected of them by actually making recommendations, taking decisions, and discovering how others react to what they do. The pressure of work is intense. Novices grope their way through. If they are smart they use the incessant round of 'chats' to learn from the mistakes of others. They discover that some ways of behaving bring smiles and others are frowned upon. Out of the cauldron of their and others' experiences, they come to know what norms are appropriate for controlling expenditure and how a good Treasury man is supposed to behave. For those who like life neat, it seems a hopelessly haphazard way of training people for important jobs. Yet there is a worldly logic to it as well. If the official has the capacity to become a good Treasury man, he will learn, and if he doesn't, no amount of instruction will help. The self-reliance and capacity for sensing out norms which are necessary to learn the job are also qualities necessary to do the job. Those who have them move ahead; the others do not.

One of the first and most obvious things learned is that the Treasury's business is to save money, not to spend it. Spending is the province of the departments. The Treasury man who comes up with ideas for programme expansion, albeit in a good cause,

3. A man who works on the economic side gave similar testimony: 'I was flung in at the deep end. I learned about exchange rates through the process of reading briefs on devaluation. I learned about budgets by making and preparing one as private secretary to the Chancellor. I did it knowing I had not the faintest idea of the basis on which the budget was put together. I did not even know what a deficit was. It came as a great flash of light when someone told me that what you did when you had a deficit was borrow.'

is likely to be reprimanded, as was one principal recently : 'you are in the Treasury. It is not your business to come up with ideas for spending money. The departments will do that on their own.' Well after the end of postwar austerity, there was, for instance, scarcely any road or hospital building programme, but anyone in the Treasury who may have thought of suggesting one would have been told that such was not proper conduct. In this sense, the Treasury is inherently reactive.

A second lesson is also likely to be difficult for those who enter the Treasury with some subject matter expertise : it is not an original research organisation. Since there are less than 30 expenditure controllers above the level of principal, they ultimately must leave the actual work to the administrative organisations directly concerned. 'One of the most important things you have to learn,' a top Treasury official states, 'is that the Treasury should not redo the work of the departments.' The Treasury's task is to see that the department does what it should. Thus a new supply division principal complains heatedly about his lack of basic data. 'I need to do some of my own forecasting, but others here say "that's not your job". They say I should criticise the departments' forecasts, not make my own.' A much more experienced principal reports, 'I almost never try to do independent forecasting, except once on [a small item]. . . . But I'll certainly discuss the department's forecasts and assumptions, particularly when there's been a problem in the past.' Or as one Treasury supply division head told a Parliamentary committee, 'It would never be for the Treasury to check the veracity of a Department's figures. We may have different interpretations but it is part of the Department's own responsibility to get these figures right.'[4]

But if the spending departments were the ultimate experts it would be difficult for the Treasury to argue with them. The Treasury, therefore, must claim a special expertise that belongs to no single department. That it indeed does so is another important part of the Treasury culture. Its spokesmen never tire of pointing out their uniquely broad perspective. One of the highest officials and one of the lowest justified this Treasury outlook in almost the same words. 'We are the only department that sees the whole picture. . . . What the spending departments don't know is how the quality of their programmes stands up at the margins.

4. H.C. 347 (1970–1), p. 80.

This can only be done by a central department such as the Treasury in constant contact with each of the actual operating departments.' The principal brought the point down to operational level: 'When [Department X] comes to me with their current proposals, [Department Y] programmes are largely an unknown quantity to them. I can find out what's happening in [Department Y] just by walking down the corridor for a chat. With everything being secret, we can provide about the only outside view.'

Only by fortifying themselves with this belief can the several dozen supply division officials venture forth to tilt against the massed expertise of the departments. 'Mostly', we were told, 'you have to develop an official norm of brazen pretence, that is, of knowing as much about everything as the department.' Arrogance? Perhaps, but Treasury men know that without it they are at the mercy of departments forever wanting more money. In one particularly interesting interview we listened to a Treasury man in the making, a young principal nine months on the job. 'The department is going to have a tougher time from me this year... Last year I was green. ... I took the view that they know more than we do. I'm now persuaded that this is the wrong approach. Last year I was far too abashed in pressing for reductions. ... This year I'm going to be far more searching in my questions and far more willing to press for reductions.'

What brings Treasury men to this view? The principal continued, 'It's knowledge and knowing the people on the other side. I have a better idea of what the department's trying to do and thus a better sense of what is factual expectation and what is wishful thinking'. There can be no doubt that the one view of departments that all Treasury men share is borne out by ample experience: the departments always want more, never less. 'I am not sure that I have ever encountered an occasion of the reverse', Sir Samuel Goldman testified, 'I would think that was rather improbable, although it might happen one day'.[5]

The natural reaction to over-long acquaintance with travelling salesmen is to develop a protective colouration of professional scepticism. In the Treasury, as several officials said, 'You have been brought up with a suspicious mind,' you are like 'a doubting Thomas,' and 'never taking things at face value.' Because he is used to dealing with people who want things they should not or

5. H.C. 549 (1970–1), p. 24, para. 103.

cannot have, the Treasury controller has an abhorrence of being taken in by 'enthusiasts' and 'wishful thinking'. Enthusiasts are spending department people who 'are not sceptical and have no balance. Anything they are dealing with is the world's top priority at the moment.' One definition of wishful thinking is the department's inclination to think it can get more work done than it possibly can; another is the belief that the Treasury will let the spending department get away with it. It is here – in juxtaposition with spending department enthusiasts, rather than in any abstract appreciation for the layman's contribution as such – that Treasury men have always found the basis for championing non-specialist knowledge. Lord Bridges, while still permanent secretary of the Treasury, declared 'the heart of the business' of Treasury control to be 'the right to call a halt when the Departmental enthusiast shows signs of getting out of hand.... By dint of practice in weighing up facts, and testing evidence and judging men, it is the Treasury man's business to form a layman's judgement on whether the case presented for more expenditure, however admirable it may appear from a particular point of view, is out of scale with what can be allowed on a common-sense judgement of things when other demands are taken into account'.[6]

To take but three subjects of the Treasury's lay scepticism, one mistrusts technical professionals. 'I think over the years we have come to apply a discount factor, as it were, to all technical advice we are given. When any scientist tells us that such and such a thing can be done within X years, we probably say $2X$; and if the technicians say the cost will be Y million, we probably say $5Y$ million. This is a sort of rule of thumb; pure experience.'[7] One

6. Sir Edward Bridges, *Treasury Control* (London: Athlone Press, 1950), pp. 27–8.

7. H.C. 347 (1970–1), p. 66. In this regard, things haven't changed much in the last century. Ivor Jennings writes that: 'When Lord George Hamilton went to the Education Department, he cut down estimates as much as he could. The Treasury then reduced the aggregate by £10,000. Hamilton pointed out that he had already reduced by more than that amount, and asked for reasons. "In reply I was informed that it always had been the practice of the Treasury to cut down education estimates by £10,000, and to that rule they intended to adhere." Accordingly, he put up the estimates in the following year so as to give the Treasury the pleasure of cutting them down.' *Cabinet Government*, pp. 161–2. An anonymous official recently described, as if it were a new game, how his department submitted Estimates 'carefully calculated to include an allowance which it knows will be pared

is also sceptical of self-serving private interests. 'In the Treasury', said a veteran of many encounters, 'you are always on the lookout for people who have been conned. There are a great many people around who are unconscious of the fact that private interests are trying to get something from the government.' Finally, old hands are dubious of sophisticated quantitative analysis from any quarter. 'You get the right technical people and they can do the quantification very precisely; they do it and we take due note, then disbelieve it. We apply our professional scepticism as administrators not merely to the estimates by other departments but to the figures which our economists and statisticians come up with. You may end up by attaching more weight to your informed hunch.'[8]

Yet the culture of the Treasury calls for something more active than mere scepticism. The Treasury role, and its prevailing norm, is to be energetically critical. Those at the Treasury learn to pride themselves on seeing through arguments that others may misjudge. A former Chief Secretary, Lord Diamond, whose public testimony reveals impressive knowledge of Treasury lore, speaks of 'wringing the water out of the figures. There is the usual procedure of reducing people's estimate of what it is going to cost to coincide with the Treasury's estimate of what that same thing is going to cost, and it sometimes happens that the Treasury's estimate is a little lower than the department's estimate'.[9] Indeed it does 'sometimes happen'.

Playing the expenditure game, a Treasury veteran observed, involves 'never saying "yes" at once. You must ask most thorough questions. You must go through the questioning process in order to see if the proposer is serious. He can't want it unless he pushes it and stands up to questioning. You also want to delay and question to see if he has inflated the estimates because you believe he does. Your job is to cut and you bargain him down to show you can cut.' If the rules of the game are followed, the department's finance officer will be able to tell his people that he got more than he expected though less than he asked for, and the

down in arguments with the Treasury'. 'The Estimates Game in the Civil Service', Letter to *The Guardian*, 18 April 1968. As we shall see, such overt padding displays a certain lack of sophistication.

8. H.C. 347 (1970–1), p. 100.

9. H.C. 549 (1970–1), p. 30, para. 135.

Treasury principal will be able to tell his superiors that he cut the department down by a certain amount, thus saving the government a specified sum of money.

Consider a typical negotiation. A department approaches the Treasury with a proposal costing £10 million. The Treasury, as usual, says no at first, especially if the ministry has been troublesome in the immediate past. If the ministry is keen to act it will ripost with a cheaper proposal, say £7·5 million, for doing essentially the same thing. Again the Treasury will say no. Then the department will rework it and come back with a proposal costing £6 million. At this point the Treasury might, no doubt with some glee, point out that the original proposal was £10 million and that by working hard the department had got it down to £6 million. If the department can work even harder and get it down to £5 million, the Treasury might be able to accept it, provided that they actually do approve the activity or feel it is inevitable.

Any such example is, of course, a vast oversimplification of the 'to-ing and fro-ing' involved. And this is just the important point: life at the Treasury calls for a sustained, dogged critical faculty rather than dumb negativism. 'You learn you don't get cuts by absolute no's', many told us. You get cuts by modifying proposals rather than rejecting them completely.

Probing is also a major device for obtaining information. Treasury officials acquire knowledge about the proposal, its estimated costs and the trustworthiness of men and departments. But they also learn how badly spenders in the department want something. For its most important proposals, the department will argue long and hard. Whether mutual education or mutual exhaustion is the main consequence is a matter of some dispute. Departmental officials, like their Treasury counterparts, know the game and take the same pleasure in playing it well. They will tell you that 'having a good case to the Treasury means that it stands up to being torn to pieces by them'. You may think you are stealing a march on them but 'even if the rocket is going up with everyone else aboard, the Treasury men have been trained to cut the link, and ask do you really mean it? These are a bunch of nasty old men with a vocational commitment to showing that you don't.'

Above all, tough Treasury probing is a norm valued for its indirect impact. Treasury men believe that departments are restrained in their spending plans by anticipations of Treasury reactions. When the immediate effort seems thankless and direct results few, Treasury men reassure themselves that 'you are justi- fied as a controller even if you never turn anything down'. Having a great deal to turn down could indicate that others are not sufficiently inhibited by your critical faculties. All of this is a long established tenet of Treasury culture, as a Chancellor pointed out three generations ago : 'The first object of the Treasury must be to throw the departments on their defence, and to compel them to give strong reasons for any increased expenditure, and to ex- plain how they have come to have to demand it. This control alone contributes to make the departments careful in what they put forward.' As usual, an official – the first permanent secretary of the Treasury – had already put the same point more succinctly : 'A great deal of the good we do in this world might perhaps be properly measured by the evil we prevent. ... We have prevented much evil without being conscious of it.' [10] Heads we win; tails we don't lose. Treasury lore, in the manner of self-protecting hypotheses, sees itself as doing good when it intends and as guard- ing against evil when it does not.

Many of these relentless inquiries must remain haphazard samp- ling, but a portion are also motivated by well-established prin- ciples – what some respondents in the institution termed 'Treasury dogma'. Violations here wave red flags before the Treasury man. He learns not so much what to look for as what to look out against. These warning signals, which generally involve hostility to hidden or built-in spending escalators, certainly do not imply that the Treasury man always gets the signals straight or that his warnings are taken by others. The maxims do suggest that there is a certain content to his critical scepticism. Here we will mention five com- mon types.

1. A high Treasury official emphasised that 'the old Treasury watchword – watch out for the thin edge of expenditures – con- stituted my major task. It was to see that no big expenditures got in unknowingly simply because they seemed small in early years.' The Treasury has had endless experience with proposals that were

10. The two quotations are Chancellor G. J. Goschen in 1901 and George Hamilton, permanent secretary of the Treasury, in a letter of 1869. Both quotations are taken from Maurice Wright's *Treasury Control of the Civil Service, 1854–1874* (Oxford : Clarendon Press, 1969), p. 346.

to cost relatively little, only to mushroom into fantastic amounts in later times. Whether this result is the outcome of departmental strategy or whether it occurs simply because no one foresees what will happen, Treasury men seek to maintain eternal vigilance against it. Departmental officials get the point. In dealing with the Treasury, they tell you, 'it is really the arithmetic that counts. What they want to see are the implications of any expenditure decision and the commitment that is being mortgaged in the years ahead.' As we shall see later, and at length, a new public expenditure survey has been designed to help prevent the thin edge from getting thicker.

2. The Treasury also has the strongest possible bias against open-ended commitments. They will resist programmes they otherwise might approve because they do not believe the administrative arrangements are stringent enough to prevent totals rising astronomically. A Treasury man spoke of fighting furiously against a certain form of programme administration that, when adopted over his opposition, resulted in tens of millions pounds greater expenditure than had been estimated because there was no way of restricting the number of beneficiaries. The Treasury will argue strenuously that bills should have financial limits in them so that there is some way to ration the money.

3. If there is any principle Treasury men learn, it is 'to avoid precedent-setting behaviour'. This does not mean what it might mean in a department, i.e., sticking closely to past lines of action, but rather to avoid making settlements with one department that will have the effect of raising expenditure in others. A higher living allowance in one programme, for example, is bound to generate demands for similar rates elsewhere.

4. The Treasury as an institution has never believed in the philosophy of economic growth. Its officials may not be against growth as such, but they are vehemently against committing resources on the basis of what one deputy secretary called 'a hoped-for, phoney paper growth rate, which only leads to false expectations, disappointments, cuts, and further disillusionment'. They want to see the colour of the money first and relish pointing out the risks of action based on hypothetical increases in wealth. People will only be encouraged to spend more money, and it will then be the Treasury's task, and an unpopular one, to find it. The Treasury orientation against public commitments to hoped for resources has

been strengthened since publication of the National Economic Development Council's 4 per cent economic growth target in 1963 and the optimistic economic expectations of the 1965 *National Plan*.[11] Rough policy statements became committed targets and led to expenditures (such as electrical generating capacity) being laid on which were geared to the over-optimistic growth rates. When these rates were not achieved, 'there was a lot of painful unscrambling to do, particularly from 1967 onwards'. The spending cutbacks and 'bloody chaos' that resulted have hardened attitudes against making expenditures the hostages to the fortune of economic growth forecasts. It is not growth but the limit on national resources that is the staple of Treasury doctrine.

5. Craftsmanlike Treasury officials do not like disguised expenditures, which by being unidentified cannot be controlled. Speaking of 'one such dogma', an official said that 'the Treasury likes subsidies clearly identified and, therefore, a loan at a false interest rate would be attacked, and the Treasury would want the loan made at the normal rate and the subsidy expressed as a grant'. Another example is government guarantees to individual borrowers. 'The Treasury is very jealous about what it will attach a government guarantee to, inasmuch as it is a measure of the government's own credit rating. You know that when something is going to be guaranteed by the government it had better be through a public organisation and not rely upon private lenders.' Norms like these, designed to protect the public purse, give direction to officials on where to exercise discretion and what to inform their superiors about if things get difficult.

All the norms discussed in this section have involved looking at expenditures as a question of money. A number of others could have been mentioned but these eight appear to be most widespread. To summarise :

1. Decide by reacting.
2. Let others do the technical work.

11. Samuel Brittan's discussion remains the most balanced account of these British planning efforts. (*Steering the Economy*, chapter 10). The targets were complete failures in terms of their intended aim of raising growth rates by raising demand expectations: they were highly effective in their unintended result of giving a new peg for spending departments' demands for more money. A highly critical review of this forecasting and planning is G. Polanyi's, *Planning in Britain: The Experience of the 1960s*, Institute of Economic Affairs research monograph, 1967.

3. You know as much as anybody and more than most.
4. Above all, be sceptical – especially of enthusiasts.
5. Probe, delay and question again.
6. As a rule, cut by bargaining rather than by absolute no's.
7. A reputation for toughness inhibits would-be spenders.
8. Be on guard against hidden and built-in expenditure escalators.

Expenditure, however, involves more than money. While learning money norms may make an adequate money controller, it is not enough to make a good Treasury man.

The Good Treasury Man

Treasury people are supposed to have a good political nose. This is one of the most important qualifications they can bring to their work. They are supposed to know or rather sense what will get the ministers into trouble.
Senior Treasury official

My job is to get the feel of political things which the Treasury ministers will be interested in. You have to acquire the skill if you are to get on in the Civil Service.
Treasury undersecretary

The senior men in the Treasury, who carry and inculcate norms, seek to reinforce behaviour that helps them perform their own jobs. The ministers they advise are busy men with limited time and special political needs. The task of the senior officials is to select out those small packages of advice that will be most helpful to men who want to make sound decisions that enhance their political reputations and avoid severe embarrassment. To do this senior officials need subordinates who are also politically alert. The good Treasury man, therefore, has a heightened political sensitivity, decides most things himself except where superiors would want to be brought in, and does it all in good form. Like the famed chicken-sexer (who can tell the gender of a chicken by looking at the egg), the good Treasury man senses the important distinctions without necessarily being able to say how he does it. 'I am supposed to know intuitively what might be of interest to the people above me and what might get a minister in trouble.' How do Treasury men come to learn what is politically important? How do they make the personally critical choices about which decisions belong to them and which ones should go up to the political masters above them? In trying to answer these questions, we will necessarily have to represent officials as being more self-conscious than they in fact are. Usually they are not pressed to reflect on these matters; indeed, it is considered a mark of the good Treasury official that he knows what to do without knowing it. His art must be artless.

The context of political appraisal is a parliamentary arena and a two-party system, in which the Opposition is always trying to catch you out, and the reputation of the government depends heavily on how well its ministers reply. What kind of question can the Opposition in Parliament ask when it ordinarily knows, and perhaps cares, little about details of the policy? The obvious thing (for here members of Parliament are not unlike Treasury examiners) is to look for inconsistencies between what the minister says now and what he has said before, between what he says now and what his government has said, and between what one department is doing versus another. 'The Opposition,' another Treasury official stated, 'is always probing for inconsistencies, and you can bet a supplementary question will begin with the phrase, "How do you reconcile this with what a colleague said?"' It is evidently important that men who advise Treasury ministers should understand customs and practices in the House of Commons.

Political sensitivity may be inculcated by giving Treasury men training as private secretaries to ministers. The private secretary spends a great deal of time in the House of Commons and, as a minister put it, 'He can see what kind of matters create trouble.' Since private secretaries are sometimes present when ministers discuss financial questions amongst themselves or with the Chief Secretary of the Treasury, they learn directly about the interests and problems of their political masters. Our attention was forcibly drawn to the importance of political training as a private secretary when we heard an eminent Treasury official criticised for political insensitivity, the explanation being that 'He never had experience as a private secretary.'

Like everyone else, Treasury people know which party is in power and what the general policy preferences of the Government are at the moment. They read the press and they receive numerous memoranda and private communications telling them what their and other ministers care about. That there is a political interest in school meals or National Health charges is not in doubt. For less obvious situations Treasury officials find that there is no substitute for concentrated 'minister watching'. According to an experienced official, 'A large part of the thinking that goes on here is an assessment of what the Treasury ministers' own interests are.' Thus certain issues 'determine themselves if a Treasury minister has expressed personal concern'.

The sensitivity of the good Treasury man, however, goes well beyond noticing issues which are or might be of concern to his own minister. It calls for the assessment of ministerial capabilities – for the official's as well as the minister's own good. 'You have to realise,' our respondents insisted, 'that it is all a struggle and it won't do you much good fighting for something till the last ditch if the minister is not going to support it. You have to know their personality and their strength in the departments to judge how well your top brass will stand up. You get this largely by experience and watching troublesome developments where ministers have gotten into a mess.' The official learns that certain ministers are weak and will give way when pressed so that he must try to shore them up. Some ministers take on too many details and must be shielded, otherwise they lose sight of the larger picture. 'Other ministers are lazy,' a well-placed observer reveals, 'which can be an advantage for a minister, but that may mean they lose arguments because they do not see their briefs.'

Being politically sensitive is a kind of art. Experience in mastering this art is one of the most important heritages the Treasury has acquired and tries to pass on. Two examples, one of political sensitivity and the other of its absence, may illustrate the general point. The Treasury, in its efforts to hold down expenditure, may oppose departmental information programmes that are designed to encourage more recipients to apply. The more people are led into the programme, the more the department can claim 'unavoidable' expansion. But the Treasury may do nothing to stop a poverty information programme because 'politically this is untouchable. You would be disastrously exposed and called immoral if people saw you trying to prevent other people from getting what they are entitled to.' Past experience has shown Treasury people that a slippery slope to ministerial embarrassment lies in taking actions – however inconsequential they may appear or however small the amount of money involved – that makes the political figure seem harsh and unfeeling. The Treasury decision to fight publicity programmes can depend on what its officials call 'the political kickback'. Judging it to be severe, they will usually hold their fire for other issues on which they have a better chance to prevail.

A second example concerns sensitivities unheeded. Protecting the Chancellor of the Exchequer, its minister, is one way the Treasury safeguards its officials and institutional reputation. By the time men rise high in the Treasury, they have learned that it is unwise for a chancellor to take responsibilities for defending specific cuts during debate in the House of Commons. An inexperienced Chancellor of the Exchequer who disregards this wisdom is likely, as Anthony Barber found in announcing the October 1970 expenditure cuts of a new Conservative government, to become embroiled in difficulties. The onus of reduction was entirely on the Chancellor instead of being spread out across the broader shoulders of his ministerial colleagues.

The ultimate judges of political sensitivity are, of course, the ministers. Sometimes they find officials more concerned about politics than they are. The political motivations of 'stop–go' economic policies in the 1950s are taken as a prominent example of top officials' overenthusiasm in bringing political assessments to bear.[12] Another Treasury minister recounted a case where an undersecretary had come to see him saying he should know about a project. It was not worth doing, the official said, but there had been so many expressions of support for it that ministers would be influenced to act. 'I said nonsense,' reported the minister, 'the political consequences can be contained. I argued it twice before a Cabinet Committee; the Chancellor said the only question was why anybody thought of wasting money that way.' The project was dropped without severe repercussions. Ministers who have to take the blame occasionally can brush aside political consequences

12. See Roseveare, *The Treasury*, p. 326. Lord Boyle has referred to several of his officials at the Department of Education and Science who were more election-conscious than he. Edward Boyle, Anthony Crosland and Maurice Kogan, *The Politics of Education* (Harmondsworth, Middlesex: Penguin Books, 1971), p. 76.

but officials, precisely because they are not vulnerable, cannot.[13] It is their political master's head, not their own, they are risking. Paradoxically, the very fact of being considered 'non-political' can heighten officials' political sensitivity.

When it is another minister's head, things may be different. Sometimes, a departmental official will allege that his opposite number in the Treasury is insensitive to his political problem. 'Let me show you what the Treasury is like. You'll be discussing something with them and point out that your minister can't get up in the House and take that line. The Treasury man simply says "That's your problem, not mine." ' Now what the Treasury man should have said is that he understood and fully sympathised but that the total financial picture required sacrifices by all. For the Treasury official undoubtedly had sounded out his colleagues and ministers, and they had agreed that since every spending minister could make similar arguments they could not accept it without gravely weakening their ability to keep spending down.

It is not enough, in other words, to cry politics in order to get your way. Everyone can and does do that. Yet in the light of limited resources, not all can prevail. The premium on political sensitivity is rooted in a fear of being caught unaware, with the attending possibility of looking foolish and unreliable; in an understandable desire to gauge the risk of surprise the affected ministers are taking; and in a need to protect all flanks, since the Opposition is there to find your mistakes. How much of this helps reconcile divergent interests, which is the business of government, and how much merely protects against the possibility of looking bad, no one can say.

A political feel for the issues and for ministers is futile unless

13. That Treasury officials have taken more than their share of responsibility is a perennial complaint by other departments' ministers. In 1875 the Attorney-General wrote on what is still a timeless theme:

I have the best reason for being certain that My Lords often know nothing whatever of these [Treasury] proceedings. In each of these cases I ascertained that neither Gladstone, nor Lowe, nor Baxter . . . nor in fact any one of 'My Lords' knew anything at all about it. . . . I for one think that of late years the assumption of authority by Treasury subordinates, and the tone they adopt towards whom they address has become intolerable.

Quoted in Ann Burton, 'Treasury Control and Colonial Policy', *Public Adminstration*, vol. 44 (summer 1966), p. 173.

Treasury officials know when to take responsibility themselves.[14] Sensitivity must be balanced by judgement. Determining politically sensitive issues by sending all conceivable cases to one's immediate superior might make certain that none were neglected, but such a practice would impose intolerable burdens on busy men. The good Treasury man does not overload his superiors. He tells them what they need to know but not more. He keeps them out of trouble by knowing what will get them into it. '... Unless I am to kill my ministers with the amount of detail I put up to them,' a Treasury undersecretary recently testified, 'I must kill a very high proportion of the work before it goes anywhere beyond me.' [15] On what grounds then, are matters sent up from principals to assistant secretaries, to permanent secretaries and to the Treasury ministers?

The amount of money involved and the rate of increase over the past year or two provide immediate starting points for sending items upward. Superiors want to know about decisions that will commit them to large expenditure now and in the future. After a time, for instance, everyone comes to know that big contracts to produce planes and submarines must go to a higher level. To be sure, 'the higher up you go, the smaller any particular sum appears; £20,000 to an assistant secretary may be like £40,000 to an undersecretary'. Although a request for more money because of forecasting error is normally not regarded as a substantial issue or sent up by undersecretaries, a substantial expenditure likely to preempt funds (some respondents mentioned items over £1 million) will go above the level of assistant secretary. An undersecretary can expect to have new expenditure issues brought to him; if he cannot settle any such general problem with other division heads, this too will be sent higher.

All officials agreed, however, that 'whether or not to send something up in the Treasury hierarchy depends less on the amount of money involved and more on the political sensitivity of the issue'. The risk of embarrassment is what counts, not the actual sum of

14. 'It was, I believe, this fear of involving ministers in unnecessary troubles which led to the pernicious tradition of writing letters in language deliberately framed so as to mean as little as possible, in the hope that since so little meaning could be attached to them, they would not lead to embarrassment.' Sir Edward Bridges, 'Portrait of a Profession', *The Rede Lecture* (Cambridge: Cambridge University Press, 1950), p. 29.

15. H.C. 347 (1970–1), pp. 74–5.

money involved. Individual cases are never sent up by principals 'unless they involve an issue of great sensitivity'. Nor will routine figures, such as forecasts, be sent up as a rule; but an unusually high forecast with a suspected political motivation will go up to the undersecretary and perhaps higher. The higher the level, the more important political criteria become. By the deputy secretary level, the official job description declares 'nearly all issues holder deals with' to be 'policy and political work' with 'actual or potential ministerial content'.

Direct contact with higher-ups enables officials to test first hand the political interest and concern of the persons involved. The Second Permanent Secretary in charge of the Treasury public expenditure side, his two deputy secretaries, the undersecretaries and an occasional assistant secretary meet with the ministers. They will be called in to prepare the minister for a Cabinet committee meeting, or they will participate themselves or brief one of their official superiors. Their access to minutes of Cabinet meetings and contacts in the Cabinet Office will provide further information on the political lay of the land.

By now it should be apparent that, like the occupant of any position with complex demands, the good Treasury man is to an extent expected to perform contradictory tasks. 'The good man can handle most things at his own level.' So everyone is told. They are told also to be critical and tough in dealing with departments. Yet a man experienced in Treasury life soon comes to understand that 'if he is too critical, if he does not compromise enough – and compromise is the basis of the entire governmental effort – the department will insist that many matters be resolved at a higher level'. The good Treasury man, it appears, is one who is critical but not too critical, one who has the respect of his department but does not get taken over by it, one who handles things at his own level while knowing when to send up matters which concern his superiors. It is difficult to combine toughness with resolving conflict at one's own level because the more critical the Treasury examiner, the more likely the departments are to challenge his judgement. Compromise between his roles no less than of his views is a necessary element of survival in the Treasury.

The strain on the Treasury man is never more evident than when he is considering his general approach to departmental requests: just how tough should he be? How often should he say yes instead of no? Outsiders, including many policy-area specialists in the spending departments, believe Treasury controllers advance in direct proportion to their negativism. There is some truth to this view – but not much. To reassure superiors that he has not been captured by the department he is supposed to be controlling, it does help an official in the supply division to show occasionally that he is very tough. Confessed one senior Treasury official, 'I begin to wonder when the departments say too many good things about [supply division officials], but then I get a slashing attack on a department and know they are still being objective.'

But pure negativism will not take a Treasury man far. Any clerk could say no to everything, and in doing so would be worthless to the Treasury. There is a tendency in the Treasury for each level to say no, but this is done so as to preserve the right for higher levels to say yes. This tactic enables each superior, up to and including the Chancellor, to have something to give and bargain with rather than being utterly negative and thereby vulnerable to complete defeat. A second and complementary tendency is a greater inclination to send upwards to higher officials one's 'no's' than one's 'yes's'. 'If I agree with something,' a principal said, 'I'm less worried about putting it up. If I disagree, and it's more than a try-on [i.e., wishful thinking from department enthusiasts] then I want to be sure Treasury Ministers agree.'

There are two broad reasons for saying 'yes' or 'maybe' rather than 'no'; first, to preserve superiors' political credit and second to preserve the Treasury's and officials' own reputations. If the Treasury official is constantly turning the department down they will try to get around him by appealing to his superiors, thus increasing the burden on them. 'You cannot say no to everything,' a Treasury official advises, 'or else the whole strain falls on the minister. It is obvious that he cannot say no to everything without tearing the government apart. So if you are entirely negative, the whole burden of saying yes to some things will fall on him.' The dilemma is one of relative political power at every level. The second reason is related to the first. Treasury controllers do not like being reversed by their superiors unless they expect it. As many officials observed, 'It's embarrassing for the Treasury to be seen later as changing its mind. What's more, it's bad for me too.' Hence, even if it is expected, officials cannot afford to be overridden too often or they will lose stature with the departments, and with their colleagues. Their value to their superiors will be lessened because no one wants to deal with men whose preferences do not count.

The official whose recommendation is turned down without being forewarned is likely to trim his sails in future actions. He will become predictably more cautious lest he lose part of his hoard of credibility. 'How tough you will be,' asserted an official who lived through just such a situation, 'largely depends on your estimation of how the Chancellor of the Exchequer will stand up to the spending ministers. On one issue recently, I said no and the Chancellor gave way to the minister for political reasons. Next time around, I will be much more cautious because it makes me look bad to get turned down by the Chancellor too often. Now the departments know they can get things taken by their minister to the Chancellor and thus get around me.'

The actions and reactions we have been describing fall into a pattern that suggests the likely course of events: aggressive Treasury analysis but ultimate yielding (though not all the way) at the final stages. The Treasury is likely to be tough in the beginning and the middle, but less so as it considers not merely what is desirable but what it can get. In the end the Treasury maintains its reputation. By being hard and critical, each level gets to say no most of the time and yes some of the time, and the department walks away with the satisfaction that it won something after a lengthy struggle.

Next to a political nose, and a logical brain, the most important skill of the good Treasury man resides in his fine drafting hand. The concise, coherent and penetrating note is the final expression of all other talents. Political sensitivity may be manifested by drafting statements that allow the minister to meet the problem at hand without getting him into additional difficulties. A logical mind is demonstrated by showing that the various aspects of the Treasury position fit together in a coherent package and, if necessary, that the opposing view does not make sense. The man who can draft a good memorandum takes the burden from his superior, incidentally showing him (as well as anyone else along the line who will read it) how able he really is. Ministers comment on the 'confident ease' that characterise Treasury minutes. There is something about the way the memorandum is written that makes ministers feel that they can identify the men 'who are about to go up and those who will never get any further'.

High officials in the Treasury look for superior grasp of the substance of issues and their expenditure implications, awareness of the opinion that has emerged in Treasury discussion, and care in avoiding recommendations that might serve as harmful precedents. All these qualities come out in drafting memoranda. Superiors rely on the drafting ability of their subordinates to set out complex issues clearly, simply and concisely. The undersecretary wants a report or a reply to a parliamentary question that he can send without alteration. 'This sounds trivial,' our respondents said, 'but is very important. The undersecretary depends on you to take over day-to-day work. The pressure at the top is much too heavy. If they are to have any hope of attending to major issues, they must be able to take your draft, initial it, and send it off.' Treasury men are also keenly aware that 'by giving a minister something foolish to say in public you can muddle up policy for years; you don't want to do that. You must enable a man to get by, to satisfy the immediate needs and at the same time find language that will not make poor commitments. This is not easy.' The man whose superiors continually have to redo his work, or who misses critical points, or who muddles up the agreed-upon Treasury position, or who overspecifies a deliberately muddled position, or who leads ministers to make commitments that turn out to be embarrassing or that enable other departments to claim similar treatment on grounds of equity – this man will soon find himself in another job.

While it is better to be thought of as too bright than not bright enough, no one wishes to be thought impudent or presumptuous. Treasury minutes may be written in a way that reveals the high intelligence of the writer but also must be marked to some extent by proper deference to superiors. You demonstrate your knowledgeability by understanding the level at which you are acting, and by playing right up to it but not over it. A principal is not expected to act like an assistant secretary, who in turn is not supposed to act like an undersecretary and so on. The moral is similar to that in the House of Commons, where an M.P. must not ask a question bigger than he is. A new and junior man, for instance, should not ask the Prime Minister whether he is aware that 'most of us' won't vote for this or that. It is presumptuous of him to believe that he speaks for his older and more senior colleagues. So, too, must the Treasury man express an opinion and make a recommendation without pretending to be more defiant and assertive than a man in his position is entitled to be. Those who do best combine a modest tone with the powerful analysis that signals promotable talent. If they succeed in this delicate balancing act, and do well in their own league, they are likely to move up to the next.

The need for analytic skills to increase confidence on the job is assumed more than specifically mentioned. Treasury controllers are supposed to 'find out how to analyse numbers and see if they really mean what they are supposed to mean'. This is part of their stance of scepticism. They are unlikely to carry out formal policy analysis in which the implications of diverse assumptions are worked out but they do, with experience, learn about the consequences of different ways of administering programmes and may even develop a certain amount of ability to consider alternatives.

The good Treasury man is an able amateur. A great deal of his behaviour can be deduced by assuming that he must make a large number of complex decisions in a short period of time without being able to investigate any of them fully. He relies on ability to argue, to find internal contradictions, to pick out flaws in arguments whose substance he has not fully mastered and of whose subtleties he can only be dimly aware.

The longer he lasts in his position, the more the Treasury man's substantive expertise grows. For most, as we shall see, this is not likely to be very long. And no matter how long his tenure, the Treasury man perforce lacks experience with the operation of programmes and with their consequences for people in society. Given the normal division of labour in the government, there are department men to look after this side of affairs. Ministers who have been in a position to observe Treasury officials find 'that rather sceptical minds did well. They often gave brilliant advice. But its characteristic was that it was coherent internally rather than necessarily fitting in with what went on outside.' Another minister confirms the impression : 'They were academically impressive. Their excellence was in logic and in qualities of mind, not in experience or in judgement.'

There may be men who can combine the most diverse and best qualities of the race. They understand intimate details of the particular, and they also have a tight grasp on the general. They are both trusting and sceptical. They care about people who suffer from cuts in funds, and they worry simultaneously about the drain on the national purse. They excel in qualities of judgement while deferring to the opinion of others when that is called for. Who, then, would play the Treasury role? No one should be surprised that so distinctive an institution as the Treasury, which has a special task in controlling expenditure, should develop men and talent tailored both to the outside demands placed on it and to its own internal requirements. The good Treasury man is not supposed to be all things to all men. He is supposed to do well at the tasks for which he was hired. Let us, therefore, look more closely at the way he performs his job.

On Making the Impossible Seem Effortless

By the time you know what you are doing you are in another job.

Treasury official

I myself don't really understand how we do it all, but the fact is the work gets done.

Treasury official

The flow of spending decisions is continuous. Thousands of small ripples form the mighty waves. The Treasury cannot simply stand aside and let these waves pass over it. If the organisation is not to be overwhelmed, it must seek to deflect and channel the currents. At the Treasury, there is no escaping decision. There is no possibility of saying one does not know. A recommendation (if not decision) on all major items is required. And yet nobody can know it all. A high Treasury official recently on the job testified that, 'the effect of dealing with these things can be traumatic. I have been responsible for complicated discussions about the future of [say, agriculture] and when I started a few weeks ago I didn't know the difference between [say, potatoes and pigs].' How then do a few dozen men make recommendations for the vast central government expenditures of an entire country?

The answer to this question reemphasises the single most dominant theme in all our talks: Treasury officials are able to do their jobs because there are relationships of trust. By their own account, the most important skill Treasury people learn is 'personal trust and where it should be put'. 'This is necessary,' as an undersecretary says, 'because you are dealing with such an enormous amount of material that you can't possibly know the whole field. You get a feeling as to who is telling you the whole truth. Very often a paper is obviously a sincere attempt to show all the implications, statistics, problems, as they really are; on the other hand you sometimes get documents with twisted contents covering up and leaving out things harmful to the case.'

In response, Treasury men have developed simple rules of decision : get close to the departments; accept proposals of those you trust; be extremely critical of those who try to fool you or who, under questioning, don't know their business. 'You are always trying to prove that what the department cites as an irresistible political need is artificial or being stimulated,' a Treasury man explained, 'This is very hard to do without internal sources of information in the departments, and here again is where staying close pays off. If you are close to the department you will find you can get parallel cases. People will send internal documents and you will learn what is feasible and what isn't and what's being generated.' A Treasury man recalled that, 'There is one finance officer who will come up on the quiet and will say that this is a weak or unjust item, and then I may write about it asking for clarification from the department.' But there are also other departments' people who are 'forever trying to bounce us. They see their job as getting things from the Treasury. When you probe what they say they do not know the details of their own case so we probe here like mad.' A number of such experiences account for high Treasury officials saying that

> In learning about the the job one relies on the knowledge of the person to a very great extent. For example, someone will call me up from the department saying we want to do this and we want to know whether or not we can. I'll tell them to wait for a half hour and then go out and talk with our chap closest to the ground, the assistant secretary who deals with the department and the man. You consult your junior people, who have more experience with these people, until you call them back with the answer.

By establishing relationships of trust, the Treasury man not only makes manageable his own calculations and is able to forewarn his superiors of development in the department, he is also often able to prevent headaches reaching the Treasury in the first place. He can head off trouble for Treasury ministers by seeing that matters which might come to him are resolved within the department itself. 'I'll say to the department officials at a meeting,' a Treasury secretary revealed, 'that I will leave it to them to raise the issue with their minister. They will make the point with him because they want our good will.'

For these reasons, it is said of the good Treasury man that 'He has weight with his department. He knows what is going on. They listen to him.' Without trust as an aid to his calculations, the Treasury controller will be unable to gain the confidence of either the department or his Treasury colleagues, he will be constantly surprised and disappointed by the department and superiors, and he will be unable to serve his ministers well. The contribution of trust to the Treasury man's effectiveness is cumulative. The better he knows his departments, the more they trust him, the more he can rely on them, and the better advice he will be able to give his superiors. Likewise, the more they accept what he says, the more important he will become, the more the department will need him.

Using department people to cut down on the cost of acquired information is one way of not having to consider everything. So is sampling. Instead of scrutinizing every expenditure, the Treasury controller may choose at random two or three over a certain amount of money. A former Treasury secretary said that, since moving to a spending department, 'I realise how terribly thin on the ground they are at the Treasury, picking out here and there what they can. But they're terribly good at it.' If those items chosen for study are being properly treated, the Treasury man can be more content that the rest are in good hands. The use of sampling, however, depends on previously having reached agreement with the department on the objective and size of the programme and confidence that the agreement is being maintained.

A rule for decision that is seemingly simple is to accept all expenditures for existing policy that are within the PESC (or previously the estimates) ceiling, and question everything above it. The first problem (as we shall see in greater detail later on) is that what constitutes existing policy is often in dispute. Even if this is agreed, the cost of last year's existing policy in this year's prices may not be agreed. Departments differ, moreover, in the degree to which their expenditures are subject to projection and prediction so that by no means all can be treated this way. Contrariwise, according to a Treasury respondent, 'It is sometimes very difficult to find out what the Chancellor's policy actually is.' Unless the situation has been made unmistakably clear, as in the period following the 1967 devaluation, Treasury people may not be certain how firm the Chancellor is on a particular expenditure limit and what particular items might be considered candidates for exceeding it. Statements that the fiscal situation is difficult and expenditures must be controlled are always made, but they do not constitute the required guidance.

Control works by comparison. This year's proposals are compared to last year's. The way a similar item was handled in the past is used to justify handling it that way in the present. The way in which an examiner dealing with another department has handled a problem may well turn out to be the way it should be handled in the present situation. It follows, therefore, that new departments and proposals for new expenditures will receive much closer scrutiny because there is no immediate basis for comparison in dealing with them. To be new is to be exposed. Departmental officials realise this, as can be seen from the finance officer who understood that 'a new ministry such as mine would have a tendency to receive the closest scrutiny from the Treasury simply because it was new. At these early stages the Treasury will concern itself more with the detailed work because it regards itself as a nanny.' The departmental tendency to try to dress up something new as something old, or to gloss over large expenditure implications of old programmes, is based on their experience of being subjected to detailed questions when it appears that they have gone beyond past boundaries.

The aids to calculation we have been considering may fairly be construed as part of the Treasury's critical approach to expenditure. They are part of the apparatus of any man who needs ways of coming to reasonable (at least acceptable) conclusions without being able to investigate a subject thoroughly. Even men who do know a certain field rather well will still use these aids to calculation in regard to that part of their work load for which they do not have sufficient time and to which they cannot devote enough attention. But there are also Treasury men who have developed substantial expertise in certain areas and who do take a positive, indeed a creative, view of their task. This is the way the head of the Treasury's Agriculture, Technology and Trade Division put it :

> I hope that after 20-odd years in the Treasury I do have something of an instinct for a bad project and a bad expenditure proposal, but it is only by having this instinct that you can have any confidence in yourself when you accept something as a sound expenditure proposal. This does happen to me frequently : A Department comes along with some proposition and this seems to me, having regard on the one hand to the public expenditure constraints, on the other hand to the country's economic situation, a sensible thing to try to do. If I think that this is right, then my job is to try to find the money for it, to try to make it fit in, to find ways and means of making it fit into the total public expenditure scene.[16]

While such men may be no more appreciated by the departments, their modes of operation also deserve some attention.

A man can develop expertise only by staying in the same place and dealing with the same subject over a period of years. If he is moved to a new job every two years or so, he will never be in a position to know enough to take positive action with any degree of assurance. Two years is just about long enough to know what you are doing but not quite long enough to develop that combination of knowledge plus experience in handling practical problems which will lead a man to venture into new paths and, equally, lead others to pay attention to him.

Treasury principals are fast on their feet. The idea is that they should get diverse experiences in their formative years. The result is a rapid turnover at the lowest levels. In June 1971 there were 41 principals in the Public Spending Group (i.e., the side of the Treasury concerned with the control of public expenditures). The average time they had been any place in this group was only a little over two years. Assistant secretaries averaged five years; undersecretaries, six years; and the permanent and deputy secretaries, four years. Expenditure experience tends to be centred at the upper middle levels, while principals are clearly exposed to little danger of losing their amateur status.

16. Ibid., p. 74.

Why are they moved so rapidly? In part because the Treasury values the infusion of bright young men, their information, and the chance to broaden departmental perspectives.[17] In part because the classic problem of budget controllers, in fact of emissaries of all kinds, also arises; longevity makes it more difficult to control the controllers. The top men in the Treasury wish to get the most experienced advice that is compatible with independence of judgement. They may fear rightly that their controllers will be captured or will develop ideas of their own that are inimical to the proper functioning of the institution and that deprive these top men of a necessary degree of manoeuvrability. The longer examiners stay on the job, the better they should be at it and the more prejudiced, or opinionated, they necessarily become. The clash between knowledge and disinterest may be resolved to some extent by knowing the proclivities of the people involved. Men of strong opinions may be put into areas where their superiors want a kind of insistent stubborness, while in other positions men who are unlikely to challenge anyone may be permitted to stay longer than would otherwise be the case. But there is no safe or certain way of maintaining a balance between the rival values that the Treasury controllers epitomise on the job.

The experienced Treasury controller is able to facilitate departmental work at the cost of being difficult to fool. He knows, so to speak, where all the bodies are buried. The inexperienced man is likely to prove a menace because he does not know the substance of the issues nor the rules of the game.

Departments usually prefer an experienced man, if for no other reason that he is a known evil. They like an opportunity to make accommodations with the examiner so that they will know what to expect from him. As a department official stated, 'The Treasury makes everyone's job especially difficult by their tendency of switching their own expenditure controllers around, often chang-

17. One of the outstanding permanent secretaries of the Treasury observed, somewhat optimistically:

This widening of experience and transfer from one job to another is a great solvent of the differences between Departments. A man with this experience behind him is likely to look with a critical eye at the departmental philosophy which he has inherited, and to be alert to correct any defects and weaknesses in it which his experience in other fields may suggest.

Bridges, 'Portrait of a Profession', p. 23.

ing them within a single year so there was little chance for the person to know what he was doing in relationship to your department.' Or, as another official put it more directly, 'Just as you know where he stands and how far you can go, he disappears.'

To observe the skilled operator – the man who knows the substance of the issues, the personalities of the department people, and the general political scene – is to see a man who is confident in his judgement and assured in his personal relationships. Such a man's experience makes him sceptical of what he hears, not only from departments but from politicians as well. 'You know by experience that you have to give a new government time to get its dogma in agreement with reality, and to get bad ministers replaced with other ministers.' A new government may say it will do one thing but the experienced man expects that conditions will force it to do quite different things. So he goes along with whatever is required, hedging his bets sufficiently, however, to have something available when the new boys begin to change their minds. 'I knew,' says one such Treasury official, 'when they scrapped —— policy that they would almost immediately contribute to the inability of the government to budget its funds.'

It must be borne in mind that none of the calculations, norms, or anything else we have mentioned reasonably allow the Treasury to claim that it knows the basis on which to allocate resources among pensions, hospitals, defence or anything else. The Treasury can justifiably say that it is the only department which collects all the claims in one place. It is all too easy to slide over from the correct factual statement that all bids for increased spending are received in a central place, to the indefensible statement that a single view, relating the consequences of each expenditure to the others, is being maintained. That the Treasury has an overview, however, that it has a perspective that is uniquely valuable and denied to others, is stoutly maintained, because without it there would be little justification for Treasury control.

Our discussion so far has been distorted by considering only the individual Treasury man. The Treasury perspective is, however, not simply a function of isolated individuals but of their interactions inside Treasury Chambers.

Forming 'The Treasury View'

> You can't speak of vertical and horizontal here. . . . It's a
> net of crossways in all directions at all times.
>
> *Treasury undersecretary*

> Treasury supply division heads live in each other's
> pockets.
>
> *Treasury official*

> We do spend a lot of our time informing one another,
> and the volume of paper floating around here is terrific.
> But really it is essential.
>
> *Senior Treasury official*

To those who have heard of the Treasury only by reputation,
it will be surprising to discover that informal, non-hierarchical
arrangements predominate within the organisation. The Treasury
is probably the most internally fluid of all government departments. It is from the flux of circulating papers and criss-crossing
conversations, not cast-iron directives, that any particular Treasury
view is formed.

For processing work, making comparisons, and co-ordinating
stances, the small size of their organisation is a positive advantage
and in the view of Treasury officials far outweighs the concomitant
disadvantage of overwork. As a supply division head recently
testified :

> One advantage of the situation, however, is that a very small
> number of heads of Treasury Divisions between them cover
> the whole public expenditure field. If there were more of us,
> each of us might have a more manageable workload but the
> loss in perspective would be very considerable ; the difficulties
> of each knowing what the other was doing would be very great.
> We are small in number, we are very closely in touch with one
> another; we meet frequently, we are all very well aware of what
> is going on in the other's field, and we exchange views and infor-
> mation very frequently indeed.[18]

18. H.C. 347 (1971–2), p. 73.

Although every division man has difficulty in keeping track of his own sector, he avidly seeks information about what is happening elsewhere. Occasionally events occurring at other places in the government may affect what his departments are trying to do. His ability to inform departmental people about such developments enhances their respect for him as a man who can be helpful to them. At other times Treasury examiners themselves may be undertaking separate actions which conflict with one another and may cause trouble, as each department claims it has been treated differently and each seeks the treatment afforded the most favourable one. If the Treasury is to have 'a view' with regard to reducing expenditures (or, for example, the extent of delegation or elimination of certain types of subsidies) it can be effective only if that view grows out of contributions from controllers with a wide range of experience, and if it is executed flexibly, as successive decisions reveal the difficulties encountered by each supply division.

Co-ordination, knowing what other people in the Treasury are saying and doing, is also a matter of pride. The Treasury is supposed to be better at such things than other departments. That reputation cannot be maintained if one arm of the Treasury is unaware of what others are up to. To be caught unaware of a parallel development elsewhere in the government would be highly embarrassing to a Treasury man who has spent so much time finding fault with departmental procedures for co-ordination. Communication matters in the Treasury.

Co-ordination depends on reinforcing mutual expectations. The better people know each other, the greater their ability to act with foreknowledge of what the other is likely to do. Most co-ordination must be tacit rather than explicit; it cannot be based on direct commands. There is simply not enough time to give orders about everything or to direct others how to adjust to rapidly changing circumstances. Thus co-ordination is fostered by a functional redundancy, as it were, of overlapping, criss-crossing and repetitive channels of communication.[19] This seemingly haphazard jumble, far from being wasteful, contains the secret of Treasury control.

The Treasury co-ordinates itself by incessant internal com-

19. The seminal work of the usefulness of such redundancy is Martin Landau's 'Redundancy, Rationality, and the Problem of Duplication and Overlap,' *Public Administration Review*, v. 34, no. 4, 1969.

munication in all directions. As one undersecretary reminded us, the Treasury is a sensitive net, pyramidic if one likes but with crossways in all directions. One obvious form of exchange is through the circulation of notes and memoranda. The subject matter is legion; it may be a report on how the annual Public Expenditure Survey is going, a forecast that is being overturned, a proposed Treasury stance, the summary of an important discussion with departments, and so on. The important point is to inform all other Treasury officials who might have an interest. To take a concrete example, an assistant secretary said, 'Last Friday afternoon I wrote a paper on [a matter of pricing] and sent this to its target, the Chief Secretary. But I also sent a copy to the Chancellor; all Treasury ministers; my immediate superior, the Third Secretary; all the division undersecretaries; and some people elsewhere in the Treasury concerned with prices and wages policy as a whole.'

This constant flow of paper is a good indication of the relative informality prevailing inside the Treasury. Any new recruit is likely to find much less rigidity in the Treasury about 'who can see what' than in the department from which he came. Usually everyone merely takes note of the papers that come across his desk. Even inexperienced principals, for example, expect to have the PESC minutes they send to assistant and undersecretaries returned simply 'with thanks' noted. But it would be a very foolish young principal who for this reason attenuated or neglected his part of the communication net. As one of the highest officials in the Treasury noted, 'I spend a good deal of my time reading. These papers are essential.'

There is not time, even if one wanted, to conduct most business on paper. Most everyday issues are settled through one of the most vital phenomena of British government, 'the chat'. And nowhere has the chat been elevated into a more pervasive institution than in the Treasury. A telephone call, lunch, a chance meeting in the corridor – almost anything can occasion a chat. Indeed, part of the delight of being at the Treasury, which compensates for its long hours, hectic pace, and difficult decisions, is incessant gossip about men and affairs throughout the government.

What do people in the Treasury talk about when they meet each other? They talk shop like everybody else. They cheerfully report the latest horror stories: they discuss new personalities and evidence concerning judgements made about old ones. They mention a department man who has done a brilliant analysis or who has executed an extremely able manoeuvre. They pass on a tip about mechanisms out of control that may prove useful elsewhere. They warn each other about events and people.

One could commit no greater error than to think that this village gossip, because it is sometimes frivolous and haphazard, is therefore unimportant. It lies at the centre of Treasury effectiveness. Co-ordination in the Treasury is based, above all, on a never ending round of personal contacts among people who know each other and who have a strong professional interest in talking about their work. No formal method of communication could be as effective as the desire of Treasury people to express themselves to one another.

The larger significance of these personal contacts lies in the learning that takes place, learning not simply about events and techniques of control, but about people. Such knowledge allows personality factors to be taken into account as an important element of Treasury co-ordination. When we wondered, for example, whether Treasurer controllers were concerned about saying 'yes' to the departments too often (for fear of appearing soft to their superiors) we were told in no uncertain terms that the question evinces insensitivity to the system. 'Everyone knows each other very well. Some are known to be tight-fisted and others liberal, and you assess what a person says on a well-informed judgement of his character.'

The 'chat' pervades all levels, but the higher you rise in the Treasury the more meetings you attend. The undersecretary who heads a supply division is constantly engaged in meetings whose purpose is to take a common line in the Treasury. Meetings are held within a single division to pass down or work out policies. Meetings are held with department officials to get their ideas. Meetings are held among the division heads to discuss issues that cut across their respective jurisdictions. Supply division heads are forever consulting one another and inviting each other to meetings. A typical undersecretary is likely to be in contact with one or another division head six times a day.

These *ad hoc* methods of communication are supplemented by more formal arrangements. Every Friday morning the Second Permanent Secretary in charge of the public sector and his two deputy secretaries, get together with the six undersecretaries – five from the older supply divisions and a sixth from the General Expenditure (G.E.) division which puts the PESC figures together. This intimate group of able men then review the week that was in public expenditure. Everyone recounts the major things that they have done and what is likely to be coming up next. Frequently it will emerge that there is a need for a common line to be pursued and this issue will then be siphoned off to some sub-group for consideration. The Friday meeting serves to bring top officials up to date. It gives everyone a sense of what is happening elsewhere, and helps maintain the feeling (not always fully justified) that the Treasury has its hand on the pulse of government spending. There is also a Monday morning meeting over coffee in the Second Permanent Secretary's office to which the two deputy secretaries and the economic adviser to the public sector group are invited. More confidential matters, including internal personnel questions, may come up here. The Second Secretary will tell about events on the economic and fiscal policy side of the Treasury, with which he is in close touch, or about contacts with Treasury ministers, according to his estimate of the undersecretaries' need to know.

At these meetings, information from several devices new to Treasury co-ordination is also likely to be discussed. The 'Running Talley' was created in 1966 by the General Expenditure division. Under this procedure the spending departments submit monthly reports, agreed with the Treasury supply divisions, as to how their planned expenditures are working out in practice. The G.E. division keeps track by department and by category of expenditure for each month. Over against this is a 'Contingency Reserve' (£350 million for 1973/4) for unforecasted spending during the year.[20] Top Treasury officials watch the monthly tallies and gradually declining contingency reserve to gain an idea of how fast money is being spent. The head of the supply division is able to see whether he is being more or less generous than others and how his pattern of actions compares with his colleagues'. Supply division people are also able to determine how much of the contingency fund is being used up. If some departments appear to be spending too fast and others too slowly, arrangements will be made to look into the matter and take remedial action. More

20. A description of the operation of the Contingency Reserve is in H.C. 549 (1970–1), pp. 86 ff.

frequent and informal returns are also used inside the Treasury to provide some foreknowledge about coming demands. These strictly internal Treasury procedures allow the supply division heads to report on what increases in the next Public Expenditure Survey will be likely as a result of issues currently under discussion with spending departments.

Wherever possible the heads of the Treasury supply divisions and their immediate superiors try to settle expenditure questions among themselves. Their task is to get an agreed position if they can. By these discussions, men from one division find out if what they are doing will create problems for other divisions. 'I might,' suggested one undersecretary, 'say to the head of G.E. division that a certain policy is costing us this much more : can you live with it? And from this you get a general idea of whether or not to make things difficult or easy for the department and who else you need to inform about it.'

According to another undersecretary, the one area, 'where things cannot be settled among ourselves is usually in the area of finance, where we have to send things up to the Treasury hierarchy to deal with the Bank of England'. The heads of the supply divisions find the interaction between expenditures on the one hand and monetary policy on the other to be slippery and esoteric. They refer to the 'somewhat mysterious' dealings with the Treasury and the Bank of England. 'The problem here is you don't know whether you are on thin ice or no ice at all.' A higher justice may be at work in all of this because, as we shall see, officials in the spending departments often feel as if the Treasury were a remote and mysterious institution whose verdicts from on high have only the most tenuous relationship to the reality in the field.

No one should imagine that the process of communication always works smoothly; it does not and it cannot. 'With so little time,' an undersecretary explained, 'the Treasury is largely reactive. Someone from the departments will ring up and say "haven't you seen the paper going to the minister next week" and you will ask to have a copy sent on to you. You might get it in draft a few hours before it goes to their minister.' There is little chance, at that late hour, that anything will be done about it, though emergency rescue operations may have to be mounted from time to time. What the higher-ups attend to is not only a function of what they wish to receive but of what they have time

P.G.P.M.—4

to hear. They are incredibly busy and must make the most drastic choices about their allocation of time. One approach they can take, depending on individual personality, is to deal with gross movements of funds, paying attention to the most deviant (and hence troublesome) trends. Another is to focus on material believed to be of personal interest to ministers or that is necessary to prepare them for Cabinet committees and presentations in Parliament. A third approach is to specialise in a few major issues each year, leaving the rest to subordinates.

Under the conditions that prevail, particularly at the top of the Treasury, a great deal of business is done off-the-cuff, on-the-run, and along-the-way. Since they are forever at meetings, the man who wishes to approach them may find it more convenient to ask a question in the corridor or drop by for a two-minute conversation. Everyone understands and attempts to get around the drastic time limitations affecting their superiors. In discussing whether his superior would make his own contribution to a draft proposal for a minister, an assistant secretary concluded that 'it depends more upon time restrictions than the merits of the case. I know that this is the usual situation and as a result I have hurried everyone along so that my boss will have time on this issue to add to it if he wants to and to study it. This is important because he is going to be the one going to the ministerial sub-committee.'

At the very highest level, the First Permanent Secretary may not wish to pay attention to the expenditure side at all. He may consider himself an expert in economic affairs or wish to devote himself to some other important question and therefore will turn over expenditures to the Second Permanent Secretary. The permanent secretary will, in any event, keep himself out of detailed negotiations unless his departmental opposite number specifically requests a meeting. 'I knew my chaps, the undersecretaries, understood what was going on far better than I did,' said one permanent secretary, 'and would be much better at negotiating an agreement. I much preferred them to clear the ground and then have the Chancellors see their Cabinet colleagues.' Permanent Secretaries of the Treasury and their masters, the Chancellors, are likely to find adjusting the economy far more glamourous than trimming expenditures – an operation which inevitably throws them into conflict with their fellow political administrators in spending departments.

From outside, the Treasury easily appears lofty and distant at the centre of British government. From inside, Treasury life is an intensely personal whirl of compromises and adjustments carried out on the run. Its power is wholly contingent, and its officials have learned how to thrive on this fact. The Treasury can influence almost every action of government and yet it is always once removed from the actual operation of government spending programmes. Treasury officials exercise extensive independence in decision-making and yet they can easily lose influence unless their independence is married to a fine sensitivity to signals from their ministerial masters. The Treasury is sceptical, dogged, actively critical, and self-assured of its unique central perspective. And yet it must largely react to what others propose and do, count on others to do the technical work, and bargain rather than rule by absolute fiat. The Treasury's supreme talent lies in its sensitivity to others. It rules indirectly by trying to shape others' assumptions, expectations and mental sets. But it is always up to someone else to take the cue. There is therefore something unreal about the Treasury considered in isolation. We must now turn to the most common expression of ambivalence in British central government – the relations between the Treasury officials, who live to control, and the departmental operators, who love to spend.

3 Village Life in Civil Service Society: Department–Treasury Bargaining

The Civil Service is run by a small group of people who grew up together.

Treasury official

The conduct of expenditure business is an eternal dialogue between the department and the Treasury....
Sir Richard Clarke,
New Trends in Government,
p. 48.

We can never have a situation like that where the Treasury says to a Department, 'We do not agree with you; go away.' I must stress this.

Leo Pliatzky, *Treasury undersecretary*, Evidence to Trade and Industry Subcommittee, Expenditure Committee (1970–1), pp. 80–1

THE TREASURY is responsible for managing the economy, departments for managing their subject matter. Since the Second World War, this theoretical distinction has been increasingly accepted by both sides and it has contributed much to the improved spirit of co-operation between Treasury and spending departments. Yet relationships between the two also constitute a mixed-motive game. Each can both help and harm the other immeasurably. They need each other but they also need to get around one another. Their conflicts are rooted in the institutional differences that separate those whose criteria for success depend on spending (and hopefully accomplishing) more, and those whose first obligation is to keep spending (and hence taxes) within acceptable limits. Their co-operation works through membership in a common society where some perform the substantive operations and others authorize the necessary funds.

Departmental views of the Treasury are suffused with ambivalence. They admire but fear it. The more droll are likely to refer half-seriously to the Treasury as 'a necessary evil – necessary and evil'. They know someone has to guard the purse and manage the economy but wish they did not have to suffer for it. They hope the Treasury will avoid concentrating on minute details, but they are not happy when it delves into major policies. All the Treasury people care about is totals, departmental people will complain, in the same breath muttering that the Treasury men think they know the department's business better than those who are entrusted with it. Department people like to feel protected in general but free in particulars. They want Treasury men to understand them but not at the price of interference. They want the Treasury to be powerful except where they differ, cynical except where they need trust, and benevolent except when other departments are depriving them of a fair share of funds.

The Treasury and its minister, the Chancellor of the Exchequer, are responsible both for raising taxes and for managing the economy. Historically the theory of the British constitution has been that the Chancellor, with the Treasury behind him, supports the interest in maintaining or reducing taxes against claims of the spending ministers who gain by doing more. The Chancellor is blamed for increasing taxes; other Cabinet members are praised for spending more than their predecessors. This division of roles is acceptable as a living reality. 'Let's be frank,' a high department official insisted, 'the Treasury's chief interest is to save themselves the unpopularity of having to put up taxes.' In the modern post-Keynesian era, the Treasury has also become responsible for managing the economy and, in particular, the huge bulk of aggregate demand supplied by the public sector. Spending departments do not always like this Treasury role either. They can easily accuse the Treasury of 'economic brutalisation by aggregation'. This means, in the words of one undersecretary, that all expenditures are treated as interchangeable. 'Since the war,' this official (along with many others) believed, 'the Treasury has always been concerned with raising money *per se* and not what it is used for.' People who spend tend to believe in what they do. They do not like the idea that for the manager of the economy, an offensive missile, a motorway or ten new hospitals may amount to the same thing.

There is, then, no chance that Treasury behaviour will be right for everybody. It is not in the nature of things for Treasury and departments to chime together in perfect harmony.[1] Yet it would be entirely misleading to begin by describing the inevitable conflicts. To talk with officials in the Treasury and spending departments is to enter a fundamentally cohesive world of insiders. Their conflicts are comprehensible only against the broader background of their co-operation. Treasury and departments live off and through each other. And they know it.

The Ambience of Collaboration

Writing in the 1930s, Ivor Jennings suggested that decisions were worked out in early, bilateral consultations between departmental and Treasury officials on a face-to-face basis.[2] The situation remains fundamentally the same. The 1950s now appear to have been one of the peaks in the periodic cycle of hostility between spending departments and the Treasury, a cycle which has been continuing for at least a century. It was in the mid-fifties

1. To this extent, there is still an important element of truth in the words of a Treasury permanent secretary who wrote 'The Treasury as a Department, if it faithfully discharges the duties entrusted to it, can never be popular....' Sir Thomas Heath, *The Treasury*, (London: G. P. Putnam's Sons) 1927.

2. Jennings, *Cabinet Government*, pp. 154–5.
... The Treasury is frequently consulted before the need for formal sanction arises, especially on large schemes and establishment matters. The appropriate departmental officer works out a scheme and there comes a point at which he says: 'It's no use going any further till we know what so-and-so at the Treasury thinks about it.' Accordingly, he crosses to Treasury Chambers to see 'so-and-so'. Possibly he takes with him the technical expert. In the result the Treasury is seized of all the facts and gets in on the ground floor.

that funds previously used in the Korean War build-up were diverted to other purposes. As spending on welfare, education, housing and other social purposes grew, the Treasury became concerned that expenditures would outstrip revenues and lead to steep increases in taxes and/or a monetary crisis. The ministers and officials of this period are those most likely to speak of the Treasury as 'narrow', 'stubborn', 'nit-picking', and tending to be inbred. By the mid-sixties high officials of the Treasury had made a serious effort to increase contacts with the departments and to gain enhanced understanding of their problems. A cooperative spirit grew. Meetings of senior officials were held both within the Treasury and between Treasury and departments. Department finance officers were encouraged to get to know one another as well as their Treasury contacts.

Yet, even in the difficult fifties, intimacy was the dominant theme in Treasury–department relations. As the Permanent Secretary at the Ministry of Agriculture said in 1957, 'The Treasury division is so close to us that I do not believe that if the head of the [Treasury] division sat in the [Ministry] office instead of near his superiors, he would know any more or be any more effective.' [3] Few practitioners doubt that this condition is the same today.

Here are the views from both sides. A permanent secretary states that 'A great deal, in fact the bulk of the work, is done bilaterally between the Treasury and the department. Although a new project going into PESC will be discussed at that time with the Treasury, it has already been talked about with the Treasury when it first came up during the course of the year.' From the Treasury side, John Hunt, Deputy Secretary at the Treasury reported that 'Behind all this [the PESC survey], the Treasury and Treasury expenditure divisions are engaged in a daily dialogue with departments about individual programmes.' [4] There is no one comprehensive paroxysm of expenditure decision-making by either civil servants or politicians.

Ministerial conflict on expenditures is like the collision of mammoth icebergs; before the tips impinge, the grinding and crunching has already been well under way below the surface. The battle

3. H.C. 254 (1957–8), question 1174. Relations between Treasury and departments in the fifties are described at length in testimony to this committee.

4. H.C. 549 (1970–1), pp. 59, 22.

begins with whomever in the department finance division is at that time dealing with his Treasury counterpart. 'If the desk man thinks the Treasury is being particularly unfair,' a permanent secretary noted, 'he will try and get up to a higher official level, and if necessary to a permanent secretary. It's an iterative process in which each upper level uses its judgement as to what issues to fight.' Selectivity is essential because, as this official remarked, 'If everything is fought, you won't get away with anything else.' There is only so much friction that anyone can cause without deeply antagonising Treasury officials and thus harming the departmental case on many issues. Clearly it is better to agree with the Treasury than to disagree, if not on each and every case, at least on the range of issues.

Co-operation is facilitated by the fact that, despite department allegiances, all officials are part of a greater civil service society. Among those at the top of the service, the bond may be particularly close. By the time they have arrived their official career paths are likely to have criss-crossed many times. Those further down may not know each other but still they know enough about each other to understand that they are dealing with 'a member of one's own group'. The statement of one Treasury assistant secretary can stand for the feeling expressed to us by most officials. 'It's difficult for an outsider to appreciate how chummy things are in the Civil Service. You've probably known each other for fifteen years – lots of informal contacts and socialising. You ring each other up and gossip about things. Not everyone agrees with this style of doing things, but most do. Formal discussion follows after informal chats.'

Members of this society feel close and, given the uncertain prospects surrounding any referral up to their political masters, civil servants are close. Few perhaps would express themselves as fervently as one man with over a dozen years as a permanent secretary. 'There's a tremendous incentive for officials to agree.... In the last resort, if you don't sort things out with the Treasury, ministers will decide and they are political animals. You don't know what they'll do.' What is at stake is less a conspiracy against ministers and more an inheritence of empathy among professionals with shared standards and understanding.

The terms 'Treasury' and 'spending department' are collective nouns suggesting discrete chunks of organisation. In terms of people, however, they are a vast flux of inter-changing personnel within the one civil service society. Discussion of civil service cohesion, usually in terms of 'elitism' has typically concentrated on the socologists' favoured themes – socio-economic background and conditions of entry to the service. We contend that a more immediate and important form of socialisation occurs by virtue of officials' post-entry movement within the government community. 'Transfer between Departments,' wrote a permanent secretary of the Treasury, is one of the most vital sources for the service's 'bond of unity.'[5] A closer look at this bonding is rewarding.

Examining the extent of turnover at the top of the civil service, we find that for the 32 permanent secretaries in office 1961–71, the average duration on the job was approximately 49 months; this time has been shortened by approximately one-quarter compared to the 66 months for permanent secretaries from 1928–38. As the figure below shows, civil servants in the post-war era

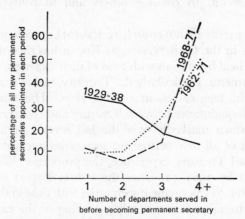

Number of departments served in before becoming permanent secretary

(Source: Data is compiled from the *Imperial Calendar* and *Who's Who* for each period shown.)

5. Sir Edward Bridges, 'Portrait of a Profession', p. 11. Studies typical of the social background approach are R. K. Kelsall, *Higher Civil Servants in Britain*, C. H. Dodd, 'Recruitment to the Administrative Class', *Public Administration*, spring 1967; Peta Sheriff's study of direct-entry principals, 'Outsiders in a Closed Career,' *Public Administration*, winter 1972; and A. H. Halsey and I. M. Crew, 'Social Survey of the Civil Service', vol. 3 (1) of the *Fulton Report*. One exception is Maurice Kogan's, 'Social Services: Their Whitehall Status', *New Society*, 21 August 1969.

are also acquiring a wider range of experience in other departments before reaching the top than did their predecessors. Whereas two-thirds of permanent secretaries appointed 1929–38 had served in only one or two departments, by the post-Fulton period (1968–71), two-thirds had served in four or more departments prior to reaching the peaks of Whitehall.

The circulation pump of career mobility in the civil service, flowing into every corner of Whitehall and back again, establishes the preconditions for co-operation between Treasury and departments. If the Treasury recruited only or mainly from its own ranks, its members would lack contact with department officials who, in the event, could hardly have found room for prior service in Great George Street. If all who once served in the Public Spending Group (the unit that concerns us most) were carried off elsewhere, there might be no spending norms to bequeath future generations other than the lament that life is flux. The flow of careers appears complex precisely because the Treasury wishes both to preserve and to pass on, to colonise others and to conserve its own values.

Career currents are not entirely reciprocal between departments. Senior jobs in the Civil Service, as Kogan has shown, are more likely to be held by officials with most of their experience in 'economic' departments, particularly the Treasury, rather than those, by contrast, with long careers in social services.[6] Thus the likelihood of mutual acquaintance between Treasury and civil service leadership has grown markedly over the last several decades. While 16 per cent of all new permanent secretaries appointed between 1928–38 had Treasury experience, the proportion had grown to 38 per cent by 1961–71. Since the Fulton Report on the Civil Service (1968–71), permanent secretaries with time in the Treasury have risen to 44 per cent, nearly a tripling of the earlier ratios. Meanwhile from beginning to end, the proportion of new permanent secretaries with previous experience in a social department such as health or education has remained constant at around 10 per cent.

The heart of expenditure control is, of course, the Treasury's Public Spending Group. A glance at a large sample of officials who have served in this section during 1961–71, (see Table 2

6. Kogan, 'Social Services: Their Whitehall Status', p. 283.

below),[7] reveals both wholesale interchange and selective continuity. Civil servants have spent, on the average, between three and four years at the jobs of controlling public expenditure, a little less than that at the lower levels and a little more for higher ranks.

TABLE 2

1961–1971	Average length of service in Public Spending Group (whole sample) in months	Average Length of service excluding those still in post (months)
Permanent secretaries	41·5	49·0
Deputy secretaries	42·0	45·5
Undersecretaries	45·8	48·7
Assistant secretaries	35·4	41·0
Principals	34·5	38·6

Most of these officials, save newly entering principals, will have worked at least three and usually more years outside the Treasury before entering into one of the various supply divisions. Nor is this capillary action accidental. In an attempt to combat the Treasury's isolation, it was Permanent Secretary Warren Fisher who fifty years ago first enunciated the principle that the Treasury 'be staffed by a continual flow and circulation of principals with two to eight years training in other departments.'[8]

Once again, however, the exchange of personnel is not symmetrical. Approximately three-fifths of those entering the Public Spending Group come from an immediately preceding post

7. The sample consists of career data for principals and above who were serving in the Public Spending Group of the Treasury at, or around, June in 1961, 1963, 1965, 1967, 1969 and 1971. Career paths of these 157 officials, as well as 19 terminated appointments have been analysed by listing previous jobs held in the Civil Service (though records are poor prior to 1961) and all service jobs held after leaving the Public Spending Group, up to June 1971. We are grateful to the Treasury and Civil Service Department for this information. We have neither asked for nor received the actual names of the officials in the sample.

8. Quoted in B. B. Schaffer, 'The British Treasury', *Public Administration, Journal of the Australian Regional Groups*, vol. 9 (1950) p. 339.

elsewhere in the Treasury. (As for the remainder, 13 per cent have come from jobs in social service departments, 13 per cent from defence, 14 per cent from industrial/technological departments, 3 per cent from Cabinet Office, and 13 per cent from other corners of the Whitehall maze.) Almost one-third of those filling the key posts of undersecretary or assistant secretary in the expenditure divisions have been promoted from within the Public Spending Group itself. These promotees of the middle ranks constitute the vital core of continuity in the control of public expenditure. While permanent and deputy secretaries of the Section are on the scene for approximately $3\frac{1}{2}$ years, promotees into undersecretary and assistant secretary posts are typically around the Group for $5\frac{1}{2}$ and $8\frac{1}{2}$ years respectively. This pattern has not changed appreciably during the last decade.

It would be entirely misleading, however, to imagine that there is anything like a comprehensive career ladder within the Treasury's Public Spending Group. The number of civil servants who have moved up from one post, to a second, and then to a third within the Group can be counted on the fingers of one hand. Their scarcity no doubt enhances their value.

Where, then, do Treasury expenditure controllers go? Officials who have been in the Group are spread out quite evenly around Whitehall. Approximately two-thirds of those leaving in the last decade immediately went to other departments (33 per cent social service, 20 per cent defence, 27 per cent industrial and 20 per cent to others), usually at a higher rank. A third take their next job in the Treasury, but a half of these had also moved on to other departments by the end of our period of study (June 1971). The Treasury could hardly be accused of inbreeding. Colonisation would be more like it. Retaining that minimum self-selection required to preserve and transfer appropriate values on public spending, the Treasury has sent the rest out to live with the natives.

None of this is to suggest that Treasury men acquire in a few years some manner of institutional-financial ideology which they then carry with them the rest of their working lives. One thing they learn is that each organisation has interests it will be in their duty (and to their advantage) to protect. Work contact does not mean that the Treasury's view will always be uppermost in their bargaining, but it does help Treasury and department officials to know how to get along and what to expect from each other. Observe the similar comments of two permanent secretaries who had held top positions in both Treasury and spending departments. 'First I knew what the Treasury was trying to do,' an ex-permanent secretary recalled, 'so it was easier to go along with it. Then secondly I knew all the chaps. Of course everybody "knows all the chaps" but I knew them with intimacy. . . . I knew how to cut corners – like who to see, who could get a problem solved.' A second permanent secretary observed that anyone in his position could 'drop in for a chat' at the Treasury but unlike him, they 'would have been a stranger.' Having been at the Treasury, 'one can read the signs and tell when the screws are really on and when they aren't.' Clearly, the civil servants' socialisation means, not that the Treasury always wins, but that both sides are more able to get what they want from each other. Familiarity may occasionally breed contempt but it always breeds mutual knowledge and increased predictability.

Co-operation in the common society of officialdom is enhanced not only by civil servants' movements but also by their working arrangements. The shadowy personal networks merge into more formal but still blurry structures. Whitehall and its vast departmental fortresses are honeycombed with joint groups, working parties, and interdepartmental committees of officials – some *ad hoc* and some formal, some meeting only once or twice and others working for several years. Treasury men are likely to be found involved in almost any major departmental or interdepartmental committee, sometimes as full members, sometimes as occasional visitors, and many times merely watching and listening from a polite distance. An organisation chartist's nightmare perhaps, but this flux of working arrangements does allow officials to meet when, where, and in the manner they deem necessary, usually with a minimum of formality.

So much is well known; but in addition, at the heart of British political administration, is a much more unknown set of committees of officials from various departments. Time and research grants could easily be wasted in discovering and naming the supposedly secret Cabinet committees of ministers. For most purposes, atttention is more profitably invested in two types of civil service groups working under the committees of ministers. First are the Cabinet Official Committees, one for each committee of ministers and usually chaired by an official at the deputy secretary level. Like ministerial committees, the official committees are rather formal appointments made yearly by the Cabinet Secretariat after sounding out the various permanent secretaries as to who should serve. Below each official committee are the Working Parties of officials (called too by various other names such as panel, committee, etc.), somewhat less permanent and more *ad hoc* but again composed entirely of civil servants. These usually will be chaired at the under- or assistant secretary level. Although formally under the official committee, a typical working party will have only one or two members from the official committee, with the remainder selected after consultation between the chairman of the official committee and permanent secretary of the department concerned.

The existence and structural details of these groups of officials are, for some reason, kept secret; they are the great unmentionables of Whitehall life. But in fact these monumental state secrets – the organisation forms – are far too schematic to be of much value. What matters is the personal fine-tuning built into these official groups. As one Cabinet Office man put it, 'Our flexibility is in fact the trick of it all. The Cabinet committee structure can be adjusted to produce the right people working together on anything that is coming up. It includes taking into account questions of individual personality.' These collaborative mechanisms are supposed to train officials in their common, transdepartmental identity. Both types of official group are usually chaired by someone from the Cabinet Office, with another (junior) Cabinet Office man probably serving as committee secretary and possibly a third (middle-rank) C.O. official as a member of the committee. The assumption is clearly that the officials will work together as a team – a group able and willing to bring out the broader issues rather than simply those advanced by each departmental protagonist (though each side invariably is represented on the committee). The man appointed to a Cabinet official committee or working party, observed another experienced Cabinet Office representative, 'is not expected to be 100 per cent loyal to the department for this assignment. You know who is working by the team spirit; you can see from their papers and statements whether they are doing anything more than regurgitating the well known departmental view.' Treasury officials as a group are exempted from this norm, although there are individually forceful characters who return to try and alter the Treasury line.

The extent to which committeemen go back to evangelise their departments with the agreed team view varies widely with the individual. 'The most useful officials,' the Cabinet Office man went on, 'say that "the department and minister will be difficult but I will support it."' But what does not vary is the expectation that the civil servant will make a fresh and individual offering rather than defensively parroting his departmental case. It is something of a mark of standing to be on these committees, and, a departmental negotiator concluded, 'the parrots don't achieve much standing, they won't get on many more interdepartmental committees.'

The greater the interchange of personnel and interdepartmental collaboration between the departments and Treasury, the better the chance that they will be able to accommodate their differing perspectives. But it would be vain to believe that they will ever reach complete understanding. Departmental needs for spending conflict with the needs of the Treasury for control. Their need for predictability in spending plans confronts the Treasury's desire for adaptability in managing the economy. Even the same need may carry a variety of meanings to different institutions. To the Treasury, security denotes being protected against surprise by sudden expenditures. To the spending departments, being secure means they can go ahead with large, long-term schemes, confident that the money will not suddenly be yanked away. There are real conflicts here and not just failures of mutual understanding. Between the Treasury's abstract claims as manager of the economy and the department's abstract claims as manager of the subject matter, there must be a concrete resolution.

Important issues are at stake. Money and subject matter merge into public policy as claims are made for limited financial resources. There is no limit to possible improvements in the quality and almost none in the quantity of government activities, especially since the demands for public goods and services are likely to grow with increased supply. Moreover, political administrators are paid to recognise not only unsatisfied demands but also areas of unmet need that may lack clearly articulated demands. Practical answers to the question of when (timing), how (standards), and what (priority) demands and needs can be addressed are usually interwoven with winning the expenditure resources to act.[9] A motorway, prison-building programme or change in the school-leaving age may be accelerated or delayed for years. Policy makers have no standards for calculating the ultimate utility of their programmes but can and do bargain over how far improvements will be made in the performance measures of government itself : numbers of nursery school places, miles of motorway, geriatric beds per 1,000 of elderly. The resources acquired affect whether some, none, or all of the aims within a particular field can be acted upon. There may be enough to raise the school-leaving age and repair primary schools but not enough for both building nursery schools and expanding higher education. Funds may be sufficient to prevent more prisoners sharing cells but not adequate to reduce existing sharing or to replace obsolescent accommodations; prison overcrowding may in turn influence the sentencing practice of courts, and so on. In the end, bargaining over public money affects issues as wide as the activity of government itself.

Strategies and Deals

Departmental participants in the expenditure process refer to it as one of 'constant haggling' and 'argy bargy'. Bargaining is incessant, and the Treasury likes it that way. The Treasury does not and, as we have seen, knows it could not, exercise control by giving flat 'no's' to the departments' proposals. If it did, Cabinet meetings would bog down as departments bypassed the Treasury and, worse yet, the Treasury would alienate its life-sustaining sources of trust and information in the spending departments. Even when it is clear to Treasury officials that general expenditure cuts are eventually going to be necessary, they would rather begin by bargaining to find out where the 'give' is in the departments' cases. Little has changed since the 1930s, when the two senior Treasury officials advised the Chancellor in the following terms.

The most candid and desirable course, if it were practicable, would be at once to tell the Departments concerned that supercuts of specified amount will be required of them. But I fear this is not practical politics. It is not merely that we cannot at

9. A number of the important points likely to be at issue are suggested in H.C. 281 (1971-2).

one and the same time impose supercuts and consult as to real economies (it is beyond the bounds of human nature to expect that a Department threatened with a supercut will not try to keep something in hand): in addition till the whole field has been surveyed we do not know where supercuts can most reasonably be imposed. ...

I conclude therefore that all we can do at present is to create an atmosphere of parsimony and financial difficulty and to ask all Departments alike to give us all they can and that any actual decision as to the use of the axe should be postponed till the end of next month: the axe, if then used (as I fear it must be), will need to be accompanied by assurances that supplementaries will be allowed if they prove unavoidable.[10]

What do departments fight about with the Treasury? Almost everything at the beginning. 'There is,' as a top Treasury official said, 'a necessary ritual dance. He inflates to enable you to cut and you bargain him down to show you can cut.' Why do you need this much? This forecast is inflated; the time schedule is over-optimistic; that section is inconsistent; another item contradicts experience. Very often the margin of accuracy being argued back and forth between Treasury and department is narrower than that on which a small business would operate. Experienced bargainers know that despite any new sophisticated expenditure techniques what often matters is not the issue but the bargaining itself. 'To the uninstructed,' a former Treasury official and department permanent secretary told us, 'it will seem like sheer rubbish to argue about £0·5 million out of £100 million. But the purpose is not the figure – arithmetically it may not matter. What does matter is to keep the idea of discipline and control.'

There is little 'artificial' inflation in department proposals. Department representatives know that to maintain their credibility they must deal in reasonable rather than wantonly incredible negotiating margins. 'If in three successive years you go to the Treasury with a range of propositions giving the costs and if in three years running they knock you down by one-third, they'll think your margins are not credible,' a recently retired permanent secretary advised. 'However, if at the end of the day there's been 2–10 per cent chopped off, you don't destroy your credibility. I

10. T. 171/317 (1934).

don't call this padding; human nature being what it is, there are simply varying degrees of satisfaction you can get.'

Strategies are what we call the departments' efforts to increase or maintain its satisfaction. Both sides know, for instance, that efforts to secure stable increases can often be begun by commissions of inquiry made up of specialists in a particular field who naturally believe that their vocation should be supported at the public's expense. All such committees – whether dedicated to admitting qualified people to university, like the Robbins Commission or some other worthy cause – recommend increased spending. The process of inquiry itself generates articles in the press and papers in the more influential periodicals. Commissions make good forums for launching publicity campaigns. Though the Treasury may clamp down on a department which uses public funds to plead for more of the same, it is not difficult to find interested groups who will carry the burden in public. Even an interdepartmental committee of officials can be expected to highlight any real need for improvement, such as a new road programme to counteract pending increases in car ownership and congestion. The result is the same: more money recommended for the favoured cause.[11]

Departments make every effort to seize upon a cause that is popular in its day. Technical and vocational education expanded, explained one departmental strategist, because it could be tied to the popular economic growth argument. A single programme can serve diverse purposes. The truth may be bent, though not necessarily broken, by finding that one rationale, among others, that will meet the public mood of the moment. In the 1950s, for instance, pollution was a topic less in vogue. One can be sure now that a variety of programmes hitherto considered unrelated to the environment will turn out suddenly to contribute to its grandeur. The economic arguments of the day can, of course, serve the

11. In this regard, little has changed since the 1880s 'economy' committees. 'It may begin in all undivided earnestness in a simple demand for a reduction of expenditure. . . . But in the process of the controversy the movement has been insensibly and irrestibly deflected from its original object. It began in a cry for economy; it has become a cry for efficiency. That is the second stage. . . . The third stage . . . becomes an agitation in favour of an increase of . . . expenditure and a more lavish establishment.' – W. S. Churchill, *Lord Randolph Churchill* (London: Macmillan) 1906, vol. 2, pp. 313–17.

same purpose. When production is slack, departments naturally will advance their capital programmes; when the economy is more fully occupied, current expenditure items are pushed to minimise claims on productive resources. Nor should the more political aspects of such opportunism be surprising, unless civil servants are assumed to be deaf-mutes, who do not hear the political music.

A favourite department strategy is targetry: to get a target established, by indirection if not by explicit ministerial statement, and seek to drive expenditures up to that higher level. The target may range from wishful thinking about how much money the department can spend to specific physical goals – so many houses, hospitals or miles of motorway by a certain date. Establishing goals for a lower pupil–teacher ratio, or a high standard of amenity in school design and construction may be worth a great deal in the long run. The Overseas Development Administration is fond of using United Nations' guidelines for foreign aid (0·1 per cent of GNP for aid grants from industrialised nations) as their standard, though they have not often managed to get the target accepted. Greater success – at least in getting targets established – has been achieved by advocates of domestic housing, road and hospital construction, though few expected the original targets would actually be reached. The Treasury zealously seeks to avoid commitment; its supply division officers take great pains to separate the department's realistic forecasts from its wishful thinking and longed-for targets.

Much bargaining is sufficiently stereotyped to have earned its own sobriquet. Departments propose offsetting savings which they know must be put back. Some officials call this 'the sore thumb' or 'beggar's sores' technique (you don't want to hit or touch it). The skilled practitioner agrees to offer compensatory savings but chooses items which are sure to reawaken painful memories of the political consequences that allegedly occurred the last time a cut was applied or proposed in this area. Ministers are unlikely to agree to it. Then it is the Treasury's turn to find counter-economies. Aside from a few old favourites (like delays in raising the school-leaving age or increasing the price of medical prescriptions) cuts are not easy to find. Besides, the Treasury does not really want to take the blame. It would rather that the department decide. The end result often is an agreement that the department will make a 1 per cent cut where it most conveniently can. During a cutting exercise, the Treasury itself is not above a little occasional 'sore thumbing' and may propose a cut in the Prime Minister's pet projects as a device for enlisting his pressure against other ministers. Obviously there is a premium in this strategy on being able to keep a straight face.

A variant of the strategy was used extensively in the late sixties against one of the more elegant and quixotic of recent Treasury ploys. In connection with the five-year expenditure forecasts based on existing policy, the Treasury also asked the department, in effect, 'What would you do with 3 per cent less or 1 per cent more money?' Surely here was a neat way, not only to increase margins for Cabinet decision, but also to obtain an agreed agenda of 'costed options' for possible expenditure cuts or increases should such be necessary. Seasoned 'sore thumb' strategists in the departments scarcely paused for breath. Apart from technical problems, a Treasury undersecretary told us, 'you have to recognise that public expenditure is a highly political game and a change such as costed options is seen as another move. For what they'd cut, departments would always put up a series of politically impossible items. For the options of what they'd do with X per cent more, departments put up the most politically attractive pieces.' Loading the first item on the cut and increase lists of priorities was only the most obvious ploy. Knowing that proposals just below the first might otherwise be jeopardised, the more cunning political administrator would put the item with political dynamite third. When the Cabinet agreed, say, that a Labour Government could not take away free school milk, the minister could reply that the items above were more important and thus increase his likelihood of retaining all three; in the same way, putting the politically most attractive items farther down the additions list improved the chances of those above. Whatever the refinements, the result was to create a natural bias for more spending. Recalling all this, top Treasury officials testily describe the several years experiment with costed options as 'a disastrous failure'.[12]

12. The official Treasury explanation is as follows:

But, coming as [costed options] did very late in the process of developing the snapshot of the cost of existing policies, which is the annual Survey, it could not be relied upon to reveal the really significant choices, which come at a far earlier stage in the continuing process of forming policy

The Treasury expects spending departments to want more money. That is their job, and no one is penalised for doing it well. But the Treasury hates what is called 'the theory of the bounce'. In American parlance, the bounce bears strong similarity to playing someone 'for a sucker' and is, at its extreme, a contradiction of the norm of trustful dealing. When 'bouncing' the Treasury, a department deliberately withholds nasty news while gaining an initial Treasury commitment. Waiting until it is up against a deadline – such as a contract running out or an international conference – the department then returns repeatedly to the Treasury, crying that more money is essential and a response is needed quickly. Here it is not simply a question of the thin end of the wedge, which Treasury men eagerly blunt, but of a cold-blooded baiting of the expenditure hook. A former Treasury principal has outlined the long bounce (from a first estimate of £150m. to over £900m.) on the Concorde supersonic air liner. 'As long as the bouncer never admits to outstanding costs which are out of proportion at any given amount during the build up of expenditure to the stated benefits of the whole project, he can lead the Treasury step by step to a total historic outlay that exceeds all possible benefits by severalfold.' [13]

The bounce is anathema to the Treasury. 'We'll do anything to punish a department which tries this too often,' responds a vengeful Treasury official. 'The Treasury's way around it is to stay close to the department so as to know what is going on.' And it would be misleading to suggest that bouncing the Treasury is in any way a common strategy. The preponderance of departmental opinion is that sharp practice is unwise. The operative rule is to present material with as much frankness as possible. 'You shouldn't make an excessively favourable case,' a permanent secretary said. 'You may get by on one or two occasions but you will get watched more closely and in the end be caught.'

Faced with Treasury demands for cuts or compensatory savings to finance a new item, departments are not above applying a form

---

and relating it to continually changing needs. Even as a device for illustrating possible marginal changes, it suffered from the natural attractiveness of additions and unattractiveness of subtractions.

'Note by the Treasury', appendix 8, H.C. 549 (1970–1), p. 219.

13. Peter Jay, 'Concord: The Biggest "Bounce" in History', *The Times*, 10 December 1971.

of 'reverse bounce'. Internal savings will be found for the first year but the rub lies in the subsequent years. By then the new item will have become established policy looking for its own money, and the offsetting savings will be a thing of the past. The supposed 'savings' may be just another name for underspending which would have occurred in any case. As the head of the Treasury general expenditure division reported, 'It is a fact of life that that is bound to occur sometimes.' [14]

Departments occasionally turn their acceptance of cuts into a strategic move. By sacrificing early rather than waiting 'you can cite your record of giving your ewe lamb for the general welfare'. But this is a temporary stance and generally department officials doubt that there is much goodwill to be gained by continuously accepting cuts without a fuss. 'If you're going to be helpful,' according to one experienced department negotiator, 'do it quickly and make a meal of it all at once.'

The following summary list of suggested practices for getting along with the Treasury, provided by several officials, would be accepted by most of their breed :

1. Consult early and thoroughly. Do not give the Treasury a proposal at the last minute and say that it has no consequences if it does.
2. Rather than trying to hide it, give the costs (in a sufficient depth of years) to show if there really is going to be a large charge.
3. Clear the line beforehand with other departments and show your awareness of the sideways effect of the proposal (e.g. if more staffing is required you'll look good to the Treasury if you show them you have cleared it with the Civil Service Department).
4. Send extensive information to the Treasury.
5. In trying to get more, preserve your credibility by dealing in reasonable negotiating margins.

What is at stake is not merely courtesy and bureaucratic decorum. Experienced members in the tightly-knit community value such rules of the game, for they are rules which help them contain very real conflicts and a game about deadly serious questions of public policy. Depending as they do on mutual confidence, political

14. H.C. 549 (1970–1), p. 86.

administrators are not likely to take advantage of the game, only play it. Caring as they usually do about the substantive issues, they will play it to the hilt.

One might think the most frequent Treasury move to counter departmental strategies is to have its minister, the Chancellor of the Exchequer, refuse requests for increased spending and carry his Cabinet colleagues with him. Treasury officials will settle for that if they must, but reliance on such overt force is not wise policy. A direct strategy bespeaks too much risk and exertion. Ideally the Treasury would prefer to circumvent all difficulties by having sufficiently inculcated norms of self-restraint in departments so as to mute the initial expenditure proposal.

As a second best, the Treasury much prefers to make departments compete among themselves for a limited sum, hopefully counteracting each others' efforts. 'The Treasury's ever-present dream,' said an ex-Treasury man and permanent secretary, 'is to foster competition and have departments scrambling for the ball while the Treasury remains on the sidelines.' The Treasury rule that 'accidental savings', that is, underspending, should not be left to the individual departments but should go into a common contingency fund, is designed to compel departments to compete against each other for limited resources. The rule is hard to enforce, however, and is mainly observed in the breach. Departments are unanimous in their resistance, claiming their own savings as a reward for restraint and as compensation for the disfavour incurred by underspending. 'The Treasury is just hanging on to the remnants of the rule,' according to one division head, 'because there is a political need for the minister to show something positive to stifle the criticism he is getting for not spending. This is how the — department got it from us this year.' Somehow the money always seems to belong to the department, hard as the Treasury tries to make believe that it belongs to everyone and therefore to no one.[15]

Moreover, the fact is that the Treasury itself is not inclined to

15. Thanks to a preoccupation with reducing the National Debt, Gladstonian finance had a specific design for budget surpluses and was much more effective in making such pooling work. Budget surpluses were deliberately planned in normal times and any windfall savings joined these surpluses to help retire the National Debt or occasionally to grant tax remissions. Between 1860–1900, the Debt was reduced by approximately £200 million.

push departmental competition very far; senior Treasury officials understand their system too well for that. It is not the department as some amorphous entity which would have to be made to compete but real people. Fostering a thorough-going competition among officials in various departments would not only be technically difficult, given the lack of comparability among programmes, but more important would endanger the fabric of understandings on which the Treasury and existing civil service society depend. In the words of a recent retiree from the stratosphere of the Treasury: 'Yes, it helps us to have the departments competing against each other, but competition didn't much happen while I was there. If you tried this, the departments [officials] would do what ministers sometimes do against the Chancellor – line up against you. Besides, policies are concerned with such vastly different things. How could you set the chap concerned with school-building against the chap concerned with hospital-building and the one concerned with road-building?'

Active departmental alliances, which are otherwise rare, will materialise when they find a common interest in assaulting Treasury rules that affect them all adversely. One Treasury device which departments initially disliked in concert is the 'relative price effect' (named Clarke's law after its Treasury progenitor, when first applied to defence spending and military pay).[16] The Treasury, bolstered by its small corps of economists, has argued that the public sector will tend to take an increasing proportion of national income as a natural consequence of government's labour-intensive activity. Whether this is because of lower productivity or problems of measurement in the public sector need not concern us here. Experience rather than theory tells the Treasury that if public expenditures and the economy grow at the same rate for five years, the tax burden will be greater at the end than the beginning because prices will have risen faster in the public than private sector. The Treasury likes to come out right in the end; the relative price effect (RPE) helps them do just that. Departments, on this theory, make notional adjustments in their projected expenditure claims on resources. While some Treasury people, like the spending departments, do not find the reasoning wholly convincing, they would rather be safe than sorry.

16. A discussion of the use of the relative price effect by Treasury officials is in H.C. 545, pp. 17 ff. and Cmnd. 4578 (1971), p. 70.

It did not take long, however, for departments to discover the silver lining. In the beginning, departments worried that RPE adjustments would make their programmes look more costly. Since that time, however, departments have discovered some small advantage in having two ways of expressing their programmes. Should Education wish to show that it is doing more, for example, it will likely include the price adjustment; should it wish to show how little is being spent, the department will concentrate on volume rather than relative costs by omitting or cutting down RPE. Maybe the lesson for the day is that budgetary strategies can rarely be static because the kind of thinking men you want in the bureaucracy will find ways to get around last year's bright idea.

To say that there are few active alliances among departments against the Treasury is not to say that departments fail to act in unison. Quite the opposite. Co-operation among departments is omnipresent, but it takes the passive form of never cutting each other down in front of the Treasury. Departments are not usually found offering up each other's prestige projects to the common cause. 'There is never much mutual attacking,' insisted an official with many years high in the Treasury and two spending departments. 'Let the Treasury carry the can is the feeling.' Just as a Treasury norm is to avoid doing the department's work, so the departments give no gratuitous aid to the Treasury by criticising each other. 'If you're a knocker,' a permanent secretary summed up, 'the search for allies is more difficult.'

The recent mergers of several ministries into new conglomerate departments (Environment, Trade and Industry, etc.) has increased the possibility that formerly independent entities might act in concert. Previously there had been an occasional tendency for one ministry to support the related expenditure proposal of another; Housing, for example, might help the Ministry of Transport when it came to the road programme in new towns. Under the new superdepartments, these alliances can become functional links within the one department's presentation to the Treasury. So far, however, this co-operation remains largely untested; the superdepartments remain an umbrella label for the old network of Treasury–department contacts and understandings. The experience of giant corporations, with their penchant for decentralisation, suggests that subunits may also develop independent goals and criteria of success. If they calculate profit and loss differently, they may bypass each other or work at cross purposes. The situation could be worse in government; the parties may be close enough to get in each other's way but too far apart to travel the same road.

If you cannot beat them, join them. Not all bargaining is incessant 'argy-bargy'. An occasional but important strategic move is, in effect, to declare a moratorium on strategic moves and to make a deal. By making a deal, the department can achieve a higher rate of growth than it might have had to settle for, together with the assurance that the new funds will not suddenly disappear during an economy drive. The Treasury guards itself against the possibility that a new programme or an expanding old one, if approved against its recommendations, will lack safeguards limiting its future growth. Each participant seeks stability in different directions. Each may be willing to take less than it might have done as the price of doing better and with greater assurance than could otherwise have been the case. The stage is set for a mutually advantageous arrangement.[17]

A deal means that the department finance officer and relevant Treasury division head (always with the complete knowledge of their superiors) may covenant that 'when everyone else is growing at 5 per cent, we have an agreement with the Treasury allowing 6 per cent'. While these conditions are not immutable, they do imply that when cuts are necessary the Treasury will work on others first and not lightly come back to the original department. The primary precondition for any such arrangement is mutual confidence.

The anatomy of a deal is worked out by parties that have a stake in reaching agreement. Suppose that the Treasury knows full well that a certain type of programme has been starved of funds and is likely to shoot up in the near future. The department hopes that it will but, having suffered unpredictable and erratic cuts in the past, would like to safeguard itself. Experienced department officials believe that, while their case is powerful, there is no limit

17. The five-year forecasting of expenditures has to some extent brought deals out more into the open for all departments to see. While publicity has undoubtedly increased the sense of fair play in the expenditure process – and this is no small thing – it has not fundamentally altered the technique.

on the improvement theoretically possible and, as they say, 'it is no good asking for the moon. Since everything cannot be done at once it must be done gradually.' In a recent and typical plan, the approach was straightforward : the Treasury would, by an exchange of letters, commit itself to securing an annual incremental rise in the programme above the increases in the cost of the operation occasioned by rising prices. There was no special rationale for the figure reached except that after lengthy discussion it seemed reasonable (that is, neither too large nor too little) to both parties. 'My basic task,' explained the initiator, 'was to convince the Treasury not simply that there is a general need but that there is more advantage to the Treasury in doing it this way.' It would cost less, his argument went, and the department would do its own policing. He went on to see 'the right chap' at the Treasury, sounded him out, found out what he wanted to know, and prepared the briefs accordingly. It was not the end of the battle, but it was a vital beginning. The risk the department took was that the programme would turn out to cost far more than anticipated, and, unable to go back on their word, they would have to transfer money from other hard-pressed activities. But at least they were able to count more confidently on a certain sum for a number of years and make plans accordingly.

When concerned with old programmes admittedly starved of funds, or programmes where targets have been formerly agreed (e.g., classroom size in education) the deal takes the form of an agreed 'improvement factor' for several years, i.e., a rate of increase above that necessary for maintenance, repair and price changes. Sometimes deals are also made when an activity is new and will evidently take time to get started. There is no point in critical scrutiny because nothing much will happen for a few years. So the Treasury might seek an arrangement to limit programme costs while guaranteeing the department a few years until a more thorough appraisal is appropriate. With a little wit, as an official related, this kind of deal was possible even in the midst of the arrival of a Conservative Government pledged to scrutinise all government activities. In this example the spending concerned a new service created by the previous Labour Government, and 'a decision had to be made on its continuation. We had to tell the new Government that it made no sense to harass this programme before it could get established. A settlement was arranged when I got – and in fact had to blackmail [the service] to get – a consultant appointed to see whether the programme was working effectively. Now that he has sent in a satisfactory report, we can keep the arrangement going for a while longer.'

A related type of deal occurs when the Treasury feels unable to judge the technical or artistic or scientific merits of a programme. So long as the item is not too large, the Treasury, rather than divert its energies into peripheral and strange paths, may agree to provide increased funds at a specified rate. The Treasury has simplified its own calculations in one scientific area by giving 'an initial dollop of money at an annual rate of increase that would at least bring them in line with the rate of national income.... Of course there is no real reason why the national income trend should be the standard. It was simply a convenience.' [18] Similarly in one government service where 'existing policy' could mean almost anything, there is an understanding to 'keep to the expenditure trend line of the last few years. This seems satisfactory and we'll say let's assume that existing policy means continuing this rate of growth.'

Deals are usually made for fairly specific programmes, not for global policy areas such as health or defence. Where and how a deal is made depends very much on the scope of the issue at stake – as well, of course, as on the inescapable questions of individual personalities. The larger the issue, the larger the number of people to be 'squared' and the more senior the negotiators will be. An agreement on a line item in the subhead of some vote will probably be settled between Treasury and departmental principals; no undersecretary wishes to be bothered with the agreed growth rate for, say, an individual research station or small training programme. At the other extreme are deals on major allocations of public money. Any consideration of substantive policy – be it in a Cabinet official committee, working party, or Treasury/department study group – is bound to involve questions of allowable spending, and any consideration of major expenditures is bound

18. There is nothing unique or necessarily irrational in this approach. Thomas Schelling's *The Strategy of Conflict*, (Cambridge, Mass.: Harvard University Press, 1960) analyses the importance of 'natural' meeting places in facilitating agreements. The point about these prominent solutions is not that they are necessarily just but that they suggest themselves as appropriate to the participants.

to involve vital questions of substantive policy. Those involved in the bargaining, assessments of climate, and weighing of merits are, until very late in the process, likely to be the so-called faceless and uncreative officials. Here is the account of a very senior official, whose deal has recently led to a new allocation of many tens of millions of pounds.

We [in the Treasury] and the department had been meeting and working at quite senior level on this for several years. As usual the department was pressing for more money but we saw that there was more than normal departmental pressure here. The group looked at the data that seemed relevant and formed a view. We tried to persuade others and our masters, or accept their modifications. There was a climate of opinion – the pressures, lobbies, in the House and outside, and sometimes these are not ineffective.

It was generally accepted that more needed to be done here. When I say generally accepted I mean accepted by people in the Treasury. There is always pressure to do something, sometimes you accept it and sometimes you resist. It was obvious that if more wasn't done here it would be disastrous in a few years.

We ended up pushing a plan for something between the largest and smallest proposals put forward. It was agreed that for a number of years ahead, three or four in fact, the major restraint would be what the machine was geared to do, not money. They could have as much money as they wanted; the question was what they could manage to spend, what could be done.

All this started long before any Cabinet decision. When 90 per cent of the work was done, ministers were asked to apply their minds to it. We of course informed the Chancellor that a view was developing in the Treasury that there should be an expansion here. We had surveyed the topic long before it ever came close to ministers. This continually happens. No civil servant is doing his job unless he has done the work and knows, if not the answers, at least the alternatives before it gets to the ministers.

Such deals constitute the great landmarks on the surface of expenditure decisions. They stand out precisely because they do not happen very often. The Treasury can always be expected to be reluctant to make what its officials call long or medium term deals because in seeking financial control, 'you want your losers' list first and maybe later a winner's list'. But they also know at the Treasury that 'it may still be worthwhile fighting a rearguard action for demonstration purposes'.

The strategic situation changes when the Treasury official involved becomes a convinced advocate of a particular programme. 'My task,' he will say, 'is to swing over the Treasury view – which I did.' Does the Treasury advance its views on substantive policy issues against the department's view of its own subject matter? Departments are certain of it; Treasury officials equivocate. In public testimony a Treasury deputy secretary has cited the high degree of substantive understanding in the supply divisions which confer daily with their colleagues in the spending departments. Asked if these Treasury officers 'are in a position to make alternative suggestions to Departments because of their specialised knowledge?' he answered, 'Yes, I think this is perfectly true.' Asked later what these specialised views might be on social services, the deputy secretary replied, 'I do not think the Treasury would normally have specific views on social policy.'[19]

A major reason for the ambiguity is the difficulty of drawing a line between an expenditure and a subject matter issue. Which is it if the Treasury should consistently favour building programmes for adult education over other education expenditure because of the former's greater impact on economic growth? Or when the head of a Treasury supply division finds a proposal of £30 million in credit facilities for the domestic ship-building industry inadequate and says, 'I personally subscribed to the figure of £200 million, which is what we wrote into the Bill'?[20] Treasury expenditure controllers do bring their own substantive policy views into the bargaining process. Their rationale for this behaviour was well expressed by the same Treasury division head, who was subsequently elevated to deputy secretary :

I think you will find it very difficult to get intelligent, educated, experienced, thinking people, as I like to think that we are,

19. H.C. 323, (1970–1), pp. 15 and 24.
20. H.C. 347, p. 77. See also pp. 72–5. On the education issue, see the comments of former Minister of Education, Sir Edward (now Lord) Boyle, in Kogan, *The Politics of Education*, p. 103.

dealing with this kind of subject who could refrain altogether from having any view of where the national interest lay in a matter like this. I am not sure whether this is a departmental role or not, but I would say it is the role of thinking civil servants to have some view, as objective and non-political as they can, about the subjects they are concerned with. I think we would be poor civil servants if we did not.[21]

No department official can be as effective in his own cause as the Treasury watchdog can be for him. The Treasury man cannot, however, give special preference to all the programmes under his jurisdiction because his sector would then be getting more than its share of the total. Advocate of department reform he may be some of the time : guardian of the Treasury he must be all the time. Department officials know they can sometimes convert their Treasury counterpart, but they are also aware that in return they may have to give him a greater say in determining their policies. Discovering that they cannot get all they want from him, spending departments must try for that extra bit without Treasury help.

So far our discussion of Treasury–departmental relations has concentrated on the situation in which the department wants more, or at least to keep what it has. Certainly this is a typical situation, but it is by no means the only impetus for bargaining. The everyday business of spending public money provides three recurrent occasions in which Treasury and department officials test themselves against each other. It is to these contests that we now turn.

Underspending, Transfers and Delegation

> ... It is the mark of a chicken-hearted Chancellor when he shrinks from upholding economy in detail.... He is not worth his salt if he is not ready to save what are meant by candle-ends and cheese-parings in the cause of the country.
>
> *William Gladstone, 1879* [22]

21. H.C. 347 (1970–1), p. 65.
22. Cited in F. W. Hirst, *Gladstone as Financier and Economist* (London : E. Benn) 1931, p. 243.

The ultimate logic of PESC is that the Treasury stops worrying about the details; the Treasury just negotiates the ceiling. But the Treasury is very uneasy about that now. Some people accept it. But other parts still delight in crawling over everything in detail and regard the delay as a victory itself.

High Treasury official

I do not think it is for the Treasury ever to be happy about anything.

Treasury undersecretary,
Trade and Industry Subcommittee,
Expenditure Committee (1970–1),
p. 92

The expenditure process contains built-in opportunities for Treasury intervention. These occur when a department spends less or more than the amount allotted to it, when it tries to transfer funds from one category to another, and when it seeks authority to make expenditure within certain limits without formal Treasury review. Though underspending, transfers and delegations appear to be technical financial topics, suitable only for desiccated accountants, these concepts involve institutional relationships that may well turn out to be decisive in determining a particular level of policy. The question of who has the right to spend may answer the question of what the money is spent on. Even if no policy differences result, the treatment of underspending, transfers and delegation tells us much about how the Treasury and departments keep conflict within bounds.

From the Treasury viewpoint, it is foolish to insist on maintaining every possibility for intervention. This is not solely or even primarily a matter of wanting to conserve time on minor matters (after all, trivialities never stopped Treasury men in the earlier heyday of Pecksniff controls). Rather, the justification for curtailing control rests on lessons learned by Treasury leadership and institutionally engrained in the post-war era. The modern Treasury not only feels more confident of its collaborative closeness to departments, but also believes that cost consciousness can be best instilled by making departments more responsible for worrying about their own cost controls. By no means do all of the 'old sweats' accept this new orthodoxy, but most see the merits of the more subtle approach to getting your own way. Thus the Treasury tries to maintain rules that allot greater responsibility to departments while at the same time allowing its own men to move in when necessary.

The spending departments, for their part, always have an interest in seeking to increase their financial flexibility so long as doing so does not put them at a disadvantage. Departments like some margin over their actual spending expectations in order to protect themselves against overspending, even if this margin does eventually manifest itself in underspending. They find it convenient to transfer money around from one programme to another, making up underspending on one item with overspending on another; by so doing, they can lessen the requirements imposed on them for precision within each category and enhance their opportunities for adapting to new circumstances. Yet the gains departments achieve through delegation from the Treasury do not always turn out to be advantageous. They may end up with less money to spend on the grounds that they can make up a deficit in one area with a surplus in another. Delegation can also mean that departments lose the convenient excuse of being able to blame the Treasury for denying them things they did not want to do anyway.

Underspending. In a strictly impartial world, underspending and overspending would be but two equal faces on the same coin of uncertainty; unexpected extra expenses would always tend to cancel out unexpected savings. In the world as it is, this is by no means true. Underspending is customary. In 1972/73 the expenditure which actually occurred was about £600 million less than the spending estimates approved, or a difference of about 2 per cent. The system is 'very strongly biased' toward underspending.[23]

Underspending is always a subject of some amazement (if not amusement) to outsiders because they assume that departments have an interest in spending right up to the last pound. And so they do – to a point. One thing that frustrates this desire is the uncertainty of the real world. Money may become available too late in the year to set up the apparatus necessary to process and

23. See, for example, the statements of Treasury witness Peter Baldwin in H.C. 549 (1970–1), pp. 80–1; and H.C. 398 (1972–3), pp. 7–18. Underspending for 1973–4 was projected at the end of 1972 to be £300 million, a figure revised to £500 million in the March 1973 Budget statement.

spend it. Men required to operate the programmes may be difficult to hire and appear too late to receive the portion allotted to their salaries. The material required may be unobtainable or have to be procured from abroad, subject to well-known delays. Should construction be involved there may be no end of difficulties in getting started and completing the work. Problems with rights-of-way, contractors, changes in design, reprogramming, and a host of other delays are likely to prevent money being spent as quickly as originally planned. Thus the £600 million underspending in 1972/73 was made up largely of underuse of certain industrial and regional subsidies, delays in nationalised industries' capital programmes, and unexpected developments in agricultural prices, housing, roads, and employment.[24] In brief, underspending occurs because men are not able to control the world in every detail, even over the short run.

These uncertainties are greatly multiplied when expenditure decisions are being assessed, not simply for the next year, but up to five years ahead. Experience with such forecasts in the Public Expenditure Survey has in fact led the Treasury since 1969 to include an estimate of total underspending, or 'shortfall'. The bald statement of spending plans was found likely to produce a false peak half-way through the five-year projection unless some corrective for total underspending was introduced.[25] This short-fall figure began at £50 m. in 1968/9 and in the Dec. 1972 PESC White Paper (Cmnd. 5178) was put at £300 m. for each year, 1972/3 to 1976/7. Clearly, however, whatever contribution the shortfall figure makes to forecasting accuracy, it gives the Treasury no new method of expenditure control or management.

Underspending is not simply a function of uncertainty but also of the administrative practices of expenditure control. It is becoming more common largely because of incentives created by the emerging system of control – the control of overspending. To be sure, department officials do not like to underspend because 'You are in the dog house with the Treasury.' More important, according to a finance officer, is 'the danger that the Treasury will not be willing to give so much money the next time around'.

24. H.C. 398 (1972–3), pp. 8–9.

25. The same tendency can be found in all defence projections of the 1930s. See, for example, the nine-year projection in C.P. 256(37), October 1937.

Treasury men have a natural instinct to cut down those who show they do not spend what they get.

But while departments may dislike underspending, they dislike overspending even more. 'Of course, if you exceed your estimate and have to go to Parliament for a supplementary estimate, you're considered sloppy by the Treasury.' And, one might add, troublesome as well. For a century the disgrace and trouble associated with supplementary estimates has been a major disincentive to overspending. This is now outdated and superseded by the much stronger disincentives against overspending inherent in the PESC process. Treasury officials seeking an explanation for the growing trend toward shortfalls now realise that the phenomena is largely due to the fact that many programmes are more effectively subject to spending ceilings. There is no better explanation than that offered by the head of the Treasury's general expenditure division:

> The regime for controlling the programmes had been profoundly altered by the introduction of specific published limits on expenditure.... There are people engaged in seeing that that limit is observed. They are there to do that, and they will exercise their strength to prevent expenditure going beyond that limit, so there is not any longer the possibility of regarding such a figure as that as being the central estimate of what expenditure will be but very much more an upper limit.[26]

Overspending is strongly suppressed; underspending incurs mild rebuke.

One conceivable consequence of these differential incentives is that departments might 'water' their expenditure plans to leave a safety margin against overspending. Indeed, the standard introductory guidebook to the civil service, published only after Treasury scrutiny, comments on standard practice in 1965 that 'the department first makes up its mind what would be likely to be a reasonable figure for the work to be done, probably adds a margin to be on the safe side, and then seeks the sanction of the Treasury.'[27]

26. H.C. 549 (1970–1), Memorandum by the Treasury, 'Public Expenditure: Comparisons with Previous Estimates', p. 80.

27. G. A. Campbell, *The Civil Service in Britain* (London: Duckworth and Co., 1965 edition), p. 157.

Treasury officials, who believe in 'tight estimating' as a creed, are confident of their ability to squeeze any such water out of the figures. 'That is known to [the departments] as well as it is to us.' [28]

Nevertheless the Treasury is concerned about underspending and seeks understandings to meet the problem. The poorly-enforced rule of pooling 'accidental savings' in a common contingency fund has been one such attempt. So too was the institution (in 1970) of what are revealingly called 'realistic midpoint estimates' in nationalised industries. To gain more realistic estimates, the Treasury has 'assured nationalised industries that they will not have their knuckles rapped for a little overspending – and this assurance is what's important to them'. By selectively reducing fears of marginal overspending, the Treasury hopes to elicit programmes less prone to underspending.

Transfers. Department officials are well aware that 'there is always a tendency to be optimistic about how quickly you will be able to spend your money'. Knowing that they have never yet managed consistently to come out just right, finance officers will try to get agreement with the Treasury that, if they overspend on some items and underspend on others, they can make transfers. Ministers discover this phenomenon when officials come to them near the end of the fiscal year and say that 'quite a bit has not been spent and here are some things that we might spend it on'. Then the minister and his officials will work together to get Treasury permission to use these funds for some other purpose. If it were possible to carry over funds, transfers would be unnecessary but formally at least, government departments must surrender any unexpended balances at the end of the financial year.[29] Although PESC forecasting can in some cases mitigate this requirement, the department's ability to act may still depend on receiving from the Treasury the right to transfer funds from one spending category to another.

Parliamentary funds for each department are supplied through a number of broad rubrics called votes within which there are a number of subheads. Since the mid-fifties, the total number of

28. H.C. 549 (1970–1), p. 81.

29. Grants-in-aid, i.e., money for private agencies to provide services directly to government or to encourage generally such services as the government thinks desirable, are given as fixed amounts and underspending can usually be carried over to subsequent years.

votes has remained at about 150, while the number of subheads has been reduced (in 1971) by a quarter.[30] In defence of the ancient parliamentary principle of 'sanction before expenditure', as well as its own interest in controlling costs, the Treasury normally cannot approve transfers of funds between votes. Only with respect to the fighting services, and then subject to reporting the fact to Parliament, can the Treasury allow transfers. However, the Treasury, and only the Treasury, is able to sanction transfers between subheads within the same vote, and it is here that it can gain leverage with the departments. By what principles, then, does the Treasury act on transfers?

Some decision rules are straightforward and have been well-established over many decades. The Treasury does not permit departments to switch funds so as to create new grants-in-aid or to increase an existing grant-in-aid. Similarly departments will not be allowed to use transferred funds for a different purpose than that contained in the vote. A department earning income will not be permitted to use it for a purpose which has nothing to do with the activity from which this largesse sprang. It is also unusual to allow transfers if the amounts involved are very large; some mentioned sums over £5 million (others, 10 per cent of estimates), but the exact allowable amount depends on the programme in question.

Where the principle clearly fits the facts, the Treasury official is on relatively firm ground. Beyond this point the whole question of principles for arranging transfers is in a state of flux because the Public Expenditures Survey has become the main instrument of Treasury control. Departments eagerly press their case. If departments are to be held to firm totals; if so much emphasis is to be put on broad spending categories that do not correspond to Parliamentary votes, why not allow departments to spend within the totals without bringing up legal niceties which the Treasury itself appears to have abandoned? The argument is difficult to resist. Departments warmly importune the Treasury not to fuss over subheads so long as the total spending figure is within the limits agreed on. 'It's really irritating,' said a finance

30. The major exception is the Secret Service, whose vote always appears as a single gross amount with no subheads and no subsequent account of how the money is spent.

officer, 'because the Treasury will say, "it's nice you got something down, but bad that the other categories are up".'

With some programmes, over or underspending can be accommodated without transfers by adjustments for subsequent years. In road building, for example, the Treasury recognises contracts as an appropriate balancing device, awarding more or less contracts the second year to balance under or overspending in the previous year.[31] But most current expenditure programmes are not so conveniently governable and the Treasury official is left with his usual devices, among them trust, political sensitivity, and consistent argument.

Broadly speaking, the permissible scope of transfers will depend on the quality of the department's own controls and the nature of the expenditure. The former is a variation on the theme of trust; the discretion allowed in transfers will tend to vary with the Treasury's confidence in the internal controls of the department. With a poor departmental record of control, the Treasury will be, as one of its undersecretaries said, 'awkward and suspicious'.

The nature of expenditures involved in a transfer covers a variety of criteria. The Treasury watches hawklike for politically sensitive transfers. On the whole it is likely to accept the department's assessment of the substantive merits of the expenditures, but will object if 'for political or other reasons, the proposed savings transferred are likely to get put back when the yells and screams start'. Again, the Treasury disapproves of precedent-creating transfers. Proposals which involve a once-and-for-all expenditure are likely to be allowed transfers. Other proposals (such as a switch from current to capital expenditure and thus eventually more current expenditure) allowing the department later to claim that something is 'established policy' are coolly received.

Perhaps the most important, and most revealing, rule of thumb is that departments are not allowed to switch from 'controlled' to 'uncontrolled' expenditures, and vice versa. By uncontrolled are meant roughly those programmes whose cost depends on factors (e.g., aged population, unemployment) apart from the spending decisions made. To invent a hypothetical example, unexpected savings in unemployment benefit (uncontrolled) because of low unemployment could not be transferred into old persons

31. H.C. 549 (1970-1), p. 58.

homes (controlled). Recognising the inertia of public spending, Treasury men know that when these temporary savings are gone next year, there will be created a permanent commitment to the higher funding level for old persons homes. But significantly, the Treasury also disapproves of switching unexpected savings from controlled to uncontrolled programmes. To do so would destroy Treasury access to one of its chief resources, information. 'We want to know,' the undersecretary said, 'why the uncontrolled item requires more money.'

When is underspending (inability to programme money) really a saving (carrying out an activity at lower cost)? When is a transfer a blatant disregard of an agreement with Parliament and when is it a means of enhancing the public interest by spending where it will do the most good? The inability to answer these questions without long and acrimonious disputes, the suspicion on all sides that precious time is being wasted, the difficulty the Treasury experiences in rationalising its position, have all led to suggestions for delegating greater spending power to the departments. If they are responsible, why shouldn't they spend and be held accountable for the consequences? To answer that question, the Treasury must assert that it too has manifest needs – for money to save or re-allocate, for information by asking 'why', for power to make its preferences effective. Significantly, Treasury men have recognised that many of their interests are best served by increasing delegation.

Delegation. It may be astonishing to learn that Treasury and Parliamentary approval of a department's estimates does not entitle the department to spend a single pound. But that is the case. In one of the few statutory references to Treasury power, the law states that audited expenditure 'shall, unless sanctioned by the Treasury, be regarded as not properly chargeable to a Parliamentary grant, and shall be so reported to the House of Commons'.[32] Despite the fact that the Treasury has already approved the estimates and Parliament voted the money, every department spending commitment, except where the Treasury choses to delegate its authority, must be approved in advance. By all account, Treasury control of the minutiae of department administration in the 1920s and 1930s was excessive. A retired Treasury knight recalls, 'The Treasury used to try to control expenditure by poking

32. Exchequer and Audit Departments Act, 1921.

its nose into everything. It was a nonsense even then.' All have their own pet examples of the absurdities involved.

After the Second World War, in seeking to re-establish its control of public spending, Treasury officials realised that preoccupation with a host of minor details had to end. Under the prodding of the new permanent secretary, Edward Bridges,[33] the Treasury gradually widened the scope for departments to manage their own affairs. A 1957 Select Committee found that delegated limits for spending without Treasury approval had markedly increased since 1950, ranging from £2000 for maps to £250,000 for individual road programmes, to no limit in some areas of spending by the Ministry of Supply.[34]

Establishment of the Public Expenditure Survey in the 1960s has accelerated this development. The corollary of the PESC concern with ceilings and totals is increased delegation to the departments. Any supply division official can cite examples of considerable increases in delegated authority occurring just within the last two years. Thus one principal recounts that 'The delegated limit in [his field] has been increased roughly fivefold and the casework of the division cut by five-sixths.'

Usually, in return for a loss of comprehensive and detailed control, the Treasury establishes a routine of periodically descending on departments to poke into details, which an official who lived through this period spoke of as 'a kind of unpredictable sampling approach'. But the need to penetrate the PESC totals leads to development of a series of informal working rules considerably more complex than those originally envisaged.

No one at the Treasury doubts the absolute necessity of delegation; physically, they could not function without it, and, more important, they believe in its psychological value for enhancing departmental cost consciousness. Against this must be balanced the danger that there may be entire categories of happenings from which the Treasury is excluded. And they do not like that. 'Although you are concerned with the global figures,' a high official pointed out, 'you have to have some sense of reality and

33. Bridges was permanent secretary 1945–56. For an account of his leadership, see 'Edward Ettingdean Bridges–Baron Bridges', *Biographical Memoirs of Fellows of the Royal Society*, vol. 16 (November 1970), pp. 37–56.

34. H.C. 254 (1957–8), pp. 236 ff.

need case experience so that you can keep the Treasury hand in.' So the Treasury always seeks loopholes which, though normally inoperative, will enable it to intervene when necessary. They will, as a Treasury man puts it, 'seek to protect their way in'.

How, then, can one explain that in certain cases Treasury approvals may go literally below £100 and in others Treasury approval need be obtained only if expenditure rises above a certain number of millions of pounds? Answers to this question reveal a great deal about the pattern of Treasury control. The essential point is that the threshold of Treasury approval is basically set in relation to a particular area, not amount, of expenditure. The fixed limit of delegated authority is intended to ensure that the particular balance of a policy cannot be upset without Treasury approval. The criteria for approval therefore is proportionate – attention is given to a sum which is significant in relation to what is being done in that area of spending. For that reason the delegated limit for capital expenditures may go into millions of pounds while that for certain types of inspections or consultantships may remain under £100.

Consider research and development spending. The Treasury, as we have seen, is deeply concerned to avoid premature commitments to large expenditures. Consequently it will require approval for various distinct phases of the research and development process so that a small expenditure in the early stages, taken without its knowledge, will not result in enormous totals later on. The sum being subjected to detailed scrutiny might, from the outside, seem pitifully small but its implications for spending are not. Research, moreover, keeps information on tap to the Treasury and supplies a rationale for delay. 'I might want to read some of the research results,' a Treasury official added, 'and maybe the Treasury could suggest other research to commission before a political decision is to be reached.'

The Treasury also wants to look at matters that might be politically sensitive, though the sums involved are small. Now no one can say for sure that a particular programme will or will not end up being politically sensitive. But there are certain signs that Treasury people have learned to use for determining political interests. One of these involves any proposals to change the law whether it costs more or less than before. The reason is that the minister involved may have to speak on the matter in Parliament and the Treasury wants to see that he speaks properly with regard to the financial aspects. Certain items in the Home Office have traditionally been subject to detailed investigation because they involve law and order and liberties of citizens. An expansion of the police force, though it might not be terribly large in total spending, is likely to be of great interest to citizens in various localities; so too will a change in criminal matters or immigration procedures. Hence discretion in the Home Office may vary from a few hundred pounds to more than £200,000 where construction of prisons is involved.[35]

Since the Treasury's idea is to 'get the feel' of the situation, it devotes considerable attention to new programmes where standards are not yet established. Thus initiation of the hospital-building programme in the early 1960s was accompanied by Treasury review of all but very small expenditure items, much smaller than in other capital programmes where performance norms were well known. By the end of the 1960s, however, there was enough experience for the Treasury to feel confident in raising manyfold the delegation ceilings.

The operative criteria for delegation are the result of repeated bilateral bargaining between Treasury and department. Agreements reached on delegation often include statements about the standard that will be used in providing funds. These vary from determining applicants' eligibility, to the number of square feet for a certain type of facility. Should the department alter its standards and, in particular, should it include an improvement factor, the Treasury expects to be consulted. Though the resulting cost in the first year may be quite nominal, the Treasury knows that over a number of years a change in standard, accepted by virtue of going unchallenged, might add up to a commitment for large amounts of public money.

No brief summary of this nature can encompass all the special considerations involved in Treasury decisions to delegate spending authority. The best way of characterising them would be to say they refer, in the words of one informant, to 'anything unusual'. Whereas a regular road scheme might not be subject to Treasury approval if it did not exceed £2 million, special financing arrangements (despite the fact that they might involve a hundred times less) will be considered at the Treasury. So, too, will safety bar-

35. H.C. 321 (1970–1), p. 67.

riers on roads. What these items have in common is that they present the possibility of political interest, or of raising a question about propriety, or simply of seeming strange and thus leading Treasury people to wonder if they should know what is happening. As these items become routine, Treasury interest in them diminishes. 'Of course,' a department official declared, 'our aim then is to get such things put into the agreed department programme as quickly as possible.' And, as always, permeating all considerations of delegation are questions of confidence. A department with a weak record of internal controls, with men and procedures which do not inspire trust, is not likely to win much margin for making independent use of its money.

There could be no greater error than to assume from all this that spending departments clamour for delegated powers, which the Treasury only grudgingly gives up. As one senior Treasury official who has lived through it insists, 'For 25 years, the Treasury has been trying to push details away from itself. The departments have generally fought delegation. They don't want it – if the authority is delegated to you, then you're responsible.' It might be more accurate, if less neat, to say that officials in operating divisions of departments want more discretion most of the time, finance officers only part of the time, and that the highest officials vacillate.

Bargaining over delegated powers is important for department officials because it sets out the terms under which they will be able to make many future decisions. They seek delegated powers to help rather than hurt them. Only those in the Treasury who have been involved in the tough negotiations realise that public statements about the infinite desirability of delegation do not completely represent the position of all departments. After all, having lived with these regulations for years, there are bound to be people who have grown used to (and found ways around) them. They may be reluctant to change to the unknown. And, above all, the requirement of Treasury sanction is protective. When there is a chance that department officials will have to take more blame for restraint than they have done in the past, the abstract virtues of delegation pale. The old tactic, so dear to the hearts of Principal Finance Officers, of shoving the blame on the Treasury (by saying that miserly old institution will not let a division do what it wants) appears specious if everyone knows that the department has the right to make the expenditure.[36] A very high ex-Treasury official, who knows whereof he speaks, is adamant on this point :

> Don't let anyone tell you that departments agreed [to PESC] because they in turn would get more delegation from the Treasury. They did not want such delegation. I had to beat departments about the head to accept responsibility which they would rather the Treasury would have. Strong opposition came from the finance people. They enjoyed controlling and enjoyed financial conscientiousness. One at the —— department was called the Abominable No Man. It was a question of the Treasury forcing departments into taking responsibility.

Similarly a young Treasury principal tells of his fight to push details back to the department because 'They don't want the sole onus of saying no to their scientists. The delegation limits on such projects has been raised to £5000 – but they probably haven't told their experts they don't have to come to the Treasury.'

Nowhere is the difference clearer between the public and private faces of expenditure community than in this question of delegation and Treasury sanction. One 'scores off others' (i.e. blames or otherwise uses fellow kinsmen and participants) on the inside, or at most at the fringes of the community, and not on the outside. The well-known doctrine of ministerial responsibility is only a special case of a much larger creed embedded throughout British government – the indivisibility of the Executive. In their public face, political administrators are thoroughly practised in making a splendid case for something they do not like. Among themselves, policy-makers find it easier to blame the Treasury, sometimes accurately but often to smooth the feathers of others inside the spending department. In some delegated areas of spending, the semi-outsiders – the interest groups, the 'pleaders' and pundits – may also hear that something cannot be done because

36. In this regard at least, little has changed since the days of Empire, when the Colonial Office habitually and peremptorily refused colonial requests for money because of supposed Treasury vetoes. The allegation was not always accurate, but Treasury officials were willing to be used in this way to allow 'a Secretary of State to do, without unpleasantness, what he might think right , but be unwilling of himself to press'. Min. by G. A. Hamilton, 14 July 1869, quoted in Burton, *Public Administration* vol. 44 (summer 1966), p. 171.

the Treasury will not cough up the money; but all department officials know that it is very bad form to go too far in this, and certainly not for publication. Experienced Treasury men realise that the price of staying close to departments, getting information, being trusted, is a willingness to be occasionally abused. Playing 'longstop' to help some men inside the departments say 'sorry, the Treasury won't have it', necessarily implies antagonising other men who have pet projects. Between the somewhat illusory public rationalisations and the internal carping at the Treasury, very few persons actually know how much of what is not done in public policy springs from the Treasury and how much from departmental leadership with delegated powers using the Treasury. Nor are many likely to know until controls are delegated further and seen to be delegated. Understandably there is a certain knowing stoicism inside Treasury Chambers.

Exceptionally, where circumstances and personalities differ on both sides, departments may make a strong bid for delegated powers. They may seek support from the Public Accounts Committee in order to remove what they consider onerous and unnecessary regulations. In seeking to get around the Treasury, department officials are not above using its favourite strategies against that august institution. They will look for anomalies, that is different thresholds for Treasury approval in similar services within a department. They may go back to the past where it is easy to show that the original rationale setting thresholds for delegation has long since been outmoded and quite possibly honoured only in the breach. Treasury men pride themselves on their consistency and, if they can be attacked from that quarter, they may well give in.

The rise of huge, conglomerate departments, joining together several that used to be separate and independent, has made further delegation necessary but also has increased Treasury fears about the effectiveness of its control. The larger the department in terms of money and men, combined with a vastly increased diversity of activity, the more difficult it becomes to penetrate its inner workings. The less the Treasury can see inside a department the more disposed it is to seek control through overall spending limitations. Treasury officials wonder if loss of internal knowledge of policy will not both defeat attempts to keep spending totals down as well as reduce its knowledge of what is going on. Is an omnibus settlement over totals in Defence a substitute for information revealed in the past by rivalry among the three former military departments? Will negotiating a ceiling with the new Departments of the Environment or Trade and Industry be an adequate substitute for serious discussion of priorities in making their internal allocations? Are not what the immense conglomerates now call 'internal' the same great issues about which they used to consult the Treasury?

Some Treasury sceptics fear that, while they have been letting go of more details, department finance offices are not necessarily picking up the slack inside the departments. 'The more you delegate control,' they fear, 'the more you rely on the auditors.' Often worried but seldom bored, Treasury officials would rather take their chances with their main allies and adversaries, the department finance officers.

Role Conflict: The Principal Finance Officer

> The finance officer is the broker.
>
> *Principal Finance Officer*

> I act as a bridge between the Treasury and the departments. One has to some extent a dual loyalty.
>
> *Accountant-General*

Since the Gladstonian financial reforms of the nineteenth century, each spending department typically has had its own finance branch headed by a Principal Finance Officer (PFO). 'The Finance Officers of Departments were regarded somewhat in the nature of outposts of the Treasury : and like other outposts, while they could give warning of attack, they were liable to be quickly overwhelmed unless reinforced.'[37] In 1920, with the strong backing of the Permanent Secretary of the Treasury, Warren Fisher, the department finance officer's position was greatly strengthened. Now he was appointed or removed only with the consent of the Prime Minister and thus, effectively, of the Treasury Permanent Secretary as head of the Civil Service. A second and more important reform was at Fisher's insistence to make the permanent secretary of each department the 'accounting officer', i.e., the

37. Bridges, *Treasury Control*, p. 10.

official with supreme responsibility under ministers for all departmental finance questions. Despite several years' opposition from some permanent secretaries, who favoured a continuing division between their policy perspective and the Treasury's financial perspective, the 30-year-old reform is now accepted throughout Whitehall as ancient tradition. Far from weakening the position of the Principal Finance Officer, this reform has ensured that his financial perspective is an integral part of the permanent secretary's own job. If all permanent secretaries do not necessarily understand very much about financial questions themselves, they will be sure to lend a ready ear to the Principal Finance Officer who does.

Today the department's Principal Finance Officer is less a Treasury outpost than the man in the middle. His effectiveness within his own department depends on establishing confidential relationships with the Treasury. He cannot serve his departmental colleagues or his minister if the Treasury does not trust him. Should he fail to achieve this trust, his fellow officials and minister will consider him incompetent as it becomes evident that he cannot gain approval for the simplest things without going through a tortuous review process. Yet should he be on the closest terms with his Treasury counterparts, all the obvious advantages may be dispelled by a feeling from below that he has sold out the operating divisions in order to get on with the controllers. Failing to get the funds they always believe their due, operating officials may suspect that their principal finance officer is working in collusion with the Treasury and against their interests. The minister, if he is aggressive and demanding, may want what he wants when he wants it. He may suggest tactics that will prove effective in the short run but would undermine the possibility of good relations with the Treasury in the long run. For its part, the Treasury expects the PFO to keep it fully informed on what is *really* going on, to honour his bargains, and to help out in times of distress – even if this means violating the expectations of department officials. The Finance Officer is a cross-pressured man. His life is never easy.

In most departments, virtually all normal negotiations with the Treasury are centralised through the department's finance office. The Treasury prefers it this way, partly due to the greater confidence it has in these men, partly to sheer administrative necessity. The Treasury has three officials to deal with the largest expenditure category: social security. Even a 'small' spending department, such as the Home Office, has 400 administrative points of expenditure with which the Treasury could potentially have to deal. Where standards are clear and agreed, as in building, the responsible department division will deal directly with the Treasury. Where there are insufficient objective tests, as in most areas, negotiations are channelled through the finance office. Otherwise said a finance officer, 'the people dealing with the Treasury will be those who are always inclined to be trying to spend more'.

The Treasury maintains a strong interest in the appointment of Principal Finance Officers – to the extent that some department officials mistakenly believe that they are in fact official Treasury appointments. Since the 1920 reform, no one has ever thought the Prime Minister influences these appointments. 'It was,' as a high Treasury official stated, 'a device used to make sure that the Treasury was consulted.'

After the Civil Service Department (CSD) was created in 1968, appointments passed to it. CSD is consulted on all appointments and postings to undersecretary positions and above, and Principal Finance Officers are normally undersecretaries. The CSD no longer seeks the direct consent of the Prime Minister, but does see to it that the Treasury is consulted. According to a man who should know, 'the purpose from the Treasury viewpoint is to make sure they get a good chap who has talent and not an old sweat who does not know what to do'. A man with a record of making life difficult for the Treasury in his prior position is unlikely to get its approval to move to a new one.

The actual appointment of a Principal Finance Officer originates with the permanent secretary of the department concerned. He normally takes a great interest in it because the successful performance of his job depends on having a competent man to safeguard the department from financial abuses and smooth the way for its programmes with the Treasury. Since the Permanent Secretary is also the department Accounting Officer, directly responsible to Parliament for both the legality and the efficiency of departmental expenditures, he is doubly dependent on his finance officer for keeping him out of trouble. When he goes to testify before the Public Accounts Committee the Permanent Secretary

depends largely on his finance officer for briefing. It is not surprising, therefore, that permanent secretaries have always liked
to keep their PFO's for unusually long periods, although four to
five years seems the norm nowadays.

Ask any finance officer and he will tell you that a major task
is 'to preserve credibility with the Treasury'. He must show that he
is in command of the facts and that the Treasury can trust him to
have gotten rid of undesirable expenditure. Credibility is enhanced,
therefore, by a reputation for toughness in quizzing departmental
colleagues so the Treasury will come to believe that what has survived the PFO probably will also pass its own scrutiny. 'I must
talk to the Treasury as if this were true,' a long-time PFO revealed,
'though it might not always be. My reputation [with the Treasury]
counts a great deal.' The finance officer will not make the difference between getting one-half or double what the department
wants, but many permanent secretaries agree with the one who
observed that 'If he inspires confidence at the Treasury, the range
of difference might be 85 to 125 per cent.' In a world of invariably
small margins, this is a considerable tribute.

The wise PFO stresses his scrupulous honesty. He reveals weaknesses in his case before Treasury people find out about them. He
wants to create the impression that he is, if anything, more zealous
than they are to see that money is well spent. With a reserve of
credibility established, the finance officer can cash it in at the
Treasury when he most needs to, providing he does not go to the
bank too often.

There does come a time when the PFO must stand and fight.
Long identification with a department may make him a convinced
advocate of a particular programme. His relationships with the
minister and departmental colleagues may depend on doing something dramatic. What does a finance officer do when he really
wants to win? According to one, perhaps exceptionally, tough
character, 'I tell the Treasury the case is cast iron. I take a poor
view of your obstruction. I may occasionally become emotional
and get bloody-minded. I may refuse to leave the room until the
talk has gone on for hours. This is a very personal business.' The
PFO, who normally appears so reasonable, deplores the ignorance
of Treasury men. 'Let me take you to a couple of our facilities,'
he would say. 'Let's have a look. If you don't want to trust me
after all these years come and see yourself.' He will try every trick

of salesmanship he knows. He will produce figures, charts, elaborate graphs, all of which will show that there is a convincing case for the expenditure. The cost of being able to act this way at the most critical junctures is a self-denying ordinance prohibiting the PFO from doing anything like it most of the time. Department officials who think the PFO should go all out for them on every conceivable occasion, no matter how unproductive this might be, are the bane of his existence.

The critical skill of a finance officer, if he has it, lies in being able to determine how far up he can push department expenditure without courting grave difficulties which will rebound against the institution he represents and himself personally. He comes to understand (and can often explicitly verbalise) that 'there is a market in politics and the experience you gain in government is ultimately directed to understanding that market'. He is constantly balancing internal demands against external conditions. To the extent that he can improve the external situation, that is, take advantage of its strategic opportunities, he can make his internal bargaining much easier. To the extent that he can convince his own department to mitigate its demands, his external relationships are improved.

The finance officer's inside task is to play essentially the same role as the Treasury does towards him. He regards himself as a watchdog. He insists upon a defensible position so that expectations will not rise beyond what he considers the plane of reality. 'The original reaction of finance,' a PFO declares, 'is probably negative. Our task is to ensure that the proposal is tied to the ground, that it is realistic in regard to what may be financially possible.'

Departmental divisions come to finance with a written note of explanation containing a justification of their spending proposals and any supporting statistics. The staff of the finance division combs the proposal for factual information. If it were not well-costed, if the financial data were inadequate or failed to pay sufficient attention to costs over the longer term, the proposal might be sent back for additional work. Getting the proposal back, the finance officer will grill the head of the division in much the same way as he has been grilled in his encounters with the Treasury. The outcome depends on whether the finance officer can shake the operating divisions' figures, whether he has his own priorities and can beat them down, or whether he has sufficient background to tell them 'it is just not on'. How does the PFO know what is on and what is not?

Every PFO tries to use his contacts at the Treasury and his reading at public and private events to estimate how tight expenditures are going to be. Experience gives him additional criteria to assess designs for increased spending, as in this informed and representative summary:

In deciding on the practicalities of a departmental proposal what you tend to do is to have a look at the programme and how it has grown over the previous years. Quite possibly there has been increased pressure to cut it from the Treasury or other departments although your own colleagues and the minister are still keen on it. You know in the long term it is going to be hard to sustain a continued rate of growth in this programme higher than the economic growth rate. You as finance officer get to feel that it is better for the department itself to slow down the rate of growth to the economy's rate, otherwise other people are going to get to criticising it.

Another common thing in terms of practicality is the likelihood of delay in spending the money you are asking for. Professionals always assume that expenditures will start much faster and earlier than they in fact do. A third element of practicality is the atmosphere of a new government that might come in. For example it is perfectly obvious that investment in nationalised industry is not something that should be pressed this year given the inclinations of a Conservative government. Finally there are changes in public fashion which heavily affect what you see as practical. Building —— right now is out of favour, for example, but there is a general feeling that more needs to be spent on ——.

Tough appraisal of one official by another, a process we have observed in the Treasury, is equally important in the departments. 'One knew one's colleagues,' a finance officer declared frankly. 'Some heads you can squeeze, others you do not want to squeeze because they were pretty reliable, they do not try things on. Other branch heads will try but you can't stop them. It is a trial of personalities.'

Conflict with department policy people can be mitigated if

the finance officer is able to show them he is looking after their interests. He tells them what the financial pressures are likely to be, whether they should be prepared for decreases or can plan on the expectation of increases. He advises them of the specific view on policies held by Treasury officials. Yet his departmental colleagues may not always like what they hear, and, what is worse, they may not believe it. One way of overcoming this distrust is to take policy officials along for discussions 'so that they can see you are not selling them down the river to the Treasury'. These operating officials can help by making their case persuasively and with expertise that the finance officer cannot match. But the main purpose is to assure them that all possible arguments have been put to the Treasury. They are only invited occasionally because to do otherwise would jeopardise the finance officer's special relationship with the Treasury, which is his most important stock in trade.

The best way to assure the department officials that the PFO is giving them support is actually to help them. 'There is an obvious and practical test,' said a matter-of-fact finance officer. 'It all depends on whether you get results that they accept as being in their interest. I may need window dressing for this purpose. From time to time when a matter is small but troubling a division, I will personally ring up the Treasury and take care of it in an hour to show that I am acting in their interest.'

No matter how hard the finance officer tries, there is bound to be an irreducible minimum of disagreement between him and his departmental colleagues. They only have to spend the money; he has to get it. His primary relations with the Treasury are only of secondary importance to them. Blocked by a recalcitrant finance officer, whom they may believe to be introducing 'quite irrational considerations of personality and politics', they are tempted to appeal over his head to the Permanent Secretary. 'The power of the principal finance officer in the department,' as they are well aware, 'derives from the way that the permanent secretary regards the principal finance officer; if it is as his departmental watchdog, then there will be no effort to go around him.' Normally the Permanent Secretary will not look at any proposal requiring funds before sending it out for the view of the finance division. As soon as it is apparent that there is no point in trying to circumvent the PFO, it becomes customary to consult him in advance.

Relationships between the finance officer and the Permanent Secretary are cordial more often than not because they depend on one another. But conflicts do break out among them. The Permanent Secretary may have different policy ideas and insist, as a hierarchical superior, that he is entitled to prevail. The finance officer, so long as he gets his say, is prepared to accept an adverse decision. But if his views are disregarded once too often the stage is set for continuing conflict. The finance officer may help people in the Treasury challenge the Permanent Secretary's views. He may, in seeking to prevent a disagreeable course of action, inform the Permanent Secretary that the Treasury or the Public Accounts Committee will object and that full responsibility remains with the head of the department. 'I tell him' a PFO revealed, 'that he has no defence and give him a warning. It is his prerogative to do otherwise but I have fulfilled my responsibilities when I have warned him.' When relationships have been embittered to that degree a department is in trouble.

Money is important not only to department officials but to their ministers. They soon come to understand, if they are not already aware, that their reputation depends on securing funds and, to a lesser extent, on spending them effectively. They will then seek out the departmental finance officer because he is in touch with Treasury opinion on important programmes. Whether a Conservative like Edward Boyle or Socialist like Anthony Crosland, wise ministers treasure a good finance officer. Boyle knew of his man at the Ministry of Education 'that when he was on the phone he got us the very best terms that he ever could...you know: "Now you don't expect me to swallow that one?" ' It is music to a harassed minister's ears. As usual, the finance officer plays his dual role, reminding the department and minister 'of just how tiresome we seemed to the Treasury from time to time'.[38]

Finance officers themselves value direct personal contact with their minister, and most will have it, at least informally. They can speak far more authoritatively to the Treasury and to departmental colleagues if they can claim direct knowledge of ministerial opinion. Yet their assessment and those of their minister may not always coincide. The PFO faces a conflict between loyalty to the minister and the insistence of the Treasury that he be financially

38. These appreciations from two recent ministers of education are in Kogan, *The Politics of Education*, pp. 124 and 167.

responsible. He may resolve the conflict by telling the Treasury he does not agree with a particular proposal that the minister insists upon and that the Treasury minister may agree so they had all better watch out. The minister, consumed with the passion to start a new programme, may be impatient with the argument that it would violate previous understandings with the Treasury. 'It can all be ironical,' an experienced officer reports. 'Ministers are much more willing than are officials to double-cross their colleagues. Ministers are a bit suspicious of officials who are on too good a basis with the Treasury. "Your job is to get what I want", they say.' What counts in the end is the minister's estimate of the balance of contributions; the PFO whose advice is right more than it is wrong will stand high with him. The more the minister can get what he wants at the official level, the less he has to use up his own resources. So he may be amenable to persuasion by a respected finance officer who in most situations helps the minister succeed.

The pattern of relationship between the finance officer and the Treasury, upon which all else depends, is now in a state of flux. The superdepartments have several finance officers and that cuts down on the exclusiveness of the relationship. As the business under their nominal jurisdiction grows, the finance officers necessarily become less expert. The Treasury supply official, therefore, is tempted to talk to officials in the departments who are in touch with day-to-day operations and can give immediate answers to their questions. But any tendency to side-step the finance division is tempered by the difficulty of getting to know and to see too many different people; in addition the Treasury man, in his own words, 'has to be careful because the Treasury does not want to be seen to be less stringent than the finance officer is internally with his own department and thus undermine the finance officer's position'. Underlying these constraints is the fear that relations of confidence, upon which the Treasury men depend so much to expedite their work, may be disrupted. Consequently, upon learning that another department official wishes to see them, the Treasury official will usually call up the PFO and say so-and-so is coming: 'Are you aware? Are you happy? Will you come too?' That is why the finance officer can be reasonably confident that 'efforts to get around me invariably come to light quickly. Nobody can really get money without my knowing it. The Treasury will always ask me for my views one way or another.'

Counteracting tendencies toward dispersion of departmental financial control is the emerging corporate spirit of department finance officers. During the 1940s and 1950s Principal Finance Officers by and large did not deal very much with each other. Each might have known who the others were but there was little personal contact or discussion of common problems. It was every man for himself. The initiative to get PFOs together came from the Treasury, which sought in this way to infuse them with a sense of common purpose and to erase the traditional view that they had no responsibility for what happened elsewhere. The frequency of contact among them has been increased by the fact that they constitute the Public Expenditure Survey Committee (PESC). As a result, a PFO will now be able to say, 'I can tell you what X, Y and Z are thinking this very moment.'

Although their behaviour has not been revolutionized, the current vocabulary of finance officers certainly is new. Taking a phrase from the Plowden Report, they may speak of themselves as 'partners in a common enterprise'. They are not, they say, expected to get all they can. The system of control would break down if they did. Accountant-Generals must balance the needs of their departments with others. The vocabulary of harmony and common interest is there but the facilitating actions are not. In the same breath that a finance officer will make a verbal nod in the direction of the general governmental interest, whatever it is, he will speak of the extra hundred million pounds he received last year 'that I take so much pride in'. Finance officers have become more ambivalent about expressing narrow departmental interests but the interests are still there. On rare occasions, when none of the extra bids is being accepted and drastic cuts are being imposed on old programmes, the Principal Finance Officers may get together to make it a little easier on those who suffer the most. A few may offer to save money in their own departments (though the amounts are small and no one is certain whether the cuts actually take place). Meeting together as they do – hardly a week goes by when one or another of them do not discuss matters of mutual interest – a certain sympathy is generated that can be used to generate mutual help. Finance officers are much more likely, however, to work together on problems that affect them all in the same way.

A consequence of regular meetings between PFO's is that they now have a heightened sense of common interest in relation to the Treasury. They are more likely to know of developments in other departments and to try and gain comparable treatment. They refuse to criticise other departments or to suggest economies that might be made in them. Each feels too vulnerable to attack others. They also know that the confidential information they now receive from other departments would no longer be forthcoming if they were to make hostile use of it. When the Treasury tries to get an auction going among them, to get them to agree that an increase for one department will mean a decrease for another, and to specify both, the PFO's will refuse to participate. They and their spending departments know when they are well off. The British system of government already provides a forum called the Cabinet for that sort of exercise. If Peter is going to rob Paul it will not be done by them; that task is reserved for their ministers. The next move in the expenditure process is up to the party politicians.

4 The Earthly City: Cabinets, Politicians and other Worldly Men

There are two types of ministers : those who get their way in Cabinet and those who don't.

Ex-minister

The primary object of every Minister is, and must be, to place his own Department, and the interests committed to him, in the greatest state of efficiency. The cost, I venture to state, will be necessarily secondary. ... What expenditure would be incurred by these Departments but for the drag of the Chancellor of the Exchequer. ...?

Permanent Secretary of the Treasury, 1869

Ministers? Who can say what difference they make, but I know if I'm a permanent secretary in charge of a spending programme, I'd rather have A than B as my minister.

Permanent Secretary

The weak minister is the despair of his department.

Ex-minister

Ministers are always in a dilemma. The public policy of their party requires restraint in spending but their political future depends on spending.

Principal Finance Officer

IF NOTHING ELSE, the preceding chapters should have helped dispel the simplistic view held by many outsiders and a few ex-ministers: the expenditure process does not turn on a minister successfully putting his case to the Treasury. We have tried to show how a vast amount of expenditure business is conducted between Treasury and department officials, men who are familiar with each other and each other's strategies. Over most of this bargaining, ministers serve as *ex officio* presiding officers.

To say this is not to advance any general theory of bureaucratic conspiracy. Ministers' limited involvement in the expenditure process is an inevitable fact of life given restrictions in their time, interests, and tenure in office. A minister (at least on the average in the last 15 years) can count on only about two years in the same job.[1] Ministers also come in all types. Some are deeply interested in forming policy on a few issues and others try primarily to manage the ongoing work of their departments; some want a shining record of legislation, while others are content with serving as their department's envoy to outsiders. One or two will inform their new departments they are to have no appointments before 10 or after 4, with Monday and Friday lunches free; most ministers will follow an exceptionally heavy schedule with a work week of 60 hours or more. But whether they are spread too thinly or they refuse to spread themselves at all, ministers have insufficient time to take a continuing part in the public expenditure process.

But there is more to it than this. Ministers also fail to become more involved because civil servants prefer it this way. And officials do so with the best intentions in the world. One man's 'decision preemption' is another man's 'conflict resolution'. Top civil servants often regard ministers as an unreliable breed, long on haphazard arrangements and short on appreciation for the department's continuing needs. 'Ministers,' said an ex-permanent secretary in a representative aside, 'are short-term animals.' Even when officials do not have this attitude, their preference is for co-operation, not conflict. Inside the department, officials will have done their best to hammer out an agreed view to present to the minister; his brief is likely to be a monolithic department tract

1. Ministerial turnover is discussed in Anthony King, 'Britain's Ministerial Turnover,' *New Society*, 18 August 1966; and Richard Rose, 'The Making of Cabinet Ministers', *British Journal of Political Science*, 1 (1971). On ministers' activity in general see Bruce Heady's forthcoming book.

in which the most vital differences are airbrushed into a light fuzz.

Outside their departments, civil servants can also be found trying to mute the natural differences which arise between their organisations. To do so they may 'co-ordinate' advice to be given ministers. They will sometimes allow feuds to smoulder for years rather than 'cause the minister trouble'. They will interpret the political will of their masters in a politic way. In Cabinet Official Committees, at working parties, over lunch in Cabinet Office mess, civil servants can be found searching for a common solution to recommend to their political masters.

The so-called Whitehall machine is the well-oiled mesh of close relationships among official department heads. They do not want ministers resigning right and left. They believe in carrying on Her Majesty's government. To take an example from recent history, the resignation of the three Treasury ministers in 1957 can be interpreted as more than an instance of Cabinet defeat for the Chancellor. Those closest to the events report that one important reason events ever reached this breaking point lay in the demorali-sation and lack of communication then rife at the top of the civil service.[2] Differences had not been mitigated by the usual official 'greasing' of interpretations and accommodations.

This creative official role stops well short of any deliberate strategy to deny power to ministers. Civil servants have their own trade-offs to make. For men whose forte is mutual trust and em-barrassment avoidance, there is no worse position than to be caught out with an agreement the minister will not back. Officials know they must balance agreements among themselves with a fine sensitivity to ministerial interests. The means for doing so consist of what is almost a normal body-function for top civil servants : intense, incessant, incurable minister-watching.

'Knowing the minister's mind', as the phrase goes, allows the civil servant to map boundaries beyond which he will not take it upon himself to negotiate expenditure bargains. As many perma-nent secretaries pointed out, officials will allow themselves less leeway if the minister is a man easily worried or insecure. If the minister has pet issues, and nearly all do, expenditure decision on these matters usually will be reserved for him. 'By knowing the

2. Some sense of this disarray can be gained from Brittan, *Steering the Economy*, pp. 128 ff., and Harold Macmillan, *Riding the Storm*, (New York : Harper and Row) 1971, pp. 363 ff. See also footnote 17 below.

minister's mind,' said a permanent secretary, 'I might cheerfully accept a delay in [to take two hypothetical examples] prison construction but not in child care facilities.' Ministers' influence is thus indirectly increased by officials' anticipations of their reactions. Politicians often 'decide' unknowingly by virtue of the anticipations they have created in officials. When in doubt, civil servants will 'take soundings' from the minister. 'The result of the soundings,' reported a permanent secretary, 'may be that you just can't tolerate a certain cut or that you write tremendous safeguards into it.'

Minister-watching is close throughout British government. The neophyte minister will find that the main bridge between him and the department is his private office – a group of two to five fairly young officials from the principal and assistant secretary levels chosen by the permanent secretary and thereby tagged as promising senior civil service material. At the same time this private office is expected to serve primarily the minister. It is a nice distinction. The new minister will find there is a strict civil service code requiring that all telephone calls to and from his office be listened in on by a member of his private office. The service expects to be in on all arrangements being made for its departments, and the minister wanting a truly private chat will have to use the few hours available outside his office. (Apparently the civil service code does, however, lay down certain terms of endearment identifying conversations on which officials in the private office are to ring off.)

Yet however close the relations between ministers and civil servants, at the day's end only the minister can fight for his department's position against other ministers. Only he can argue for that supreme guideline coveted by all civil servants, a favourable Cabinet decision.

The minister's indispensability for inter-ministerial bargaining explains the universal observation of officials and ex-ministers: civil servants invariably prefer a strong to a weak minister. Margins in expenditure decision-making may be small but everyone wants his share of the bit that is going. Given a choice between someone who passively accepts their advice and someone who can effectively protect and advance the departmental interests, officials in Treasury and spending departments would unanimously choose the stronger character. In part this preference stems from the officials' need to make accurate anticipations; the strong minister who knows his own mind gives clear signals which others can safely interpret. He is predictable. But an equally fundamental reason behind officials' desire for strong ministers is departmental advantage. Baroness Sharpe, an outstanding post-war permanent secretary, has emphasised the value civil servants attach to ministers who can influence others. 'The thing you ask of your Minister is that he should be able to get his way in Cabinet. He must know what he wants. He must be decisive. And he must have weight in the councils of the government.'[3] An ex-minister summed up the situation: 'Civil servants hate a weak minister. He reflects badly on the department. If he waffles in debate or is getting kicked about by his colleagues it affects the department. His permanent secretary, when he goes to the Reform Club, will be embarrassed and pitied by other permanent secretaries.'

Officials may wince at a shouting, 'knockabout' minister but he will be much more highly valued than a perpetual loser in the struggle for resources. Ministers', like civil servants', reputations are common currency in official society. Cabinet minutes (prepared by the Cabinet Office) are typically circulated to senior civil servants down to deputy secretary level and provide a ready guide to who is winning and losing in Cabinet.[4] Superficial displays of ministerial strength, e.g. trying to show who is in command by insisting on new office furniture, mean little compared to the hardheaded judgement of seasoned minister-watchers. 'If you've been a minister before,' Anthony Crosland observed, 'officials in your new department will know on the Whitehall grapevine in considerable detail what you are like.'[5]

But what does it take to be considered a 'strong' or 'weak' minister? How do ministers struggle for money and how does this interaction produce one allocation among the virtually illimitable purposes for which public money might be spent? In short, what is the reality of Cabinet government in the expendi-

---

3. *The Listener*, 1 October 1970.

4. 'Sometimes as a member of the Cabinet you don't realise that you lost the battle; it was not your impression of what happened. But once it is there, written in the minutes, it *has* been decided – against you. This is, perhaps, the great secret of Cabinet government – the development of the decision-drafting technique.' Crossman, *Inside View*, (London: Jonathan Cape) 1972, p. 48.

5. Kogan *et al.*, *The Politics of Education*, p. 154.

ture process? For answers to these questions we must turn to the major ministerial protagonists – the spending and Treasury ministers.

The Spending Ministers: Fighting your Corner

> You fight your corner as Churchill said.
> *Spending minister*

> Every minister worth his salt pursues salami tactics.
> *Spending minister*

> It's a Turkish bazaar really.
> *Permanent Secretary*

Spending ministers do not acquire the name for nothing. They head the departments that spend most of the funds consumed by the national government. In most postwar Cabinets, one-half or more of the members have been ministers and secretaries of state heading departments with significant expenditure responsibilities, that is, at least five per cent of government spending; among members of the Government who are not in the Cabinet, spending ministers (a term we shall use to include secretaries of state) have usually bulked at least as large. In the Conservative Government formed in 1970, for example, there were sixteen Cabinet members in addition to the Prime Minister. Of these, ten headed major operating departments spending public money. Obviously some of these ministers spend much less than others (the Minister of Agriculture, for example, dealing with less than one-tenth the money going to the Secretary of State for Social Services), but this does not mean that their funds are any less important to the smaller spenders. It can just as easily mean that they fight all the harder. The money ministers spend and the increases they seek matter greatly to many people in society. They deal, not merely with money, but with the things money can buy. In a way, they are merchants of human happiness, providing one believes that the money is well spent and does not dwell overly long on those who pay the taxes to support it.

Whether one calls it the Collectivist Age, Welfare State, or positive government, a general consensus has grown up in post-war

Britain that is favourable to spenders, if not as a group at least individually. The minister faces an asymmetrical political environment inasmuch as spending and cutting are not equivalent alternatives for obtaining public favour. It is not, of course, spending for its own sake which is applauded but spending for something – roads, schools, hospitals, pensions, industries, regions and the host of other claimants. Those few who have made political reputations as cutters have only reduced rates of spending increase, and even they have usually emphasised, not the absolute savings, but the improvements – that is, more money – made available elsewhere in their programmes. During economically difficult times, the Prime Minister and Cabinet may be forced to institute spending curbs which require ministers to incur the enmity of large sectors of society. Spreading unpopularity, however, can never be the norm but only an exception in a democratic government, and the minister or government undertaking to deprive citizens of their customary indulgences can expect few rewards.

Inside his department, the spending minister who is uninterested in increased spending is likely to be viewed, if not with distaste, at least with despair. Officials expect him to support the large objectives with which their lives are identified. Moreover the minister himself, after an initial period during which he may revise his predecessor's policies, easily identifies with his department. Ministerial responsibility means that the department's successes and failures are also his own. The normal way to gain respect and advance himself is to enhance some of the great purposes of his department. And great purposes usually cost money.

This rule of ministerial advocacy knows no party boundaries. The Chancellor of the Exchequer may gain by reducing taxes; for the spending minister to expect rewards for doing likewise would be almost a contradiction in terms. Who will know or give credit to the head of a major department for not spending money on this, that, and an infinite number of other crying needs? The tendency was put to the test in 1970. Few governments can have started out more devoted to government economy than the Conservatives, with their business-minded reforms in education : charges for school meals and an ending of free school milk. But a year later the economising Minister of Education, like other Conservative spending ministers, could be found in the usual political operation of commending herself to a client audience by citing increased spending. 'I have,' she said, 'done everything possible to show my confidence in the future of higher education. In my monthly battles with the Treasury, I managed to get another £76 million for student grants and last week announced the biggest ever development programme for further education and polytechnics.'[6] Few objective measures exist for judging a minister, but ability to hold his own and perhaps do better than his colleagues in gaining funds is one of the most well-worn touchstones in Whitehall, in Cabinet, and in the outside public.[7]

The minister may accept sacrifices imposed equally on all his colleagues without serious blemish but he cannot accept inferior treatment without being considered a lesser man. 'The spending minister who does not put up a fight loses authority forever.' That statement was echoed by countless other ministers. The lesson has been drummed into them by their own experience and by observing what happens to others who violate this precept. Everyone has his favourite cautionary tale. We have pieced this one together both from the minister who suffered under the situation and from other ministers who watched what he did (or did not do) and his subsequent loss of reputation. The minister involved was disposed

6. Speech of Mrs Margaret Thatcher, at the Royal Festival Hall, reported in the *Daily Telegraph*, 23 November 1971. For similar ministerial claims of success as a function of spending more money, see public assertions by the Conservative Secretaries of State for the Environment, *The Times*, 15 July 1971; for Defence, *The Times*, 14 October 1971; and for Social Services, *Financial Times*, 9 February 1972.

7. So widespread is the acceptance of ministerial advocacy that even tough Treasury officials can be led to forego their prerogatives in its favour. For example, Sir Edward Playfair, a retired permanent secretary with 30 years experience mostly in the Treasury has reported, 'I agree – and it was a politician, David Eccles, who converted me to this view – that the old arrangement by which the University Grants Committee dealt direct with the Treasury was wrong. As he put it: the universities in present circumstances cannot succeed unless there is a Minister whose political reputation depends on his getting the money that they need.' ('Who are the Policy-Makers?' p. 260). Ministerial advocacy has changed little over the years. In 1933 the Chancellor urged the Cabinet 'to dismiss from their minds the question of whether there would be a surplus in the coming Budget and if so, of what amount, and to consider the question in the abstract'. The Home Secretary, Minister of Labour, President of the Board of Education, and President of the Board of Trade saw things a little differently. Cab. 23/77 (1933), pp. 226 ff.

to be co-operative in helping the government maintain a lower level of expenditure to serve its economic goals. The Chancellor, in an atmosphere of economic crisis, proposed a substantial cut in his departmental funds that would affect a vital programme. The minister went to the Chancellor and said that this was intolerable. He would accept only half the cut, possibly throwing in a little extra out of capital expenditure. Now let the minister describe it in his own words: 'I made this agreement with the Chancellor and told my officials to find where we could most easily get the sum we had to cut. The Chancellor, of course, did not tell other ministers he had first wanted larger cuts that would have affected the programme more severely. No one knows I made an agreement with him to reduce this. So when I went to the Cabinet and did not fight, I looked bad. It made me very unpopular because word leaked out and some people informed journalists that I did not fight and this gets around to the —— lobby. There has to be trust, and, having made the agreement with the Chancellor, I believe I had to keep it. But one looks very bad.' Ministers who observed this episode were emphatic in stating that the man had crippled his reputation. Department officials considered him weak. His Cabinet colleagues believed that they could easily run over him. The interests affected no longer wanted him to deal with their subject. Other interests who wanted a strong minister to look after their affairs would be upset if he came into an office affecting them. According to his fellow ministers, the chances of this man ever having a major department again were considerably reduced. He should not, they thought, have accepted the Chancellor's initial bargaining position as unshakeable. If he had to give in, he should have done so only after a lengthy struggle in open Cabinet where his efforts to prevent the worst could be known to his colleagues. The minister who appears to give up without a fight loses credibility all around.

Gaining respect among one's colleagues depends on doing things, not on leaving them undone. The specific impetus for a proposed spending increase can come from almost any quarter – department officials, the minister himself, interest groups, parliamentary questions, and so on. Our concern is not how this impetus begins, but what happens to it once it does occur. Normally, a spending minister becomes actively involved in the expenditure process through strategy sessions with his top officials when there is a new spending proposal to advance or cut to resist. By this time of course feelers will have already been put out at the official level to see, as one top official said, 'how fierce Treasury resistance is before engaging in battle at the ministerial level'. Whether it is a cut or an increase that is at stake, the point at which civil servants' advice and politicians' judgements intercept is the minister's briefing. To begin understanding what spending ministers do we must look more closely at the information they receive.

The Minister's Briefing

The brief is designed to enable the minister to hold his own, whether he is in personal talks with Treasury ministers, in Cabinet committees, or ultimately in the Cabinet itself when the final battles are being fought. The document produced for the minister is for strictly internal consumption, because it reveals as explicitly as possible the basis of what the department wants and (often) its strategy for getting it. As Treasury review has become more highly structured under the PESC procedure, departments have responded by forming more or less informal groups of senior officials to deal with the PESC bid before and after its submission. The members of the committee typically will include the permanent secretary, division undersecretaries, the finance officer and probably the establishment (personnel) officer.[8] If the preliminary PESC report prepared by the Treasury says the department has to cut anything substantial this group reconvenes. 'What we do then,' a participant said, 'is brief the minister to fight like mad.'

But it is not quite this clearcut. A permanent secretary summed up the feeling of most : 'With the best will in the world, briefing a minister becomes an editing job. You're affected by the nature of the client for whom you're doing the job and by the impression you want to make.' Preparing the brief materialises the senior civil servants' standard dilemma. On one hand, their reputation as competent people depends on being able to reach a certain amount of agreement among themselves; leaving too many matters to be decided by ministers suggests they do not know their business. 'The consequence of not settling most things between

8. A description of one of the more formal such arrangements in the Ministry of Technology, when Sir Richard Clarke was senior official, is in H.C. 410 (1968–9), p. 64: 'Memorandum by the Ministry of Technology'.

officials,' observed a permanent secretary who reflects the mass of opinion among his class, 'is that you as a civil servant lose credibility, and the minister himself loses credibility with the Cabinet and Chancellor.' Ministers are normally the last resort, not the first. They and the Cabinet are unpredictable, so that officials would usually settle for less if they could be more certain of getting it.

On the other hand, officials have not worked in their area of policy so hard and so long to sit by and watch their best ideas die for lack of funds. Experienced department officials believe that ultimately the nature of the brief depends partly on the case but more importantly on the minister. With a strong minister, they are always willing to try for something extra. More unhappy experiences than they care to remember cause permanent secretaries to repeat endlessly that in deciding what goes up to the minister 'first and foremost is the quality of your minister as an advocate and how he stands in the Cabinet and with the P.M. If he is hopeless in this sense, there is no chance and you may as well not bother.' Another more aggressive senior official asked rhetorically, 'Is the minister a man of strength? Does he have the support or can he force the support of other colleagues to get a bigger slice for himself? If you have a minister who is quite sensible and bright and pleasant but will not fight with his colleagues and recognise the personal political realities involved, there is no point in forcing the issue.' The minister who is not only unaggressive but also dull will be kept out of sight as much as possible. His officials will go to great lengths to settle matters with their Treasury counterparts; they will seek a deal, make an arrangement, accept losses they would rather not take – anything but let their feeble lamb go up to the slaughter. The bright minister who will not fight can at least get the substantive arguments straight and officials will concentrate on those. The interesting strategic problems emerge when they judge their minister to be capable of making a case and winning over his colleagues if only the right approach can be found.

Although the brief is a suit of armour tailored to the client, a number of uniformities can be identified in fitting out the minister to do battle. The department brief is first of all designed to convince the minister himself. If he is a forceful man, with high standing in his party and good relations with the Prime Minister and/or Chancellor of the Exchequer, he is also likely to know his own mind. Once the minister himself is convinced, he will have an easier time persuading his colleagues. The brief attempts to marshal the facts in a clear and well-argued way. The merits of the case, in so far as they may be known, do matter even when they are not all that matters.

The official brief goes on to warn the minister of weaknesses in his case. It identifies the chinks of vulnerability which could be brought up by others and particularly Treasury ministers, who are briefed on the same issues by their officials. Comparison with other departments' past allocations and rates of growth may be made either to show how the department is behind and should catch up, or to explain why – though it looks like the department is doing better than others – this is not so, or, contrariwise, deserves to be so.

The brief often suggests a set of trade-offs. Certain items can be jettisoned without significant loss and others the minister must stick to at all costs because they are central to the departmental programme. Some items may be offered up as loss-leaders – gestures used to show that the department is already accepting sacrifices and should not be asked to do more. Only a few of these can be represented because it is not good practice to suggest that there are activities currently being carried out that are expendable. During the heat of battle, however, when the time comes to strike a final bargain, the minister must know where he can retreat and where he must stand firm.

Many, but not all, official briefs will mention strictly political arguments, usually in a suitably demure phrase ('the Minister may care to reflect...') at the bottom of the page. Thinly veiled references may be made to party advantage, election pledges, public reactions and so forth. For the seasoned politician, such comments are often 'touchingly wrong' but civil servants will, as they told us, 'try to make good for a minister who can't put forward the political arguments'. Even seeing no need to suggest political arguments, senior officials will still recognise and emphasise the need to marshal argument in a politic way. The comment recorded from permanent secretary Herbert Andrew to his Minister of Education is typical:

> The important thing is not the arguments which convince you and me and how best to put these arguments to the Cabinet – the important thing is to try to visualise the way in which some

other members of the Cabinet will view this subject. What are the blockages, that may make it difficult for some of them to see why it is so important? Approach the discussion by looking at the subject from their end, as well as from our end here.[9]

All briefs and 'bull sessions' between minister and civil servants will review some or all of the standard strategies discussed in previous chapters – false cuts, sore thumbs, targetry, and so on. Should it be a period of expenditure restraint, as is usual, the minister and civil servants will plan whether to achieve reductions with several large items or with a series of small cuts; the political temptation, as an ex-minister said, is always to do the latter since 'small cuts are harder for people to notice'.

One strategic option – getting a snap commitment from the Cabinet without going through the official channels – is not discussed in official briefs. Putting ideas that are considered 'bad form' into writing is not the done thing. Though officials recognise the dangers of violating protocol, they also believe that 'sometimes you simply have to go to the minister and say that we are not going to do very well. The others are ganging up on us and are going to cut us because we have done so well in the past. Then about all you can do is try and get the minister to pre-empt things by getting an early commitment from Cabinet because the issue is of such importance.' The decision to follow this course of action may be based on timing. 'When there are lots of other axe grinders on the job,' a permanent secretary explained, 'you may be able to get the Treasury on the run or, if you choose a particularly slack time, you may steal a march on other people and beggar your neighbour.'

The most important gap in the spending minister's document is competitive briefing, and its absence speaks volumes about politicians' preparation for Cabinet government. The minister is likely to be briefed, as his civil servants say, 'only for defence, not offence'. He will not be told how to leave more for himself by holding down others and equally, he will be offered little advice on how to assess other ministers' proposals. Politicians' collective deliberations on allocating public money are rarely serviced by their departmental officials. This self-denying ordinance among civil servants stems partly from ignorance. 'There's the feeling,'

9. Sir Edward Boyle, 'Who are the Policy-Makers?', *Public Administration*, 43 (1965), p. 253.

said one permanent secretary, 'that you don't know enough about the other chap's programme to do this.' A more important reason, which should be clear from preceding chapters, lies in the closeness of civil service society. There may be snide remarks in some briefs ('this is consistent with that department's record of unsound proposals'), but unless you are in the Treasury it is considered 'not on' to make one's way by criticising other departments. In addition, officials can justifiably console themselves with the thought that it is not their job to get their minister in trouble by picking gratuitous fights with other ministers. The comment from one combative permanent secretary makes clear the circumspection which even the most aggressive officials exercise:

> This question of squeezing down other departments is very much a matter of ministerial strength and is the one thing that has to be discussed with the minister very carefully. [Why?] Because it is his career that is at stake with his ministerial colleagues if he tries to squeeze them down too far.

The struggle for resources may be a contest, but it is far from a free-for-all.

The Minister as Combatant

Some ministers accept the brief much as it is put before them, merely varying the emphasis here and there to suit their preferences. Other ministers will make more substantial alterations, citing their superior knowledge of the political situation. A very small minority takes no interest in expenditure problems, dutifully reading the brief as underlined (in red for the more hopeless ministers) by the permanent secretary. Few ministers, however, are an entirely neutral influence; they affect their department's expenditure cases for better or for worse. While the personal qualities of politicians have an effect only at the margin, they do make a difference. One minister effectively summed up the situation: 'Public expenditure decisions are not the smooth technical operation presented in the White Papers and published accounts. These [personal qualities of ministers] are the things this smooth current flows around.' What then does the spending minister himself bring to the expenditure process?

All participants agree that one of the most important contributions made by a minister is his political 'standing'. But the source of this standing is not self-evident to an outsider. From talks with politicians who are (or were) ministers we can go somewhat further. Little advantage accrues to a minister merely by virtue of his prior position in the party, either inside or outside Parliament. The man who has been popular in the constituency organisations or cuts a major figure in the parliamentary party enjoys no automatic authority for getting his way on expenditures in Cabinet. Of course, a key figure can threaten to resign but such threats are rare and unlikely in the normal course of spending decisions. (It is, however, indicative of the importance attached to ministerial advocacy and the spending process that over half of the fifteen or so voluntary resignations of ministers during 1950–70 were associated with disputes on expenditure stringency.)[10] Instead, a minister's standing is a more composite political image reflecting the Cabinet's assessment of his success as minister. Here are typical comments by two former Cabinet members. 'What matters is the minister's general public standing and image, not his position in the parliamentary party. If he's regarded as a shining success at his department, he gets a very good hearing.' And again, 'If a man is known as popular and a successful minister, the Cabinet will look on him more favourably. This is human nature. If a minister is slipping, if he is under attack, then he will not do so well.' A minister's standing is a collage of his reputation among all those judging how he is doing – officials, backbenchers, interest group leaders, journalists. But in the final analysis, standing depends chiefly on the judgement of ministerial colleagues. The close contact ministers have with one another and their incessant evaluation of each other's capabilities makes it difficult for a man to stand on the opinion of outsiders.

So far we have come only a little way in understanding why some ministers tend to prevail and others are regularly thwarted in their spending plans. The core of the matter was well summed

10. Obviously any single-cause interpretation of resignations is an over-simplification of ministerial behaviour. Included as resigning for questions of expenditure, questions which as we shall see later are inherently bound up with substantive policy, are: Bevan, Wilson and Freeman in April 1951; Thorneycroft, Powell and Birch (from the Treasury) in January 1958; Mayhew in February 1966; Herbison in July 1967; and Longford in January 1968. A general discussion of the complexities of resignation is in P. J. Madgwick, 'Resignations', *Parliamentary Affairs* (winter 1966), pp. 59–76.

up by a man with experience as both a spending and Treasury minister. 'What really counts is absolute firmness combined with the sensitivity to know when to give way a little.' Which is to say, to be an artist. From a variety of sources one can piece together the following 'identikit' picture of the successful minister in the contemporary expenditure process.

First, he is supremely well-informed in presenting his own case. The strong minister realises that the Cabinet and Treasury ministers are quick to discount anyone who is confused and tentative. Colleagues will respect a minister's plea only if he is knowledgeable about what matters to him and can defend his position. 'You need to have the whole score in your head,' a minister states. 'You should not look at your notes. You should be able to respond to anything that comes up. You should be able to play whatever balls come your way.' Behind the air of easy mastery, to be sure, may well lie a significant amount of preparation and sometimes even rehearsal in the departmental briefing, but the outcome can be worth it. The results, according to another successful minister, is that 'by knowing your own brief through and through, you can shoot down every objection; the Prime Minister and others are impressed'. A number of political 'glamour boys' have found out to their regret what all experienced political administrators know: 'It is no use thinking that a man who comes along with a nice little brief and waffles – however successful he may have been on the hustings or even in the House – will carry any weight with his fellow-Ministers.' [11] Cabinet government is not a beauty contest.

Second, the successful spending minister can talk beyond his own brief and knows, as one put it, 'how to mobilise the political argument'. He is able to drive home the political consequences of proposed actions by showing, for instance, the loss of public sympathy in instituting fees on a certain group while other groups not overly warm toward the Party continue to be heavily subsidised; recalling that a particular service was conceived by the Party and is now 'regarded as our baby'; discussing the loss of seats in local elections; arguing that a delay in something already programmed will offer it to the tender mercies, or electoral credit, of the next government. The inventive spending minister can lay hold of any number of such political sticks.

11. Sir Edward Playfair, 'Who are the Policy-Makers?' *Public Administration*, 43, 1965, p. 261.

Above all, the successful spending minister is a fighter – tough, persistent, formidable. Political associates know how much a minister wants something only by seeing how hard he fights for it. 'My Secretary of State is doughty,' an admiring official declared. 'He never gives up.' The minister referred to observed, 'Maybe the most important thing was will and stamina, to keep on nagging when everyone else was tired. This fighting is what prevailed and others knew it. [Name of minister] said to me that only when cuts had to be made in [his ministry] was he moved from being its minister because everyone knew how hard he'd fight.'

There are, of course, many shades of aggressiveness and pugnacity. The minister with high standing has a somewhat easier time of it. He does not need to play the part of the windmill fighter who bowls everyone over and bleeds every step of the way. He gets what he wants by virtue of who he is, by selective tenacity, and by his ability to bring others along with him. But the expenditure process is still the great divider of ministers, and fight he must if high standing is to pay-off in more funds. There is also the more fearsome minister who, according to a participant, 'fights only for his own corner and fights like hell. This is so they can let it be known outside the Cabinet – to their own group in Parliament – that they've shown the colours. They are afraid that if they don't fight, someone will let it out.' These more aggressive spending ministers feel themselves little constrained by their officials. Quite the contrary. 'I always wanted to do more, much more,' a spending minister asserted, 'and my officials were restraining me by saying, "well, Minister, I don't see you getting Treasury authority for this".' Regardless of any such variations, the fact remains that ministers who are fighters – subtle or brusque – are recognised on all sides as doing the best in the expenditure decisions in Cabinet. Anthony Crosland, generally accepted as a strong minister, accurately summed up what is the situation in either Conservative or Labour Government: a minister gets resources for his service 'by persuading, arguing, cajoling, exploiting his political position … above all by being persistent … whether you can exhaust your colleagues before they exhaust you. It's an endless tactical battle which requires determination, cunning and occasional unscrupulousness.' [12]

Although he is tough, the strong minister is also temperate; he

12. Kogan *et al. The Politics of Education*, p. 167.

P.G.P.M.—6*

does not become so obstinate as to cause annoyance. A fighter, yes; a disrupter, definitely not. At a minimum he must know his 'Cabinet manners' well enough to recognise that 'anyone who talks too much is a bore'. Said one experienced minister, 'If such a man isn't a central figure he'll likely be dropped in the next Cabinet reshuffle.' Much more important to success is the good sense to compromise when you must – but on what you choose. 'Absolute intransigence,' as a wise ex-minister said, 'only puts the others' backs up.' Just as the minister who is ready to trade anything soon becomes known as a man insensitive to the merits of his case, so the man who never compromises makes life difficult for his colleagues; they may conclude there is no point in giving in to him since he will only ask for more next time.

For a few, but not many, sheer stubbornness may pay off. 'There was nothing you could do with ——,' a Treasury minister revealed. 'He refused to take any cuts. He would argue doggedly for increases and was absolutely unyielding. Almost invariably he got his way. There was fear of reaction in public opinion if the row should get into public view.' By his very determination such a minister may make it costly for his colleagues to deal adversely with him, but the minister who, like Henderson the Rain King, insists on demanding 'I want, I want', everywhere and at all times soon annoys his colleagues. They cannot have what they want if he is so damned insistent. They get tired of and annoyed with his bullying tactics and are likely to regard him as a public nuisance who must be disabused of his self-important notions. Still, if he is a man willing to take what the future will bring, he may yet prevail because his colleagues cannot find an opportune time or a satisfactory way of cutting him down.

Selective monomania may not be necessary for the successful minister, but it is helpful. The minister with a clear idea of what he wants and who pursues it tenaciously from one season to the next, has a good chance of ultimately getting it. Ministerial colleagues may want many things and diffuse their energy while he saves it all for the one thing he wants most.

To what extent does the successful spending minister form alliances ('you scratch my departmental bid, I'll scratch yours') with other spending ministers? There is a certain amount of 'arranging for colleagues to back you up'. But even more than toughness, logrolling must be used very selectively. It cannot be a regular strategy nor always carried out with the same allies. 'Otherwise,' as one ex-minister observed, 'the losers will gang up on you, and there's always more of them.' Formal bargains between ministers are rare. When the time is right, a special appointment may be made for the purpose or (in the midst of the usual gossip) there may appear a few well-chosen sentences about the earth-shaking significance of a programme for which funds simply must be found. The minister who receives these entreaties may mention in an offhand way a project that is also dear to his heart. A's expenditure increase could be delayed to release funds for B; in return, A needs support for a major new plan. Nothing further need be said; the spirit of mutual gain at Cabinet time has already been created.

The scope for such alliances is, however, extremely limited. Ministers not in the Cabinet have few such opportunities. 'I attend Cabinet only when an issue affecting my department is being discussed,' a non-Cabinet minister explained. 'I cannot engage in horse-trading. I cannot say I'll help you on this, meaning I would like help on that, or if I get help now I would return the favour later.' Moreover ministers tend to act unilaterally because they are too busy to do anything else. 'There are too many issues, too many departmental matters, too much business in the House, too many meetings,' a minister stated, 'to do very much other than follow the procedure.' A spending programme must, therefore, be of extraordinary importance before a minister will invest energy in forming an alliance.

Logrolling is generally rejected as a tactic because spending ministers believe it will not help them. Strong ministers generally can get what they want without it. 'No, I don't contact other ministers beforehand,' such a minister declared, 'but then I did not often get a "no" answer either.' Other ministers may need allies but feel constrained. 'If they are spending ministers,' said one politician, 'it will do you no good. They are interested in their own spending. The non-spending ministers will not take your word because they know there are other things involved.' Persistent horse-trading is also considered a variety of unseemly importuning more likely to raise hackles than expenditures. 'Those who do it,' said a minister who did not like asking for favours, 'usually do not succeed. It is not good form to be known as lobbying around.' Since one's 'own sort' does not do that sort of thing, many ministers' first thought is that lobbying does not occur at all. 'There is no systematic lobbying,' they would say, though on being pressed they would add that 'sometimes other ministers did mention projects in conversational tones during informal meetings.' A casual word may not appear 'systematic' to the listener but it may nonetheless get to colleagues. Propriety matters though, because it enhances respect for the advocate.

All these elements can be brought to life in the words of a man generally recognized as a successful minister.

You simply had to fight for what you wanted – like a bulldog only on a slightly more intellectual basis. Maybe the most important thing was physical stamina, to keep on barking when everyone else was tired. This fighting is what prevailed and others knew it.

You had to give officials the political lead because they didn't know what sort of political appeals would have good effect. I got [my programme] increased and increased. Now to do this I couldn't count on the [X] lobby because they're all with the Opposition. My colleagues would look and say what a high rate of increase was occurring in [X] compared to [Y and Z]. You'd point out what disastrous results would occur otherwise. One spent an enormous amount of time getting the telling information from a mass of statistics.

You couldn't do things by pure hammer blows – you could not go on so much to weary or annoy Cabinet colleagues. What you're after is the telling phrase and fact. When the economic mood was tough I'd use nice statistics. I'd say 'do you realise the rate of return on this programme – what's your rate of return?'

Then at other times you'd play for political kudos and hang the economic return. Another time it would be more appropriate to make a demagogical appeal – another time you might try to make a dirty deal with another minister, though this did not always work.

For the spending minister who is sufficiently keen on an issue, there are more exceptional – and risky – courses outside the prescribed channels. Department officials are supposed to bargain with the Treasury; ministers are expected to make their case before other ministers. But deliberate attempts to galvanise public opinion and direct appeals to the Prime Minister occupy a different status: these tactics are not exactly illegitimate but neither are they accepted as general practice. Ministers who engage in them must be aware that their behaviour may cause antipathy among colleagues who consider it out of line. The cost attached to such lobbying limits its use. Still, knowing that his colleagues read the signs of the times, spending ministers sometimes seek to create or manipulate a few auguries of their own. They talk to interest group leaders in private and go to annual conferences where they exhort the assembled believers to create a favourable public climate for education, the environment, welfare and the rest. Ministers indirectly sponsor meetings which end by recommending the higher spending for which they were assembled in the beginning. Letters and articles may spontaneously appear in the newspapers and weeklies claiming to show that certain programmes have been starved for funds. Shocking conditions are revealed that must be remedied. To take a recent example, one government service 'had been ridden roughshod over for years by the Treasury'. Against the advice of his officials, the spending minister decided to publish a report on a series of recent scandals in the service, knowing that under the traditional doctrine of ministerial responsibility, he would be held accountable. The gamble paid off. 'After that,' our informant said, 'the Treasury and Cabinet couldn't deny him more money in this area.' Given the time and risks involved, such tactics must be the exception not the rule.

Discretion and sense of timing are, if anything, more vital when it comes to lobbying the Prime Minister. The obvious thing is that he must be a court of last resort. The Leader would collapse under the strain if ministers continually solicited him; his Chancellor would not stand being regularly bypassed; every special arrangement made for one minister would constitute the basis of a claim by others for special treatment. There is always a big mental sign advising CAUTION to the spending minister before approaching the top man. Still, the importance of having the Prime Minister on your side can hardly be exaggerated. He might persuade the Chancellor when a minister could not. He can argue the political merits more authoritatively than anyone else: if he says the party requires a programme it will be difficult to resist him. His summation of a Cabinet discussion can turn the tide of opinion. Except on the most vital issues, other ministers will think twice before opposing him. Persuading the Prime Minister, if it can be done, is a trump card.

There are two approaches to a Prime Minister: direct assault and enveloping action. The direct method involves going to see him and putting the case; the indirect one seeks to weave a cocoon of favourable opinion about him. Close associates are approached in the hope they will put in a good word. The minister involved will seek every opportunity to make his case. He will drop a word during a party rally or after a Cabinet meeting. Upon being called in to discuss a different issue he will find a way to link it up with the subject closest to his heart. By and by the P.M. will get the idea that the minister cares deeply; better still he will begin to think that something positive has to be done. A few ministers in any government can be found playing trumps.

Most ministers follow a self-denying ordinance and do not bother the Prime Minister with their expenditure problems. Some will not approach the Prime Minister because their personal relationships are strained. Membership in the Cabinet is quite compatible with mutual dislike, and the minister who lacks a personal footing for approaching the Prime Minister does not go near him unless asked: 'My relations with him never allowed it.' Other ministers may have good personal relations with the Prime Minister but fear losing them. 'You can't imagine how easy it is to annoy a Prime Minister,' said a veteran of many skirmishes. 'One demand too many is likely to prejudice future requests.' A politician who has lived with four Prime Ministers observed, 'Prime Ministers tend to divide ministers into two classes: those who economise the Prime Minister's time and those who consume it.' Taking in events at a run, forming judgements from the briefest encounters, the Prime Minister will be put off by the man who grates on his nerves by seeming too insistent.

Spending ministers conclude generally that 'the Prime Minister has enough on his plate. My job is to fight my own corner.' Prime Ministers and their colleagues know that inherent in the structure of British Cabinet government is the fact that only exceptionally and on small issues can he take sides against the Treasury ministers. To do so regularly on major spending issues is an operational definition of a government crisis. The Prime Minister and a few civil servants whose duty it is to protect him ward off potential lobbyists by letting it be known that he will not be receptive. Consequently, most spending ministers at most times are forced back to the usual process that funnels their demands through the Treasury ministers. To these powerful politicians we must now turn.

Chief Secretaries: Unsung Makers of Major Choices

I say no.

Ex-Chief Secretary

Your brief is to make yourself awkward.

Ex-Chief Secretary

I feel, also, as is well known to you and your colleagues that the argument is very rarely about how much a particular programme shall be reduced. It is always the other way around.

Lord Diamond, Third Report from the Expenditure Committee (1970–1), Minutes of Evidence, *p. 30*

To understand the Treasury minister's role in the expenditure process, one must begin, not as many would think with the Chancellor of the Exchequer, but with the Chief Secretary. Created only recently, the Chief Secretary's post is little known to outsiders. Any minister who has tried to increase spending or avoid cuts in the last ten years knows it only too well.

Since 1852 there has been a Financial Secretary to the Treasury, a junior political minister who handles the government's day-to-day financial business in the House of Commons. Little-noticed changes in 1961 did not alter this arrangement but produced an entirely new ministerial post at the Treasury – a senior colleague of the Chancellor known as the Chief Secretary. To be appointed Financial Secretary is to be labelled promising ministerial material; to be Chief Secretary is to have climbed higher. Indeed, a good Chief Secretary is so invaluable to Chancellor and Prime Minister that in hard economic times he may be regarded as indispensable and denied a departmental post he more eagerly desires.

The need for two ministers to take the Treasury viewpoint grew out of the vast increase in government expenditures and the decrease in the amount of time the Chancellor could, or was prepared to devote to them. As expenditures rose after the Second World War the Chancellor's interest in them went down in favour of trying to manage the economy. According to one who took part in creating the office, 'the whole object of establishing a Chief Secretary in 1961 was to relieve the Chancellor; we thought it was absurd that with his wide responsibilities he should have to argue individual expenditure items. The Chancellor would have to study the brief 15–20 minutes and then spend 30–45 minutes arguing with the minister – in all maybe one and one-half hours of his day on something that wasn't critical to the management of the economy or budget.' The result is that the Chief Secretary now represents the Treasury in most ministerial bargaining on spending.[13]

While the Chief Secretary is not necessarily a regular Cabinet member, he has invariably possessed full Cabinet rank. Not only does he argue the Treasury case bilaterally with individual spending ministers and multilaterally in Cabinet committees, but he also attends all Cabinet meetings dealing with spending decisions. The reasoning is obvious. 'The Chancellor needs someone well-briefed in Cabinet to back him up,' observed an experienced Chief Secretary. 'In any committee a lone voice is very lonely and two people arguing a case is much more than two times as effective as one.' Only during the annual summer expenditure review and on the largest issues is the Chancellor likely to become the main protagonist in Cabinet spending decisions, and even then he will work in close co-operation with his ministerial ally. 'During the rest of the year,' as a Chancellor said, 'most issues are settled by the Chief Secretary. I see the main papers for information only, initial them to show that I had read them, but I would not make any decisions.'

13. The announcement of the post's creation, 9 October 1961, prescribed that the Chief Secretary would, 'under the general direction of the Chancellor, deal with the whole range of public expenditure, both current and prospective, including the scrutiny of departmental estimates and the framing of forward surveys'. Quoted in Bridges, *The Treasury*, p. 163.

Since the Chief Secretary is given not merely the Chancellor's busy work but an important part of his power, the working relations between the two men clearly are crucial. In 1961 it was the Prime Minister's and new Chancellor's suggestion that there should be no appeal from the Chief Secretary to the Chancellor, only to the entire Cabinet itself. Despite some wobbling in the interim, this remains true today. A more junior Chief Secretary, possibly without major ministerial experience, begins with narrower discretion than others, and recognises that on highly sensitive and/or sudden expenditure problems, it is the Chancellor's word that must prevail. But on the huge range of issues still remaining for even a junior man, Chief Secretaries and Chancellors are adamant that the principle of no appeals to the Chancellor should remain intact, briefing their successors – of whatever party – on how to make the necessary arrangements.

These arrangements are likely to pay special regard to the nature of the issue involved. On matters which have remained solely within the Treasury the Chancellor is likely to feel a little freer occasionally to overrule his Chief Secretary, usually in the direction of being a little more generous on this or that (Chancellors have been known to bestow minor beneficences when feeling in an expansive mood on Christmas Eve). Even these interventions will be rare if there is any danger perceived of undermining the Chief Secretary's position with senior Treasury officials or his own self-confidence.

Where the matter involves a bilateral dispute between Treasury and spending department, and particularly if the Chief Secretary has taken a firm position, the Chancellor will almost always support his colleague fully. Chancellors know (or usually have soon learned) that if the Chief Secretary is to ease their burdens, they must refuse to be lobbied directly by other ministers. For as one spending minister explained 'if the Chancellor is firm, if he says "go and see so and so" and insists on it, others know they can't get around the Chief Secretary'. Before 1961 every minister had a right to see the Chancellor. Nowadays, a minister seeking such an appeal normally will receive a letter saying that the Chancellor has spoken to the Chief Secretary and agreed to follow his advice. Occasionally maintenance of good relations with a strong Cabinet colleague requires the Chancellor to relent, but even then, Chancellors as a working rule will, in the words of one, 'hold only a *pro forma* interview knowing in advance that I will stick to [the Chief Secretary's] judgement'.

When an issue has escalated into multilateral argument before the Cabinet, arrangements between the two Treasury Ministers must be particularly delicate. Quite likely there will be an understanding that the Chief Secretary can have at least 'one go' before Cabinet colleagues. Since, as we shall see in a later section, complete success can never be guaranteed, both Chancellor and Chief Secretary are also likely to be agreed that some fallback position may be necessary. They must then agree on when and how the Chief Secretary may surrender.

Whatever the permutation of circumstances, the important point is that the Chief Secretary's position be buttressed by the Chancellor's behaviour. The Chief Secretary's authority is a function of not being overruled unless he expects it. By following a self-denying ordinance in regard to the few matters of special interest to the Chancellor, he can insist on support in the broader areas clearly reserved for him. Said one Chief Secretary, 'I would be a fool if I were to allow an issue on which I knew the Chancellor and I had a disagreement to get to Cabinet.' The Chief Secretary will, therefore, make accomodations to the Chancellor's occasional view in return for the Second Lord's imprimatur. Preoccupied with the drama of economic management and repelled by constantly importuning spending ministers, Chancellors scarcely regret what outsiders might consider a loss of power.

The capable Chief Secretary is a boon not only to the Chancellor above him but also to the officials below him. 'Treasury people,' a minister reports, 'have a tendency to be excessively tough because they fear their ministers will give way on appeal. With Jack Diamond [Chief Secretary 1964–70] things worked the other way round. If a department official said he could not accept a certain limitation, Treasury officials only had to say his minister should take the matter up with Jack Diamond. It was a case of sentence being increased on appeal.' That a good Chief Secretary is invaluable to Treasury, Chancellor and Prime Minister is accepted by all; that his is the most difficult job description in government is suspected by some, especially former Chief Secretaries.

Success in any ministerial position varies with the personal qualities of the office holder. But some are peculiarly dependent on the special skills (or the lack thereof) of the minister. Bright or dull, brutish or charming, a Chancellor of the Exchequer is sometimes less powerful than he might be but he will always be a man of some importance. The Chief Secretary, however, will be a total failure if he does not measure up to the job. If he cannot understand the intricacies of expenditure, he will be unable to cope either with Treasury officials or spending ministers. If he does not retain the Chancellor's confidence, spending ministers will try to bypass him, reducing his influence to the extreme situation in which they act literally as if he were not there. (As far as we can tell, this alternative has not yet arisen.) If the Chief Secretary is a man of parts, however, combining an ability to master the issues with personal adroitness, he can influence a larger number of more important decisions than almost any other minister. Only in the last few years have political men woken up to the fact, that, as one expressed it, 'The Chief Secretary increasingly is becoming a very powerful man. He is quietly making decisions on roads, loans to students and so on that in other contexts would be regarded as subjects for major political choices.'

How well a man does as Chief Secretary depends in part on how much he likes the work. One man's career may be hurt by being placed in a position where he has to deny some important and senior colleagues things close to their hearts. They hate him and he hates his job. Another man can gain as Chief Secretary by using the many opportunities offered for serving on an endless number of Cabinet committees (even when formally not a member of the Cabinet) and for seeing more of the working of government than virtually any other minister. He who indulges other men is not surprised to find warm regard; he who can win their affection while depriving them of worldly goods has reached an extraordinary height of diplomacy reserved for a few.

Chief Secretaries take pains to say they do not glory in the negative role. It was not all restrictiveness, they will say, as they recall singular instances in the job that allowed them to act positively. The very language they use suggests the degree to which everyone concerned has come under the influence of the belief that spending is positive while cutting is negative. Nevertheless the approach of the Chief Secretary soon becomes a reflection of his Treasury allegiance. 'You do get caught up in the atmosphere of the Treasury,' a former Chief Secretary said, 'and that means taking a critical view of expenditures.' Asked how he spent his time, he replied that 'I was in over thirty interdepartmental committees arguing for the less expensive course.' Hard experience leads the Chief Secretary to believe that 'only one person will put the non-spending, savings point of view and that is the Treasury minister. All the others propose spending.'

A reputation as a stone-waller can help a Chief Secretary by encouraging departments to make settlements with officials lower down. But a reputation for being harsh will do him no good if he wishes to maintain the personal good will of his colleagues, to keep the government working in some sort of harmony and, perhaps not least, to rise further in the party. Any new Chief Secretary quickly learns that his colleagues in the Government see his job, like most other things, in terms of their departmental responsibilities. A little flexibility in meeting at least some of their needs can help him in the long run. 'I lost one time,' said a Chief Secretary, 'because I was too intemperate. I should have recognized some of the points that were being made and sensed better the mood of the chairman [of the Cabinet committee].' A former Chancellor observed, 'You can get a civil servant if all you want is somebody to say no. You need somebody to make suggestions, to find ways around difficulties. If the Chief Secretary is regarded as a bottle-neck people will go round him.' Chief Secretaries must become experts at turning people down in a nice way. 'The hardest part of my job,' a Chief Secretary reflected, 'was to maintain good personal relations with my colleagues. You have got to be sympathetic, to show understanding. You must always realise it is a minister's whole involvement and investment. You are dealing with something about which he feels very deeply. One of the best things people said about me was that I said "no" more nicely than anybody they had ever come across. But you still must say no.'

Turning a minister down gently requires a good deal of effort in order to show understanding (and hence sympathy) on the substance of issues. Tact is required to avoid appearing to know more than the department. The criterion for decision must be those of special Treasury expertise on which the Chief Secretary can speak with authority. One Chief Secretary, a man who helped to shape the present-day job and was sensitive to the personal nuances surrounding his office, tried to work it this way: 'When I first came to the Treasury as Chief Secretary I quickly came to the conclusion that I couldn't exercise very much control simply by saying no. I could only exercise effective control by establishing mutual confidence with the department. [The preceding minister] had had to be very tough in expenditure decisions and hadn't worked especially hard at establishing this mutual trust. I did it by trying to really explain why I couldn't approve something and point out what the repercussions would be.' Such a man will lay out the whole of the Treasury position, showing the parallel demands which others would be encouraged to make, and so forth. He will try to build mutual understanding rather than 'make ministers feel they had just had an unlucky dip'. Financial secretaries of the old days, i.e., before 1961, could afford to say that 'the only way to reduce spending is to take the victim by the necktie, back him up against the wall, and tell him that either your department functions at this lower level or I'll knock your teeth out!' They knew that the Chancellor could be left with the mangle of spending ministers' appeals. The Chief Secretary today cannot afford such an attitude. 'If you make a flat dictate and say no,' observed a Chief Secretary, 'then you are at war with every spending department. What I tried to do was make them realise that I appreciated their position but overriding considerations required us, say, to meet them only half way.'

The care and feeding of unhappy ministers must necessarily vary with the circumstances and the man. The Chief Secretary already has been briefed by Treasury officials about the submissions made by the department. Unless a proposed expenditure seems bad beyond redemption, the Chief Secretary is likely to sympathise with its purposes. This warmth is not difficult to generate because the Chief Secretary may wish also that any number of good things could be done, and there is hardly a proposed expenditure that does not help someone. He thinks the scheme is grand but, alas, there are insufficient funds. Perhaps, if the department did it another and less expensive way some good might still be done, though not of course as much as the minister had originally hoped. The minister may counter by urging the high priority of his programme. The Chief Secretary does not doubt it for a moment but it turns out that many others feel the same way and their cases also are good. The spending minister must be careful lest he suggest that the programme is useless unless accepted *in toto*, for the Chief Secretary may then regretfully say that he would not harm the people by doing part when all must be done, hence the government will maintain its integrity by doing nothing at all.

The reaction Chief Secretaries like to create was summed up in a character judgement by a spending minister '[The Chief Secretary] was cold, hard, self-righteous, but very nice.' By being known as exceptionally tough, the Chief Secretary can afford to make occasional concessions without weakening his bargaining position. But they are exceptional. A spending minister tells the story of a small research grant for which the department had continually but unsuccessfully fought with Treasury officials. 'All the officials told me it was no good seeing the Chief Secretary – the Treasury simply wouldn't back it. I won by personally drawing up a six-page memo and taking it around to [the Chief Secretary's] flat at 8 a.m. He eventually gave in, as he later told me, because I had taken the trouble to do such a thing and it must therefore be important to me.' All this for a sum of money in the five-figure bracket.

The Chief Secretary very quickly learns the meaning of incrementalism. Old expenditures roll on blocking the course for most new ones except the fortunate few that manage to squeeze through. His main effort is thus centred on new spending. 'I'd simply look to see if there was any large rise over the previous year,' a Treasury minister recalled. 'If so I would note it and argue each point with the department.' The number of new proposals, or substantial increases in old ones across the range of modern British government staggers the imagination. The workload of the diligent Chief Secretary is enormous and never-ending.

Since he is there to take the burden off the Chancellor, the Chief Secretary cannot go far in determining his pattern of activity. His work is set for him by the demands of the situation. The top Treasury officials who are his workaday colleagues – the Second Permanent Secretary (public sector) and two deputy secretaries – bring him virtually all expenditure issues which require a ministerial answer. These civil servants must perforce handle many of the political issues themselves; a typical job description at this official level specifies that the office holder will generally oversee negotiations with departments for 'the necessary adjustments'. But they will also decide 'in more intractable cases' whether to refer them to Treasury Ministers for bilateral negotiation with

Departmental Ministers, or to leave them for later identification in the formal PESC submission to Ministers collectively. Civil Servants like to get ministerial cover, and therefore everything the Chief Secretary handles, except for mere formalities, turns out to be 'a special case'. Possibly the item has sensitive political implications, meaning that the reputation of a minister is implicated or that it is likely to get into the press and will require explanation in Parliament. Possibly the Chief Secretary will be aware that a programme has been the subject of intense disagreement among his colleagues, and he must take a hand. Or a matter may simply be one of the few open to discretion requiring new judgements for which ministerial approval is essential.

The Chief Secretary who processes all such issues will get no rest and little sleep. He will have no time for reading (except for official briefs and not always them) and a dearth of opportunities for reflection. He must, in truth, live off the capital fund of ideas he brought with him. The pace of office is incredibly swift. At any moment he is sitting actively on a dozen Cabinet committees (with two dozen others held in abeyance), handling ten to twenty decisions a day, and always ready to be told that the Chancellor cannot make a meeting and the Chief Secretary must go, reading his brief as he rides, for the session is already under way. No wonder that when a Chief Secretary does well, Chancellors fight to hang on to his invaluable services. The Chancellor saves his energy for the coming battles in the Cabinet. With the understanding that many of the duties to be discussed will, in practice, often fall on the Chief Secretary, we now turn to the most publicised figure in the expenditure process, the Chancellor of the Exchequer.

Chancellor of the Exchequer: Victim or Victimiser of the Spending Ministers?

> The control of the Treasury is neither more nor less than the personal influence of the Chancellor... upon the Cabinet.
>
> *Winston Churchill*, Life of Lord
> Randolph Churchill, *vol. II, p. 184–5.*

The one thing that matters is the Queen because she counts for all the pawns. If the P.M. supports him then the Chancellor will certainly win.

Ex-Chancellor

The spending ministers ganged up against me.

Ex-Chancellor

There's the question of actually controlling expenditures but the big thing is how does the Chancellor steer the economic ship.

Ex-Chancellor

The lot of the Chancellor is rarely a happy one. His every move in the economic sphere is watched by critical eyes. He is second-guessed on all sides: within the Treasury, by his ministerial colleagues, by financial interests, and by a myriad of reporters specially designated for the task. A look through the major book on Chancellors' postwar economic management (Samuel Brittan's *Steering the Economy*) suggests that in retrospect Chancellors rarely do the right thing and, if they do, it is often for the wrong reasons. They inflate when they should deflate, cut when they should expand, act when they should do nothing. The outsider begins to wonder if the British economy is that precarious or if perhaps these men are being called on to make adjustments too delicate for the kind of knowledge at their disposal. Be that as it may, the public preoccupation with the Chancellor as manager of the economy suggests an important truth: 'The big role of the Chancellor,' as a former occupant of that position put it, 'is not expenditure but as minister of the economy.'

If he is fortunate, the Chancellor will have a Chief Secretary who knows or is willing to learn about controlling expenditure. If he is extremely unfortunate, the Chancellor will find that neither the Chief Secretary nor the Permanent Secretary of the Treasury have their heart in the expenditure side of the business. The fact remains that modern Chancellors basically are not interested in expenditures; they are interested in the economy – productivity, employment, interest rates, money supply, exports, balance of payments, anything and everything but spending. The result is that spending limits are part of their economic policy rather than an end in themselves or a means of allocating resources in a better way.

The Chancellor's greatest specific interest is taxation. He receives the credit for reducing taxes; only spending ministers get credit for increasing expenditures. Behind all the discussions that Treasury officialdom has with the departments and all the negotiations the Treasury ministers undertake with spending colleagues, lies the Treasury's and Chancellor's overriding interest in taxation. This, indeed, is the substance of British constitutional practice : a balance between spending and saving is to be maintained not by some abstract formula but by giving specific individuals, standing at the head of concrete institutions, an interest in promoting these rival claims.

The following section deals more fully with the key locus of political decision-making and any Chancellor's activity – the Cabinet. In preparation for this discussion we can begin here by describing the basic features of the Chancellor's (and by implication Chief Secretary's) position. The Treasury ministers are few and the spending ministers many; fortunately for the former, the would-be spenders do not usually have to be faced all at the same time.

'The Chancellor has a lot of cards to play but he needs all of them', a former Chancellor philosophically reflected.[14] As the Chief Secretary depends on the Chancellor, so the Chancellor's ace must come from the Prime Minister. An ex-premier and ex-Chancellor from different parties used almost the same words to describe this need. 'The P.M. must appear impartial but broadly backing the Chancellor. The spending ministers always outnumber the Chancellor and unless the P.M. backs him, he'll always lose.' Another occupant of one of these perilous positions stressed that 'Because the majority of the Cabinet is inevitably against the Chancellor he depends very directly upon the Prime Minister's support. Without it, he's bound to go under.' So long as the Chan-

---

14. Even in the allegedly Golden Age of Gladstonian finance, it was always an uphill fight for the Chancellor, (particularly with regard to the one major expenditure item, defence). Cabinet meetings on expenditure estimates were frequently heated; Gladstone confided to his diary that 'Estimates are always settled at the dagger's point', and at another time, 'in regard to the Naval Estimates I have no effective or broad support ... My opinion is manifestly in a minority.' Quoted in John Morley, *The Life of William Ewart Gladstone*, (London : Macmillan) 1903, II, p. 140.

cellor has the support of the Prime Minister, that majority of two is ordinarily sufficient to determine most outcomes, though there must be some general willingness in the rest of the Cabinet to accept expenditure limitations. At the same time the Prime Minister will typically acknowledge that the Chancellor cannot come to be regarded as his 'stooge'. Should that occur, the Prime Minister's independent position in the Cabinet is ruined. Thus preliminary meetings of the utmost confidence will usually be held so that each man knows where he stands, the Chancellor sketching a cluster of spending claims, the Prime Minister advising on political realities. Both know that the Chancellor's position, and eventually their government's stable operation, requires that the Chancellor not be overturned too often – certainly nothing approaching half the time. 'What is really at issue,' said a participant to such talks, 'is which one of perhaps four proposals you're going to give way on.' Few, if any, Cabinet members will know of the secret meetings held between Chancellor and Prime Minister well before both the Chancellor's talks with spending ministers and Cabinet meetings. There is no more delicate or vital relationship in all British government.

Every Chancellor knows that the climate in which negotiations are conducted also has enormous impact on their outcome. His task is to depress expectations by creating an overwhelming atmosphere of stringency. Experience has taught all Chancellors that 'agreement was much easier to reach in the background of crisis.' The easier the economic situation, the more abundant the resources, the more difficult it is to convince spending ministers they must do with less. Once storm clouds gather, the Chancellor can rise to his full height and prevail by saying that the economy demands restrictive measures to prevent flood and famine in the country and/or an intolerable increase in taxation.

Outside the pressure cooker of crisis, which homogenises opinion and pulverises dissent, the position of a Chancellor in Conservative and Labour governments may differ. The Tory Chancellor is battered by his colleagues and back benchers on the question of tax relief. He is supposed to restrain spending and reduce taxes. The Tory Chancellor is less able to talk about the larger purposes for which funds are spent. Budgets are great political occasions and the pressures on a Chancellor are intense. There is less pressure on a Labour Chancellor for tax reduction (except immediately before a general election) but there is more for spending. Traditionally his party has been committed to a broad range of social expenditures and it is not easy for him, especially since he may well have advocated them in the past, to argue they should be excluded on what appear to be unfeeling technical arguments about something as exotic as the balance of payments or excessive liquidity. Some observers also perceive a tendency in Labour governments for the Chancellorship to go more regularly to the number two man in the party than is the case in Conservative Governments. But regardless of any such variations, the crucial fact is that in both parties the Chancellorship invariably will go to one of the handful of leading politicians in the Government. The number of outstandingly powerful leaders in both parties is small. Officials in every spending department hope for one but can only wait for the luck of the draw. 'The great strength of the Treasury is that it is almost certain to have one of these outstanding politicians as its Minister.'[15]

The style of negotiation chosen by a Chancellor depends on his knowledge of his own abilities and limitations. The Chancellor who is hard-working and solid rather than flashy and brilliant may not relish an excessive amount of personal negotiation. He will downgrade face-to-face discussions in favour of committee meetings and Cabinet sessions, in which he will defend his total with all the force at his command. A different Chancellor, who excels in personal argument and backstairs work, will do more of that. By the time he is finished his colleagues may decide they would be better off taking up the matter in a larger group. But regardless of these stylistic variations, the essential similarity of the task before them lends a certain sameness to all Treasury ministers' negotiations. Their colleagues want more and they cannot give it to them. Outsiders are tempted to think that creative politicians find approaches and arguments that would not occur to the ordinary person. This is largely untrue. Only a few things can be said and the standard responses are limited.

The Treasury minister of course will have been briefed by his officials on the department's expenditure and places where 'give' can be expected in its figures. Whether he realises it or not, a spending minister trying to short-circuit official channels by

15. D. N. Chester, 'The Treasury, 1956', *Public Administration*, vol. 35 (1957), p. 17.

approaching the Chancellor directly will have his proposal quickly
sent down to the knowledgeable men of the Treasury supply divisions. Their penchant for practised scepticism will be given full
scope. To this the Treasury minister adds his own political judgements. The criteria used by one Chancellor are pretty much the
same as those used by others :

> In deciding upon a minister's spending proposal and my bar-
> gainings with him on it I looked at several things. First, and
> most important, was my view of capital investment and the
> movement of economic aggregates. Second, if I gave in to this
> minister there would not be enough for the other ministers.
> Third, the proposal should be in line or at least not contradic-
> tory to the political strategy of the government. Then you
> always ask yourself, if you can get it through the House of
> Commons. By this I mean not so much getting it past the oppo-
> sition but your own supporters. It is useful to provoke the
> opposition. You don't want peace across the House because the
> opposition from the other party will help you with your own
> supporters. Nothing makes them rally round so much as being
> attacked by the opposition party. A fifth thing was whether or
> not the minister was able to make a good case, but this was less
> important than the political case. Finally, there was the man
> himself, his trustworthiness. There were two aspects here : the
> prestige of the man, that is his standing and reputation. Then
> there is also the department's reputation in the past as having
> been financially responsible.

The personal relationship between the Chancellor and the
minister largely determines the initial approach. Men who have
been friends for years do not need to go through the entire song-
and-dance. 'I did well,' a minister reported, 'probably because I
had a good relationship with [first name of Chancellor]. I would
tell him, [first name] you really can't do what you are contemplating. I made no desperate attempt to argue with him. I would
say that Treasury officials might not like it but there were reasons
for it. I said I absolutely had to have this thing or that. He would
say you have to find a saving elsewhere. And we would engage in
political bargaining at the margins.' Though not every minister
can trade on personal friendship it is important to remember that
these men are all well known to each other. In all likelihood they

have served together in the House of Commons for at least a decade. Each has a clear estimate of the strength of the other and is aware of tendencies toward accommodation or stiff-necked insistence that the other has shown in the past.

Chancellors can expect to hear all the well-beloved political arguments we have already identified with spending ministers. The final political argument of course is a threat to create internal difficulty in the Cabinet. The minister will say that the Treasury is being intolerable. 'If we have to have a terrible clash over this it will raise political passions and I can't accept the decision of the Treasury officials. You know how I hate to take this to Cabinet but I will have no choice and it will have repercussions.' There are, of course, severe limits to this approach. 'A weak minister does not threaten to carry matters to Cabinet,' a stronger colleague explained, 'because he can't argue and everyone knows he will lose.' Only a small number of issues can profitably be carried to the Cabinet. 'You lose your credibility if you try very often. If you come to a great big issue, you have done your case harm if you have taken four previous appeals on minor matters, because people will discount what you have to say.'

The Chancellor may be tempted to argue the merits of proposals. He may do a quick study and feel that he can out-argue a minister on the substance of departmental proposals. But this substantive approach is extremely perilous. He may be wrong and discover that the minister inevitably knows more about his special area than can any Chancellor. Even if the argument goes well from the Chancellor's side, all he may win is debating points. Spending ministers who would accept a negative response of general economic policy are likely to become angry at the implication they do not know their own business. Rather than risk having continually to appeal to the Cabinet in an atmosphere of unnecessary rancour, most Chancellors most of the time will concentrate on their own departmental brief – the state of the economy and public finances.

The Treasury minister is also a politician and he understands the power stakes involved in discussions about money. He knows that spending ministers will lose in reputation if they do badly.[16]

16. A Chancellor who prided himself on understanding the ways of politicians was approached with the argument, 'I have got a big [field of ministry] banquet and I need £5 million extra to have something to tell

He knows they see spending as an opportunity to make their mark in the world. The wise Treasury minister (and not all manage this) evinces a flow of empathy for the spending minister's predicament, but he knows the total picture and cannot give in. A Chancellor described an exchange : 'The minister would say "if you ask me to cut I can only do it by eliminating welfare milk which would be bad and politically unpopular." I would reply that a run on sterling would also be politically unpopular and that he could do something else that might meet the situation.' He may try to suggest delay or other alternatives to a spending minister, but when pressed the Treasury minister will revert to form : 'I could try and squeeze the minister and this is often effective,' a Chancellor recalled, 'by saying "all I can tell you is that I am not willing to allow a pound more – now you tell me where you could cut your own programme to create the money you want for this new proposal".'

When the expenditure lid is clamped on tight and spending ministers see their cherished dreams squeezed to nothing, the negotiation process can easily degenerate into childish outburst. They are all adults but they are also tired and frustrated after endless rounds of bargaining. The Chancellor may come to feel that he faces spoiled brats who are making a worthy father's life miserable by incessant whining. 'You know,' one revealed, 'I would in fact stop at nothing. Sometimes it was like dealing with small boys and you had to warn them that if they weren't good you would tell the Prime Minister.' The boys may be small but the issues are large. They will often go a long way before admitting defeat.

What is a Treasury minister to do if his best efforts come to naught? Hour-by-hour during Cabinet meetings or month by month in the normal business of government, he may observe a dissipation of his carefully contrived agreements. As a decision is reached – always upon apparently exceptional grounds – to increase the total for one particular department, other ministers claim comparable treatment. The Prime Minister, whose support for spending limits once seemed so firm, begins to waver. No one wants to raise taxes, and no decision has been made to raise the

---

them about.' The Chancellor asked if this was like the Mansion House banquet for Treasury people. The minister who reported this incident said yes; the Chancellor immediately understood what was going on and agreed.

expenditure total. It is just that the amount allocated keeps creeping up. Emergencies arise and new commitments are made at short notice. Departments which agreed to live within certain totals end up spending more because, they claim, of events beyond their control. By the time the next year rolls around an entirely new level of expenditure has been reached, which the departments then defend as their existing base for new increases. It is not surprising to find that Chancellors who have gone through this experience begin to feel that the spending ministers have successfully ganged up on them.

The idea has gained such currency that few stop to ask precisely what is meant by ganging up against the Chancellor. Does it mean that ministers entered into a conspiracy to raise their own total? Not likely. The big spending ministers are ordinarily in too much of a competitive situation to act jointly. Ganging up generally means that spending ministers can rarely be found opposing each other's proposals; the result, as many experienced political administrators observed, is that 'by the nature of things the Chancellor is left friendless'. As we have seen, the nature of things is that the spending minister is expected to serve as departmental advocate, arguing for his corner from an essentially defensive brief. The implicit character of this process helps explain why ministers who were active under the post-Suez Macmillan government, when allegations of ganging up were at their height, steadfastly deny any such thing took place. They all accepted the need for limits on government spending and the Chancellor's role in achieving that result. 'We look to the Chancellor to keep spending down', they would say. There was therefore 'no question of ganging up against the Treasury'. Knowing that each participant was only playing his traditional role, convinced that there was no collusion among them, these ministers thought the idea of ganging up was a fiction. The end result of each one playing his appointed part, however, can be that the Chancellor loses out. The rare but sufficient condition for Treasury weakness is either a Chancellor who himself believes in greater spending or a Prime Minister who will not back up his Chancellor on spending issues. Both conditions were fulfilled by Harold Macmillan and dramatically demonstrated by the resignation of Chancellor Peter (now Lord) Thorneycroft in 1957.

The case is puzzling only if we ask why a Chancellor would

resign over an apparently trivial sum. Thorneycroft and his two Treasury secretaries, Nigel Birch and Enoch Powell, demanded a £250 million cut for prospective expenditures in the forthcoming 1958–9 fiscal year. Amid the usual moaning and groaning the Cabinet produced cuts of £200 million. Many, including a number of top Treasury officials, thought a resignation over £50 million was not only a silly but dogmatic rejection of the normal give and take of real-life expenditure bargaining. The resignation makes sense only as a protest against a series of adverse decisions in which Treasury ministers had systematically lost in Cabinet and Cabinet committees because of Prime Minister Macmillan's lukewarm support. The impact on the Treasury of a process in which spending limits were steadily eroded was devastating. Charges of ganging up on the Chancellor were most rampant in the Treasury because the authority of its officials was being undermined. Admittedly, under Powell's influence, the Treasury ministers were in the unusual position of being more doctrinaire than their top officials on the issues at stake. But seeing himself as consistently denied Prime Ministerial and Cabinet support, it has always been the Chancellor's prerogative to call it a day.[17]

The unusual experience of Thorneycroft can be contrasted with the more typical term of Roy Jenkins as Chancellor, when the

17. There is another aspect to the resignation of Thorneycroft which, though neglected in the published accounts, was important for the future history of Treasury control. Economists in the Treasury might debate endlessly whether it was a demand or a cost inflation but the Chancellor felt he had to act to curb it no matter what it was called. The other Treasury ministers, Nigel Birch and Enoch Powell, achieved a meeting of minds with the Chancellor about inflation. They wanted to reduce the supply of money, an unorthodox approach in those days for which there was no supporting Treasury doctrine. By the autumn, the three men had also agreed that holding expenditures to the previous year's absolute level was an essential anti-inflationary measure because of its psychological effects. In effect, Treasury ministers and the highest level permanent officials were operating separately. The civil servants were disposed to be more passive; they believed that the reductions were too severe to be maintained. The middle ranks of the Treasury were torn between the control orientation of the ministers, to which they were accustomed and dedicated, and the deference they owed to the officials at the top. Morale suffered. The cutting exercise was differentially supported at varying levels. The usual effort was not made by Treasury officials to rally the highest level civil servants behind the policy of Treasury ministers.

whiplash of economic crisis created agreement on the need to hold down spending. A close observer of spending policy reports that 'the Treasury won consistently. Jenkins refused to allow appeals. The Cabinet accepted the necessity of cutbacks and the Prime Minister supported it.' The entire balance of relationships in Cabinet government, the array of political strengths and weaknesses, are involved in determining whether Treasury ministers (and with them the Treasury) enjoy substantial authority.

So far we have treated the expenditure process in fairly sectional terms. Treasury officials–department officials; spending ministers–Treasury ministers. We have done so because our evidence suggests this is the way most things happen. Once the Treasury and a department bilaterally agree, whether through ministerial or official bargaining, one can be 95 per cent sure of only perfunctory Cabinet discussion; for the Cabinet to reopen more than one or two such agreements in any one year would violate most political administrators' view of how business gets done. Hence our discussion has only skirted around what most would consider the key arena where politicians collectively decide – the Cabinet.

The Cabinet Carveup – Getting What There is To Give

The Cabinet can tend to be a bit of a jungle. All ministers are out to further their own ministerial image at the expense of others. A weak minister gets squeezed out by his colleagues. This is part of the operation of collective government.

There is a tremendous pressure to keep things in line with colleagues. You know you have to make the government a success because your own political career depends on it.

Cabinet discussion was poor, ghastly, nightmarish, traumatic. Everybody was absolutely desperate to get every extra bit they could. The arguments were very dishonest. There was a lot of give and take. The Chancellor would give a million to a minister and hope to get support to cut off larger expenditures elsewhere. The Chancellor would try to buy support one way or the other.

In discussing these matters in Cabinet we have done it all before; many of us have been on both sides of these matters; we are experienced men and the thing went rather quietly and expertly.

It is an atmosphere operating, not on rational decisions, but on fair shares.

When a decision comes to Cabinet you have to consider exhaustion as a very strong factor. I got sixteen million for [my area] primarily because it came up at the beginning of August at the last of a long series of meetings and everyone longed to go away on vacation. At something like 1.00 a.m. the Chancellor said all right and let's forget it.

The Cabinet is the great projective test of British politics. Each person's experience seems to him unique. He finds in it his own personality writ large or a magnification of his pet theory concerning British politics. No two members precisely agree on what the Cabinet is like, but all tend to agree that the outsiders cannot understand the Cabinet's way of doing business. The quotations displayed above are all from present or former Cabinet members and should suffice to explain why no statement about the Cabinet is immune from criticism that the observer does not really understand.

A major barrier to understanding is the fact that the Cabinet is a variable institution which responds differently to issues and circumstances. A crisis in foreign policy undoubtedly projects a different Cabinet image than an every-day political expenditure decision. Moreover reports on the Cabinet can come only from partisans, none of whom have seen it all or experienced it in quite the same way. Among other things, the Cabinet often decides not only what but who gets carved up. Those who are satisfied are more inclined to attribute qualities of rationality to chaotic proceedings than are the disgruntled who believe that their failures could have been avoided by saner methods. By the same token the man without a plan may look on the Cabinet as a disorderly house, whereas the man whose strategy succeeds may see in it the work of a cunning hand. Participant observers disagree on whether Cabinet meetings are calm and judicious or hectic and jungle-like. Fortunately there is more agreement on specific aspects of Cabinet behaviour than there is on the vaguer question of what the Cabinet is really like. These specifics we can try to knit into a general account of the Cabinet's role in spending decisions.

The Cabinet can and does become involved in the expenditure process at almost any time in the year – whenever a minister feels aggrieved and wishes to appeal a Treasury minister's decision. Usually, however, there is a fairly standard yearly routine for Cabinet involvement. Even the series of emergency cuts in the Wilson government became something of a mid-year custom, timed around the half-yearly balance of payments forecasts. Our discussion will centre on the normal round of Cabinet decision-making in expenditures, recognising that these standard procedures can be upset in everyday political life.

The Treasury and Chancellor Prepare

Two estimates prepared by Treasury officials bring the expenditure process to a head each year. One is an economic forecast that projects likely trends for investment, private consumption, employment, the balance of payments, and other economic indicators. The second is the PESC report (or its earlier and rougher equivalents) that projects the level of spending for the next several years on the assumption that existing policies will be maintained. These two statements go to the Cabinet in June of each year and while the hope always is that the Cabinet will make its cuts or increases during July, the normal requirement is for three to five long Cabinet meetings extending into October or November. In the background is a third element to come before the Cabinet, a list of 'bids' from spending ministers for any new money available. In considering these three statements, what is the Cabinet actually deciding about?

In essence, the Cabinet has before it a projection of the cost of existing policies and a Treasury expenditure judgement as to whether this is too large or if there is room for growth. In the normal course of events, the total considered allowable by the

Treasury is almost always less than the collective demands of spending ministers for more money. To cut it down is the problem for Treasury ministers and officials.

The details and formulation of the PESC report on cost projections of policy can be deferred until the next chapter, since this is a given factor which scarcely involves the Cabinet as a whole. The Treasury expenditure judgement and departmental bids, however, are crucial and flexible variables by which the Treasury and Chancellor prepare – and in fact largely predetermine – the ground for Cabinet decision-making.

Treasury officials at the highest level develop a position on the desirable level of public expenditure. 'Normally we had a view of the total,' said one. 'We sought to convince the Chancellor, and he the P.M. to adopt something of this order of magnitude. If either the Chancellor or the P.M. were not prepared to support and to clear the ground it was no good going on with it.' But the Treasury judgement is not quite so cut and dried as this suggests. Chancellor and Prime Minister are of course likely to quarrel with the official figure of how much is allowable and how much must be cut; as proposals flood in, it is not surprising if these top politicians' ideas about spending for specific programmes filter into their notions of desirable total expenditure. Treasury officials can also bide their time waiting for events to help them get more of their way.

Behind such give and take lies an important consideration: Treasury officials' expenditure judgement is (and can only be) a compound of knowledge, hunch and intuition. As hard as the parliamentary committees may look for the magic figure, the Treasury has no automatic equation or fixed numerical relationship to determine the allowable size of total public expenditure.[18] What the Treasury does have is its economic forecasts (or as some in the Treasury prefer to call it, economic assumptions) on the expected expansion of the economy, balance of payments, inflation, and employment. 'It's like a litmus paper test,' a top Treasury official equivocated. 'You hold expenditures up against assumptions on the economy. It may be clearly all right or clearly impossible, but it often turns neither colour, varying with which

18. See for example the responses of Second Permanent Secretary (public sector) Sir Samuel Goldman before the General Subcommittee, Committee on Expenditure, H.C. 450 (1971–2).

assumption you make, and politicians have to decide what to risk.' Since precise judgements on the basis of economic forecasts are difficult, rough rules of thumb must usually suffice. 'The important point,' reported one Treasury economic adviser, 'is that all the measures taken in regard to the economic variables should point in the same direction. With a balance of payments problem, for example, monetary policy, taxes, and public expenditures should be working together.'

The economic assessment tends, of course, to give special emphasis to points where the economic shoe is pinching hardest at the time. For the last half of the sixties, the balance of payments forecast occupied stage centre, and one may be sure that by 1971/2 unemployment trends were particularly prominent in the Treasury expenditure judgement. But throughout all economic variations and changes in government, the single most important factor to have developed over the last ten years is the Treasury assessment of the rate of growth in 'productive potential'. This is not so much a forecast as an historically derived average (going back approximately ten years) showing the growth in economic output if demand were held level at full employment. Neither the exact economic calculation of this figure nor its validity need concern us here; what does concern us is that by laying the growth in productive potential alongside the proposed growth rate in public expenditure, the Treasury has an important standard for saying how much is allowable. Herein lies the highly-summarised remains of the doctrine, enunciated in the 1961 Plowden Report, that the prospective size and pattern of public expenditure must be judged against whether it 'is likely to outrun the prospective resources available to finance it'.[19]

Even if the reading on these economic dials gave an unambiguous pointer to a single, 'proper' level of public expenditure – which no one believes they do – the forecasts themselves are uncertain.[20] The ability of forecasters to predict demands for goods and services, exports, investment and other crucial variables has not been exactly overpowering. The problem does not lie with

19. Cmnd. 1432 (1961), para. 16.
20. An excellent discussion may be found in Sir Alec Cairncross, 'Economic Forecasting', *Economic Journal*, vol. 79 (December 1969), pp. 797–812. See also Samuel Brittan's strong criticism of overreliance on forecasting, *The Financial Times*, 16 August 1973, p. 17.

incompetent people but with lack of knowledge and inability to do better, except for those who, like the great Professor Hindzeit, are always wise after the fact. To begin, the forecasters must first forecast where they are – no simple matter. All data is not only out of date, but out of date to different extents. 'Today the forecast of where we are,' a Treasury advisor observes, 'is often as wrong or more wrong than the trend lines.' Yet the official Treasury view of necessary expenditure cuts – usually between £100 and £500 million – are small in relation to the national economic magnitudes and typically within the margins of error in these highly tentative forecasts. (One estimate of total public expenditure in 1972–3, for example, is over £27,000 million and, depending on the assumption used, average *annual* increases in gross domestic product between 1971–7 could be £1970 million, £2900 million or some place in between.) Although some Treasury economists reflect that 'this is one of the snags in the whole game', the Treasury expenditure judgement is nevertheless based on a single midpoint figure within the range of error. Does this mean that the margin of error contained in the Treasury view is equal to or greater than the scope for ministerial decisions? 'Yes. Of course,' an official stated candidly. 'I wouldn't say that to the Expenditure Committee in Parliament. Some rabble-rousing M.P. would take it out of context and say "it proves they don't know what they're doing".'

Whatever the uncertainties, the official Treasury expenditure judgement is almost inevitably taken as the point of departure for what the Cabinet considers its own range of decision-making. Let us be clear; we are not saying that the Treasury sets out to dictate to and overrule a democratically elected government. But the Treasury expenditure judgement *is* the given factor around whose centre the official and ministerial bargaining takes place. Modified, increased or decreased, the Treasury economic view is the assumption worked upon. This view is a judgement about what risks to run with the economy. The theory is that the Cabinet makes its own judgement about what risks – political and social as well as economic – to run in relation to what cost (in terms of reduced expenditure plans). In practice, ministers usually consider themselves to be, and in fact are, adjusting a Treasury figure rather than bringing a wholly separate judgement to bear. As an experienced Cabinet member observed, 'It's always a question of marginal changes and the margins are always measured against the basis of the Treasury figure.' Or as a very senior Treasury official put it, 'There's no "right" answer here; equally, there's the advantage that you can't be proven wrong. I'd not say we're taking decisions, but *de facto* I suppose we are. We certainly are having a tremendous influence....'

This influence manifests itself in a number of ways. Both the Wilson government after the 1967 devaluation and the Heath government accepted as their parameter the dictum that growth in public expenditure should not exceed the rate of 'productive potential'. Earlier both parties had publicly espoused the standdard of holding expenditures in line with increases in Gross National Product, but they could not avoid wildly optimistic estimates.[21] An important reason for the Treasury shifting attention from the GNP growth rate (given such prominence in expenditure planning from 1963 to 1966) is the volatility of this standard; while GNP growth could quite reasonably be put at anything from 2 to 6 per cent, 'productive potential' hovers warily around a safer level, usually at about 3 per cent, and shows little change on a monthly or even yearly basis.[22] Using this pedestrian but operational guide, Treasury officials know they are more likely to err on the side of caution than to make spending plans hostage to the uncertain fortunes of GNP. And, to put oneself in their place, a constant is much easier to work with than a variable. For expenditure controllers, it is an attractive trade-off.

The Treasury expenditure judgement makes itself felt well before Cabinet meets. It permeates the formulation of bids by spending departments. At the beginning of the year, when officials start to confer with their ministers on proposals for new spending, they have in all likelihood already been given a general Treasury assess-

21. Cmnd. 4829 (1971), p. 6; Cmnd. 4578 (1971), p. 7; Cmnd. 3936 (1969), p. 4; Cmnd. 3515 (1968), p. 12; Cmnd. 2915 (1966), p. 4; Cmnd. 2235 (1963), p. 10.

22. The Treasury has good reason to look for a more stable standard for expenditure control than GNP. Although all were supposedly measuring the same thing, three measures of GNP (expenditure, income, and output) between the first quarter of 1966 and 1967 rose 2%, fell $\frac{1}{2}$% and remained unchanged, respectively. Cairncross, 'Economic Forecasting', p. 803. By mid-1973, the Treasury cautiously began to accept the view that the annual growth rate in productive potential may have risen to $3\frac{1}{2}$–4 per cent, rather than the old standard of 3–$3\frac{1}{2}$ per cent.

ment that they cannot have more than a certain amount, or at least that the economic prognosis is unfavourable. When political administrators say that 'the battlefield is fairly easily laid out', they are implicitly recognising the force of the initial Treasury deployment. From this base, officials return the list of department bids to the Treasury (or, more accurately, the Cabinet Secretariat), arguing for their highest priorities. Informal official and ministerial chats will let it be known that the Treasury can let down on some things but not others. The results are now prepared to go to the Cabinet.

In so far as total allowable spending is concerned, the Treasury view is bound to prevail. By the nature of divided responsibility, the Chancellor and Treasury are presumably the experts on the economy. Other ministers may claim to know more about current conditions in their departments but the Chancellor is the one who is in touch with the latest and best advice on the state of the economy. If he says that a balance of payments deficit of such a magnitude is in prospect and that it would have unfortunate consequences unless government spending were held to a specified level, there is really no good way of arguing with him. Observers from all sides of the expenditure picture confirmed this view. 'The Cabinet spends scarcely any time discussing the Treasury view of total cuts necessary as such', a spending minister asserted. A top Treasury official explained that 'If his colleagues don't accept the Chancellor's basic view of the economy it may be a resigning issue for him. He has all the expertise and can say, "granted the figures are uncertain but here is our central estimate which is justified for this and that reason".'

Which is not to suggest that the Treasury figure on allowable expenditure is expected to be accepted *in toto*. Sometimes, a Treasury official recalled, trouble is caused when someone in the Cabinet 'argues that given the magnitudes and errors in the forecasts, it's ridiculous worrying about the expenditure trimming proposed'. During the devaluation crisis the Cabinet revolted against the Treasury's proposed much larger cuts and eventually agreed to 5 per cent. Every spending minister suspects that the Chancellor 'has some money tucked away for the compromises', and they are probably right. According to one who has watched all these Cabinet moves for a number of years, 'There's a lot of fencing that goes on. In practice the Treasury's original target of how much had to come out would always go down in time.' A disillusioned Cabinet member agreed in more vehement terms :

The Treasury was very dishonest. It would put up a kind of cursory macro-economic paper saying that the total has to be so and so and giving a few arguments. The Cabinet members were incapable of debating these economic issues in any sensible way. Then after a few months or some period of time when officials discussed it at their level and ministers talked to the Chancellor, they would drop, say, from £500 million reduction to £450 or £400 million and the Cabinet discussion would go on from there.

The resulting decision on the total cuts necessary may be a compromise, but it is a compromise *on the Treasury's figure*.

To support their bruising economic argument, Treasury ministers are outfitted with two big sticks. The first is a strategic option which not all Chancellors have used but which appears, through hard experience, to have become the norm. Before 1968 the desirable spending total was debated alongside individual items. Arguing the general against the particular is never easy and is now recognised as a poor strategic choice for Treasury ministers. The sequence was changed. The Chancellor first puts in his paper saying expenditure is 'X', will be 'Y', and asking for cutbacks to allow a certain growth rate. Once the Cabinet has this basic figure or some variant thereof, the Chancellor then begins bilateral bargaining with spending ministers. His hand, as Treasury officials and ex-Chancellors told us, is immeasurably strengthened by this sequence. With the total figure agreed 'everyone can be made to feel he must each do his bit'. Worried about the uncertainty of the underlying economic forecast? With the total settled 'individual departments can't argue that given the error margins it's ridiculous to worry about their few million'. The strategy of totals agreed in advance was less necessary under the reflationary mood of the early 1970s, but has reappeared during subsequent periods of greater expenditure restraint.

The other club behind the Treasury's expenditure judgement is far more ancient than strategic sequencing, but it is by no means weak with age. Taxes are the favourite weapon of Treasury ministers. If the Cabinet does not hold down expenditures they threaten the members with having to put up taxes. When the Cabinet does protest against the Treasury view of the allowable expenditure total, it will be told, as one spending minister paraphrased it, 'Very well then, this is by how much you will have to increase taxes. You can't escape the political odium.' Of course, just as there is no automatic test of how high government spending should be, no one can say what are the proper levels of taxation or public borrowing. The limits are political, for politicians can always be relied upon to dislike having to raise taxes. While Conservatives are often thought to be more reluctant to raise taxes, there can be no doubt that the 1964–70 Labour Cabinet also was constantly worried about how far to push their political popularity by raising taxes, particularly when it became clear that the low economic growth rate was creating little surplus for new spending.

The force of the Treasury tax weapon lies not merely in the threat of having to increase taxes but also of having to overturn another sophisticated and independently arrived at economic assessment. In its post-war role as steerer of the economy, the Treasury acknowledges taxation and public expenditure to be two sides of the same coin; the cutting edge where they meet is in economic management. If expenditure plans are too large and taxes not increased, the economy (assuming full-employment) will allegedly be overheated. Thus, the Treasury weapon, and also Cabinet choice on total spending, becomes triple-edged : reduce expenditure projections – or raise taxes – or destabilise the economy.

To many it will be surprising that we have not had to consider taxes earlier. Surely prospective tax revenue is a factor in the Treasury's long-term expenditure judgement? The short answer, despite some recent efforts, is that the Treasury does not use revenue projections for this purpose. The government first published projections of total receipts (taxes, revenue, charges, etc.) in relation to public spending projections in 1968, with the justification that any statement of future gross expenditure would be misleading without the revenue side presented at the same time.[23] Although he had not necessarily favoured publishing projections, the fresh intellectual impulse behind this new approach was due largely to Sir Richard Clarke (Second Permanent Secretary public sector at the Treasury until 1966) and stemmed from his view that

23. Cmnd. 4234 (1969), table 1.2. See also Cmnd. 4017 (1969), 'Public Expenditure: A new Presentation', paras. 20–2, 30.

a rational consideration of prospective expenditure can only be made in relation to prospective resources '... and thus to the consideration of what changes of taxation will in the long-term be likely to be needed in order to enable the economy to accommodate the growing public expenditure.'[24]

Within two years, this forecast of total receipts had ceased being published, although rough estimates have always been used inside the Treasury for economic purposes other than expenditure control (such as estimating costs for servicing the national debt). Part of the reason for omitting these figures are said to be technical problems concerning the greater uncertainty of revenue compared to expenditure projections. But the more fundamental reason – accidentally aired in public when Treasury witnesses were recently pressed on the technical problems – is that the projections of total revenue are not used to form the Treasury expenditure judgement.[25] Figures on total revenue projections were a presentational device prepared solely for the 1968 White Paper to round off discussion of particular receipts for particular net expenditure items. 'The fact is,' an official participant recalled, 'that the revenue figures as published just weren't of any use in the Government. It's a matter of fact that nothing hangs or has ever hung on projections of revenue. For internal purposes expenditure is looked at in relation to the economic assessment, not to revenues as presented there [in 1968]. The conclusion we reached was that the figures were of no use, and it was nonsense to publish them.'

Public expenditures may be projected five years ahead but there is not and never has been any medium term (i.e., more than one year) tax policy with which they can be juxtaposed.[26] Taxes are settled independently in the great Budget ritual each year. They are settled in a firm Keynesian assessment of how much, under the prevailing economic conditions, needs to be 'given away' or taken back in tax changes in order to provide economic stability at a high level of employment. Aside from the evident political

24. Sir Richard Clarke, 'Management of the Public Sector of the Economy' *Stamp Memorial Lecture* (London: Athlone Press) 1964, p. 24.

25. Sir Samuel Goldman, H.C. 549 (1970–1), pp. 44, 46, 47; and H.C. 545 (1970–1), p. 18.

26. H.C. 549 (1970–1), p. 50. Revenues are uncertain, among other reasons, because of this frequently changing tax policy, pp. 15 and 42. A brief review of Treasury revenue orthodoxy is in Samuel Brittan, 'Tax Cuts the Treasury will Prescribe', *Financial Times*, 2 March 1972.

implications, revenue changes are solely a tool of macro-economic management, considered separately by the Treasury, and announced to the Cabinet by the Chancellor – in practice for information, not approval – just before the Budget is publicly presented in March or April.

This independence of revenue considerations from expenditure does not imply the reciprocal; quite the opposite. Cabinet expenditure reviews in the summer and autumn are heavily conditioned by the previous spring's revenue decisions. Whatever the economic conditions or tax rates, the existence and yearly refreshment of the government's independent, short-term tax policy means that expenditure decisions always confront a very strict view of the economically correct tax rate. Thus in preparing his Budget, the Chancellor has – with virtually no Cabinet interference – also prepared a powerful weapon for dealing with any quarrels over his latest expenditure judgement. Those who do not like it can bear the onus of raising taxes already calibrated several months earlier to the needs of the economy. The situation was well summarised by a spending minister : 'In practice, the Treasury view on the tax rate allowable is firmly fixed, and it will argue that tax rates are up against a ceiling. So if the Cabinet refuses to cut total expenditures as suggested and the Chancellor says he can't accept an increase in revenue, a government crisis would again result.' That the classic doctrine of a yearly balanced budget of income and outgo is defunct does not mean expenditures have been freed from the force of revenue calculations. It means expenditures are subject to a sovereign revenue programme of short-term economic management.[27] Under existing arrangements, revenue policy is and only can be a constraint serving to enforce in Cabinet the Chancellor's and Treasury's expenditure judgement.

Backed by a generally agreed limit on growth rates, by an advance influence on expenditure bids, by the Chancellor's inevitable status as a major politician and sole interpreter of economic needs, by the ability to sequence strategic decisions, and by a predetermined revenue standard, Treasury ministers and officials can feel

27. This overcoming of traditional revenue concepts was one of the major contributions of outside economic advisers such as Nicholas Kaldor in the 1964–70 Labour Government. Inventing the Selective Employment Tax and tax recovery (clawback) of family allowances from the better-off allowed the Government to bypass traditional Treasury arguments on the tax rate ceiling – for a little while.

secure that their preparations have not been in vain. Yet security in setting the boundaries of Cabinet decision-making scarcely means that the political battle is over. Though the major economic guideline is likely to go by default to Treasury ministers, spending ministers still want their portion of whatever is going. They and their department officials often share a resentment against what some describe as the Treasury's 'rationing approach'. Apart from certain economic technicalities (such as differential demand effects of different types of expenditure), a pound is always likely to be a pound to the Treasury – whether it is spent on a hospital, submarine or road. Though its officials often have their own policy preferences, these are necessarily subordinated to keeping the totals in line, which is, after all, the Treasury's main task.

To departmental advocates all expenditures are most assuredly not the same. How, they will ask, can you eliminate, cut back, or hold down programmes without understanding their purposes and consequences? Whatever the basis for action, however, Cabinet members must reach agreement on some allocation without splitting the government and party. The first step is to follow routine and go through Cabinet committees.

Cabinet Committees

Unnecessarily subject to secrecy, the operation of Cabinet committees is always somewhat mysterious. Lacking authoritative lists of committees and their members, the investigator must try to reconstruct them from incomplete accounts. The committees, moreover, change rapidly in membership, name and function; a description correct today is likely to be woefully out of date in a few months.[28] Amidst the shifts in Cabinet personnel and arrangements, however, we can discern several patterns with important implications for spending decisions.

Every Cabinet, at least for expenditure purposes, is led by an inner group rarely dignified by any formal committee title. It is obvious from what has been said earlier that this group must consist of the Prime Minister and the Chancellor; depending on personal relations, one or two other Cabinet members also may be present. They meet to agree on the main strategies towards the economy and spending. In a typical interchange, the Chancellor

28. For a general description of Cabinet committees, see Patrick Gordon Walker, *The Cabinet* (London: Jonathan Cape) 1970, pp. 40 ff.

and Prime Minister will first sit down and talk about the memorandum expressing the Treasury economic strategy and expenditure judgement. Expenditures, for example, may be projected to rise at 2·6 per cent and resources at 2·2 per cent so that they must agree to borrow or to cut out the difference. When both have agreed to this total, and they usually do, the Chancellor (or more frequently Chief Secretary) will begin preliminary talks with spending ministers, trying as usual to whittle down or reject their spending bids. At a later stage, when the Chancellor sees the general shape of these bilateral dealings, he will return to the Prime Minister and talk about tactics; what to push and whom to shove.

Now is the hour the Prime Minister brings the sensitivity of his own political judgement to bear on expenditures. 'You're going to have a rough time in Cabinet,' he will say (unnecessarily). 'Here is what I think will go through.' Certain things, he suggests, will not be stomached by the Cabinet and should be taken off the table. Occasionally the Prime Minister will suggest compromises on other items, such as going for a reduction of £7 million rather than £10 million. On a few issues the Prime Minister probably will have his own sense of government priorities and personal preferences; on these he will refuse to go along with the Chancellor.[29] 'For the rest,' the Prime Minister says – and must say for the Chancellor to retain credibility – 'I'll back you.' Thus, well before the Cabinet meeting, the Chancellor has a good idea of where he will be upheld and where let down, where to become awkward and where to give up gracefully.

29. Prime Ministers' preferences may have changed (or have they?) but not their ability to pre-empt the Treasury on certain items. Upon first taking office, Disraeli told his private secretary,

There is one thing I want you to understand clearly: The Treasury, under Gladstonian influence, is imbued with a dreadful spirit of economy, and they will come here asking us to agree to cut down various sinecures with four-figure salaries, and I want you to understand this, that so far as patronage is concerned, I give up nothing. The Government of this country cannot be carried on without a number of sinecures over £1000 a year.

Whatever their formal names, there will usually be regular Cabinet committees in the areas of defence, agriculture, economic policy and domestic affairs. Their job is to deal with substantive

Quoted in Henry Higgs, 'Treasury Control', *Journal of Public Administration*, vol. 2, April 1924, p. 126.

policy, and on the traditional grounds that a Cabinet which wills the purpose must supply the means, they usually will review expenditures in their area. *Ad hoc* committees on spending also will be created from time to time to reduce the burden on the Chancellor in Cabinet. Committee members who cannot agree still may be able to get together on a presentation of rival positions that will facilitate Cabinet discussions. Most committees meet about once a week and are attended by senior ministers at the Secretary of State level, always including the Chief Secretary or Financial Secretary.

Collective government means that each minister has a right, though he will not always choose to exercise it, to ask for the full Cabinet's judgement. Of course, he may be better off accepting less in committee than suffering a resounding defeat in Cabinet. Prudence also suggests that he save his appeals in Cabinet for the most critical issues and accommodate himself to committee views on lesser matters. Cabinet committees are useful to the Prime Minister and Chancellor, not because they settle everything, but because enough is settled there to bring into bold relief the questions that the Cabinet alone can answer.

Everyone knows that certain items are destined for the Cabinet and that committee meetings are only one of a long series of skirmishes which lead up to the final battle. There is the Farm Price Review, which passes through the Agricultural Policy Committee and which can always be counted on to generate disagreement between the Treasury and the Agricultural Ministry. Housing has typically been a sensitive political issue and ended up in the Cabinet. Committee sessions on issues destined for Cabinet take on an almost wholly tactical quality. Faced with a persistent difference of opinion, the chairman prepares a memorandum setting out the pros and cons, circulates it to members for approval, then sends it on to the Cabinet.

And, for our purposes, this is precisely the point: major disputes float up to Cabinet, but much bargaining on expenditures is sectionalised among the half dozen or so Cabinet committees. The Treasury expenditure judgement on the total, now usually agreed beforehand, typically is broken down by departments, each with a rate for 'natural' and 'improvement' increases, or what one minister called 'bargaining counters to play with'. The departments take these away to their committees, there to begin thrashing out an accommodation among themselves and the Chief Secretary. One committee dealing with social services and another with industrial policy will have almost no contact with each other. Each has its own budget to discuss among its own members. In the normal course of events, therefore, hospitals will confront schools and not industrial subsidies or agricultural payments. There is no established capacity for one committee to argue its expenditures against another.

Disheartening though this sectionalism may be for those seeking a more comprehensive allocation, it has advantages. Departments know that they will be bargaining with others sufficiently close in subject matter for there to be some sympathetic understanding. Full Cabinets have notoriously little interest in department details; one spending minister was typical in being able to recall only two semi-knowledgeable Cabinet discussions about substantive issues of a major department during his three years as its minister. In the committees, however, departments can be sure of at least some empathy with the cherished purposes of each other's spending. Here all expenditure pounds will not be treated as interchangeable. At the same time the Treasury is interested in holding down Cabinet conflict and knows that while departments' spending bids can still be played off against each other, conflicts based on ignorance and misunderstandings will be minimised. If bargaining occurs across groups, where there is less sympathy for each's purposes, conflicts will proliferate. 'The Treasury realises' a perceptive minister concluded, 'that faced with a conflict between two powerful spending ministers, the Cabinet is likely to let each have his way. Sectionalism in ministerial bargaining suits the Treasury book like nobody's business.'

Surely, some men have reasoned, there must be a better way. After all it is not just the Chancellor but the government as a collectivity which is responsible for controlling expenditures. Cannot a Cabinet committee of senior ministers – ministers without departmental spending axes to grind – look dispassionately at major spending proposals and consider each against the other in the context of limited total resources? This was in fact one of the major ideas proposed by the Plowden Committee in 1961.[30] A

30. Cmnd. 1432 (1961), paras. 31, 32. The unpublished version specifically commended the idea of a committee of non-spending ministers. Thirty years earlier, the May Committee on Economy in Government had pro-

little-known experiment in Cabinet government, tried once in the early 1960s under Conservatives and again in the late 1960s under Labour, can add much to our understanding.

On these occasions, the Plowden idea, with Treasury support, became translated into a committee of non-spending ministers who were presumed to be more objective because they had no departmental responsibilities or their departments did not spend a great deal. The committee was composed of the Treasury minister, the Chancellor of the Duchy of Lancaster, the leader of the House of Commons, and a few other ministers without departmental responsibility or, like the Foreign Secretary, with only a minimum amount of spending. Such ministers have always sat and provided a measure of disinterest on standard Cabinet committees. Now they were to be assembled into one committee able to give objective judgements on the relations among whole and parts. All participants – officials originally in favour and those opposed, Labour and Conservative ministers – agree that this common-sensical experiment was a failure.

Behind the smooth language of Plowden was a down-to-earth justification for this Cabinet committee innovation: declared a top Treasury official of this period, 'By the nature of the system the Chancellor is facing a group of brigands. Our idea was to get a group of senior, non-spending ministers to share the grilling with the Chancellor – to deal with the problem of his having no friends.'[31]

---

posed a similar standing Finance Committee in the Cabinet 'which would be kept fully informed of the state of national revenue and expenditure and would examine all schemes submitted to the Cabinet', *May Committee Report*, para. 572.

31. To hold back the accelerating expenditures, particularly in defence, the Treasury attempted a similar strategy in May 1939. The words of the Chancellor's memorandum can stand as a permanent lament for his breed.

I constantly receive new schemes involving heavy expenditure.... Many of the schemes, I do not doubt, are admirable if we could afford them ... but it would be, I submit, the greatest misfortune were the Cabinet to continue to consider these matters as the individual schemes come along on the basis mainly of their individual merits in contributing to national security. We must face hard facts.... There is a limit to the rate at which we can raise money, and that limit, in the best of my judgement, has been reached. [The Chancellor] is entitled to something more than the consideration of his financial difficulties by the particular colleague who wishes to spend further money.   *[Footnote continued overleaf]*

The expenditure committee of non-spending ministers failed for three interrelated reasons, none of which should come as a surprise to the reader by now. First, and least important, there were not enough ministers with time to do the work. It turned out that the non-spending ministers were too few in number and the Committee, therefore, had to include 'little spending' ministers. Hence there was trouble in dealing with the expenditures of their departments, however small, within the Committee. Placing ministers on committees in which they do not have a direct interest also raises the difficult problem of adequate preparation. One of the weaknesses of Cabinet government, acknowledged on all sides, is that ministers are largely taken up with departmental, House of Commons, constituency and extra-Parliamentary party business. However hard they worked, there was not enough time for most ministers to become informed on the numerous issues which came before such a committee, spanning as they must virtually the entire gamut of government activity. 'You can't expect busy men not directly concerned,' said one of the officials active with the committee, 'to give the attention and make the effort required.'

The second reason for failure goes to the heart of the Cabinet government. It is best expressed in the acquired political wisdom of another senior Treasury official :

[The Committee] didn't work because Ministers live by supporting each other. Dog doesn't eat dog. I say this even though I wanted it and worked hard for it at the time. Any big spending operation is a political operation. This is something Plowden overlooked, or underestimated with its technologist view. Who will you get as 'non-spending' ministers. The Foreign Minister? He knows he needs the support of his Cabinet colleagues for things he wants to do, even if he's not spending a

---

The Chancellor proposed that a small committee of Cabinet members be appointed to examine substantial new spending proposals in relation 'to the whole financial conspectus'. The Prime Minister gave strong support, observing 'that when the Chancellor put financial problems before the Cabinet there was hardly anyone who was in a position to consider these problems against a background of financial knowledge'. With the new committee 'there would be at least six members who would be informed of the [general financial] position'. The committee was established with four non-spending and two of the smallest spending ministers. Its fate was sealed three months later with the outbreak of war. C.P. 118(39) and Cab. 23/99 (1938).

lot of money. What's more, the Cabinet is a personal business. There may be four or five 'non-spending' ministers the Chancellor can try to line up, but they may hate his guts – you know what I mean.

To say the least, non-spending ministers were reluctant to create difficulties for themselves by telling one minister he was getting too much and another that he was not getting enough. What was in it for them?

When the Committee did manage to bring forth its 'objective' view of an allocation, it only fired resentment among the spending ministers in Cabinet. This third reason for failure reflects the quintessence of decision-making on expenditures. 'The political reputation of a minister depends on how successful he is at moving forward and fighting for his department,' said one such battler. 'He won't have other ministers depriving him of a chance to fight. No two or three or four others can preempt your right to put your case to your colleagues. My whole authority with the [policy interests of his ministry] world depends on fighting hard for expenditures. You are fighting for interests including your own.' Ministers, it turned out, did not want these important questions decided by a small group *in camera*. Some idea of what happened may be gleaned from the account of a Labour minister. 'No one sitting around the table in that committee had experience in [my area]. It meant you did not have a friend! Then this thing would get to Cabinet and the supposedly objective ministers would not hear of any alteration, arguing that if one part was altered, then the whole package could break up and have to be renegotiated. I created some almighty rows.'

Multiply this minister by a half dozen or more and the failure of the committee of non-spending ministers becomes wholly explicable. As unhappiness accumulated and passions rose, the spending ministers called upon their ancient prerogative – a jury of their Cabinet peers. They still may have to admit defeat; but they will be damn well certain they fall in complete battle regalia, in open field and in full view of the assembled hosts. 'The whole basis of this committee,' a participant accurately concluded, 'was a political error.' Treasury officials too have also learned their lesson. They are unlikely in the future to call for any mechanism to set expenditure priorities short of the entire Cabinet.

The Cabinet Meeting

The tendency of Cabinet meetings to disgruntle losers and confuse winners, including those who firmly believe they understand it best, suggests the advisability of starting with the end results. Except in the rarest circumstances, what will definitely *not* emerge from Cabinet is a comprehensive consideration of overall priorities within the total spending figure. The intention that the Cabinet as a whole should take such decisions under the current PESC system – which might be thought to distinguish earlier Cabinets from later ones – has not impressed most ministers that way. Though each bit may be related to total expenditures, only rarely will one set of expenditures be weighed against another. To understand the British expenditure process, it is essential to know why this is so.

Despite recent talk about priorities, strategies, and rational allocation, the British Cabinet is unable to consider and decide upon any clear overall allocation of expenditure resources. A few of the reasons have been recounted by the Treasury itself.

[Allocation] is not a separate process from the determination of the total. In the first place, the total impact on demand is important in relation to the economy generally, and the same impact may be made by, say, a smaller total comprising much demand-intensive expenditure, or a larger total with less of that kind of expenditure. Second, the total may be directly affected when inescapable new expenditures arise while other expenditures cannot acceptably be adjusted at the same time to make room. Third, there is a balance to be struck between the extent of the provision which is desirable for each of the programmes and the consequences of the resulting total for the rest of the economy. The aggregates for the public sector and the individual programmes then eventually represent the particular balance which the Government, with its own view of social and economic priorities, desires to see.[32]

32. H.C. 549 (1970–1), pp. 20–1. The Treasury has also commented on comparing alternative expenditures: 'In either type of case, the policy and its resulting cost as part of the general body of "existing policies" has to be determined at a far earlier stage than Ministers' consideration of the total costings of existing policies expressed in the annual Surveys. If, therefore,

A more down-to-earth summary of barriers to the Cabinet's taking decisions on the broad range of spending priorities can be set out by recalling some of our previous points and anticipating others.

First, taking all outstanding issues together is a Herculean task and no one knows how to manage the calculations involved. Even a total agreed in terms of the Treasury rationing approach (i.e., all pounds are the same) could, as the Treasury memorandum points out, be composed of an almost infinite variety of programme allocations and still have the same resource impact on the economy. Looking at the one piece of hard data available – rates of increase or decrease in spending within the total – gives no reliable standard for judging priorities; contextual differences between programmes (e.g., absolute size of programme, demographic factors, compensation for past cuts, etc.) make such figures incomparable. The Treasury also knows that there is no objective 'technique available for determining whether more or less resources should be used on roads compared with, say, hospitals'.[33]

Secondly, simultaneous consideration of spending bids is difficult when they do not occur at the same time. There is, as we have seen, no one season for expenditure proposals and although Treasury officials may not like this temporal diffusion, they expect it. Observed deputy secretary Douglas Henley, '... by the nature of things it is not possible to confine all decisions or all requests for additional public spending or a change in the balance to a major exercise once a year.... I do not think we find that departmental ministers are normally slow at putting forward proposals for new policies which do cost substantial amounts of money from time to time....'[34] During his time in office, every spending minister has seen a plea for financial stringency and zealous economy campaign negated by flows of new expenditures committed at random points throughout the year. 'Why sweat your guts out over the last million pounds,' a minister told us, 'when some-

---

the Subcommittee is interested in the real issues of policy choice, there is no short cut that can be recommended to them ...' 'Costed Options', ibid., appendix 8, p. 219.

33. 'The Determinants and Objectives of Public Expenditure': Memorandum by the Treasury, H.C. 549 (1970–1), p. 53. Curiousy, the Treasury had earlier criticised the 1961 system on the grounds that 'there was no systematic way in which priorities between programmes and proposals could be established and settled', p. 17.

34. H.C. 321 (1970–1), pp. 10 and 19.

thing just came up far greater than that and went right through.'

Finally and overarching all other barriers to weighing expenditures against each other are the behavioural norms against mutual attack. Sectionalism among Cabinet committees reflects and reinforces such norms, but far more important is the political-administrative culture itself. Greasings by civil service society will already have muted most interdepartmental squeaks before Cabinet meetings. Department briefings will do their best to prepare the minister for protecting his own case but offer little scope for analysing others' claims. Reciprocity in ministerial discussions (you leave my programmes alone and I'll leave yours alone) is the counterpart of reciprocal neutrality among civil servants in relation to each others' spending. Spending ministers' reluctance to criticise each other's proposals is a standing guarantee that the sequence of decisions usually will not be disturbed by explicit trade-offs or cross-references.

The preceding list of barriers to comprehensive Cabinet allocation is, necessarily, an abstraction from the complex interactions of real life. Important operations of the Cabinet are easily obscured by making its deliberations seem less messy than they in fact are. There is some value, then, in looking more closely at the details of Cabinet bargaining. The fact that a spending total is apparently agreed on by the Cabinet does not mean that the expenditure pattern has been accepted or that the programmes within the total are consistent with one another. The existence of a co-ordinating figure no more means that co-ordination has been achieved than does the mere existence of a Prime Minister signify that leadership is being effectively exercised. Following discussion and agreement on the Treasury expenditure judgement and on individual Cabinet committee reports, the Cabinet will move through the departments one by one and consider the outstanding individual expenditure disputes.[35] The Treasury, under the PESC

35. The only recent published account of this confirms our independent interview reports. 'When the whole programme comes before the Cabinet, each proposal for a departmental economy would be discussed in turn and separately decided. The Cabinet is always conscious in regard to such matters that each saving forms part of a packet which must in the end be decided upon as a whole. Tacitly or explicitly Ministers who accept or bow to cuts in their Estimates reserve the right to reopen the issue if savings proposed by the Chancellor in other fields are reduced by the Cabinet.' Walker, *The Cabinet*, p. 116.

procedures, has agreed to so much for each department and they, in turn, have expressed certain disagreements. The unagreed margin between the Treasury figure and the departmental proposals forms the focal point of initial Cabinet discussions. The Chief Secretary, or if necessary the Chancellor, argues that the department must cut and, with the briefing of supply divisions, proposes items. The spending minister, in substance, says 'over my dead body'. 'If your department comes late in the bargaining sequence,' a spending minister reported, 'the Chancellor may truly be running up against his real limits and you will have a very tough time. He may say I've now given £50 million and absolutely can go no farther, which means he has only £10 million left to play with.'

Settling the expenditure allocation is not the work of an afternoon around the Cabinet table. Cabinet decisions on expenditure are an endless iteration resembling the labours of Sisyphus more than the thunderbolts of Zeus. Choices are not taken at once but through a series of meetings, some informal and others in the Cabinet itself; decisions are made, remade, postponed and brought up again until exhaustion sets in and an end is reached. Unless the Chancellor were to announce all decisions at once and permit no alteration, which is hardly credible in collective rule, there is no way of avoiding sequential decision-making.

One or more weeks are likely to elapse between these Cabinet meetings on expenditures. Time is required to heal wounds, to permit the Chancellor to hold discussions with aggrieved ministers and to help ministers get used to the prospect of having less to spend than they would like. Tension is high and all hope that the passage of time will work a soothing influence. Often the two Treasury ministers will have agreed that the Chief Secretary should go all out in arguing the Treasury case at the first several meetings. While the Chancellor will support his colleague against the spending minister, this division of labour means that the Chancellor is also in a position to propose a compromise at a later date without loss of face. A Chancellor described what is a common move: 'If it looked as though Cabinet opinion, including neutrals whom I respected, were rather against us, quite often we would adjourn the matter, discuss it between ourselves, and [the Chief Secretary] would expect me to propose a compromise.' At other times the Chancellor may be able to settle major claims that bring all the others into line. In the last Labour government it became common practice for the Chancellor to do a deal in advance with the Minister of Defence;[36] they agreed by how much defence would be cut and the Minister then backed the Chancellor in Cabinet against the other spending ministers, saying in substance, 'I have my expenditures under control, why don't you?' Changes in the economic picture can also reinforce the Chancellor's hand. But time often knows no friends and may equally well make everyone a little more desperate.

It is important to pause and recognise how much the expenditure process has narrowed down the impossibly heavy decision agenda since those first meetings between Treasury and department officials. If nothing else, the *ad hoc* sequencing in Cabinet has distilled out for attention the major residue of disagreement. Bargaining in open Cabinet meeting also allows each minister to see how much others are getting and giving away. Original expectations may be altered as the pattern of settlement is higher or lower than expected. Despite careful preparation and sounding of opinion, ministers may be surprised to discover greater or lesser support for their programmes than they had thought. The Chancellor and Chief Secretary are trying to cut a certain amount from past totals or to hold the rate of increase down to a certain level. Every Treasury minister knows, and will certainly hear repeatedly from his top officials, that 'allocation is not a separate process from determination of the total'. A series of innocent individual decisions can easily add up to a debauched total sum. Each one wonders how hard and how far he should push. The meetings drag on; trial by ordeal now begins in earnest.

Agreements in Cabinet are easiest to reach when they are made across the board: every department either increased or cut by roughly the same proportions. Sacrifices are (or appear to be) equally shared. There is more grumbling when reductions have to be absorbed but they are easier to take when all ministers suffer equally and none can claim that he did better than the other. The problem with so-called equality of sacrifice is that not all programmes and departments are in fact equal.[37] Some are better

36. An abbreviated account of the Chancellor's deals in defence is in Wilson, *The Labour Government 1964–70*, pp. 479–80.

37. Once publicly acknowledged, such a self-evident principle as 'equality of sacrifice' easily becomes a strait-jacket for future decisions. The slashing cuts during the 1931 economic crisis, cuts which included teachers'

able to absorb cuts than others. To take a few examples, the Home Office will have only decreases in police to offer for immediate savings; housing will have a great many short-term victims to tempt cutters; unless benefits are to be reduced social security will have almost nothing to give. Capital programmes have the most flexibility in the sense that no existing personnel, salaries or benefits need be hit; but a capital programme also has the longest time lag in delivering its yield of savings. And, needless to say, some policy areas also figure more prominently in election pledges and are dearer to the hearts of party members. If politics inside the Cabinet suggest that equal treatment will make life easier, politics outside the Cabinet imply the reverse. Across the board, flat-rate cuts remain a rare strategic move in Cabinet, resorted to 'only with reluctance' and in the direst economic emergency.[38]

The more normal situation finds all achieving marginal increases over past allowances, but some doing better than others. Disagreement over purposes and rivalries among ministers may still combine to ensure heated discussion and bruised egos. Yet, when each minister can tell his clientele that he has done better for them than before, though never as much as he hoped, the worst conflicts are mitigated. No one has lost out entirely and everyone has got something. Partisans realise that their party has a policy (and should have if it does not) and this means that some programmes will be favoured over others. Under these reasonably benevolent circumstances ministers may privately admit that the decisions taken were appropriate if not perfect.

The most difficult Cabinet meetings – those that remain enshrined in ministerial memory as bitter and unmercifully long – invariably involve deep cuts that are applied unequally. Most ministers must lose and only a few can win. Ministers whose programmes have been favoured at the expense of others become

---

salaries and unemployment benefits, were sold under this slogan. While recognising the humbug in the phrase, senior Treasury officials had found by May 1932 that any further large economies were 'quite impractical' unless they were part of a comprehensive scheme 'designed to impose "equality of sacrifice" anew'. Cuts would have to be applied to the same items as before, taxation increased to impose a similar sacrifice on the better-off, and any cuts in social benefits were considered to be politically impossible without 'partial' repudiation of interest on the national debt'. T. 172/1790, 6 May 1932.

38. H.C. 321 (1970–1), p. 17; see also H.C. 549 (1970–1), pp. 63–5.

targets of envy if not outright hostility. Did they make secret arrangements with the Chancellor to sell out their colleagues? Are they being groomed for advancement to which other ministers believe themselves better entitled? On these occasions the dividing line between paranoia and politics may be exceedingly thin.

These difficult strategic situations can help us realise how much scope for agreement normally exists and is facilitated *precisely* by the Cabinet's failure to engage in a simultaneous, comprehensive and consistent allocation of resources. Consider the experience after the November 1967 devaluation when sets of expenditure actually were weighed against each other. The Treasury economic memorandum in December, first agreed privately between Chancellor and Prime Minister, argued that about 14 per cent had to be switched from domestic demand (i.e., private spending and public expenditures) to exports and investment. Cuts of around 10 per cent in public expenditure were probably suggested. For once there was little opportunity for sequential decision-making. All priorities had to be considered together. The story is best continued by several of the participants.

These expenditure cuts were made essentially at marathon Cabinet meetings held during December 1967 and January 1968. Of course it was good form for every minister to show his department doing a little in the way of cutting back expenditures but the major decisions were about party priorities. The Party's programme as a whole was debated at Cabinet meetings and the bulk of resulting cuts were made in accordance with the decisions on priorities which were reached. This package of cuts, for example, decided first that education would bear a heavy part through postponement of the promised increase in school-leaving age, second that overseas defence spending would be heavily cut through an accelerated withdrawal, third that the F-111 would be cancelled.

Disagreements proliferated. What were the Party's real priorities? Who says so? Why not more here and less there? Tempers rose as sincere men and women disagreed on their view of the worthwhile. Collective government became brittle. The former Prime Minister recounts the tempest:

Cabinets do not proceed by counting heads. I had been trained by Attlee. He was usually able to sum up, as I was, by saying that the Cabinet view was thus and thus, and it was rarely challenged. Both he and I frequently ended a discussion by saying there was no decision, but that one judged that if this or that particular point were dropped, the Cabinet might well be disposed to agree....

But in this review so much was at stake, and views were so evenly divided, that any attempt to express a consensus or, indeed, a majority view, would have been challenged. It was the only time in six years that colleagues seemed to be keeping their own tally of the 'voices'. And such were the strains that I was reading day by day in the press that the 'vote' was eleven to ten, or twelve to nine on this or that particular proposal. As I said, every Government goes through such a period; we did not have to face it again.[39]

The one and only time during six years that the Labour Cabinet had to resort to voting was when all expenditures were weighed against each other. 'If we voted,' any number of ministers insisted in nearly identical words, 'that would be the beginning and end of Cabinet government.'

In the absence of any objective technique to decide trade-offs, the bargaining process in Cabinet also provides rough indicators for setting priorities; what is important is what people will fight for. The Prime Minister and his colleagues cannot be expected to know about everything. How hard a minister fights tells the Cabinet something important: a political associate wants something badly. More disinterested members of the Cabinet depend on others to push their preferences so that there is some idea of the best case that can be made before disputed issues are decided.

We can now appreciate why some spending ministers do better than others in Cabinet. In the first place, ministers do not start from positions of equality. Events far beyond their control have created different opportunities and disabilities for them. Luck matters. The pattern of departmental spending, not merely in the year the minister takes office but for a number of succeeding years, may already have been determined by demographic changes and inherited policies. All he may have to do is sit back and watch his programmes grow and his expenditures increase. Another minister's programme may be growing much faster than most and

39. Wilson, *The Labour Government 1964–70*, pp. 480–1.

therefore be regarded as particularly vulnerable. Events may occur during the year, such as a well-publicised disaster or a study of deplorable conditions, that will lead to common recognition in the public and among ministerial colleagues that something must be done. His officials need only submit a proposal to meet the situation. Some ministers have programmes which can be expanded, and stopped, faster for purposes of economic management. The selection of Cabinet members, whatever its basis, may turn out to be skewed in favour of one or another type of programme. No minister can plan on finding an extraordinarily large number of former school-teachers in the Cabinet but if he does so and is in the Education Ministry it may help him. Governments come into office committed to certain traditional party stands and to certain lines of policy – hospital construction, housing, regional aid, etc. If what the minister wants for his department fits in with the general party opinion, he can do much better. Obviously one of the most important givens affecting any minister's chance for success is the quality of his officials and their relations with others. 'Because it is the officials that fight his case for him in their battles with other officials,' as a former Chancellor and spending minister observed, 'a minister forced to rely on ineffective people is in immediate trouble.'

To all these situational constraints, the minister makes his own independent contribution of skill and forcefulness. If he is able to advance his case in a knowledgeable, flexible and tenacious way appropriate to political circumstances and his audience, his chances for success are good. Creating an aura of urgency and inevitability surrounding his position, he can hope to hear the final accolade from his fellow ministers: 'I'm not sure I fully understand or agree but I am awfully clear that this is vital.' However good or bad his situation, the minister's own ability can make it better or worse.

Ministers will always be concerned with standing and reputation, and spending ministers will always find ways to make their interests manifest in the expenditure process. There will always be fighters, moderators and weaklings. The problem is not that ministers are narrow – they are paid to defend departmental interest – or that a broader view no one possesses is ignored. Rather the vital question is: how can these proclivities be structured so that ministers have strong incentives to behave in more productive ways – ways actually leading to better policies with better consequences for the people they are designed to help? With so much of national income absorbed by government spending, it is not only ministers but citizens who lose if policies are not analysed and challenged from different perspectives.

Spending ministers do have second thoughts. They wonder whether there might not be some better way to allocate resources. They will play the game to the hilt but they are not always certain it is the right game to play. Occasionally they have experiences that start them thinking. One of the most combative ministers of recent times, both by self-rating and the judgement of others, ultimately decided that 'just fighting for your department was not enough. I remember time and time again I would go through a heartbreaking battle for money and come back to the officials and say "at least I got half and now what has to go?" And time and again the permanent secretary would say that we really did not need all this expenditure for this or that item. Everyone does this.' He ended up supporting the PESC procedure, though of course he works just as hard to get around that as he did the old way of doing things.

Attempts to respond to such second thoughts and to embody answers in institutional form have been made in recent years. The essential purpose of the PESC procedure is to provide information on the likely levels of government expenditure over the next five years and by doing so to get a general idea of total commitments and available margins for new expenditure. The PAR process (Programme Analysis Review) is supposed to select major issues in both new and old spending programmes for sustained analysis so that choices within the available margins can be made in a more intelligent way. The Central Policy Review Staff is designed to supplement these procedures by providing Cabinet members with independent non-departmental analyses of major issues. No one with the experience of the Cabinet committee of non-spending ministers in mind should underestimate the difficulties in making these innovations work. Implicated are not merely alterations in expenditure procedure but also major changes in relationships among political administrators and hence the entire spirit of Cabinet government under the British model. Let us see how well these new machines are working, the better to gauge their prospects.

5 PESC and Parliament: New Machines for Old Problems

Like it or not, anyone who wishes to claim even the meanest understanding of how Britain is governed must first comprehend the dual apparatus of PESC and PAR, whereby national political priorities are set and implemented.

Peter Jay, Economics Editor,
The Times, 31 January 1927.

Public expenditure decisions should never be taken without consideration of (a) what the country can afford over a period of years having regard to prospective resources and (b) the relative importance of one kind of expenditure against another. This may appear to be self-evident, but in administrative (and, we would hazard the opinion, in political) terms it is not easy to carry out.

Plowden Report, Cmnd. 1432,
para. 7.

The essence of the Chancellor of the Exchequer's problem is the relation of a particular piece of proposed expenditure to the whole financial conspectus.

Chancellor John Simon, May 1939
Cab, 23/287.

In practical political terms you can't really survey the whole ground, give Jane a sweet and Jack a smack on the behind. You can't make it work unless you have complete control over all decisions. The Prime Minister will make a speech some weekend and you've had it chums. In crude terms people say 'take it out of politics'

– you may get the huckstering reduced but you don't take it out of political decisions.

Department deputy secretary

People adapt themselves to any game.

Permanent secretary

BRITISH GOVERNMENT during the last ten years has been particularly fecund with new mechanisms in the expenditure process. Claims for these innovations vary from the totally euphoric to the utterly cynical; a recent PESC white paper has been variously described as 'probably the most important state document of the year' and 'flogging a dead mouse'.[1]

This ambivalence should not be particularly surprising. Every innovation is born into a hostile world and depends on its enthusiastic advocates for survival. At the same time, any mechanism for dealing with spending priorities must show dreadful weaknesses. Little is known about the consequences of programmes, and there is no agreement on the value of one expenditure compared to another. By the time the Committee of Non-Spending Ministers had run its course, the skeletons of forlorn hopes and failed aspirations littered the corridors. Since no one likes to be reminded of past carnage, there is always an inducement to try a seemingly new mechanism or to drop the matter for awhile until old wounds heal.

The first and most important new mechanism has already cropped up throughout our discussion and is by far the best established in the government community. PESC takes its name from the Public Expenditure Survey Committee, the interdepartmental group composed of department finance officers and Treasury officials (chaired by a Treasury deputy secretary) which reports on the projection of public expenditures. The yearly PESC report seeks to show the future cost of existing government policies if these policies remain unchanged over the ensuing five years.[2] The stated aim of the exercise is to provide a clearer perspective so that political administrators can weigh (1) the total spending

1. House of Commons debate, 9 December 1971.

2. A general description of the PESC exercise is contained in the Treasury memorandum, 'Public Expenditure Survey System', in H.C. 549 (1970–1), pp. 17 ff.

implications of present policies against the financial resources likely to be available and (2) different expenditures against each other.

The annual PESC cycle will come into sharper focus if we outline the steps involved and the approximate times of the year when each occurs. Sometime in November or December the Treasury sends the departments a statement about the economic assumptions on which to operate in preparing their individual spending forecasts. These operating assumptions typically will include the likely growth of productive potential, consumer expenditure, industrial production and fixed investment. By the end of February, the spending departments submit preliminary returns to the Treasury, laying out their five-year expenditure projections for existing policies. The Treasury makes a computer tabulation and sends the results to its relevant spending divisions. From March until May, the Treasury divisions scrutinise and discuss the figures with spending departments in order to reach some agreement on statistical assumptions, on what existing policies are, and on their probable future cost. As we shall see, agreement on these three important issues is by no means a bureaucratic formality. The interdepartmental PESC committee meets in May to write a report projecting the cost of present policies and specifying remaining areas of disagreement.

This preliminary report then goes to the Chancellor in June with copies to all departments. At this time the Chancellor and top Treasury officials juxtapose the PESC report with the assessment of economic prospects and decide whether there is, in their view, room for this total of public expenditure within the limits of economic resources likely to be available (i.e., the Treasury expenditure judgement described in the preceding chapter). In June the Cabinet then hears what the prospects are, whether cuts are necessary or whether there actually will be enough room for greater expenditure. Cuts are usually necessary. Between June and November the Cabinet takes its decisions which later appear publically in the annual White Paper on Public Expenditure during November/December.

It is important to recognise that the yearly PESC report and government White Paper on PESC are not the same thing: the former is the raw material for Cabinet decision, the latter is the resulting product. The PESC report is a mid-year costing of existing policy before ministers act. As such it is secret and never published, for to do so would bare the innermost compromises through which a government reconciles conflicting pressures.[3] The PESC report is compiled by the General Expenditure Division in the Treasury and shows the level of current expenditure, assumptions on which spending projections are based, proposed expenditures over the five-year period, explanations by the departments of these figures, and percentage increases by department. A Treasury supplement will also include a list of alternative reductions that might be made to keep expenditures at their existing levels. The report is basically a Treasury document, with an overall appraisal section written by the General Expenditure Division, edited commentaries on the figures written through the usual supply division/department negotiation, and footnotes containing departmental objections.

The purpose of PESC is not to agree on any particular expenditure level or allocation of resources among the departments. Rather, it is supposed to produce agreement among officials on the present and future costing of existing policies. Most of the time in the PESC interdepartmental committee is therefore spent on the methodology of projection and presentation. The only serious arguments take place over issues in which the finance officers have a common interest apart from that of the Treasury. Thus there may be some discussion on the size of the contingency reserve to be included in the Public Expenditure Survey and on the conditions for access to the sum of money involved. No serious consideration of the relative merits of departmental proposals takes place. 'PESC is in no sense the place for trade-offs,' members of the Committee state unequivocally. 'Bargaining is almost invariably done on a bilateral basis with the Treasury.' All is usually harmonious in the Public Expenditure Survey Committee precisely because substantial disagreements are reserved for direct dealings between department and Treasury.

As a result of bilateral discussions with the Treasury, it usually is possible to obtain an agreed statement on the financial conse-

3. Quite by chance, the arrival of the Conservative Government in June 1970 coincided with the PESC report and, in desiring to portray the situation before they acted, the Conservatives published what was in effect the totals of the previous Labour Government's PESC report. Cmnd. 4515 (1970), tables 1 and 2; Cmnd. 4578 (1971) appendix A.

quences of existing policies and alternative cuts. Officials try hard to reach agreement because ministers depend on them to ascertain the overt meaning of the figures and what goes into them. If ministers had to debate these abstruse points, officials would be thought to be doing a poor job. Agreement on the costing of a programme is also possible because it does not in any way imply that Treasury and departments agree on its desirability or relative priority.

No nation in the world can match the sophistication or thoroughness found in the British process of expenditure projection. In their offhand way, Treasury officials are more than a little proud of it. But what does it mean in practice? PESC is one of those phenomena which can be best understood by examining its genesis and growth. Indeed, some participants have become so enamoured with current technical refinements that only a dip into history can separate the basic things PESC does from its sophisticated veneer.

The Coming of PESC

> PESC made it more respectable to think about the cost.
> *Principal Finance Officer*

> With PESC, power is shifted to the centre, that is, to the Treasury.
> *Treasury official*

> I am sure my colleagues would agree with me when I say there is nothing we would like better than to strengthen the hand of the Treasury!
> *Sir Samuel Goldman*, First Report Select Committee on Procedure, 1968–69, *p.* 5.

> The entire rationale of the Plowden Committee was an attempt to find a basis on which the Treasury would not be defeated.
> *Treasury official*

A wise man said that every constitution is written to thwart the last usurper. The original appearance of PESC and its subsequent modifications may be traced directly to the unsatisfactory experience of Treasury officials in trying to control expenditures in the 1950s. To a lesser degree these officials were joined in their views by ministers who felt that the expenditure system was out of control. There was, of course, no unanimity among either civil servants or politicians about how to read history or to interpret their own experience. Treasury officials did not agree whether or not the Chancellor (and hence the Treasury) was being regularly defeated and politicians differed over whether expenditure control was an illusion or in fact too stringent. In the end, however, Treasury officials such as Richard Clarke, David Serpell, Matthew Stevenson, William Armstrong and others won out because a strong feeling crystallised in the Treasury that it was being defeated far too often. Spending, the victorious faction believed, was not being controlled by anyone. These men acted on the basis of their understanding of the recent past. If we are to understand why they acted the way they did – that is, why PESC emerged and took on its current shape – we must look at the past through their eyes.

To many Treasury observers, the 1950s were notable for their contrast with the 1930s, the Golden Age of the Treasury. The departments proposed and iron Chancellors disposed. No one can read the Cabinet documents of that decade without being struck by the fierce hold of deflationary economics. As one civil servant active in the 1930s observed: 'The idea that it was a strong Treasury holding down spending between the wars misunderstands what was happening. It was in fact an economic doctrine permeating everywhere – Parliament, ministers, officials, press – everyone. Even to Labour and trade union people the economic laws seemed clear-cut. They really believed these economic laws and were ready to cut expenditures.' Without stopping to debate the power of the Treasury in the 1930s, it seems clear in retrospect that public opinion had opposed expenditure. The minister who wanted to spend had to pass through any number of obstacles. It was assumed that expenditure was not justified except in unusual cases. Not only the Treasury but the Cabinet and Parliament also were opposed. The committees set up to pursue economy in government during the 1930s have had no counterpart in the post-Second World War era.

If the 1930s were golden, the 1950s seemed to consist entirely of base metal for the Treasury. The basic difficulty pointed out by all our informants was that 'spending became popular'.[4] Huge expenditures were incurred during the Second World War and nothing terrible happened. Why not spend during peacetime? The post-war Labour Government naturally favoured spending in line with their social welfare philosophy, and the arrival of a Conservative Government in 1951 did not alter this trend. To many inside government it seemed that people no longer cared much about taxes, but apparently they did care about expenditures. The change in public opinion was reflected in Parliament. A few voices might be heard for economy in general, but all voices were in favour of expenditures in particular. According to the prevailing Treasury view, forceful spending ministers were able to push through their programmes piecemeal, willy nilly, and with little thought for the morrow. The Chancellor and Treasury seemed to have lost authority.

But the difficulties went deeper than any supposed change in opinion. As the public expenditure side of the Treasury fell into eclipse, its economic side became more prominent. After the war the weight of the Treasury shifted into managing the national economy. The new concerns were not expenditure control but full employment and stabilising the trade cycle and balance of payments. Keynesian doctrine had taken hold. Under that system, however, there was no mechanism for integrating traditional expenditure control and modern macro-economic management. The old pre-Keynesian view had been very easy to work for expenditure purposes: you balanced the budget. If you wanted to spend more, you put 6d on the income tax. Post-war acceptance of

4. This lament has a long historical pedigree. A permanent secretary of the Treasury observed in the 1890s that

> Public opinion has changed and it no longer puts much stress upon economy; that change at once finds its reflection in the House of Commons, and I should say that from that time [the 1880s] the wind was in the sails of the spending departments and ... the effective power of control in the Chancellor of the Exchequer proportionately diminished.

Quoted in Basil Chubb, *The Control of Public Expenditure* (Oxford: Clarendon Press) 1952, p. 65.

Keynesian economics meant that expenditures were not to be measured immediately against revenues but later against unemployment. The old standards were gone with no ceilings to put in their place. During the 1950s, Treasury officials gradually came to see that the absence of a self-evident link between expenditure and revenue meant that some new measure was necessary to bring expenditures into line with economic resources.

Several recurring events convinced many that, in the words of a senior Treasury official, 'the old estimates procedure had come unstuck'. Future expenditure commitments seemed to be mushrooming with little or no Treasury control. The problem was not just that the Chancellor lost now and then; losing in one year might be overcome by winning the next. But even when the Chancellor 'won' by reducing a spending proposal, the controlled figure was for next year only and gave no idea of the total expenditure committed for future years. Vast sums were thereby being committed on the basis of apparently small initial expenditures. Defenders of the *status quo* could argue that the upward trend of expenditures on social services had been matched by the downturn in defence. But the worriers prevailed. They drew a gloomy picture of an upcoming 'scissors' crisis. Talk with any of the Treasury agitators from this period and you are bound to be referred to this one dominant image: with post-Korean defence cut-backs finite and civil expenditures growing faster than GNP, it was only a question of time before total public expenditure devoured the entire national output.[5] As soon as the 'surplus' taken from declining defence expenditures was used up, Treasury officials contended, the nation would find the rate of spending rising more rapidly than economic growth could support. Severe financial trouble lay ahead. The Treasury, said the proponents of change, could no longer play its traditional role. Reform was essential.

A related weakness was perceived through the series of 'stop–go' crises in the 1950s. If the gradual but insuperable growth rate in expenditures showed the reins had been dropped, the economic crises suggested that a sledgehammer was the only tool available for stopping the runaway. And the results were no better than anyone would expect if he had to use a hammer on a horse; they

5. This preoccupation was clearly reflected in the Chancellor's Budget speech in 1961. House of Commons debates, 17 April 1961.

usually missed each other and when they collided you wished they hadn't. The 1950s were punctuated by economy drives whenever financial conditions worsened. Lacking any better technique, governments periodically resorted to flat per cent rate cuts, supposedly a method of sharing the misery equally. But few programmes had the short-term flexibility to accommodate such cuts without some distortion. Spending would build up rapidly and then have to be reduced by ham-handed methods such as percentage reductions in civil service staffs or halting construction work already underway. Departments attempting to make these reductions found them 'ridiculously wasteful'. Their work would be thrown out of gear and the cost of beginning again or laying off people would often turn out to be greater than the so-called savings involved. And even then, the cuts would not become effective for two or three years. Treasury controllers in the era of active government found that the requirements for cutting expenditures and growing asparagus were much the same : 'have the trench prepared five years before'. Departments became increasingly irritated and evasive because they needed more continuity to phase out their activities in an orderly manner. The Treasury was hesitant because it wanted to oversee the necessary reductions but also knew that its actions were neither wholly rational nor effective.

Along with senior Treasury officials, certain ministers were coming to the same view. An extended comment from a former Chancellor of the Exchequer sums up the reasons for growing disenchantment with the existing state of affairs :

The real impetus behind trying to get a longer-term control lay in the fact that several times during the 1950s and 60s the Treasury was trapped and had to learn by bitter experience about the tendency of costs to rise in future years. The old idea was that with a new piece of legislation the Treasury had costed it when it gave the cost of the proposal in the remaining part of the existing year and added that into its cost for one full year.

Increasingly in the 1950s we learned that the cost in the second or fifth full year may not be at all related to this supposed uniform standard of 'full year cost'. In new weapons for defence you tended to find the cost underestimation factor something like five times what you had approved in the first instance. This was true of a great many other areas particularly in education and in national insurance.

Drawing together the threads of experience in the 1950s, top Treasury officials began to look for a spending system that would avoid the major difficulties. Since cuts could not be made effective in a single year it would be necessary to project expenditures over several years. The pioneering work was done in defence (where the need for cost projections running from five to ten years had first manifested itself) and in certain 'rolling' programmes in roads and nationalised industries. Since the Chancellor was being cut up in Cabinet, piece by piece, programme by programme, the expenditure system had to be reformed so as to consider the total first and then make individual proposals compete for a share of it. 'The purpose of PESC,' as a Treasury official observed, 'was to avoid this system of being nibbled to death.' Thus the indictments against the past and present suggested the shape of future reform : continuous, multi-year projections within a restricted total would allow the government to relate spending rates both to the capacity of the economy and to the willingness of political leaders to trade off one expenditure item against another.[6] The stage was set for PESC.

6. Long-term expenditure projections were scarcely new. In January 1931 Chancellor Snowden used four-year projections for each item of the Civil Supply Estimates to urge expenditure restraint on his Labour Government colleagues, and the road programme of the 1930s was typically organised in terms of projected five-year expenditures. T. 171/287, (1931); C.P. 7(38), appendix; and P.C.E. (37) 10. There were also close strategic precedents for the discipline of a prior total. With defence expenditures almost double those of the previous year, the Chancellor in June 1937 sought to reassert Treasury control by 'correlating the rising total burden of Defence liabilities to the whole of our available resources', and seeking defence projections for a period of five years ahead. Prime Minister Chamberlain concurred with words which could have just as easily been uttered in the early 1960s.

The Prime Minister said that when the matter had been before him as Chancellor of the Exchequer, what he had in mind was that it would be necessary to arrive first at a global total of the expenditure contemplated by all the Defence Services. The next stage would be to obtain from the Treasury some idea as to the amount that could be spent. . . . Probably a discrepancy would be shown between the two figures, and then a second process would arise as to how the available money was to be subdivided between the various Departments.

C.P. 165 (37) and Cab. 23/88 (1937), and Cab. 23/90 (1937).

The first task in changing the expenditure system was to sway opinion in the Treasury itself. A participant in this campaign recalled that :

> Internally, the Treasury was constipated by the annual estimates approach and tied to the yearly cycle of Parliamentary business. It was a hard task convincing the Treasury, and I did it really by marshalling the arguments which had led me to the idea – namely, if you're going to try to control anything, you can't do it by looking at annual estimates. 98.5 per cent of next year's money is already committed. The second argument was, of course, that next year's cost was no sure gauge of what the total real cost would be in the end. A third argument was that if people were anxious to reduce expenditure, then this was the way, not only to control, but to cut.

A few men with an idea are more than a match for a large number of men who are unsure of where they have been and cannot tell you where they are going. The ideas behind PESC triumphed in the Treasury because you cannot beat something with nothing.

Efforts to sway opinion reached across from the Treasury into the House of Commons. The House Select Committee on Estimates, properly briefed and encouraged, issued a report decrying the lack of rational consideration of public spending and recommending that 'an independent inquiry' look into the matter.[7] Probably more important in getting an investigation established was the fact that senior Treasury officials had convinced the Chancellor and several other top ministers of its value. Concerned that an outside committee, as suggested by the House Select Committee, might prove embarrassing, the Conservative government in the summer of 1959 set up an internal Committee on the Control of Public Expenditure chaired by Lord Plowden.

Three members from outside government sat with Plowden and signed the report in 1961,[8] but the ideas expressed came from inside. The committee members were bright and the evidence interesting, but outsiders had few specific suggestions about what to do. Senior Treasury officials sat as assessors with the Plowden Committee, and it was they who imported most of the key ideas – writing the major substance of the report in virtually one weekend. That was how the doctrine of Treasury Deputy Secretary

7. H.C. 254 (1957–8).   8. Cmnd. 1432 (1961).

(now Sir) Richard Clarke – 'that decisions involving substantial future expenditure should always be taken in the light of public expenditure as a whole, over a period of years, and in relation to the prospective resources' – was embedded in the core paragraph (7) of the final report. The Committee's public recommendations called for a committee of officials (the present Public Expenditure Survey Committee) to make five-year projections; a private recommendation was that the Cabinet should establish its own PESC committee to receive the officials' report and to make recommendations on the division of expenditures within an agreed total – the ill-fated Cabinet committee of non-spending ministers discussed in the preceding chapter.

Publication of the Plowden Report made it possible to encourage discussion at the upper echelons of the civil service and among interested scholars and journalists. The support of all permanent secretaries but one (who himself had extensive Treasury experience) was won. Did these department officials understand what they were letting themselves in for? We shall return to this intriguing question when we have a better idea of what PESC actually does. It is sufficient now to observe that no one, not even those in charge of making the new procedure a reality, understood precisely how it would turn out. They improvised for several years, sometimes buffeted by events, other times seizing on an unexpected opportunity. Life still had a few surprises in store for everybody.

Annual PESC exercises began under a Conservative government in 1961.[9] The first published version, showing expenditures for 1963/4 and projections for 1967/8 appeared in 1963 and was occasioned both by a challenge from the Labour opposition that the government had no expenditure projections and by fears that Labour plans would bid spending much higher. By that time, both parties were beginning to talk about how high rates of economic growth would make life easier all around. The Labour Party, which came into office in 1964, also brought with it a particular interest in planning, increased welfare spending, and the idea for a new, pro-growth organisation separate from the Treasury – a Department of Economic Affairs.

9. An authoritative (if somewhat antiseptic) account of the stages in PESC's development is contained in evidence from Peter Baldwin of the Treasury to the General Subcommittee, H.C. 549 (1970–1), p. 152.

Institutions that worry about running out of money and institutions that worry about increasing investment to expand the economic growth rate are found within the same governments throughout the world. The one prophesies doom if expenditures exceed the total, and the other if they do not rise above it. Each one typically considers itself as the representative of wisdom, the other as hopelessly misguided. Because everything done by the one interferes with the other, they are rarely able to work out a satisfactory division of labour. The idea in Britain was that the Treasury presumably dealt with short-term affairs and the DEA with long-term planning. Yet it soon appeared that one was never out of the short-term; the important was invariably comprised by the urgent. Decisions taken immediately had long-term implications, and any decision predicated on longer-term considerations necessarily had to work with the raw materials of the present. The DEA wanted to be in on the present, and the Treasury wanted to get in on the future. The important fact for our purposes is that the Treasury became distinctly upset by the DEA's targets for annual growth in Gross National Product. The original PESC exercises assumed an economic growth rate of 4 per cent or more each year, and this hope did not materialise. The DEA might be expressing only its optimism about the future, but once a growth rate was postulated (first the 4 per cent of the National Economic Development Council in 1963 and then the DEA's $4\frac{3}{4}$ per cent), the Treasury found it difficult to control public spending. What was the point? Everyone argued that the alchemist's magic of economic growth could accommodate their spending plans and dissolve the hard choices of the past. It was not to be so. Not only did the optimistic growth rates go unmet but the Labour Government allowed public expenditure to climb faster than the economic target which had been missed. As the following figure shows, by 1968 public spending was absorbing more of the national output than it had during the Korean War and committing nearly all of the growth in Gross Domestic Product.

Treasury officials are now emphatic that the 1964 and 1965 PESC exercises 'were vitiated by the DEA's exaggerated economic targets. Apparently there was enough for everybody. It was terribly misleading.' The Treasury could not publicly say that the target was unlikely to be met; insisting on a lesser target would make it appear to be selling the country short. It would distort the Treasury position to sugest that it wanted a more accurate rate of growth postulated in the National Plan; the Treasury saw little virtue in the entire exercise.

RATIO OF PUBLIC EXPENDITURE TO GROSS
DOMESTIC PRODUCT, 1952–1971

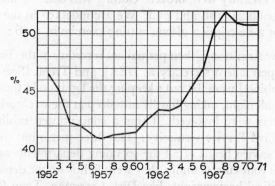

Source: Sir Richard Clarke, 'Parliament and Public Expenditure', *The Political Quarterly*, April–June, 1973, p. 139.

The Labour Government's original thesis upon coming into office in 1964 had been that the economy could grow out of its problems. By 1966 it was clear that the economy was not growing fast enough. The Government was hard pressed to meet its political commitments for major social programmes and PESC operations became more onerous than anyone cares to remember. Balance of payments crises recurred in 1966–7 and signalled a series of *ad hoc* expenditure cuts completely outside the PESC timetable. PESC seemed to have failed. It had concentrated, as Plowden had suggested, on expenditures in the current year and on a projection five years hence, disregarding the outturns in between. The Treasury catch-phrase for this had been 'forward planning'. Well before the final climax of devaluation and its vicious expenditure cuts at the end of 1967, Treasury officials had realised that 'proposals from certain quarters were making a monkey out of the fifth year target'.

But the circumstances that were pressing the Labour Government provided the opportunity for critical changes in PESC. Out of the depths of its weakness the PESC system emerged with renewed vigour. What was bad for the country turned out to be good for PESC. Senior Treasury officials, the very ones who had been the strongest backers of PESC, reflected critically on its performance during the difficult years of 1966 and 1967. Cuts in those years, as one recalled, were done in ways 'totally contrary to the rules of the game. Undertakings entered into in a proper way with the Treasury were broken. Cutting was done by horse-trading, by political push and pull.' We are indebted to the *Sunday Times* for a description of one cutting exercise in 1966 :

By now Armstrong [then permanent secretary of the Treasury], Roll [permanent secretary at DEA], and Trend [Secretary to the Cabinet] were flat out : keeping the lights on in the Cabinet Office all night, taking hardly any sleep at the weekend. . . . No Ministers were involved. It was a concentrated exhibition of pure Civil Service virtuosity : The three men rang round the Civil Service heads of all the spending departments and said: give us your cuts. Cannily, they went lightly on the departments of political heavyweights like Dick Crossman, Tony Crosland and Barbara Castle.

Minor figures like Dennis Howell, the Minister of Sport, had their appropriations wiped out without a tremor. (Last week Howell still did not know what had happened.)

Trend, Armstrong and Roll had another sleepless night on Tuesday : preparing the [£500 million deflationary] proposals for the Cabinet meeting on Wednesday morning. And the Cabinet went off almost without a hitch : except for the ominous silence from George Brown. . . .[10]

The inability of PESC to work adequately during the emergencies of 1966 and 1967 might have constituted evidence against its continuance. Instead these unsatisfactory experiences were interpreted to mean that PESC was more essential than ever. 'The balance of payments crisis [of 1967],' according to one permanent secretary involved, 'was an excuse for what we had believed all along. You were spending too high and you must cut it. We had to violate the system in order to do it. This showed that the financial control procedure was not good because you could not use it when you needed it most.' Labour spending ministers, who had

10. 'How the Bubble Burst', *Sunday Times*, 24 July 1966, p. 9.

seen their fine plans of 1965–6 blown to tatters when paper targets crumbled, were receptive to the idea. The Government needed more discipline, not less. It needed not only to set total expenditure targets but also to get beneath and behind the totals to ensure that the target was hit and that when necessary, intelligent reductions could be made. No one sat down in isolation to think up bright ideas for improving PESC. The changes flowed from the practical problems of government.

The most important change in PESC after 1967 was not inherent in the exercise but in the way others saw it. As soon as the Chancellor was able to impose a strict spending limit for the coming year and hopefully for the immediately succeeding years, the projections of existing expenditure demands became much more significant. This time the exercise was for real. For PESC to work, the projections had to be made complete. Instead of an estimate for only the first and fifth years of a programme, now costs were also to be projected for the intervening second, third and fourth years. 'Forward planning' was transcended.

The great symbolic phrase inside the Treasury, given official blessing in the White Paper of January 1968, became 'planning the path as well as the whole'. It was not a case of recasting figures in order to make the growth rate of expenditures lower by the fifth year, but of laying down a publicly proclaimed path, year-by-year, for each department. The Treasury officials in charge of PESC believe that working along an expenditure path is a more effective method of exercising control than setting a distant goal in the fifth year toward which to work; only if intervening years' figures are controlled can there be any meaning to the fifth year projection. This doctrine is so well-established that, as we have seen, Treasury officials can now be found engaged in a month-by-month monitoring of each department's alignment with the proposed spending path.

Another innovation unveiled in 1968 was the doctrine of the 'focal year'. As part of the effort to interest the House of Commons in expenditure control, the Treasury (and in particular its Chief Secretary 'Jack', now Lord, Diamond) had argued to the Select Committees that the House was understandably uninterested in next year's estimates; only years further ahead contained sufficient flexibility for real decision-making. Considering year three as the focal year was thus partly a presentational device. Partly too it was a seat-of-the-pants compromise in determining the path to year five. 'You can't have ministers crawling over each of the five years making allocations', Treasury officials argued. Since years one and two were heavily committed while four and five were vague, year three was chosen as the key focus for decisions. That year, as Goldilocks might have said, was just right. Expenditure decisions would be made fairly firm for year three but only provisionally for years four and five.

Around 1970, however, the focal year doctrine was itself transcended as too simple-minded. Departments were attaching unrealistic hopes to years four and five and necessarily vitiating the meaning of the total five-year target. Moreover degrees of flexibility were found to vary with the spending programme in question. For some with especially large capital elements, years four and five might be largely committed, while other programmes might not need to commit year three at all. The denouement is a current conception of PESC more in line with the way expenditure decisions are actually taken. As one Treasury official put it, 'The figures are in general simply more provisional the farther ahead you look – we've tried to make clear to the departments and get them to understand that these figures for years four and five, although provisional, are approved and are important. They aren't cast in iron but they are to be taken seriously.'

The election of a new Government dedicated to further spending or suspicious of new-fangled techniques would have created havoc for PESC. An unwillingness to set ceilings or capriciously raising them to vastly higher levels would have nullified the control aspects and reduced PESC to a worthless paper exercise. A Government hostile to PESC could have abolished it. As luck (or misfortune, depending on one's preferences) would have it, the advent of the Conservative Government in 1970 proved a boon to PESC's supporters. The Government was dedicated, at least temporarily, to lowering taxes and reducing expenditures. The PESC procedure fitted well into a frame of thought determined to bring spending under control.

Apart from any political party changes, other refinements since 1968 have occurred and been recounted in previous chapters. The monthly running tally has been supplemented with an even shorter-term intelligence return within the Treasury concerning emergent spending issues; a discount factor, the 'relative price effect', has been used to take into account the tendency for public sector prices to rise faster than other prices; the 'resource impact effect' has tried to break away from the tradition of counting all pounds as equal and to show the varying degrees of economic resources absorbed by different types of spending. Anyone out of the Treasury for even a few months is likely to find himself antiquated by the latest embellishment on PESC's doctrinal rococo.

Not the least important of these changes has been the decision to publish in considerable detail the PESC expenditure projections – though not the PESC report or economic assessment behind the Treasury's expenditure judgement. When Treasury ministers and senior officials give out information it rarely stems from an unqualified desire to be informative. In this case, the publication of PESC White Papers was designed to lend more realism to the expenditure projections. 'It's important to the Treasury,' as a senior official told us, 'that the White Paper be published. Before, while it was solely internal to the Government machine, ministers could leave a lot of things fuzzy.' Hopefully, a public document would commit the Government to what it said. The Treasury then would have an anchor to restrain the tendency of spending ministers to set the figures adrift.

Despite the increasing publicity PESC has received, it is not wholly understood in political circles. Socialists who suffered under it, though few can specify how or why, are prone to echo the ex-minister who wailed, 'PESC proved the Treasury is Tory'. Some Conservative ministers have to be hand-carried through the procedure – not once but every time it is brought up. No matter how often Treasury officials appear before the House Select Committees, patiently explaining the ABC's of PESC, they never seem quite able to overcome the puzzlement of Members. Even inside the Treasury, some voices are heard to the effect that PESC has become over-elaborate and should be simplified. Is it possible that the Treasury is not only the guardian of the purse, but also keeper of the secret of understanding PESC? Or is PESC difficult to understand because it is not one, but many different things that vary with the needs and perspectives of the user?

The Politics of Projection, or Rashomon Revisited

How did you, as Chief Secretary, find the PESC process? ... I found it a very valuable exercise and an absolutely essential one.

*Lord Diamond, Expenditure Committee
70–71, Minutes of Evidence,
22 March 1971*

Really, I and the financial officer regard PESC as a tiresome gnat.

Permanent Secretary

It was part of the Treasury's aim in this note to try to explain the essentially dispassionate character of the inter-departmentally agreed figuring and recommendations to ministers about the costs of changes.

*Sir Samuel Goldman, Second Permanent
Secretary of the Treasury*

Facts are, of course, facts, but on this scale and in this complexity they can be presented in many different ways, and it is no light task to get the agreement which we normally get on this so-called factual presentation.

*Douglas Henley, Treasury official
in charge of PESC*

Rational decision-making is a chancy business, as chancy as non-rational decision-making. Everyone wants to know what's in it for them.

Senior Treasury official

PESC has a deceptive appearance of simplicity. You start from where you are and ask what it would cost to continue your present activities in the next five years. It would be easy to assume that the Survey is a straightforward technical operation that produces figures on programme costs within an allowable margin of error. But this is not so.

Let us return to the simplest statement of PESC: a cost projection of existing policies. It turns out that there is often disagreement about what each element – cost, projection and existing policy – actually means. These issues, argued out between department finance offices, Treasury principals and assistant secretaries, are of course technical matters – or are they? Every participant knows or soon learns that, in the words of a Treasury official, 'there is a great deal of advantage in getting one's own figures into the PESC Report'. Disagreements arise partly because of unresolved technical problems but also because each member of the community has a stake in securing a favourable outcome. The Treasury naturally projects low and the departments invariably project high. A large part of the PESC process is devoted to bargaining to arrive at an agreed figure. By discussing the elements of PESC we can begin to understand the shadowland between technical operations and the politics of projection.

Trial by Technique

What is existing policy? Surely everyone knows. The fact is that there are continual battles in the bowels of the bureaucracy on this issue with, as one participant put it, 'the department trying to fiddle it up and the Treasury saying that ministers haven't agreed to this.' Is existing policy that which is agreed upon, or that which is done despite the fact that no one agreed? Is the Treasury's understanding of past agreements the same as that of the department? Does agreement mean a formal concordat or traditional acquiescence? When new circumstances arise, who shall interpret the vague agreements that were made before any of the disputing officials were on the scene? When a policy has 'existence' is a subject for profound thought; if decisions did not have to be made it could appropriately be left to metaphysical philosophers and semanticists. 'Existing policy,' concluded a finance officer, 'is one of those delightful phrases that one exploits as well as one can.'

In the first place there may be no present policy under which expenditures can be projected. Ministers may be undecided, their opinions contradictory or vague and, while officials do look diligently for signals, there may be none to see. Similarly what is casually called existing policy may be in flux. Its general outlines may be in a continual state of modification so that it appears quite different, depending on who is doing the looking. Take the case of political promises. Suppose that a Government had a target of building so many thousand homes. This target might fail to be met because the Government did not know how to achieve it, or the private sector did not come through, or because the Government later decided to use its resources elsewhere. The department can argue that it should be able to spend the housing money elsewhere, while the Treasury will say that a change in policy has occurred. In one sense 'existing policy' is not to build the houses but in another sense building them evidently is the latent policy, even if events temporarily have prevented it from coming to fruition. Another variant occurs when a money programme, though not necessarily a policy, is being phased out. A particular industrial subsidy may be terminating but the existing policy remains one of supporting that industry. The PESC contingency fund may make up the declining wedge of old subsidies before new programmes start but the question lingers on: what does existing policy say about new money for future subsidies in the same industry?

Another difficulty lies in distinguishing 'natural' increases from policy changes. Does existing policy mean only what was done last year, or did it always anticipate a gradual increase in the quality of the services or facilities provided? The PESC projection can include both maintenance and improvement of existing standards (such as pupil-teacher or doctor-patient ratios, or space per classroom or hospital beds). Early in the 1960s, for example, policy called for an excess electricity generating capacity of 14 per cent but deficiences led to a rise of 17 per cent; with larger plants now operating, the excess operating margins are necessarily more 'lumpy'. Does, then, the request to reflect this fact in larger expenditure margins constitute a new policy? The Treasury may wish to challenge the formulas by which old standards are expressed in practice or to suggest that the standards themselves have been set too high. The department will insist that existing policy covers the standards and is usually able to prevent their deterioration. But the departments also will insist that an improvement factor is built into current policy. It was assumed, the department will argue, that standards would alter with the general expectation of the citizenry for a higher level of performance. The Treasury will say that an improvement factor was not agreed on or has lapsed and that the proper level of projection is whatever the department bought in the first year.

Or again, suppose that for some reason a programme that cost so many million pounds a year has suddenly shot up to twice that amount. The Treasury will say that the increased cost was the product of special circumstances and that existing policy dictates that the programme return to its original level. The department will argue that the proper base for projecting its future expenditures should be the higher total or at least some amount between the lower and higher figures. The end result is less likely to be agreement on some supposedly correct figure than a deal on an in-between amount with which both parties believe they can live.

The Treasury controller may be particularly hard put to determine whether an increase in spending is due to a growing demand for services under existing policy or a deliberate departmental change in that policy. It will help us to see how the problem looks from the standpoint of the Treasury official:

In a PESC submission this year I see that a proposal is going to cost 30 million pounds the second year, 60 million the third and 120 million in the fifth year. Now this trend line leads me to question whether or not this is existing policy. What I do then is look for the causes of the increased trend, whether it is being done with the encouragement of the departments or whether it is a result of public demand. If it is the latter I can't do very much, but I am beginning to have doubts if the department is not really encouraging public demand in this. A second way to identify departures from existing policy is to study the circulars that go out from the departments to their regional administrative offices. A third area is uncalled-for improvements in standards. For example, if a building has to be replaced with a new building there is a natural increase in standards but it is very difficult for me here at the Treasury to make this stick as a change in existing policy.

New money is always more difficult to find than old. New programmes are subject to criticisms that old ones escape. Departments, therefore, have an incentive to claim that what they want to do is part of existing policy and not a new departure that calls for intensive scrutiny. For this, if for no other reason, spending departments generally prefer to accept small cutbacks in a variety of programmes rather than see any one item entirely eliminated. It is useful to keep at least the tip of the camel's nose under the tent.[11]

Failing to secure agreement with the Treasury, a department may have its minister take the matter up with the Chief Secretary or the Chancellor of the Exchequer. From time to time the department will register a memorandum of disagreement so that the Cabinet will be required to decide between it and the Treasury opinion. The PESC process manifestly is not one in which there is agreement across-the-board on the costing of existing policies but rather, as a department official said, of 'marginal but nevertheless important haggling' throughout the year.

One can understand that the precise detail of existing policy is unclear. But surely its general outlines and configuration are understood and agreed upon. Is this not another example of pettifogging bureaucracy? Not at all. In expenditures, one man's margin is another man's profit. The tiny differences which may seem unworthy of argument yield the little extras that make life worth living. Policies, as we have seen, are bargained out precisely on these margins. A few per cent on hundreds of millions of pounds may make the difference between sufficiency and stringency, contentment and dissatisfaction, elbow room and the straitjacket. A strength of the PESC exercise is that it goes on year after year. Eventually most initial disagreements are negotiated and differences between the Treasury and the departments narrowed down to more manageable proportions. To be sure, new disagreements arise continually but they are more readily resolved in the context of a pattern of past settlements. Over the years a record of understandings about the meaning of existing policy is built up. For the departments, this record serves to protect them against departures from their accustomed income. The Treasury also can be more confident about the foundations of the five-year projections on which it has staked so much. For each participant, uncertainty is reduced and security is increased. The price of this security lies in giving away the right to challenge. Thus the margin for change in an already constrained system is reduced.

11. This is naturally a well-worn tactic. In 1934, for example, the First Lord of the Admiralty was willing to reduce total spending by £150,000, but only if he could retain a core of £50,000 for the shipbuilding programme. Cab. 23/78 (1934).

A second large area of technical–political argument is the price basis for costing whatever definition of existing policy is agreed upon. The prevailing view that spending forecasts should be based on constant pounds has considerable intuitive and political appeal. How can any comparisons be made unless the objects compared – expenditures – are placed on the same basis? But PESC is also a five-year projection rolling forward each year; the constant prices used one year are in no way directly comparable to the constant prices used next year. Comparing current prices would overlook changes and exaggerate the rate of real increase. But a succession of yearly projections, each on its own particular constant price basis and with no clear method of translation between the current and previous years means that it is extremely difficult to monitor and verify past projections. Only in 1972 did the Public Expenditure White Paper begin showing comparisons of actual out-turns over several years and even then the figures concerned only the most general spending aggregates. Since the amount of each programme category is not in terms of pounds whose value is constant over time, there is no easy way of comparing departmental performance from one PESC exercise to another.

In this respect, PESC in its early stages has taken a step backwards from the much-maligned annual estimates procedure. When control was exercised through estimates prepared for Parliament, there was a kind of inherent monitoring process. Since staying within the estimates was important, and since the accounting system was geared to that end, there was a tendency to look at what actually had happened in the past year or two. Departments which deviated markedly from their proposed estimates could be held to account. As the Treasury began to tell departments that they no longer needed to pay so much attention to the estimates, that one meagre feedback operation fell into disuse. In PESC there is more forecasting but less monitoring.

The Treasury is, of course, aware of these problems, but in the ongoing debate with departments, the field for squabbling about 'true' costs and price changes is immense. Even if the monitoring problem were solved, each programme has its own distinctive set of component prices. Moreover, to compare a change between only two years can involve looking at prices at the beginning of year one's projection, or its out-turn, at the time of year two's projection or its out-turn, or at any time in between and in any combination thereof. Most finance officers would agree with one of their colleagues who suggested that 'The annual updating of PESC covers a multitude of sins.' Every department will make a strong case for a generous updating and recosting of its existing policy and deny that any new policy is involved. Treasury officials recall 'the tremendous battles with departments' over the supposedly technical problem of revaluing 1969/70 expenditure figures into 1970/71 prices. The department that wins a higher price adjustment gets more money without a change in the PESC figures to alert others to its recent success. After all, the difference between underspending, overspending, and coming out right depends heavily on the prices at which one chooses to look.

Others offer a more radical critique of the constant price projections. A former Treasury minister lamented that 'Control in real terms is the work of the devil. When you hear that term, real money, [or constant pounds] you are round the bend. Real money is the signal the Chancellor and the government have given up and accepted inflation. You can only exercise control over regular money. Real money means you are accepting the very thing you must fight.' We need take no position on this question, except to observe that the technique appropriate for economic processes which require measurement in constant pounds may be a poor, and possibly counterproductive, instrument for limiting the absolute growth in public spending. The higher the denominator, the larger the numbers seem but the lower the fraction really is.

If there is disagreement over what constitutes, first, existing policy and, second, its cost, there can scarcely be agreement on the projections that follow from these disputed premises. Despite the unwarranted aura of scientific precision and mathematical objectivity which outside observers sometimes attach to projections involving numbers and formulas, the people who make those projections know that their assumptions often are open to question and that their conclusions are subject to wide margins of error. Projections (and the formulas for making them) do not fall from heaven; they are made by men, subject to the usual limitations of human knowledge and men's natural bias toward protecting the interests entrusted to their care.

Projections require either (1) theories accounting for the growth rate of certain expenditures, theories which are in scarce supply to say the least; or (2) extrapolations from past trends, which may prove fallacious under future conditions; or (3) conventions about costing that have little but convenience to recommend them. Projection may be better than untutored judgement, but it is still more art than science. Disagreements over projections have deeper roots than (though they may be compounded by) technical problems of computation.

The difficulties of projection vary with the kind of programme involved. In some, governmental priorities, past trends in expenditures and the important variables determining future costs are all known. The expenditure projection takes the form of a *forecast*, i.e., what the government thinks will happen. In certain cases the facts are sufficiently clear for the forecast to be a firm postulation of how spending will develop. Possibly a deal between Treasury and department on the growth of capital expenditures has settled the major issue and the remaining variables are open to little question. Given a few demographic facts, such as student enrolments, and assuming a few bargains on the improvement factor involved, educational expenditures generally fall into this class.[12] Projections of housing expenditures, to turn to a more problematical area, are largely a function of forecasts for housebuilding; but this is a less certain area than school attendance and, as we have seen, Treasury officials are eager to separate factual forecasts from wishful targetry. Projection is easier when the amount of business involved remains fairly constant so that the cost associated with it in earlier years may be confidently extrapolated into later ones. Where social services or other programmes relying on public applications are involved, predicting future costs depends on being able to assess future demand. In addition to questions about whether the demand has been artificially stimulated by the department, the number of people applying, say for hospital care, will depend on factors – the economy and employment, climatic conditions, appearance of new diseases or new treatment for old ones – that no one knows how to predict. These projections are not estimates so much as 'guesstimates'.

12. For a discussion of the varying degrees of certainty among programmes and among items in programmes see the testimony of D. O. Henley to the Employment and Social Services Subcommittee, H.C. 323 (1970–1), p. 9.

In a second type of programme, conditions are so uncertain that there is really no attempt at forecasting. The projection becomes an arbitrary *convention*. In agricultural supports, for example, PESC does not try to anticipate the annual farm price reviews or market prices; it merely projects the level of support agreed at the last price review. The cost to the government of debt interest similarly is projected on the assumption of fixed interest rates. Staff ceilings certainly are not known five years ahead; the projected staff costs, always an important item in lesser spending departments such as Employment, are based on a purely 'notional number of staff'.[13] The largest of all public expenditure programmes, social security cash benefits, also rely heavily on conventional projections. Demographic trends are used, but rates of benefit are assumed to remain at an unchanged constant value (although internally in the PESC report, officials do play about with the effect of likely price movements on National Insurance benefits). The published PESC figures project the cost of benefits at their current level, disregarding future changes in the schemes.

A third category of projections, a hybrid of forecasts and conventions, is based on a purely hypothetical government hope or *target*. Projection in this case spells out some particular desideratum. To take a prominent example, projections about the cost of unemployment and redundancy benefits depend less on demography and more on the state of the economy. The five-year projection of these costs from 1970/1 showed a decline and was based on a statistical-political assumption about unemployment. This assumption was 'consistent with the government's view that the present level is too high'. In practice, the government based these projections on its hope that the unemployment level (then 3·1 per cent) would return to the 2·5 per cent level prevailing in the previous five years.[14] By the same token, when the government

13. Sir Denis Barnes and A. F. Sutherland, testimony to Employment and Social Services Subcommittee, H.C. 323 (1970–1), p. 114. For a general discussion of such conventions, see Sir Samuel Goldman's testimony to the General Subcommittee, H.C. 549 (1970–1), pp. 37 ff.

14. Testimony of Sir Denis Barnes, Permanent Secretary, Department of Employment, and Miss M. Riddelsdell, Second Permanent Secretary, Department of Health and Social Security, H.C. 323 (1970–1), pp. 100 and 124. Similarly the introduction of new housing subsidies was expected

says its new import levy scheme will save £150 million, the projected 'cost of agricultural support therefore assumes, on a quite arbitrary basis', that savings will gradually rise from £25 million in 1971/2 to £150 million by 1974/5. Or to take another example, a new system of prescription charges leads projectors to calculate savings by taking past trends and 'simply applied the figure which we knew the government had in mind. . . .' [15]

A final category, hopefully entitled 'miscellaneous', generates its share of Treasury–department argument. Rather than having to try to project the future courses of diverse and numerous items, departments are encouraged to lump them together and project their total, possibly in the hope that the various errors will cancel each other out. The time spent, as is so often the case, does not depend on the importance of the items but on the room for disagreement and manoeuvre. The Treasury may say that the projection of existing policy with regard to all these items means that amount which was spent on them last year; the department will not agree.

These seemingly technical difficulties could be multiplied at length. Clearly the PESC figures do not automatically add up to a total as if they were untouched by human hands. The PESC projection is neither a simple forecast, convention, or target but some indeterminate combination of all three. The inherent ambiguities of existing policy are only accentuated by debatable interpretations of price movements. All these basic elements of PESC are subject at the margins, where crucial decisions are made, to fundamental uncertainties and thus to human volition. At that ever-critical margin, moreover, it is difficult to distinguish a projection that falls to one side of the possible and a postulation that pushes the numbers in the desired direction. Technique is not neutral.

Since the end of the sixties, the Treasury mood has changed appreciably; Treasury people now realise that the PESC figures are more rough and ready than was once thought. A contingency reserve was introduced in 1969 to cover some of the uncertainties, but it is a relatively small sum and used up yearly. A few Treasury

---

to save £100–£200 million. PESC fixed on £150 million to be saved by 1974–5 and arbitrarily subdivided that figure for the years in-between. Testimony of I. D. Janes, H.C. 321 (1970–1), p. 43.

15. The quotations are taken from Cmnd. 4578 (1971), p. 20; and testimony of H. C. Salter, H.C. 323 (1970–1), p. 75.

officials now harbour suspicions that they need larger margins in PESC projections than they could ever get away with from the Cabinet. According to one of them, realistic margins 'would mean the Treasury having to say to politicians, "Look, we don't know why but we'll be needing this extra money. We need to keep resources free." Of course politicians want to use up whatever money there is available.' Recognising the difficulties of arguing the general against the particular, Treasury officials get what margins they can and deliberately avoid claiming too much for the precise accuracy of their PESC figures.[16] But in all of this area, we are speaking only of the supposedly technical issues. Political bargaining is far more overt in the substance of the PESC process itself.

Payoffs and Punishments

A finance officer recalled to us that in 1967 his predecessor had briefed him with a long description of the annual estimates cycle. 'To my successor now, I would say nothing of the estimates and speak only of PESC.' This reorientation is significant and representative. PESC has become an integral part of the process through which government funds and policy priorities are allocated in Great Britain. Those who feel they benefit by it try to make it work; those who feel they lose out try to cushion its impact. All participants in the PESC procedure are aware that the politics of public policy is being played out under their eyes. PESC is not only a way of helping some participants make better decisions, it is an arena for decision in which strategy is more important than producing an elegant report.

This is not to say that PESC has worked out as intended by its Treasury founders and as proposed in the Plowden report over a decade ago. Practice has thwarted many of these original hopes. One can now hear it said in the stratosphere of the Treasury that PESC's founders 'were schematic people. They thought in flow

16. Testified the Treasury Deputy Secretary in charge of PESC (D. O. Henley), '... A lot of the figures in this White Paper and other publications on public expenditure do have the look of a fine degree of accuracy which is not really justified by what I have been saying, but it is rather difficult to produce completely rounded figures when you have a whole range of uncertainties so we have to give figures to a greater degree of accuracy than is justified in some cases.' H.C. 323 (1970–1), p. 9.

charts, organisational models and such things. They believed that if you set out the right organisation you'd get the right decisions.' Although the preceding description is unfair to the founding fathers, it does indicate that the men who have lived with PESC's everyday problems realise that expenditure control is not so neat and tidy as was once thought.

Nowhere has the original rationale for PESC been more confounded than in its efforts to weigh particular expenditures against each other. Experiments with Cabinet committees of non-spending ministers have, as we saw, consistently failed. Little-known attempts in 1968/9 to organise an interdepartmental group of senior civil servants to promote a similar competition came to nothing; ministers know they are responsible for fighting for their departments and will not have this right pre-empted by any other group. Any number of people with experience under PESC recognise that, as a permanent secretary put it, 'it has not in any sense altered the fact that the big stuff is settled by ministerial bargaining'. Or, in the words of a minister who observed Cabinets over a long period, 'the Plowden concept of making ministers rivals has never worked. PESC does let the Chancellor say that the projected total of existing decisions is so much money, but it is still not forcing ministers to weigh proposals against each other. PESC has been of value at the official, rather than the ministerial, level because the tendency is for big expenditure projects to be taken up separately by the Cabinet.' Every Treasury minister must work diligently to create a simultaneous and competitive rather than a sequential and collaborative decision process. Between 1967 and 1971 the balance did move in the former direction, but by and large it still seems true to say that most Cabinet bargaining is a sequential operation in which major expenditures are each considered serially rather than all together at the same time.

When political administrators sometimes say that 'for all practical purposes I disregard PESC', they do not mean it quite the way it sounds. They do participate in PESC and try to do their best there. But they are also conscious of aiming to get a more favourable decision out of the Cabinet. 'PESC inevitably came out of the Cabinet larger than when it went in,' one official reported. 'Ministers doing the worst try to get their improvement there.' Ministers and officials use the last or the next PESC exercise as a launching platform for their particular spending plans.

It is just one more move along the long road toward getting one's way in Cabinet. 'Only the naïve list all their preferences in PESC as they actually stand,' said a sophisticated minister. 'Weak ministers don't understand PESC. Tough ministers get most of what they want.' PESC, with its once yearly overview, may initiate or record the results of Cabinet bargaining but it is not that bargaining itself. Outside pressures, departmental strategy, and/or ministerial forcefulness can result in a Cabinet decision and pre-emptive strike on resources at any time; the 1971 White Paper, for example, showed £365 million in policy increases since the previous year's PESC settlement.[17]

The disaggregation and lack of comparison among spending decisions is not the result of sheer ministerial wilfulness. Even Treasury controllers, who would like to see expenditures counterpoised, recognise the inherent difficulties. 'The reason they can't do this,' a veteran official mused, 'is that new demands come up from various quarters at all times of the year and get settled individually. You don't get a comparison of alternative uses of resources but something on health in June and roads in December.' There is no reason whatsoever to believe that this process will change, unless one is also prepared to believe that emergencies (real or apparent) will disappear in the future and not play havoc in Cabinet as they have in the past. Every Government has things that matter to it at the moment. Indeed, ability to respond to emerging conditions is supposed to be one of the hallmarks of a successful government. But adaptation also means that expenditure decisions are not made comparatively and finally at any single point of time each year. 'PESC is, in fact, no jamboree of decisions once a year, after which time it is put away and filed,' a senior Treasury official who has lived through the evolution of PESC concluded. 'The problems are simply too big and continuous for this. Most of the real work gets done in the on-going system of continuous contact between the Treasury and the department.'

The preceding quotation suggests another important, indeed vital, reason for the limited realisation of PESC's original hopes. The Treasury itself is of mixed opinions about the value of PESC for its everyday work of expenditure control. PESC, strictly con-

17. This excludes Farm Price Review and social security increases. Cmnd. 4829 (1971), para. 11 and 12.

ceived, is only a set of figures and aggregate figures at that. There are few things more likely to arouse the practiced scepticism of Treasury men; many have already spent much of their adult lives, particularly in the supply divisions, looking for the substance behind superficial totals. Some near the top of the Treasury now speak of what they consider as the 'heresy' in the idea of PESC's founders 'that all you need is overall control of expenditure totals. A total is practically meaningless. We have got to know a lot about details. That is why it is necessary for the Treasury division head to live in close association with the department.' It is here, bilaterally between Treasury and department political administrators, that substantive meaning is given to existing policy, projections, improvement factors – in short the whole panoply of considerations involved in the department's spending proposal and the Treasury view on the subject. In Treasury eyes much more is at issue than the question of whether there is 'money in the kitty' for a spending plan. Our earlier chapters have tried to suggest how much more Treasury controllers actually want to know. The Treasury official immediately responsible for PESC has made the point as well as anyone :

It is tempting when figures are laid down in anything like a White Paper to come to the conclusion that the totals set out are the controlling mechanism. They are in certain cases but the underlying point really is the agreement in the Government as a whole on the constituent policies in each of these fields. . . . As between the Department concerned and the Treasury there has to be an understanding about the policy content of each programme in a fair degree of detail, so one does not rest, as it were, on figures to determine the relationships between Treasury and Departments as the main basis of their relationship.[18]

Perhaps the evolution of PESC has revealed a subtle but important conflict in Treasury norms between procedures and people, between the belief that rationality is linked to performing certain quantitative calculations and the view that the quality of personal interaction is what matters.

Anyone who works on PESC knows that it is part of, and not

18. Peter Baldwin, testimony to Employment and Social Services Subcommittee, H.C. 323 (1970–1), p. 12.

a substitute for, the ties of kinship and culture between department officials and their Treasury counterparts. Most Treasury officials pride themselves on the close relations their supply divisions have with the departments and consider PESC as providing only one part of the framework within which these negotiations are conducted. Hence, both Treasury and department officials emphasise that PESC machinery is not so much a way of taking decisions as a means of recording them. 'Essentially', a department official said, what PESC does is to ratify bargains which have already been reached, with some little scope for "argy-bargy".' All officials involved know that the impact of these bargains will be felt for years to come. According to a Treasury official speaking in 1971,

> PESC registers the year-long series of haggles. You cannot get away from what is inherited in these haggles. For example, the ministers in this government wanted to do things in [X policy] but they really could not have done much without the preceding discussions which have occurred bilaterally on these questions between the Treasury and the expenditure divisions of the departments in the last Government. The discussions which we are having to fight now bilaterally with the departments won't really be important in expenditure terms for quite a while. But the specified aspects which we are looking at will probably appear in expenditures 1975–6 or later.

The Treasury concern for policy content will, therefore, often outrun or pay little regard to the somewhat arbitrary five-year period of PESC projections.

It PESC is not a scale, is it nevertheless effective as a ceiling? If it cannot count on weighing expenditure decisions against each other, can PESC still be rated a success in holding individual spending programmes down to a prearranged and fixed total? There is, alas, no simple answer to this question. But unravelling some of its complexities can help us understand more about the expenditure process.

Few programmes are subject to control in the narrow sense of a 'ceiling', i.e., a fixed sum projected ahead and under which the programme must at all costs stay.[19] Rigid ceilings have been found practical only in those few programmes where the central

19. A brief discussion is in H.C. 549 (1970–1) pp. 89, 153; and H.C. 398 (1972–3), pp. 12–15.

government has complete control over both the finances and the determinants of the expenditure. Both in research councils and in overseas aid, for example, money is allocated largely at the government's will (though not entirely without pressure by beneficiaries and their friends). Parts of the defence, road, hospital and industrial aid programme are of a similar nature. But in a great many other areas an absolute PESC ceiling is impossible. Local authority and agricultural spending are subject to their own external determinants, from changes in the political winds to the effect of rain on farmers' crops. Social security expenditures are based on statutory entitlements and depend on numbers of beneficiaries, rates and conditions. Housing subsidies and improvement grants follow automatically from the number of accommodations meeting fixed requirements; control consists in assessing the accuracy of building forecasts, not in setting financial limits. Nationalised industries have independent commercial criteria to meet and their current expenditures are not controlled by the Treasury. Since 1969 their capital investment plans have been included in PESC, but the next three to five years are more in the nature of probabilistic forecasts than control figures.[20] Added to all these difficult-to-control areas are a vast range of individually small but collectively large programmes where strict individual ceilings would require more fine-tuning than PESC can produce. As the Treasury controller for one department said, 'Really, you know, the spending we're concerned with is so relatively small that it's never possible to say that because something is over the PESC forecast, they can't have it. It would be laughable to say the money can't be found. In the days of balanced budget and fixed revenue maybe you could say, "I'm sorry, we've looked in the Exchequer and there isn't any money left", but you can't do that today.'

The fact that only a minority of programmes have absolutely fixed ceilings is, however, scarcely the end of the matter. PESC's origins clearly show the intentions of its founders to introduce, if not an oak-beamed ceiling, at least a springtop lid on expenditures.

20. For nationalised industries' investment plans in a given year, PESC means that so much can be spent on year two at given prices. Generally for year three the Treasury allows the industry to commit a certain proportion (e.g., 80%) of its allocation for that year. Years four and five comprise a statement of what the government sees as a reasonable presumption for planning purposes; the industries are not required to plan on the basis of these figures.

The spending implications of individual decisions were to be spelled out for the future and related *in toto* to likely resources. In this aim the Treasury has been moderately successful. PESC *has* altered some of the important cultural norms in the expenditure community. Our previous comments – about the role of the Treasury's expenditure judgement in Cabinet deliberations, about the post-1968 emphasis on paths rather than simply a fifth-year target, about the unequal pressure for underspending rather than overspending – have suggested the important part which PESC has come to play. But the best evidence comes from the participants themselves. Most political administrators believe PESC is taking hold and would agree with the permanent secretary who contended that 'PESC's value is not really in its precise forward-look, but in teaching people to look at the value of resources to be used over time.' Agreeing that cost consciousness has seeped into his department, a PFO observed that 'what PESC has done is to provide a big gun in the financial officer's arsenal for dealing with officials in the policy divisions. Now you can always cite last year's agreed amount in any argument with them.'[21] While most of the real work continues to be done in bilateral bargaining between Treasury and departments, PESC means that this argument goes on within the agreement that there will be some total. In essence, PESC has made it much more difficult, if not impossible, for departments to argue the merits of their case to the Treasury without considering the implications for total expenditure and the costs five years ahead. The mechanics of PESC may be a bookkeeping exercise but the figures are now kept in one book and over five years. The strategic environment for bargaining has thereby been subtly but significantly altered.

Even local authorities operating in the area of their greatest ostensible independence, current expenditure, have felt the impact of this new bargaining environment. Before the end of the 1960s

---

21. The Finance Department of the Home Office, for example, has expressed the formal doctrine in this way:

> The Public Expenditure Survey each year is a framework within which expenditure is expected to be contained. In the normal course proposals for new policies or extensions of existing policy are not put forward between Surveys unless the estimated cost can be met within the agreed forecasts, e.g., by making compensatory savings.

Memorandum by the Home Office: 'Public Expenditure on Home Office Services', H.C. 323 (1970–1), para. 17.

local authority current expenditures had been growing by about 6 per cent annually in real terms. The slowdown imposed after the 1967 devaluation was a temporary and only partially successful expedient seeking to contain their spending to a point where it would absorb the rate of price increases. The 1968 negotiations between central government and local authorities began to change this situation by presenting a brief economic paper showing why the national economic situation could allow only so much to be given to local authorities (in terms of the Rate Support Grant). The next biennial negotiation in 1970 went further and included local authority representatives in the working parties of central departments to agree on forecasts on the cost of existing policy, likely needs, and the expense of marginal changes. Negotiations in 1970 and 1972 expressed the central government's determination to limit local authority current expenditure to a 4 to 5 per cent growth rate in real terms, still above the 3 per cent guideline of productive potential but lower than before. (The government also negotiates the proportion of local authority current expenditure it will support, usually changing this marginally by 1 or 0·5 per cent a year and going up to 58 per cent in 1972). There is, of course, no neat, rational formula for arriving at this figure. 'We have the feeling,' says a key government negotiator, 'that this is about the marginal change which can occur to contain this degree of pressure – public demand, need for improvement, and so on.' The point is that the local authority portion of public expenditure is now more effectively constrained between, on the one hand, the authorities' reluctance to turn to their own hard-pressed rates (taxes) and, on the other hand, a clearer view of forecasted costs and spending totals to be observed.

But the major impact of PESC has been within central government. Those who know PESC best are fully aware of the deficiencies in their projections, the ambiguities of existing policy, the pliability of supposedly agreed totals and costs. They are likely to speak of it as 'technically awful', 'full of terrific cheating', 'intellectually unsophisticated', and 'lacking in follow-through'. The men who operate the PESC system fight a rearguard action trying to get departments competing for shares of the total and any pooled savings. They try to force additional expenditure plans into bidding for the contingency reserve this year, but know also that this reserve is itself an uncertain amount likely to be altered next year. While it is true that PESC is essentially a reporting exercise representing a cumulative result of continuous haggling, neither this nor other difficulties render PESC ineffective.

Experienced Treasury men are willing to trade statistical exactitude for getting the argument into their own terms. If PESC is less than a total system for making expenditure decisions, it is far more than a blank sheet of paper on which contending armies total up the results of their battles. Only the simple-minded worry about exact figures for expenditure control. What matters most is what people take for granted. Let us listen to one of the Treasury officials who did most to help PESC take hold in the 1960s:

> If people fuss that the figures aren't good, I don't care and I never did care. What is important is the framework – creating habits of mind.

> Let me show you what I mean. When I first came to the Treasury, in the 1940s, people would say about an expenditure, 'It's either on the vote or below the line.'[22] The system was well understood only by the high priests in the know. It had been thought of in this way for a century and what mattered was that everybody did think of it in this way.

> Our idea was that if we could get PESC embedded in minds in this way, it didn't matter if people didn't actually comprehend it all. If you get people saying about issues 'it's not in our PESC allocation', then you're home and dry. This sounds cynical, but it doesn't matter that the system isn't understood by the man who makes this remark or the fact that he's unaware of the technical machine behind it. What matters are the mental reference points. The questions he knows he'll have to answer are much more important than the figures themselves, which are never right anyway.

In this basic intention, PESC has succeeded. Every department now accepts that, in the words of a permanent secretary, they face a 'rolling restraint. It's harder for us to say "We didn't think

22. The reference is to the traditional budget form which held sway in accountability control before PESC. 'Above the line' is the organisational classification of yearly departmental estimates. Expenditures set out 'below the line' in the financial statement are those financed out of loan transactions, not direct parliamentary grants. Ursula Hicks, *Public Finance* (Cambridge: Cambridge University Press, 1955), pp. 336, 348.

of this last year, can we have the money for it now" ' Another permanent secretary pointed up the contrast with 'the Fifties [when] we were always in grave doubt about what total we were supposed to be observing'. 'The PESC machinery,' said a third, 'has given the Treasury something to slap down in front of the government and say "Here is the whole ruddy picture. These are the implications of expenditures as presently approved." ' Granted, the limits agreed to are not absolute; the Labour government entered into the 1970 election with the clear understanding that upon its victory, the last set of PESC projections would be reformulated with new spending proposals. The important point to note is that even then the debate would have been in the Treasury terms of agreed expenditure paths and a view of the resulting totals. 'PESC has made it harder to get money,' an experienced department head summed up. 'The Treasury is going to want to know about financial effects in the years ahead. It's also reduced taking *ad hoc* spending decisions with an undeliberate total. Now it's harder for a sharp-witted minister or official to get away with something in isolation.' The Treasury reformers of the 1950s and 1960s may feel some just satisfaction.

But every innovation also has its unintended effects and new strategic possibilities. PESC is no exception. The interest of the departments lies in making their projections as high as possible. The more room they leave themselves for future expansion, the easier they will find it to accommodate new activities or expand old ones. But the strategy of bargaining for the highest possible projection will only work if a few departments practice it successfully. If every department comes in too high, the total will scare Treasury officials and their ministers and may well precipitate an economy drive. Estimating spending too high can be counterproductive if it leads to deeper cuts and more detailed Treasury scrutiny. So each department needs to know something about the behaviour of others in the same position. More careful consideration may lead them to modify their objective: come in on the high side, so as to have room for manoeuvre in the future, the revised version states, but not so high as to generate an economy drive. Deciding how high is too high is difficult. When in doubt, departments would rather live with the problems of largesse than stringency, of trying too hard, than of not trying hard enough. To this end, they have worked out approaches to help them gain the increments they value so highly.

PESC is meant to control spending. It is, thus, peculiarly vulnerable to tactics that claim alleged savings. Treasury doctrine, which recent governments have accepted, is that if you want to do X you must save in Y. But interesting forms of bargaining are still possible. Under the old system, departments knew they would have to fight and they would end up with a certain figure for the year immediately ahead; the Treasury might require offsetting savings, but these were always real savings to materialise in next year's out-turn. With PESC, said a department official, departments 'are being tempted to use larger amounts in the first of the five years and promise to be good boys later'. Departments may readily accept shadow cuts in years four and five so they can get more earlier on. Sufficient unto the day is the increase thereof, is their motto.

The reader must try to imagine the fanciful possibilities involved in sacrificing a set sum of money in year two for one in year three, about which little is known, or for another in year five, about which virtually nothing is known. Fortunately we do not have to rely entirely on our imagination. The Conservative Government of Prime Minister Heath was not slow to pick up the intriguing prospects which PESC opens up for new men. How, the curious may ask, was a Conservative Government able in the autumn of 1970 simultaneously to claim both modest increases and substantial reductions in defence allocations? He who follows the explanation closely will be rewarded. He must understand that when the Labour Government left office it was not overly concerned with the fifth year of projected costs in defence and thus may have let them go higher than otherwise would have been the case. In any event, the Heath Government found that new costings showed the Labour projections were too low and had to be revalued upward. Here is where the savings materialise magically before our eyes. Projecting its slightly higher level of expenditures into the future against the newly revalued Labour projection, the Conservatives argued that by year five hypothetically they would still be spending less than Labour had projected. Now you see it, and now you don't!

Suppose, for example, that a minister wants to increase the rate of replacement for old primary school buildings. He (or in this instance, she) goes to the Chancellor of the Exchequer and says that the department will save on its spending projections for higher education by cutting down other projected expenses. (Perhaps the moral is that it takes one kind of projection to beat another.) Brandishing this 'saving', she will ask the Chancellor to provide the rest in new funds or out of the contingency reserve. Any minister who has done his or her share can always justify getting a piece of what is up for grabs. Of course, the more politically sensitive the projected saving (e.g. cutting free school milk), the greater the likelihood of success in persuading Treasury and other ministers to support a supposedly more essential expenditure (e.g. a new nursery school programme).

Playing off expenditure commitments against the projected savings of future years reached a fine art after 1971. Until this time PESC had developed in an unremitting atmosphere of economic stringency. Spending was always too high. In 1971, unemployment began climbing toward one million, the spending climate began to be assessed differently, and the emphasis on ministerial approval or offsetting savings for going above the PESC ceiling was relaxed. By 1972 the Prime Minister was citing large increases in government spending to help deal with unemployment. Treasury officials argued publicly that this increased expenditure had not altered the five-year PESC totals already projected; it had merely shifted the path upward earlier, with a compensating decline in later years.[23] In 1973 the pressure for a spending restraint revived. When in May 1973 the Chancellor announced cuts to make expenditure £535 million lower for 1974–75 than it would otherwise have been, the parliamentary Expenditure Committee rightly queried if the cuts would be 'real' or estimating changes, particularly given the £600 million underspending that had occurred in 1972–73. Expressing a similar scepticism, some Whitehall circles term such tentative future savings 'fairy-gold'. Whether these conjectural savings – on hypothetical expenditures – in an

23. The Prime Minister's speech is reported in *The Times*, 25 January 1972. See also Treasury testimony in H.C. 450 (1971–2); H.C. 149 (1972–3); and H.C. 398 (1972–3). The 1970 White Paper projected an annual 2·1% expenditure increase for 1971/2 and 2·0% for 1974/5; the 1971 White Paper showed 3·9% for the former year but reduced the projected future

uncertain future – will ever materialise is problematic. Nor is anyone likely ever to know whether or not they did. As the man said, the annual updating of PESC covers 'a multitude of sins'.

Incrementalism to the nth Power

PESC has proven susceptible, not only to the strategist of projected savings, but also to the strategist of the well-applied nibble. PESC may make it harder to get money but it makes it easier to keep money once gotten. Consider the following representative comments : 'PESC makes the starting points well established,' a PFO noted. 'It lends itself to a system of incremental planning.' 'What PESC does,' the head of a supply division declared, 'is prevent chopping and changing policies and ensures change will be at the margins. One hopes and thinks that this is right.' 'The best thing,' a Treasury man concluded, 'is that each year the arguments with departments do not start afresh.'

In short, PESC has enshrined incrementalism with a vengeance. It is incrementalism to the nth power. If PESC helps prevent departments from going beyond established bounds, it also commits the Treasury in public to keeping their expenditures going at the projected rate. Both sides find it more difficult to depart from the historical base. If PESC makes it less likely that new monetary programmes with large spending implications will be introduced inadvertently, it also helps to assure departments that their on-going programmes will not suddenly be disrupted. 'It's harder to get new items injected under PESC but it's easier to keep old ones from being ejected', reported a permanent secretary. PESC is like a fast merry-go-round : it is hard to jump on but once you do, it is equally difficult to be pulled off and there is every incentive to hang on.

To see this incrementalism in action we must return to the basic linchpin, the official in a Treasury supply division. When he uses PESC, he will do so by trying to get a forecast of the five-year trend for a new expenditure or, if it is a once and for all item, to obtain some idea of the year in which it will affect the

rate for the latter to 1·4%. Thus the wonderful result is a smaller average annual rate of spending (1971/2 to 1974/5) *after* the 1971 reflation than before. Cmnd. 4829, table 1.1.

total. PESC may be used to see if past forecasts were sensible and to generate feedback about the expenditure climate. Offsetting savings will be called for. 'We may', said one such official, 'help stop an extravagant expenditure, but not its gradual growth.' By the same token the major value of PESC for the spending departments, as any number of their officials told us, lay precisely in this stability. Under PESC they are better able to let their administrators and clientele know what they can count on getting. Another term for the same thing is inertia.

Incrementalism has been reinforced through PESC by making each department more conscious of its own fair share of the total and more aware of other departments' departures from the expected rate of increase. In this sense, PESC has increased openness by reducing the scope for backstairs deals between Treasury and spending ministers. Vastly increasing a programme or switching priorities must be registered (if not arranged) in the open. And this, as a senior Treasury official believed, can help make the Treasury minister's job easier 'because it lets people see that there's fair play.... If the department wants something the Chancellor can say "my heart bleeds for you but I can only give £50 million, for the other £50 million we'll have to talk to the others in PESC".' But fair play can easily come to mean a standard of equal marginal changes. 'Before PESC,' a permanent secretary suggested, 'no one had a good idea whether he was being treated generously or cheaply.' A contemporary and critical Treasury view is that 'PESC has simply enforced an earlier tendency for each dog to get its share. Thus, each permanent secretary can test his virility for next year by seeing whether he got the required x plus percentage like everybody else.' They are all professionals on the Public Expenditures Survey Committee and they all know what to look for. The comment of one department finance officer was typical:

There are three kinds of things that are especially likely to antagonise other departments. First, an unusually high rate of growth in your expenditures. What everyone in other departments looks at is that last column, year five, to see if your allocation is going up very sharply apart from the usual trend of drifting upwards. A second thing likely to antagonise other departments is if your proposal will pre-empt a large sum of money over the future years, for example, if you are creating contractual obligations or entitlements. Finally, what others are concerned about is to see if there is any substantial change in your expenditures over what was agreed originally in the last PESC. This aura of legitimacy for the last figure, of course, creates tremendous inertia.

With the PESC report in hand, department officials find it easier to brief their ministers because they can tell them about claims being made by other departments and how these impinge on the suggested total. Officials also are in a better position to know whether other departments will be after them or whether their big programme is likely to pre-empt several others that are being pushed equally hard. Normally it is far easier to keep nibbling away with unobtrusive increments like everyone else.

By this time it should be clear that the diverse meanings and effects attributed to PESC are a product not merely of disagreement about its consequences but also of the varying functions it performs for different people. The actual use made of PESC also helps explain why this device for supposedly increasing Treasury spending control has been so readily accepted and implemented by the spending departments. The Treasury's desire for increased control and the department's desire for increased security were a powerful parlay backing PESC.

The smooth adoption of PESC has been greatly helped, first, by the fact that it was a forecasting machine before it was a control mechanism. PESC could thereby creep up on the departments. Departments were used to hearing about forecasting operations that did not amount to anything. The apparent triviality of PESC and its obvious weakness in the early years meant that few people, as one hostile Permanent Secretary put it, 'realised this monster was looming at their back'. A departmental official recalled that 'no one had much interest in the beginning. [Sir Richard] Clarke was regarded as something of a figure of fun. What a bore, people would say. We left it to the PFO to deal with. Eventually it got so far it couldn't be stopped.'

As PESC developed fitfully in its early years, perceptive department officials began to see that it could have advantages for the longer haul. 'What appeared to be most important to them,' a Treasury minister observed, 'was that once a department was successful in getting a programme injected into the PESC cycle, there was very little risk of it being cut out.' No one has had to educate civil servants on the power of inertia. The fact that a Treasury concern with spending totals might increase departments' delegated power was not merely secondary but actually often opposed by a great many departments. What did matter was the security, as can be gathered from the Treasury official who did much of the selling of PESC to the departments:

If you're in charge of a programme with short-term inflexibility, as all are, you're a bloody sight better off if you have – not a precisely agreed programme – but some indication of where you're going and what you'll have. Whereas before, as a spending department, you were at the mercy of the next year's estimates cycle and there was always the danger of a Chancellor deciding on cutbacks to help the economy. This was especially true if the Chancellor was strong and your minister weak – I'm not saying your programme would be cut to ribbons. The amounts cut would be small, but just these small sharp cutbacks is what put your programme in a hell of a mess. Most saw they'd be better off [with PESC].

Had department officials taken PESC seriously in the beginning, they might well have been against it as a restriction of their freedom of action. Once it already existed they could find ways around PESC where it pinched and ways into it where it gave aid and comfort. No one could have foretold how PESC would re-emerge from its earlier obscurity to become prominent in a Labour Government that desperately needed to hold down expenditures. Perhaps it is fitting that an approach which enshrines incrementalism should have crept up on everyone unawares.

PESC is not a self-contained, isolated process and there is something misleading about even applying a distinctive noun to what has happened. PESC is embedded in the pre-existing culture and kinship of British political administration. It is the use of the ordinary community relationships to focus and bring up to date yearly the bargaining system we have described in earlier chapters. The Treasury's achievement in establishing and making PESC work is substantial. It has been accomplished, not because the Treasury knows how to manage public money better than anyone else, but because it knows better than most how to manage men and their community relationships. The adaptability to emerging expenditure problems, the appreciation for departments' needs, the strategic prudence which aimed at creating habits of mind rather than lock-step obedience – all these features say much for the sensitivity of the men involved. PESC may not have revolutionised the expenditure process but, as a Treasury veteran observed, 'it's a bloody sight better than what was going on before'.

Yet some political administrators have also begun wondering if PESC has not become too successful. Treasury proponents of PESC are well aware of its weaknesses. Has security in expenditure planning and all-round marginal increases overbalanced the need for asking fundamental questions and staying in touch with policy? Are not the virtues which departments find in PESC also its vices? Treasury men hope that Programme Analysis and Review – discrete analyses of individual programmes within departments – will create an impetus for change within agreed ceilings. In their more optimistic moods, they even hope for assistance from the new Parliamentary machinery sired by PESC.

Parliament: Who Cares?

> The proper officers bring in the estimates; it is taken for granted that they are necessary, and frugal; the members go to dinner, and leave Mr. West and Mr. Martin [the Joint Parliamentary Secretaries to the Treasury] to do the rest.
>
> *Lord Chesterfield, 1759*

> In prehistoric times there might have been some [parliamentary] control over the expenditure but there certainly has not been in my parliamentary experience.
>
> *Arthur Balfour, 1905*

> ... We thought in a minor way they [the Parliamentary Select Committees] might provide occupation to our frustrated back-benchers. ...
>
> *Richard Crossman, 1970*

Looking back, the Select Committee on Expenditure seems to have been of more use to the Treasury than to Members of Parliament.

A founding member of the Committee, 1972

The great difficulty is getting the chaps at the other end to show an interest. It's difficult to see how we'll get Parliament off the ground.

Treasury official, 1973

Ministers can sometimes be found nursing visions of arcadian Cabinet meetings spent elaborating clear strategies and consistent lists of expenditure priorities. Members of Parliament outside the government are more likely to direct their reveries to a halcyon past when Parliament had real control of government spending. The most comfortable thing about golden ages, past or future, is that no one ever lives in them. Recent attempts to revive Parliamentary involvement in the expenditure process generally are trying to revive a corpse that never lived, but the historical references no doubt have their presentational value. So far, the recent Parliamentary reforms – a two-day debate on the PESC White Paper and creation of the Select Committee on Expenditure – have come to little, but a review of the Parliamentary expenditure domain does provide another prominent surface for refracting a beam of enlightenment on the political administration of public money.

Our account so far has been able to bypass traditional maxims concerning Parliament's power over the purse for one straightforward reason : Parliament plays little direct part in expenditure decision-making. Following the completion of an expenditure, the Public Accounts Committee in Parliament and the expert staff headed by the Comptroller and Auditor-General review the accounts to ensure financial responsibility. The preceeding supply estimates are considered and approved virtually automatically. In the modern era of party discipline, any other outcome is likely to be considered by the Government as cause for resignation. So automatic has this approval become that the fiction of Supply Days for approving departmental estimates has been dropped and renamed Opposition Days to signify the set-piece partisan debates that take place between Government and Opposition on any and everything other than finances. When even the British constitution drops a fiction, it is a telling sign.

The preceding chapters have suggested that any part played by Parliament is at least once or twice removed from the legislature itself. Ministers and civil servants trying to assess the expenditure climate frequently will use their reading of Parliamentary opinion as one barometer. Political climate in Great Britain refers mostly to predispositions within government and, unable to get a grasp of what the public at large may think, officials occasionally use Members of Parliament as an acceptable surrogate. Similarly fashions for this or that type of programme often are nurtured in the legislature and can provide would-be spenders with a tactical advantage in bargaining with the Treasury.

Parliament is used to help weigh people as well as issues in public spending. The standing of department ministers, and thus an important part of their weight in the bargaining process, is affected by what happens within the House. The assurance of the minister in debate and his avoidance of embarrassment under questioning is an obvious testing ground. Equally, if not more, important is the less structured gossip which washes throughout the Palace of Westminster and concerns ministerial performances inside government. X is making his name at Environment, Y is as dismal as expected, but isn't Z doing surprisingly well at Employment. With political life so heavily concentrated in London, it is not surprising that opinion in the House is sometimes regarded as public opinion itself.

One of Parliament's most important roles in the expenditure process is essentially passive. Mutual confidence, we have observed, is crucial in the interactions of those making expenditure decisions inside the government. Parliament is the ever-present outsider, a political-counterweight sustaining trustful behaviour within the executive. By agreeing – implicitly or explicitly – on what Parliament will and will not be told, political administrators evince their trust in one another; by keeping to their agreements, they reinforce that trust. The government as a whole and ministers individually are of course answerable to the House, but the reciprocal of answerability is assumed to be Executive impenetrability. Official advice to ministers is held confidential; the Cabinet official committees and working parties, the deals, bargaining and conflict of the expenditure process are interdicted subject matter for the legislature. By confirming and reconfirming to themselves what is proper behaviour toward outsiders, political administrators strengthen their own internal ties of mutual confidence. Parliament is the permanent and proper stranger whose very presence indirectly helps nurture the sense of community within the Executive.

An unconscionable conspiracy? Any such conclusion is facile. Or at least if there is a conspiracy, it is one in which the vast bulk of the victimised MPs deliberately conspire. There are opportunities to have it otherwise. Not all have been content with the indirect and *post hoc* nature of Parliament's contribution. Efforts to reform Parliamentary machinery led to the creation of a Select Committee on Expenditure in 1970 to replace the old Estimates Committee. Briefly reviewing a little recent and ancient history can tell us much about the nature of executive-legislative control over public spending.

Any unsentimental exploration reveals that the golden age of 'real' parliamentary power over expenditures was little more than a brief interlude – roughly 1850–80. Then, as now, it was less a question of Parliament forcing its spending will on the executive and more a question of its being used as an ally by one segment of the executive against another. Then, as now, M.P.s as a whole remained distinctly uninterested in the spending process, and they had 600 years of precedent to reinforce this feeling. Despite the host of qualifications which should be made in any detailed historical study, the fact remains that the creative tension between executive and legislative powers – a struggle generally conceived to lie at the heart of the Englishman's liberties – has had its source in questions of revenue and not expenditures. The power of the purse has concerned consent to taxation and safeguards against its arbitrary use. Public spending, if considered at all, has been dismissed with the somewhat curious idea that you cannot spend what you haven't got, a sanguine view that is disproved during every Christmas shopping season. Revolts against taxes have been endemic in British history; revolts against wrongful or excessive expenditures are historical curiosities. (The only one which historians can generally call to mind is that of Robin of Redesdale in 1469, not one of the more prominent dates in the island's chronicle).

While government remained small and expenditure items customary, taxation and expenditure were almost indistinguishable; those willing the means willed the end. Medieval taxes and special levies were typically earmarked for particular purposes (such as Danegeld for buying off Norsemen) and the closer the earmarking, the more a legislative decision on a tax also took the form of an appropriation. Although such allocation of specific sums for specific purposes was an inherent feature of feudal revenue, it would be a mistake to think that these precedents created unilinear progression toward Parliamentary control of expenditure. Even in the mid-fourteenth century, when appropriation of extraordinary grants had become established procedure, the legislative interest in public finances was directed toward ensuring only that the King lived effectively on his own resources and did not lightly approach Parliament for tax revenue. Parliament was scarcely interested in or equipped to deal with spending decisions on a continuing basis.

The major landmarks in British constitutional history have, therefore, concerned disputes on the power of the executive (which had usually found its own income and borrowing capacity inadequate) to impose extraordinary taxation rather than disputes on the uses of that taxation. From the formative struggles between Barons and Crown, to the difficulties of the Stuarts with Parliament, to the Protector's fiscal headaches, the issue – far from implicating legislative participation in spending decisions – presumed that Parliamentary interest lay exclusively in the scope and duration of tax revenues. Despite the temporary appearance of annual supplies, appropriation and audits immediately after the Glorious Revolution, Parliament soon became content to authorise bloc grants for all civil administration expenses and to do so in perpetuity for the reigns of William III, Anne and George I. Gradual replacement of the Crown's hereditary revenue with the Civil List was consistent with the tradition that once having got the funds, the executive disposed of them as it wished. Military spending did depend on annual Parliamentary supply after 1688, but by the eighteenth century even these estimates generally were accepted uncritically, with neither Treasury nor Commons exercising anything but the most formal control. From the idea that the King 'lived off his own', it was only a stone's throw to the notion of executive control over the spending process.

The growth of British public finances meant that tax revenue increasingly became a general resource tied to no distinctive spending programmes, and thereby curtailed even the *de facto* role of Parliament in appropriation. At the same time, as political responsibilty passed from royal to civilian ministers (with their subservient majorities in the eighteenth-century House of Commons), there was little inclination to change the presumption of exclusively executive control over the determination and allocation of public spending. There is no better indication of this than the fact that within 25 years of the Glorious Revolution, the standing order still operative today had been laid down: Parliament could receive 'no Petition for any sum of Money relating to public service, but what is recommended from the Crown'. With this rule the Treasury was not only 'rooted in the leadership of the House', but eventually afforded primacy in the business of the government itself.[24] The emergence of a Prime Minister's office was to be through financial control and the Lords of the Treasury rather than through any of the powerful Secretaries of State.

The eighteenth and early nineteenth century rise of Treasury power within the executive and of Parliamentary scrutiny over public spending were far from separate coincidences. At first the general pattern was for Parliamentary investigations to show up glaring organisational and procedural deficiences within the executive. Departments could be found blatantly misusing appropriated funds; unappropriated expenditures by departments escaped all scrutiny; records were confused, out of date, and incapable of ensuring accountability of the spenders. As usual, however, the aim of Parliamentary criticism was to make the executive mind its expenditure business more efficiently – a new version of the King living off his own – rather than to gain a part of that business for itself. The House would do its duty by 'holding the Treasury responsible for every act of expenditure in each Department'.[25] Increasingly, Treasury authority advanced through unsolicited increments of power from the latest reform and Parliamentary commission pressure. If reformers in Parliament

24. Roseveare, *The Treasury*, p. 80. Basic historical reviews of Parliament's role are in Basil Chubb, *The Control of Public Expenditure* (Oxford: Clarendon Press, 1952); and Paul Einzig, *The Control of the Purse* (London: Secker and Warburg, 1959).

25. *Select Committee on Income and Expenditure*, vol. 5, 1828, p. 8.

(usually from the Whig Opposition and always a minority of the membership) were interested in promoting centralisation and co-ordination within the executive, it was not a campaign the Treasury was likely to shun.

By the mid-nineteenth century, the Treasury was no longer the junior partner to Parliament in urging improved expenditure controls, but partners they still were. Reform within the Executive had advanced to the point that it was possible for the Treasury to make more deliberate use of the House of Commons as its ally; indeed, only when the Treasury had made a good beginning at co-ordinating estimates, appropriation, and audit procedures within the executive could the House be expected to help scrutinise these operations. Now it was Parliamentary reform that was seen as a vital means of increasing control over departmental spending. Here was one of the oldest strategic moves in British politics. As the thirteenth-century monarchs had summoned the Commons in order to appeal under the heads of the difficult-to-tax Barons, so the governmental centre in the mid-nineteenth century sought a Parliamentary ally against the feudal strongholds of the spending departments. This is the background from which we must view the reforms that resulted in the fleeting interlude of direct Parliamentary control over expenditures.

The impetus for Parliamentary reform was not, to be sure, solely a question of Treasury strategy. Utilitarian philosophers and an active minority within Parliament worked energetically for a new system of Parliamentary control. But it was work in which the Treasury found advantage and gave its active support. Changes in Parliamentary procedures were to supplement the struggle for effective expenditure control within the executive. One of the first landmarks in modern Parliamentary scrutiny occurred in 1832 at the initiative of the executive rather than Parliament itself. Trying to control his unruly department, the First Lord of the Admiralty decided it would be advantageous to present the detailed audited accounts to Parliament each year. In 1846 the Treasury instituted the same requirement for the War and Ordnance Offices, and in 1861 for the revenue departments. By 1845 a Treasury committee had concluded that reports of its own Audit Board were being laid before Parliament without result and that effective control depended upon establishing a special committee in the House to examine the accounts. The arrival of Gladstone as

Chancellor of the Exchequer in the 1850s crystallised the Treasury's interest and the pressure from a small number of reforming M.P.s to push for another Parliamentary investigation.

Again, the Treasury's enthusiastic co-operation and proposals were revealing. The Finance Clerk of the Treasury re-emphasised the contention that a special Parliamentary committee was needed to ensure adequate attention for the audited accounts. Indeed, the proposal of Treasury officials went farther than any other by suggesting a guaranteed debate in the House on the accounts and report. Although details of the Treasury plan, including a guaranteed debate, were not accepted, the basic idea was. The Treasury warmly supported establishment of a Public Accounts Committee in 1861 and remained one of the strongest advocates for its permanent status. '... The very capable permanent Treasury chiefs had given the matter much thought and had come to the same conclusions as eventually had the Parliamentary investigating committee. The Public Accounts Committee looked like strengthening the Treasury's already strong hand.' [26] The Comptroller and Auditor-General who serviced the committee became a Treasury appointment, although responsible solely to Parliament; and the working relationships between Treasury and Committee necessarily became intimate. In time, Committee and Treasury representatives literally began to sit on the same side of the table, that is, opposite the spending departments called in to account for their actions. If the Treasury has thereby become obligated to implement the Committee's strictures, they are strictures likely to be in line with the Treasury's natural interest in economy. When the Public Accounts Committee criticises the Treasury, it will be for not following its own inclinations strongly enough.

Parliamentary reforms of the Gladstone period have provided the blueprint for the last century of Parliamentary expenditure activity. In this scheme of things, Parliamentary votes the money requested by the government but becomes actively involved only in post mortem examination of completed expenditures. For a brief period, Parliament did scrutinise departmental estimates in

---

26. Chubb, *The Control of Public Expenditure*, p. 33. One of the few people to object that parliamentary control should be based on suspicion and not confidence in the Treasury was the soon-to-be unemployed Comptroller-General, a semi-judicial official independent of the Treasury and responsible to Parliament.

some detail before granting approval; on seventeen occasions between 1858–72 the legislature reduced the estimates despite government opposition. Usually, however, the amounts were trivial (involving less than £5000 in all but three cases) and in any event, the flush of Parliamentary interest quickly faded as party discipline increased, implying that any such defeat on the estimates was a vote of no confidence in the government. By the turn of this century, Parliamentary debates on the estimates had shrunk in time and content to what they have remained – *ersatz* election campaign attacks by the Opposition on the Government. The Public Accounts Committee has continued its painstaking examination and auditing of accounts. The various estimates committees (first established in 1912) began with a brief to examine 'what' if any, economies consistent with the policy implied in the Estimates should be effected'. In 1960, the Committee's terms of reference inched forward to examining 'how, if at all, the policy implied in the Estimates may be carried out more economically'. Even such reviews of past administrative performance were chosen from 'a list of possible subjects ... compiled after informal contact with the Treasury.' [27] Usually the sub-committees chewed over some minor programme which struck the chairman's fancy. Parliament has been allowed to ask if the government has spent the money as intended, with accurate accounts and economical management. Except in the general terms of public debate, Parliament has most definitely not been there to examine government policy and help settle the total amount or allocation of forthcoming expenditures.

The new Parliamentary debates and committees which came into effect at the end of the 1960s were intended, at least among the handful of enthusiastic M.P.s involved, to break out of the undertaker's role of presiding over terminated expenditures and to get in on the act of creation. Parliament, the reformers argued, had not kept pace with changes within the Executive, in particular with the introduction of PESC. There was, no doubt, a good deal of self-flattery involved in the assumption that Parliament had ever been effectively in touch with the spending process before PESC, but it was a convenient pad for launching reform. Now a third element was to be added to the older pro-

27. Memorandum by the Chairman of the Public Accounts Committee, 'The Estimates Committee', H.C. 410 (1968–9), pp. 87–8.

cesses for examining means (reflected in the annual estimates) and retrospective scrutiny of ends (expressed in terms of value for money). Parliament would 'consider systematically the merits of proposed expenditures compared with alternatives and with resources likely to be available....' It would undertake a 'discussion of the Government's expenditure strategy and policies, as set out in projections of public expenditure several years ahead'. These were heady days. 'It is heartening, indeed, for once to witness a process where events and practices not only appear to be moving in the right direction,' Peter Jay wrote, 'but also to be doing so primarily because that is the direction in which reason points.'[28]

To implement these ideas, there was now to be an annual two-day debate in the House on the PESC White Paper to thrash out the choices and priorities reflected in the expenditure projections. Here would be the 'main opportunity for the influence of the legislature to be brought to bear on the programme of the executive. It should be among the most important events of the parliamentary year.'[29] While it is far too early to declare this experiment in Parliamentary involvement with expenditures a failure, it is obvious already that performance has fallen well below the founding M.P.s' original hopes. Several of these founders in fact have turned from such committee work to, in the words of one, 'more political struggles – areas more suitable for a Government backbencher'. One leader of the Expenditure Committee reported that 'our subcommittees are not doing the job intended, they're not thinking about priorities, only the narrow subjects just like the old estimates committee'. In 1971, the supposedly great debate in Parliament on the PESC White Paper – a debate intended to rank among the top Parliamentary occasions of the year – ended in abject failure. Opposition Labour members refused to sit through the debate, others complained that they felt as if they were at a gathering of bridge enthusiasts, and the vaunted debate petered out without a vote.[30] A number of reasons for the

28. Ibid., p. viii; and Peter Jay, 'Public Expenditure and Administration', *Political Quarterly* (April–June, 1970), p. 195.

29. H.C. 549 (1970–1), p. vi.

30. The failure to take a vote was explained by Douglas Houghton for the Opposition. 'I make no bones about it. The explanation is that last night we had to revise our judgement about the nature of the debate. It has not been a political debate but a discussion between practitioners, craftsmen,

failure can be offered – poor timing of the debate, absence of Opposition leaders, long preceding debates with three-line whips on another issue – these occasioned but they did not cause the failure. The underlying difficulties go deeper. If the PESC figures truly do summarise the heart of the Government's programme, why has not Parliament seized the opportunity to discuss them? Why does Parliament brush aside its one opportunity to discuss those wonderful things – priorities and strategies? Partly because there was more behind Parliamentary reform than the hopes of reforming M.P.s and academics, partly because their hopes were quixotic.

We can better understand what has happened to these hopes by looking more closely at their origin. The proposals for reforming Parliament's role in the expenditure process stemmed from a failure, or at least a setback, in another area of Parliamentary reform : the preceding establishment of specialist subject matter committees (in agriculture and science and technology) during the mid-sixties. By the 1967/8 session of Parliament, it was clear that the short-lived experiment in parliamentary specialist committees to scrutinise particular subject matter was stultified. The agriculture committee was disbanded in February 1969, and the Government made clear that the number of specialist committees would not be increased. Any replacements would in all likelihood have a life of only one year. The Government had tolerated this experiment, partly as a means of occupying the frustrated younger backbenchers, partly as a cosmetic for its reformist image, and partly because of the convictions of several members in the Government. After a year or so, many senior ministers and officials were annoyed by the specialist committee experiment.[31] Within

---

accountants, quantity surveyors, forecasters.' Other Opposition members observed more candidly that enough members could not be driven in for the vote with only a two-line whip. The Chief Secretary concluded for the Government with the hope that 'the serious work which will continue in the Expenditure Committee will enable us to make better use of parliamentary time in debating the essential subject of public expenditure than has been the case in the last few years and tonight.' Hansard, *Parliamentary Debates*, vol. 827, 9 December 1971, cols. 1622, 1639, 1640.

31. One account of the story behind the specialist committee experiment is John P. Mackintosh's 'Specialist Committees in the House of Commons: Have They Failed?' *The Waverley Papers*, Occasional Paper no. 1, University of Edinburgh.

the House itself, the number of M.P.s firmly in favour of specialist committees had probably never numbered more than a hundred, and the guiding forces in the movement could be counted on the fingers of one hand. Several of these reformers now decided to try and rescue the idea of specialist committees by looking at financial procedures. PESC was being given increasing prominence by the government. Expenditure cuts for balance of payments reasons were making a mockery of the Labour Party's earlier plans. Public spending, it seemed, was something for Parliament to get its teeth into, or at least to exercise its gums on. But how to begin? Certainly not by trying to awaken and organise other M.P.s on the issue. Rather than starting with the mobilisation of M.P.s, the Select Committee on Expenditure got under way at a lunch between a few Parliamentary reformers and several Treasury officials. 'We knew that if we took the idea to the Chancellor of the Exchequer, even the preliminary idea of an investigation on the question, he would say "Let me ask my officials." So they had to be squared first. We found that a number of middle-range Treasury officials were on our side.'

For the parliamentarians the reasoning was obvious; with the effective focus of the spending process shifted from yearly estimates to PESC projections, the House of Common's annual authorisations of expenditure for one year ahead had become more irrelevant than ever. But there was another side to the affair. If not exactly pushing reform of Parliamentary procedure, Treasury officials nevertheless were, as one remarked, 'ready for the idea'. First, it could help the Treasury in dealing with spending departments if Parliament became interested in advancing PESC. 'The points they [the Expenditure Committee] could make,' said a Treasury man, 'would help the Treasury. Now we can say to the departments "there is Parliamentary pressure – we must go on developing PESC".' A second and related advantage was that publication and public debate could also help clarify the commitments of ministers and spending departments to certain expenditure limits. 'These things are cumulative. Some people go along with you right away but others don't. Unless the first move is followed up, as with the publication of PESC,' the Treasury official continued, 'one doesn't get 100 per cent advantage. If a holdout sees others going along, he'll feel himself exposed.'

The Treasury also had an interest in promoting a more informed climate of public discussion. This need was borne home with particular forcefulness immediately after the November 1967 devaluation. Reduction of public expenditure growth rates to $3\frac{3}{4}$ per cent (at constant prices) had been widely publicised in January 1968 in an attempt to reassure foreign creditors and shift resources to export production. One month later the Parliamentary vote on account revealed a 10 per cent rise in central government expenditures for 1968/9 and sent a renewed shock through the foreign exchange markets. Embarrassed by this misunderstanding between total public spending and central government supply estimates, senior Treasury officials were open to the argument that henceforth Parliament should receive the total public expenditure figures in PESC. 'Because of these out-of-date estimate figures, public expenditure was said to be out of control,' said one Treasury veteran. 'It was a poor show.' Before Parliamentary reformers could produce their proposals, the Chancellor, in April 1969, had brought forth the Treasury's own proposal: to present annually to Parliament the PESC White Paper on public expenditure prospects.

The Treasury interest in enhancing parliamentary activity – up to a point – continued a historically well-established partnership. It was the Treasury which had a century earlier sought unsuccessfully to ensure a debate on the audit reports. In 1965, the Chief Secretary to the Treasury had expressed a similar conviction that Parliament should seek the publication and debate of PESC expenditure projections, both their rate of growth and allocation.[32] The Select Committee, unlike its successor in 1968, failed to take the hint. Though somewhat exaggerated, there is therefore some truth in the remark of a Treasury official closely connected with these events. 'One can fairly say that the growing publicity and Parliamentary concern is due to Treasury effort. In essence, what has been happening is the Executive pressing this information on a Parliament showing few signs of interest. You just can't pretend that the annual PESC publicity and debate has been produced at the request, much less pressure, of Parliament.'

M.P.'s efforts to increase Parliamentary involvement in public spending have therefore been curtailed in the first instance because Treasury men as well as Parliamentary reformers were in-

32. H.C. 303 (1965–6) appendix 1 and testimony pp. 101 ff.

terested in the shape of the outcome. The changes often have not been an outstanding success because the parties involved in creating them had different ideas about the uses of Parliament and different definitions of success. To take only one example, the handful of interested M.P.s had urged that a debate on the spending total and priorities should be held in June, before the Cabinet had considered and agreed on the PESC report; the Executive was adamant in restricting the debate until November–December, i.e., a retrospective discussion following the appearance of the annual PESC White Paper. 'We wanted to be in on the formulative stages,' said an M.P., 'but the government would have none of it.' The 1968 Select Committee on Procedure, which proposed the 1970 reforms, should have been left in little doubt. Senior officials (and a number of M.P.s) made it clear before the reforms were introduced that they did not regard Parliament as entitled to the information behind ministerial decisions. This raised 'some fairly major issues of the position of Ministers vis-à-vis Parliament. ... This takes us into deep waters. You talk about enabling Parliament to make decisions.' [33]

The same divergence between reformers' aspirations and the Executive's sense of Parliament's proper place has followed the work of the Expenditure Committee itself. Requests for the economic assessments, which are juxtaposed to suggest ceilings in public spending, have been clumsily skirted; sometimes they are discounted as unimportant and at other times the assessments are said to be too important to be trusted to Parliament. To reveal this internal information would, the government fears, expose the Executive to the risk of being impaled on its own projections. The costing of options and advice going to spending ministers have been ruled outside the bounds of proper Parliamentary concern and potentially embarrassing to ministers and officials. The Central Policy Review Staff has refused to testify on the grounds that internal advice in the government cannot be discussed with Parliament. While the subcommittees of the Expenditure Committee were established to try and get inside spending departments – assessing their development of objectives and priorities, the spending implications of their policy choices, and their success in obtaining objectives – the departments have been more than a little reluctant to participate in such self-exposure. Not only the

33. H.C. 410 (1968–9), testimony 12 March 1969, p. 79.

PAR reports, but even the list of yearly PAR topics has been regarded as outside the preserve of Parliament. In essence, the Expenditure Committee has been told that decisions about public spending are the business of the Executive and the Executive alone. '... This is a process which all Governments up to now have preferred to do behind closed doors,' Sir Samuel Goldman, then Second Permanent Secretary of the Treasury, told the Committee. 'I do not believe that Ministers would want to show either to Parliament or to the public at large that they had found it necessary to cut back the original [PESC] projections as put to them, by something on the order of £500 million and they choose to do it in this, that and the other way. This is something that goes to the very heart of Government and, indeed, of politics.' Embarrassment would result from 'a Minister having to justify in a much wider and less informed arena his actions'.[34]

Apart from any questions of arrogance, retentiveness, and self-protection in officials – present though these sometimes are – there are important principles at stake. Since officials believe in keeping the machine running smoothly, they are not interested in seeing important community relationships and understandings among political administrators upset. Since the Treasury believes in controlling expenditures, it is not interested in exposing the compromises necessary to such control. These sentiments, as well as the customary postulation of the ancient Treasury–Parliament partnership, were well expressed by the Second Permanent Secretary of the Treasury:

I think every Government would be less successful in achieving Parliament's purpose of containing public expenditure within a desirable figure if each minister's discussions and each minister's achievements were to be searchlighted.... If every minister of every department were put in the position that he had to justify every single step... he would insist, as far as it was

34. Sir Samuel Goldman, Evidence to the Expenditure (General Sub-committee), H.C. 549 (1970–1), pp. 24–5, 33–4. There was something touching in the Committee members who inquired a year later if officials might be embarrassed by having to supply information both to Ministers and to the Expenditure Committee. There was something telling in the reply of the Treasury Second Permanent Secretary: 'I do not regard this as an embarrassing question at all. I have no hesitation whatever in replying that officials can only serve one master, their Minister or the Government collectively.' H.C. 62 (1971–2), p. 63.

open to him, on every single item of departmental expenditure being included. If anything was of public political controversy, he would insist to the point of resigning and you would have an enormous turnover of ministers, a much increased public expenditure and the result would be pretty chaotic.'[35]

Certainly not all officials inside or outside the Treasury would agree with this argument but enough do to ensure that the Executive volunteers no information about its internal spending deliberations. Parliament might be useful for generating pressures to bring the spending departments into line; it might help reduce ignorance and misunderstanding of the Executive's spending plans. Parliament is not to become a contributing member of the expenditure community.

Our account would be totally misleading, however, if it suggested that the Executive has been a fatal constraint either on the Expenditure Committee's work or on PESC debate in Parliament. What the evidence does indicate is that the withholding of information has scotched any euphoric idea that the Executive would welcome Parliament with open arms into the formulative stages of expenditure policy. But apart from this refusal, the Executive –and civil servants in particular – has actually offered the Expenditure Committee and its six subcommittees an unprecedented amount of raw material for doing its own work and analysis. Far from being churlish, the Treasury has gone to unusual lengths to accommodate requests of the Expenditure Committee for a great deal of new information. The 1971 and 1972 PESC White Papers, for example, took great pains to point out the recommendations of the Expenditure Committee which had been followed : estimating changes were separated from policy changes in spending projections, one version of the medium-term economic assessment was provided, receipts were specified, and a beginning was made at comparison with earlier years. Treasury officials know that refusing other information, and particularly the equivocation surrounding economic assessments, has meant that 'we are left in an unsatisfactory and suspect posture. We appear positively bloody-minded.' But even less would the Treasury like to be in the cut and dried position of asserting what definitely never can be supplied to Parliament. As much as possible, they want to keep

35. H.C. 549 (1970–1), pp. 33–4.

their options open; moreover many officials genuinely believe that the expenditure process will be improved if Members of Parliament can be helped to understand and support PESC and the improvements that the Treasury desires. As always, they know the value of trustful dealings. 'Our feeling is,' said a Treasury official closely concerned with Parliament, 'that if we can keep the system moving, showing that we are keeping faith, then we can put up with our not-very-good superficial appearance. Others will see that the thing is gradually evolving and that we're gradually giving them what they want. This year you'll see we've gone to a lot of trouble to give the Committee the tables they want and a full written explanation of the figures they've asked for. We try to make a tolerable response to what they want.' He might have added that those who complain loudest about the lack of information are usually those who have not bothered to glance at the wealth of data already produced for the Expenditure Committee in its first several years.

Want of information has certainly been only a minor reason for the failure of Parliamentary reform to live up to the expectations of its founders. Far more important is the fact that these expectations were themselves based on a largely idealised, unrealistic version of the Executive process with which Parliament was supposedly trying to keep pace. The following appraisal formed the basis of the 1969 Parliamentary proposals for the two-day PESC debate and Expenditure Committee: 'In [the Executive's expenditure planning], priorities will be increasingly chosen after analysis by function or objectives – that is to say, by reference to the real object of the expenditure – and after consideration of the possible alternative priorities and the benefits to be expected, of the resources likely to be available and of the phasing of the expenditure over years.' From the evidence of the preceding chapters, this scarcely can be regarded as anything more than an over-intellectualised caricature of the real-life expenditure process. Within the Committee's own minutes of evidence there was ample evidence from seasoned officials concerning the limited prospects for systematic comparisons of alternatives and decisions on priorities. Asked about the possibility of presenting Parliament with the alternatives presented to ministers through PESC, Sir Richard Clarke observed that 'alternatives very rarely arise in this way.... It is terribly difficult for Ministers to have that argument in public in the form in which they originally had it.' In discussing new analytic techniques, such as cost–benefit analysis and output budgeting, Sir Richard had a tempting line trailed before him. 'In effect then, Sir Richard, you are saying it is not that you do not think there is a future for applying this kind of thing to your Ministry [of Technology], or to a large part of your Ministry, but that as yet the technique has not yet been perfected?' His answer was to the point: 'We do not know how to do it, and it will be a long time before we do. It is a useful discipline.'[36]

A similar preoccupation with finding the simple key to expenditure decision-making has characterised much of the subsequent work of the Expenditure Committee. Give us, the Expenditure Committee has said, the lists of costed options lying behind expenditure choices. By now, the response should come as no surprise to our readers: there are no such meaningful lists; there is only the continuous process of expenditure decision-making. 'The Treasury could recommend no short-cut to us; the possible choices emerge from the full consideration of each individual area of policy.' What, the M.P.s had asked, is the magical formula that determines the acceptable trend of public spending in relation to economic resources? Probe as they would, the Committee could obtain no clear answer from Treasury officials. '... Private consumption, public investment, the requirements of the balance of payments ... unemployment ... productive potential ... [spending] plans are not rigidly determined by these prospects in any numerical sense ... The relationship is a tenuous one ... an elastic one ... We are trying to say that you have not got a uniquely determined solution when you have said those things ...' The Treasury certainly does have an expenditure judgement and this does seem to set the context of ministerial decision, but officials are not dissembling when they deny the existence of any simple formula for determining total public spending. There is none.[37]

The Committee also discovered that there was no straightforward interpretation of the expenditure figures themselves. The

36. Quotations are taken from H.C. 410 (1968–9), pp. vii, 80, 83, 84.

37. Quotations and paraphrases in this and the following paragraphs are taken from H.C. 549 (1970–1), p. xv.; evidence to the Education and Arts Sub-committee, 8 March 1971, H.C. 545 (1970–1); and evidence to the General Sub-committee, 3 May 1971, H.C. 549 (1970–1), and 28 February 1972, H.C. 450 (1971–2).

series of percentage changes scarcely provides an accurate picture of priorities, depending as the figures do on the age of the programme, demographic change, climate and a host of other factors. Similarly, whether or not expenditures are committed turns out to be an uncertain judgement along a continuum ranging from statutory requirements, to spending consequent on previous decisions, to a willingness to accept the costs of a change, to moral commitments, to a chance undertaking given by a minister over the weekend. Understanding, much less participating in, the expenditure process turns out to involve more than peeking through the Executive keyhole, however much M.P.s assume government omniscience.

Ultimately the main limitation on the scope of Parliamentary expenditure reform stems less from Executive secrecy or unrealistic views of reformers and more from Members of Parliament themselves. Most do not care. One of the founding members of the Expenditure Committee summed up his experience after two years' service: 'The chief enemy of our work has been that the majority of Members don't want it or are ambivalent.' In part the reason lies in a poor choice of original topics for Committee investigation; evidence on the measurement and verification of public expenditures has little chance of interesting any but the most devoted financial buffs in the Commons. But there are much deeper reasons why M.P.s are likely to be uninterested in Parliamentary intervention in spending decisions.

A great many, probably most, backbenchers want to be in the government. They care much less about Parliament getting in on the Executive's act than in themselves joining the troupe. Numerically, the chances of doing so are good for the M.P. of the majority party. In 1970, there were no less than 79 paid posts and another 32 Parliamentary Private Secretary posts available in the government for appointments from within Parliament; with almost a third of M.P.s in any majority party bound to be appointed to some post in the Government, the attractions of the Executive are obvious and alluring. At the same time it is not obvious that service on a Parliamentary committee advances the M.P.'s chances for getting ahead. Some may feel that marked prominence in committee work is a way of impressing leaders, especially in opposition, but the point is debatable. At least as many are likely to feel it is a good way of becoming known as too clever, troublesome, and permanent backbench material. Besides, a reputation as a sharp debater may serve political career prospects just as well and quite possibly better.

Politics is, of course, about more than policy and Parliament is, among other things, a running partisan battle between Government and Opposition. With a little exaggeration and much bitterness, one of the originators of the Expenditure Committee idea declared, 'The problem is that for most of my colleagues [in the House of Commons] the main function is to continue the party conflict. Parliament is admirably suited for supporting or opposing, for making scenes rather than participating in policy creation.' Undoubtedly the political battle matters to all M.P.s and to some it is almost all that matters. For the Opposition, the primary aim is not to become involved in policy making but to take over the full range of executive power after the next election. Through constant teasing, chiding, and searching out chinks through which to stab home some political embarrassment, each side tries to demonstrate its own competence and the other's incompetence. Members instrumentally inclined toward policy are likely to find many colleagues on the Right, Left and usually apathetic Centre far more interested in scoring political points than in understanding the intricacies of spending decisions and narrow options open to any government. One M.P. recalls the comment of Michael Foot from the Left : 'not knowing the facts has never hampered me up to now, so I see no reason to change my views.' The same orientation can be heard from Enoch Powell on the Right : 'I should be prepared to argue that the more information Members have the less effective they are likely to be in debate. . . .'[38] Knowing too much can inhibit repartee.

But it would be a mistake to conclude that M.P.s as a group are interested only in the partisan uses of spending and policy questions.[39] Some Members have a concern as abiding as any political adminstrator's in the allocation of public resources and even the most analytically comatose M.P. is at some time on some issue likely to worry through a piece of substantive policy. Backbenchers nursing their career prospects often want to affect some

38. The quotations are taken from Macintosh, 'Specialist Committees', pp. 11–12; and H.C. 303 (1964–5), p. 81.

39. We are particularly indebted to Professor Anthony King for his helpful comments on this subject.

course of government action once they arrive in the government. Likewise, a portion of the chiding and probing in the House seeks not only to embarrass ministers but to affect a particular aspect of government policy. In fields such as education, hospitals, housing and regional policy, many M.P.s press important policy questions and occasionally achieve results. Yet among even these M.P.s there is apparently little interest in the expenditure decisions affecting education, hospitals, housing and regions. How can one account for this paradox?

There are undoubtedly some Members who miss the connection and have yet to learn the lesson which has been gradually and painfully acquired within the Executive, the lesson strongly reinforced by PESC: policy ends and spending means are not readily detachable from each other. Those who want to influence public policy and leave expenditure decisions to others are likely to be incapable of significantly affecting either. Many other Members, however, see the connection but are likely to feel that it is worth their while to ignore it. Analysing policy and expenditure choices calls for sustained, full-time attention. It meets no constituency needs (at least not directly), generates very few headlines, and scores no points for the party. M.P.s may be interested in subject matter but they are also interested in a number of other things. For those facing the full-time demands of part-time legislative, constituency and party work, policy analysis can seem an expensive luxury.

In one respect, Parliament is to the Executive as the Treasury is to spending departments: it must depend on others to do most of the work and provide most of the information it needs. But while departments are also dependent on the Treasury, it is less certain who needs Parliament's active participation. Certainly little is likely to change unless Members themselves feel the need for a more active expenditure role. No Government can ever be expected to yield up the internal information and policy analysis behind its spending decisions, but there is considerable raw material potentially available to hard-headed questioning and analysis. Co-operation from political administrators will obviously vary but the comment of one senior Treasury man was to the point and echoed by other officials: 'The fact is that in the Expenditure Committee system they have all they need – short of spoonfeeding them information they can't expect the government to give. They have the machinery but they must work it, formulate their own choices and get the information. Except for the General Subcommittee we have had very little feedback. The other subcommittees are tending to behave as the old estimates committees, choosing something of interest to the chairman and spending all their time chasing down little alleyways. How does one get these chaps to look at big things?'

Meanwhile, the handful of M.P.s who value the possibility of a direct role for Parliament in the expenditure process continue throwing their frail lines across to political administrators. Here and there links or even mutual confidence may be found, but Parliament is far from being an active participant, critic or ally in the expenditure community. The closer this or that M.P. becomes involved, the more likely he is to be turned on by his fellow M.P.s and labelled a technician, accountant, empire-builder and/or Government lackey. In his darker moments, any such Member must invariably ask himself, why bother? It is not a new question. The M.P. most actively involved in establishing the Public Accounts Committee in the mid-nineteenth century, Sir Francis Baring, continually lamented 'that the House showed so little anxiety with regard to this subject'.[40]

40. Quoted in Chubb, *The Control of Public Expenditure*, p. 28.

6 There Must Be a Better Way: PAR and the New Rationalism

We made a big mistake as to the realities of power.
Businessman consultant to the Government

Mr. East [businessman-adviser in the Treasury] will say how we ought to go about it and Mr. Couzens [Treasury undersecretary] will say what we are in fact doing.
Treasury Deputy Secretary introducing PAR to the Expenditure Committee (Steering Subcommittee), 27 January 1972

You're always wondering if you shoot off your mouth about somebody else's department the next minute you'll meet that chap in committee or tête-à-tête and you have destroyed your relations with him.
A minister

It appears to us that adequate provision has not been made in the past for the organised acquisition of facts and information, and for the systematic application of thought, as preliminary to the settlement of policy and its subsequent administration.
Report on the Machinery of Government, 1918, Cmnd.9230, p. 6

To ASK 'how shall public money be spent' and 'what should government do' are kindred, though not identical, questions. Decisions about public expenditure shade imperceptibly into decisions about public policy and more subtly still into judgements on the general welfare of society. No person in the British Isles is immune from the consequences of these decisions.

Political administrators know and appreciate this connection better than anyone else. Contemporary governmental reforms express their efforts to find better ways of linking expenditure and policy decisions. Like PESC, Programme Analysis and Review (PAR) and the Central Policy Review Staff (CPRS) are changes at the core of British government, changes about which the public knows almost nothing. Like PESC, these reforms are firmly rooted in insiders' dissatisfactions with the immediate past. No public outcry has created them. PAR and CPRS are largely self-induced changes.

If the organisation of policy advice and analysis were merely a question of proper management or expert knowledge, it would scarcely be a problem of British Government. But efforts to improve (that is, make different) policy/expenditure decisions necessarily run up against the most fundamental political issues. To reform the procedures for advising ministers raises questions about the working relationships not only between ministers and civil servants, but between some ministers and other ministers, between some senior officials and others. If what the Cabinet needs is a collective briefing to complement its aggregation of individual departmental briefings, there are profound implications for the pecking order of ministers and for the future roles of the central departments. The politics of advice is pervasive because both advice and advisers impinge on the established ties of kinship and culture in the Executive community.

For students of British central government, the PAR procedure and CPRS think-tank provide invaluable opportunities. No outsider could have devised such appropriate natural experiments. For if one wishes to know how departments relate to each other, what could be better than compelling them to expose their inner working to one another? PAR is supposed to do just that. If you want to know how to break into the Cabinet system, then what could be better than watching Lord Rothschild and his CPRS attempt to do it? By observing how the operators of PAR and CPRS have attempted to make their will felt, we can learn » great deal about how power treats knowledge in British government.

These recent innovations are deliberately shrouded in mystery. The secrecy is not inadvertent and peripheral but purposive and central; it covers far more than the content of advice, an understandably sensitive area. Even the most mundane procedural facts, such as the membership of the PAR Committee, are treated as deep state secrets. No outsider is supposed to know how (if at all) PAR helps ministers decide about each other's programmes. No one is supposed to know how (if at all) CPRS helps the Cabinet function as a collectivity. The politics of advice to ministers, singly or as a group, is decreed to be forbidden fruit to the public. Presumably, the worry is less that the public will fall from grace by eating from this tree of knowledge, and more that political administrators, naked in a sinful world, will lose their aura of original innocence.

So what? No one appears determined to know. If Cabinet ministers are willing to accept the incredible notion that they cannot be informed about vital economic decisions in the Budget because of the remote possibility of a minor leak in regard to tax rates, there may be very little that anyone can do for them. Likewise, better advice is likely to be wasted on those who feel comfortable with the idea that the chairmanship and even jurisdiction of Cabinet committees must be state secrets on the grounds that Members of Parliament might somehow think that these chairmen rather than the departmental minister are responsible for the subject matter. No one, it seems, stops to ask whether ministerial difficulties might not in some way be connected with the practices they seek to shield from public view. The furtive approach to the politics of advice has resulted in a quagmire of inconsistency and supposition. Silence does not heal all wounds; it only helps them fester. In the end, it is not merely the outsiders who are misled, but the insiders who are confused.

Government Reform, British Style

By the end of the 1960s, few insiders were particularly happy with the way their machine was working. Public commentators were preoccupied with the Fulton Report and its analysis of civil service manpower; academics were tabulating officials' social background, educational record, and reading habits to demonstrate – of all things – civil service elitism. But those closest to events were privately raising more relevant questions about the organisation of Cabinet Government and ministerial decision-making.

Labour ministers felt they were being badly served and had the scars to prove it. Particularly distressing after the 1967 devaluation was, in the words of Lord George Wigg, 'the age-old system which permitted Treasury ministers to take decisions affecting Departmental Ministers without effective consultation with them. Every Minister to whom I talked that weekend felt acutely that the Treasury were solving their own problems regardless of the difficulties being created for others.' [1] To deflect these criticisms, Roy Jenkins, Chancellor of the Exchequer from 1968, began talking privately to key ministers in order to get their reactions to his proposed policies before they were announced. But the bitterness over devaluation, the sense of helplessness in which ministers found themselves propelled toward courses on which they could get no independent advice and which predetermined so much of what happened, meant that this sort of informal gesture, though better than nothing, was still not good enough.

Labour ministers were too busy to do much about these complaints, but not so the unemployed Conservatives. The Opposition had not only time but a vested interest in demonstrating how much more they could do to improve the government machine. One reason Labour had bad policies was that they had bad procedures; solid Tory business sense would put it right. But unknown to the politicians, the origins of PAR and CPRS were also being weaved from another strand of experience – senior civil servants themselves. They too were dissatisfied with what looked like drift, improvisation, and diminishing margins for political decision at the centre of British government. They too were looking for ways of improving the machine's performance. If the Conservatives had not already been working on their new style of government by the 1970 election, PAR and CPRS would never have been started so quickly thereafter; if the civil service had not already been inclined to and working toward similar ideas,

1. Lord George Wigg, *Memoirs*, quoted in the *Sunday Times*, 30 April 1972, p. 33.

the reforms would have never gone so far. To say this is not to prejudge how far and how quickly any real change has occurred. The result has been something which neither Conservative Opposition or civil service gadflies intended when they started out.

What was wrong? The standard critique ran something as follows: (1) Ministers and the Cabinet agenda were overcrowded with detail; (2) there was insufficient time to discuss major strategic issues and priorities; (3) no central capability existed for analysing these major issues for the Cabinet as a whole; (4) ministers lacked sophisticated information and analysis such as that used in United States programme budgeting. The result was that resources were being allocated without much reasoned deliberation. Policy wavered and was largely reactive to events. The yearning for 'the smack of firm government' caught the mood nicely.

There was not much new in this indictment. The history of the British Cabinet since the First World War has been studded with attempts to grapple with some of the same problems. The creation of the Cabinet Secretariat and Lloyd George's 'Garden Suburb' of advisers during the First World War, the standing Cabinet Committee of Civil Research and 1918 Report of the Machinery of Government Committee, the 1929 Economic General Staff, Prime Minister Churchill's own Statistical Section under his personal adviser (F. A. Lindemann) in 1940, the 1951–3 experiment with 'Overlord' ministers above several groups of departments – all these and more were attempts to improve the capabilities of the centre and to organise information and men more effectively toward the 'big' issues.

The historical results had not been altogether encouraging for reformers. The Cabinet Secretariat and Garden Suburb of the First World War quickly encountered hostility because both were staffed by outsiders whose relations with career civil servants were, to put it mildly, strained. The Prime Minister's advisers of the Garden Suburb faded with the flowers of St James's Park. Only by threatening to resign and winning the new Prime Minister's personal intervention was the Cabinet Secretary, Hankey, able to defeat Treasury efforts at absorbing the Secretariat.[2] The Committee on Civil Research added little to the Cabinet's work;

2. A candid, if one-sided, account of the struggle is in Stephen Roskill, *Hankey, Man of Secrets* (London: Collins, 1972), II, 309–20. On Cabinet

the vague thought that there was greater potential for rationality was no substitute for specific applications. The Economic General Staff of 1929, with John Maynard Keynes and Ernest Bevin as members, was no lightweight, but the reactions to it were instructive. 'It looks to me,' wrote the Cabinet Secretary to the Deputy Secretary in the Cabinet Office, 'like a feckless duplication of work already done quite efficiently by departments. I hope the Cabinet Office will be able to keep clear of it.'[3] Despite the efforts of Keynes and Bevin, the General Economic Staff came to little. The lesson, presumably, was that a new advisory machine does not do much good if no one knows what to do, or if the Nation's leaders are in the grips of a fallacious theory; Cabinet documents amply testify to the profound impact of deflationary economics.

Prime Minister Churchill's Statistical Section owed loyalty to him alone and dissolved when Churchill left. Churchill's later attempt to institute Departmental Overlords in peacetime was even less successful. Amidst heated Parliamentary debate, it turned out that the Opposition believed the difficulty lay in naming specific people (particularly peers) as co-ordinators; Parliament knew who they were and yet could not question them about their duties. Churchill argued that publicity concerning men who dealt with such large issues of policy was desirable, but was repeatedly beaten back with the assertion that formal ministerial responsibility to Parliament was being weakened. That was that. Parliament gained a famous victory by insisting it be kept in the dark; if told nothing, Parliament would be owed less. Cabinet committees can proliferate and real decision-making authority move to them, but so long as the name of the chairman is not announced, nervous observers will not be shaken out of the fictions about who holds power. Those who insist that no news is good news cannot expect to be enlightened. But at least we now know why governments say they cannot announce the chairmen of Cabinet committees.

---

reform in general, see D. N. Chester and F. G. Willson, *The Organization of British Central Government 1914–1964* (London: George Allen and Unwin, Ltd, 1968); Hans Daalder, *Cabinet Reform in Britain, 1914–1963* (Stanford: Stanford University Press, 1963).

3. Thomas Jones, *Whitehall Diary*, (London: Oxford University Press, 1969), II, 219.

In the post-war years, economic advice to the government invariably has been concentrated in the Treasury and Chancellor of the Exchequer. The Economic Planning Board of 1947, begot the National Economic Development Council of 1961, begot the Department of Economic Affairs, begot the 1965 National Plan, begot.... Well, several officials from the defunct DEA have become prominent elsewhere in government, but what remained at the end of the 1960s was a strengthened Treasury, a Cabinet Office which had made itself an integral part of central administration, and the same sets of problems that led before to dissatisfaction with these official arrangements.

No matter what was done the economic situation did not appear to be improving. Although the civil servants were evidently loyal to announced governmental decisions, there were sneaking suspicions that they might be less than eager or able to propose the kinds of alternatives that governments needed to hear. Ministers could not say just what these alternatives should be like or they would not have needed the advice. Ministers were still rewarded for pursuing departmental interests, but the sense of collectivity remained a will-o'-the-wisp. Under attack, ministers would give assurance that a government-wide sense of priorities existed but in private they expressed doubt, even to the point of acknowledging that their own actions contributed to the difficulty. There had to be a better way.

To the Conservative Opposition, management science offered that way. The Conservative loss of office in 1964 coincided with the period of euphoria on programme budgeting and systems analysis in the United States. Bright young men, such as Mark Schrieber from the Conservative Research Department and David Howell from the new crop of M.P.s, could be found poring over accounts of programme budgeting in the Ministry of Defence. During the next two years, the Conservative Systems Research Centre and Public Sector Research Unit were founded to try and interest politicians in systematic analysis. Computer routines were established to help politicians see if some preference were obtainable within the context of their other preferences and resource constraints. At one time there was even rumoured to be a computer console in Edward Heath's room at the House of Commons. What was British government coming to?

As new Leader of the Conservative Party, Edward Heath was

eager for new ideas. It was largely thanks to his efforts that the new breed of technicians did not disappear under the weight of opposition from individuals in the Conservative Party Research Department and sceptical Conservative politicians. 'Heath stuck his neck out and fought for us,' the researchers stated. 'He had to virtually take on his own staff and defend us.' In March 1966 a press release from the new Leader declared his own faith that a war on waste based on studies of American systems analysis techniques would result in dramatic savings. Heath proposed a three point plan: '(1) A Central Cost Effectiveness Department, responsible to the Prime Minister will be set up; (2) Every Minister will be instructed to work out a cost reduction programme for his Department; (3) Any undue secrecy which Whitehall imposes on the discussions of policy will be swept away.' (Press release 10131, Conservative Party, 21 March 1966.) Efficiency studies were winning out, but policy analysis was not yet in.

Sound business sense was still more relevant to the Conservatives than new-fangled computers. Government, they reasoned, like big business, required modern management; party leaders decided that they needed a team of businessmen to help create new government machinery and procedures. Two of the Nation's leading firms of business consultants were hired to advise the leadership, and forty-one large corporations were asked to recommend managers it would hurt to lose but who could be available on a part-time basis before the next election and full-time afterwards for perhaps two years. Eighteen businessmen were finally selected from such firms as Shell International, Marks and Spencer, RTZ, and Hambros. In the autumn of 1968 a two-week seminar was held in a country retreat with a dozen or so members of the Shadow Cabinet, approximately an equal number of businessmen and younger M.P.s, several ex-permanent secretaries and ex-ministers. The politicians talked about their experiences and problems; the businessmen suggested how principles of corporate planning would help.

During the eighteen months prior to the June 1970 election, two small working parties of consultants, businessmen and several young Conservatives, analysed British government. One group dealt with procurement and hiving-off government activities; another group of four, and the one of concern to us, dealt with the reorganisation of central government. Their original idea was to imagine two separate parts of government : a planning activity to decide objectives and a funding activity to disburse money. It was an ill-starred division. The management experts began by looking at the Treasury and at its system for controlling expenditures. They liked what PESC did, but they also believed that the expenditure process was oriented to inputs and did not analyse the quality of programmes. The businessmen also looked at the structure of the Cabinet Office (in so far as anyone could tell them what that was) and 'found they did a damn good job on process and procedure, seeing to it that the agenda did not overburden ministers, and that they had the relevant papers. But there was no analysis, the work was almost purely secretarial. Thus, there was obviously a need for an analytical facility at the centre.' What about the Treasury? 'It was doing this by default without anyone telling it to. It didn't seem entirely right because the Treasury had its own special financial interests.' Thus the Cabinet appeared to the businessmen to be missing a collective political dimension in policy advice.

Fortified by the belief that there was a general theory of resource management that could be applied anywhere, the business team pulled together the ideas that eventually became Programme Analysis and Review. One of their members was dispatched on the obligatory trip to the United States, where he soon discovered that some of the bloom had gone off the rose of programme budgeting. Officials in the United States were having their own difficulties resolving similar problems – how should the analytical role be split between Presidental advisers and the Office of Management and Budget (or between the Cabinet Office, the Treasury and the departments). Nevertheless programme budgeting as then practised in America was the only show in town, and the British businessmen modelled their original suggestions on it. Each department was to produce a comprehensive programme structure ahead of the annual PESC exercise. This structure would somehow show how departments' various activities were related to each other. Ministers would then be able to select and authorise specific, in-depth studies (PARs) of policies within that broader context. These analyses would force departments to justify their existing programmes, enforce costing by objectives, and provide lead time on decisions.

PAR was only part of the story; it was meant to fit into a larger scheme in which a Central Capability Department would do for government what corporate planning allegedly did for business. The politicians in the study group wanted a means both of reminding government about its election promises and of holding the administrative apparatus faithful to them. That is why, in one reformer's words, they felt that creation of a central unit 'at the highest political level with the job of analysing and pushing departments into self-analysis across the whole waterfront' was 'the key instrument in establishing the new style of government'. Since the departments were down below making proposals for programmes, and the Treasury was in the middle checking their analysis, the business/political team reasoned there was a need for a central unit above it all to look at the whole picture. Originally the idea was for this central capability to be composed of the public expenditure side of the Treasury, the management functions of the Civil Service Department, and the Cabinet Office, topped off with the creation of a new Central Capability Unit reporting directly to the Prime Minister and the Cabinet. Strategic planning and expenditure control would be joined.

A final concern of the businessmen was stillborn. They had found that 'an appallingly large number of ministers were people whose training as journalists, teachers or barristers 'left them totally unsuited for major decision-making'. Most of them had never learned co-operative behaviour, or delegation, or 'self-administration' to arrange their time priorities. The business consultants saw the training of future ministers in decision-making procedures as a crucial problem. Politicians seemed to feel that they could do without this advice. There were a few attempts at organising more seminars but these came to nothing. Forced to choose in their evangelising between the education of transient ministers and the continuous influence of officials, the businessmen would eventually, as one later said, 'opt for continuity. The civil servants are always there, ministers aren't.'

As it happened, the surprise election in 1970 made any idea of training future ministers purely academic. The businessmen were unable to meet with the incoming ministers to discuss PAR and CPRS at any length, let alone remould the personal habits of these politicians. Incoming ministers probably did not understand or fully appreciate the kinds of behaviour on their part required to make PAR and CPRS work. Conservative politicians, or at least the Prime Minister, had agreed to something, but no one could say whether they knew what they were getting into or whether, once they found out, they might not try to get out of it.

Meanwhile, back at the civil service, parallel events and discussions were taking place that would have at least as much impact on PAR and CPRS as the businessmen. Events jumped ahead of theory in 1968 when the Labour Government, in the wake of devaluation, took a serious look at controlling the size of the public sector and converted the small steps that had followed since the 1961 Plowden Report into the powerful PESC system. It was a change of historic dimensions, but by 1970 it was clear to many Treasury officials that PESC needed further development and that this should entail an increased effort at evaluating individual programmes and their results. PESC, as we have seen, entrenches old policies against new ones. Whether or not an activity should be performed at all does not get settled – indeed it is actively suppressed through PESC. Once the businessmen did get into government, they found that the Treasury was well aware of PESC's limitations and that their earlier criticisms of the input rather than output orientation 'was a bit unfair. The Treasury,' recalled one consultant, 'was getting deeper into dialogue with the departments than we thought and this led to more questioning of programmes than we thought existed.' The Treasury was eager to extend PESC into analysing individual programmes and their results, but as always it was difficult to arouse political interest.

The Treasury too sent its emissaries to America, sceptical men who returned full of caution at the immense size of the task and the powerful resistance to be encountered in introducing programme budgeting. There was something to the ideas but the Treasury did not swallow as much about programme structures, output budgets, etc., as did the businessmen. They would start slowly, encouraging a few of the departments with bright and interested young men to try their hand at programme budgeting in limited areas of policy. If it came to nothing, not much would be lost. Treasury men were prepared for a long campaign and the usual, steady accretion of change.

As luck would have it, the new Conservative Government held strong views about the need for more policy analysis of individual programmes. The Treasury found itself 'pushing against an open door'. Officials at the Treasury wished to grab this opportunity with both hands, but they also wanted to avoid falling into the errors they observed in the United States – over-ambition, form in favour of substance, and hostilities from departments. They also did not want to lose the power they had in the guise of strengthening it. They would resist the efforts of the business–political team to split off the Public Spending Group and to give it additional analytical capability. The Treasury preferred to work with their own undersecretaries who already had experience and to rely, as always, on gaining the co-operation of the departments.

A third line of development had proceeded with little knowledge of what the Conservatives in opposition were doing. Conversations among a group of senior permanent secretaries identified three major gaps in the Executive's decision-making machinery. The largest gap was the difficulty of finding out what the government as a whole wanted. The Treasury did not formally have a view on individual programmes and seemed more interested in totals than specific expenditure purposes. Yet, as the only central analytic capability, the Treasury was in a position to be blamed for everything that went wrong. The PESC system, they believed, was informative about the cost of policies but not about what a department should do if it were forced to subtract or add several per cent to its base. The whole thing was done by push-and-pull among departments. A related gap involved policies that did not make it worthwhile for the Treasury to bother or had only an indirect effect on expenditure. Penal policy, for example, involved sentencing and treatment of prisoners, and while not leading to immediate spending, ultimately effected enormous expenditure on prisons. Yet such policies did not receive the PESC treatment. The third gap concerned matters over the five-year time horizon of PESC. Certain longer-term policies, such as pensions and education, were being analytically short-changed. The senior officials wondered whether the Treasury might be compromised by trying to provide more analysis for the government as a whole; departments might reckon that this was just a device for screwing expenditures down further. Perhaps new arrangements outside the Treasury were desirable.

What should be done? The senior officials played with the idea, modelled somewhat on the Executive Office of the President, of creating a Prime Minister's Department out of the Treasury's

Public Spending Group, Civil Service Department and Cabinet Office, somehow welding them all together. All these central units would be responsible to the Cabinet as a whole, but first and foremost to the Prime Minister and the chairmen of Cabinet committees. The officials concerned were preparing to test these ideas when the 1970 election intervened. They, too, discovered that their views and those of the new Government were convergent. Some PAR-type procedure seemed necessary to ask fundamental questions about ongoing programmes; some sort of central capability/CPRS seemed likely to improve the collective deliberations of ministers.

At this early moment the exact organisational structure was in some doubt. PAR lay in a limbo somewhere between the Treasury, the Civil Service Department (CSD), and CPRS. Six businessmen, led by R. J. Meyjes of Shell International, had been brought into government and were initially housed in the CSD, so that it appeared to be the place to get PAR launched. At the same time, while the form of CPRS was still being hotly debated, it appeared sufficient to say that the new unit might deal with analytical questions that were not within the purview of a single department. When, after a good six months' delay, Lord Rothschild was appointed head of CPRS, he was not overly enamoured of PAR, and so the connections between the two mechanisms were placed further in doubt. Something was about to happen, but only time would tell what it would be.

PAR Meets the Machine: Or, the Fine Art of Obtaining Pearls from Clams

> *Prime Minister Heath:* What we are trying to do is to take each aspect of work in a department and say: 'Right, for this year we're going to analyse this, see what its origin was, what its purpose and cost are.'
>
> Then when it's been analysed by the PAR team, Ministers collectively can see what this department's up to. So this is also a major means of seeing the particular activities of individual departments.
>
> *Interviewer:* What's Whitehall saying about all this revolution?

Prime Minister: They find it rather exciting.
Evening Standard, *1 June 1972*

Why was PAR moved out of the Civil Service Department? 'I can't say, it's a sensitive matter.'
Treasury official

It's like sticking sand in an oyster shell; the departments have got to do something about it.
Treasury official

PAR did not develop as the businessmen had first intended while working with the Conservatives in opposition. Any idea of a super-central department under the Prime Minister had – as we shall see in the next chapter – quickly floundered. Who then would be in charge of PAR and its fundamental requestioning of government programmes?

Immediately after the June 1970 election, PAR had followed the team of businessmen into the Civil Service Department. But the businessmen soon found that they could not make PAR work where it was. 'Putting PAR in the CSD caused the Treasury to be anti,' one explained. 'The Treasury wanted to take it over. They saw, as we did, PAR as an extension of PESC, but they were against it if the CSD was mucking about.' Another explained that 'we tried to do something outside of the power centres. The CPRS was new and CSD was not in a position to help. The only person with real teeth was the Treasury. It was a bit dumb of us not to see that.' [4]

What occurred was scarcely a one-sided, power-grab by the Treasury. Most of the businessmen themselves soon became convinced through hard experience that PAR would not happen without the Treasury in charge. (Far from being alienated by the takeover, the businessman directly responsible for PAR indicated

4. The businessmen received the usual introduction to the Treasury. 'On the first day of the new government we businessmen all had a meeting with the Treasury officials. They rubbed their hands. "Lovely to have you here. We're so looking forward to it – great work to be done. Now we're sure you will want to get stuck into it right away, so we have prepared these papers (stacks 3 feet high) to tell you how we work – books on the Treasury, Select Committee hearings, etc." ' The outsiders replied they had read all these things and on this and that page had these questions. 'If we had crawled back in our hole with those papers, we'd have never come out again.'

acceptance of this view by moving from the Civil Service Department to the Treasury.) Here is how one businessman described his experience. 'In dealing with departments, we discovered they had great internal problems involving reorganisation and that they were very busy. The CSD comes along and the departments say "this is all terribly interesting but we really can't take it on board now". When you didn't have the Treasury with you the departments would resist. Not that they love the Treasury, but they do listen.' A number of departmental officials confirmed that 'The breakthrough in PAR occurred when the Treasury took it over. Most of us felt it was here to stay and would become a serious part of our activities.'

The management experts had rediscovered that British government community is a loose federation of departments. 'It depends,' as one businessman observed, 'on an existing network of personal relationships and only the Treasury has this network throughout Whitehall.' The Treasury's value was not that it could give imperative commands to other departments; far from it. As former line officers in their companies, most of the businessmen spent several months unlearning ideas of hierarchical command. Their turn to the Treasury was consistent with acting like consultants, who persuade others what to do, rather than like managers, who issue marching orders. In the Treasury, PAR had a chance of becoming an established part of civil service society by being linked to the one solvent of government – having to pay the bills. The migration of PAR also signalled the businessmen's final reliance on civil servants rather than retrained ministers to carry through the new ideas. 'PAR will not be as good in the Treasury as we had first wanted,' said one businessman at the time, 'but there it has a chance for continuity and survival.'

Original fears that departments would suspect the Treasury of seizing on the information gained through PAR to promote cuts proved secondary to more serious concerns. Why should they be worried about the Treasury finding out things, departmental officials told us, when there is so much exchange of information and personnel that the Treasury knows most of what is going on ('the little lies and that sort of thing') anyway? Might not the information from PAR studies be used against you? 'When you talk to the Treasury, it is on the understanding that it will always be used against you. Everything is a basis for negotiation.' What the departments did not like was the idea of having two centres to deal with on financial matters. Perhaps they preferred the known evil.

Once they understood that the departments strongly desired to deal with one central point, that the Treasury had the influence, network and manpower, and that Lord Rothschild would do nothing to take PAR into the CPRS, the businessmen went along with the inevitable. PAR became the province of the Treasury. Its centre of gravity shifted into the same Public Spending Group we have high-lighted as being so important in the general expenditure process. 'In the final analysis of sheer ability to do the work,' said a businessman, 'the engineroom of PAR is the undersecretaries of the Treasury, the chaps who know the substance of policy, the same ones who operate PESC.' Repeated Treasury testimony before House of Commons expenditure subcommittees, to the effect that PAR is a logical, inexorable development of PESC, is today the only remaining trace of the struggle to find a home for policy analysis.

There were more casualties. The management experts' idea of a comprehensive programme structure for each department, every part of which would be subjected to in-depth PAR studies, quickly proved unworkable. Since the businessmen proceeded, as one put it, 'in ignorance of United Kingdom government' (working mostly on the basis of American and United Nations' material on programme budgeting), it is not surprising that the edifice they recommended was not imported into British government. The characteristic experience of department officials attempting to develop programme budgets was that even if there was enough manpower, which there was not, the structures 'broke in our hands. The young people who were doing it very reluctantly admitted that they couldn't make it go. It was a complete waste of everybody's time.' A fair comment from one Treasury man is that 'PAR is like programme budgeting without a programme budget.' By that he means that the over-arching framework of categories, into which the individual programmes are supposed to fit, is missing but that there is analysis of one or more departmental activity each year. Official Treasury word is that work on programme structure is continuing, as indeed it is; but it is safe to say that no one is now contemplating using these categories to make actual decisions. When the ideas for PAR were laid before the Conservative Cabinet, ministers agreed that programme structure notions were too ambitious. Prompted perhaps by cautious voices from the Treasury, ministers asked, why not try to analyse a dozen or so major policy issues, bring the results to ministers, and see if the debate on them proves useful? The frail PAR craft was launched on its way.

From its outset, therefore, PAR has departed from many of the original hopes behind its creation. Location in the Treasury means that PAR is likely to exclude analyses of subjects lacking significant and immediate expenditure content. Invariably PAR is also run by the same old faces, people who are familiar with each other's problems and assumptions through the normal expenditure process. PAR has not fallen to a detached, independent group of long-term thinkers.

The Treasury is willing to give up a good deal of formal sophistication in return for winning departments' co-operation. Hoping to borrow from the successful history of PESC, the Treasury established a PAR Committee (PARC) composed of designated departmental representatives and Treasury undersecretaries and chaired by the Treasury's head of the Public Expenditure Survey Committee; about half the departmental representatives are in fact the same finance officers sitting on PESC.[5] While PARC has little important power, it does decide on the administrative housekeeping arrangements for PAR studies. The Treasury is wise enough to ensure that grievances, small in themselves but important to administrators, do not escalate to threaten the substance of the exercise. Thus PARC officials quickly decided to abandon the businessmen's flow-chart in which all PAR studies started at the same time each year, flowed up to ministers for decision in autumn, and then simmered for a month or so while officials argued about what the PAR decision meant in the money terms of PESC. PAR reports are now dealt with flexibly as they are finished at various times in the year.

There is nothing particularly unusual or new in this Treasury

5. Needless to say membership in PARC is secret, though why this is so remains a mystery to anyone who does not automatically assume that nothing should be made public. Using modes of analysis advocated in PAR studies, the amateur analyst can easily determine that a minimum of five thousand people (everyone in the department at undersecretary level and above, everyone working on a study, making at least a hundred people in each of ten departments, each with five friends) must know most of the members of PARC.

strategy. PARC and the joint discussions of PAR subjects and procedures is another instance of getting people involved together in order to increase communal pressure on the hold-outs. Nor is it lost on the departments that making PAR a 'public' process (public, that is, within the political administration) increases the pressure to participate and to do a responsible job at it. The kind of reverse bargaining involved was expressed by one permanent secretary who did not want to participate but did. 'It's a cynical point but if you go around the table and five people say they'll do a PAR, it makes it very hard on you to hold out and say you won't.' By 1972 those who did not want to do another PAR felt an obligation to go at least as far as doing a joint PAR with another department.

As a further milestone in the degeneration of government language, PAR is now both noun and verb (programmes are 'PARed'). Programme Analysis and Review has become another esoteric piece of British statecraft suggesting that the government is in possession of some wonderful ability and, if not super-wise, is at least more knowing than anyone else; the myth of the mullahs is intensified by the secrecy which lays down that no mortal in the ordinary public should know how PAR actually works. The fact is that there is little agreement on the nature of analytic studies. If men have difficulty defining what is good policy, then they are likely to be hard-put to state precisely the ingredients of a good analysis leading to better policy. Mostly there exist conventions calling for the specification of objectives, attempts at quantifying the resources involved in trying to achieve them, specifying the criterion for choice, and working out on paper how alternative programmes might be expected to operate. To say that an analysis is to be done, therefore, is only to indicate that empty spaces will be filled in and says little about the content of the resulting work.

Analytical studies under the PAR process are not the only ones around. Many more are being done in departments for their own purposes. How, then, does a PAR study differ from any other? The honest answer is that the substance of a PAR cannot differ much from the kind of analysis that has been done for years, if only because no one pretends to have discovered any new way of arriving at bright ideas. Looking at a study of energy policy that is not labelled as a PAR and the study of higher education that is called a PAR, one would be hard put to tell which is which.

Without being entirely certain of what it should be like, the Treasury is trying to provide the departments with a gentle initiation into systems analysis. Without being overly demanding, the Treasury is trying to get departments to do more than they have done. Departments are encouraged to discuss objectives, certainly not ultimate ones like peace and prosperity, nor myopic ones, like decreasing the welfare case load the next year, but something in between. Inputs can often be measured but outputs are more difficult. The Treasury line is to try and see what can be measured. No department is asked to compare different objectives because no one knows how to calculate social returns; what is compared are alternative ways of meeting similar objectives. There is talk about constraints and about concentrating on variables that are amenable to intervention by policy makers. It all adds up, hopefully, to some kind of model, a term designating a theory in which elements are related to one another so that one can determine the consequences of choice, providing he can devise a suitable criterion for making his way among the alternatives. At the Treasury, of course, words like 'criterion' and 'model' are not used. People fear someone might think they were being overly precise or, perish the thought, addicted to jargon. It is, however, all right to talk about options and guidelines for choosing among them, which comes down to the same thing.

Guidelines for a PAR analysis are thought of as proceeding in five parts. First, departments are expected to assess demand for their programmes by looking at the determinants of expenditure in the chosen area. Is it the number of criminal offences, motor-car population, number of children moving through primary school, or whatever, that is driving their expenditures up? Secondly, the department is asked to make an inquiry into the 'stock position' (or the resources being used) in carrying out the programme, such as numbers and capacities of hospitals and schools. What are the standards for determining the value of this stock and what changes can be expected over the next several years? The third area of questioning concerns the composition of current expenditures among man-power, transfer payments, commodities, and so on. The department is requested, fourth, to appraise the impact of the programme on the problem to which it is directed. What will present policies do to meet the need? How does supply compare with demand at least for five years (or longer if an outline agreement has been made with the Treasury to do so)? Fifth and finally, departments are asked to specify the options available to obtain different mixes of supply and demand, or to alter the concept of need or to consider alternatives that are not entirely within their control.[6] There is room for disagreement on all five elements and each is subject to the usual negotiation inside the community.

For whom is all this analysis being produced? PAR is almost invariably for someone else. Ask a minister and he is likely to tell you that PAR is for the department officials – very useful in clarifying their thinking. Department officials will tell you that it is the muddled ministers who need PAR, or the Treasury, or CPRS, or some other department with a dreadful lack of analysis. Things are so bad there that they actually learned something from it, but over here, we have been doing this sort of thing for years. Most department officials will insist, as did one permanent secretary, 'PAR is not set up to help departments. Let's face it, any minister or permanent secretary has a bloody hell of a time running his own staff and his own business. Unless I felt passionately about something I would not get involved with —— department. I might need him later and I don't want him buggering around in [mine].' PAR complicates their lives when they desperately wish to simplify them. 'If you just look at individual departments,' another secretary insisted, 'they get nothing out of it at all. All they do is expose the information to others. The idea of PAR must be that it strengthens planning at the centre, where they need it.'

The refrain – 'PAR is not designed to help me' – is heard everywhere. And the reason is clear. PAR, like any mode of formal analysis, is an insult to the organisation concerned. It suggests that they have been sitting around for years mindlessly carrying out their activities without ever asking whether what they were doing was worthwhile or whether there might not be better ways to do the same thing. To say that an organisation does not analyse is to accuse its officials of being stupid. Thus it is not surprising they would deny there is anything new in PAR. One minister emphasised the typical view of political administrators in the departments. 'Of course you look at an important topic in the round and its effects elsewhere; of course you look at emerging problems and

6. See R. J. East's testimony, H.C. 147 (1971–2), p. 19–22, 29, for a formal statement on the type of analysis the Treasury would like to see.

alternatives. They would be bloody poor civil servants and this would be a bloody poor department if we didn't.'

The Treasury is the one institution that knows that PAR is for it, or rather (since the Treasury has no inclination to 'PAR' its own policy activities) everyone else's PAR is for it. Treasury men do genuinely believe that it is a logical development of their system of expenditure control. In hindsight it all looks so clear: the annual estimate led to the Plowden fifth-year forward look, which led to the five-year path to the target. Since 1971, the Treasury has tried to move into a new, far more ambitious stage of expenditure control. According to an actively involved Treasury official:

> One wants to know a great deal more than what are the changes of policy required to remain on the path. One wants to know fully, by a very detailed analysis, precisely what the objectives are, whether the expenditure is properly related to them and whether those objectives have in fact been obtained, and so on. So that beyond the general controlling of the pattern of future expenditure there is a much more detailed conception of control. . . .[7]

Yet the Treasury realises that if PAR is for it alone, essential co-operation from departments will prove most difficult to elicit.[8] On the face of it, most Treasury officials are aware that 'PAR is an inroad into the Department's prerogative by the centre, that is Treasury and CPRS.' It doesn't take a genius to understand that 'ministers feel sensitive about this. They don't want the Chancellor crawling all over their programmes.' Moreover unless the Treasury were to change character by growing much larger (and this it has steadfastly refused to do) the sheer logistics of the situation demand that the departments do the actual analytic work. The Treasury's aim, baldly stated, is to get the departments to do what it would like done without actually doing the work itself.

The constitutional position, so to speak, so far as the Treasury is concerned, is that analytical studies belong to the departments. They are given the lead in initiating and working on them with the

7. Testimony of Peter Baldwin, H.C. 549 (1970–1), p. 152.
8. 'Although PAR has great relevance to the centre, . . . unless it is seen by Departments to produce things for them, I do not think it would ever be successful. . . .' Deputy Secretary John Hunt, H.C. 147 (1971–2), p. 15.

Treasury providing advice and a push now and then. Thus the Treasury would not dream of dictating to departments whether it is finance officers or planning officers, or someone else who undertake PAR studies. Departments are entitled to set the thing up any way they find convenient. Ever fearful that procedure will overwhelm purpose, officials emphasise that 'the important things are the intangibles, the co-operation between departments and the strong rapport between them and the Treasury'. Ask a Treasury man how his work on PAR will be evaluated and he is sure to say that 'First, I think considerable store will be set on the good relations I am able to work up.' The guiding principle that 'You need to approach the department with tact and win over the senior personnel' is firmly engrained.

Still, the Treasury does not wish to be confronted with a study about whose directions it is ignorant or whose analysis it considers worthless or which does not broaden alternatives beyond those already favoured by the departmental minister or his officials. After a topic has been agreed upon, the department draws up a synopsis saying what it will look at, how the topic will be approached, what options will be initially considered, and so on. Discussions are held with the Treasury and CPRS to settle the methodology of the PARs and to determine the stages at which the departments will check back. At the same time, the Treasury officials may consult the history of this or that administrative programme, written chronicles which its own researchers have compiled and to which the departments do not have access. Usually the Treasury and CPRS will try to see a draft of the PAR three or four months before it is presented, discuss the adequacy of the options presented and ask for others to be considered if necessary.

Let an undersecretary now describe how negotiations about the content of studies are conducted :

There is a meeting, customarily in the Treasury, among undersecretaries. There would be myself, the CPRS, a Treasury undersecretary. We would all be on christian name terms. They would say that you promised to do analysis that covered certain questions. 'Yes, yes,' we would say, 'that is so.' Treasury would say that it was disappointed that we did not put so-and so into the study. 'We disagreed with you in 1967 on this point,' the Treasury would continue, 'and we've had a running battle ever since.'

People are well versed not only in the subject, but on each other's views. Sparring with the Treasury goes on forever. The discussion takes place in shorthand terms. 'Yes, but dammit all, when you got [Programme A] a condition agreed to by your minister was that [X, Y and Z] would not take place.' 'Yes, I know but you interpret it one way and we interpret it another.' Pinning down these points is what the fight is about. The points on which the two sides agree are not very interesting.

They are all professionals and they will arrive at an agreement with which all can live, at least for the time being.

In discussions with department officials about the quality of their PAR submissions, Treasury negotiators face a delicate problem. If they are too critical they may discourage departments from trying to do better in the future or otherwise damage their relationships. The Treasury man is not likely to neglect the human dimension of analysis and is running true to form when he says, 'We cannot have a grand jamboree in which we say these studies are good and those are bad, and play one department off against another. Only a few people are involved; it is a highly personal matter.' And yet if the Treasury says everything is all right, it may continue to receive worthless analyses. Its initial approach has been to give at least modest praise to anything that looks like a decent attempt has been made and to come down hard on sham efforts. With the passage of time, standards are expected to grow higher. Because the sanctions are informal, no one should underestimate their influence. Men who value their reputations inside the community are affected when others let it be known that their work is not up to standard. Department officials do not care for it to get around that their analysis, and indirectly they themselves, have been 'rumbled' by the Treasury or the CPRS.

The quality of the analysis, like any other creative work, depends on getting talented people to do it. To say that trained staff to do PAR studies is not superabundant would be an understatement. Training takes time and until recently there has been little interest and less support. Worse, perhaps, than the shortage of professional analysts are the officials who think they already analyse policy, by which they mean sifting through arguments and searching for inconsistencies, but not working to make their judgements more reliable. The Treasury's approach to the lack of trained staff provides another revealing glimpse into its philosophy of management in the public service. It has not set out staffing requirements and insisted that the departments hire new people right away. The best thing was to get the undersecretaries and the permanent secretaries interested in it so that they would later be willing to acquire staff. What point would there be in getting new people unless higher officials really believed there was something to be gained from their efforts? In the third year of PAR, small efforts began to encourage the recruitment of better-trained staff.[9]

Out of all this to-ing and fro-ing come PAR studies. Whether the experiment will survive, much less prove valuable, depends on whether departments are rewarded for being open and analytical. If those who dig deeper and expose more of themselves find that ministers collectively or, what is more likely, the Treasury, are harder on their programmes, they will have little reason to continue that practice. If good work and candour are rewarded in the tangible currency of cold cash, the moral of the story will not be lost on others, who will wish to trade at the same bank. 'The basic problem for PAR in its early stages,' a Treasury official thought, 'is that when you talk to departments they don't see the colour of the money they get back for their investment. It has to prove itself by results.'

The blunt opinion in about half the departments is that 'there would be no point and no interest in undertaking PAR if it did not already exist'. The other half hedge their response with an important qualification: 'For practical purposes these studies we would do anyway are the same as PAR. The difference is that they would be subject to our own choosing, not the Treasury's or CPRS, and we would do it our own way, though we would tackle problem areas of equal importance and do them

9. The lack of relevant cost-accounting data is also a considerable handicap in doing analytical studies. This difficulty exists everywhere, for any way of presenting information cannot be useful for each and every purpose one has in mind after the fact. We have considerable doubts about the wisdom of investing the huge amounts of time, energy and money required to alter accounting systems in the vague hope that they will one day provide data that someone will actually put to use.

equally systematically.' Whether they want to do it or not, department officials and their ministers know that the Government of the day wants PAR and they must do it. Their problem then becomes one of mitigating any harmful effects in the worst case and making it serve their own purposes in the best. The remainder of our commentary on PAR may be read as variations on the theme of making PAR work for you rather than against you.

PAR in Action: What Good Is It?

> These developments were a bit starry-eyed – these things always are – and we haven't done too much yet, but I still have hope.
>
> *A businessman in Government*

> There's been a dog-fight every time. The person in the department with the least resistance is the one whose policy gets reviewed.
>
> *Treasury undersecretary*

> How do you judge PAR this far? 'How does a child walk? Pretty good for a child.'
>
> *Treasury official*

> Socrates was the first person to do a PAR. He did it on Athens, going around asking fundamental questions. Athens put him to death. That's why I don't want to do any more PARs.
>
> *Department undersecretary*

It is too early to offer final judgements on PAR. The first studies began in 1971 and no doubt we will all be wiser five or ten years from now. But before the early experience with PAR is lost in the mists of history and subjected to retrospective glorification or vilification, there are useful things to be learned from it about how British public policy and expenditure decisions are made.

How good are the PAR studies? An interim appraisal by the Treasury describes the results as 'patchy', and that seems a fair judgement. Since neither the subjects chosen nor the analyses completed are considered fit for public eyes, an outside opinion is difficult. From discussing three PAR studies with the participants, we would hazard a guess that two of the three were hopeless and the third might prove useful. This is a ratio with which we believe most participants would agree. The summary by an official in one department was that 'The first PAR was an absolute disaster. It was a purely defensive piece. The second PAR was very minor; it involved bringing to a minister's attention analytical work already done. Since the idea was politically unattractive, nothing more was heard of it. The third study is aimed at encouraging people to think more analytically, with a certain amount of outside support.'

The technical defects of the PAR studies are not surprising. A department is likely to send up an admirable historical statement of how its objectives have evolved over the years but equivocate on what objectives are now and whether they should be maintained. Given the type of men who must do these studies, analytic virtues are likely to be logical rather than empirical. Various parts of their analyses fit together but there is little sense of involvement with the people affected or of search for data on the consequences of programmes. When the technical level is reached, the result is likely to be a narrow-gauged operations research type of study which, even if it is true, would still change very little. The best pieces of work seem to have contained several ideas that one might not have thought of, together with some illustrative data, a few suggestions, and a brief assessment of implications for how things might be done differently.

We can better evaluate this new rationalism in government by trying, in a minor way, to 'PAR'-analyse PAR itself. What are the objectives of this exercise? Summarising the recent testimony of the Treasury Deputy Secretary then responsible for PAR, there are basically two. PAR's first purpose is to aid collective ministerial decision-making. The results of a PAR are intended to focus issues for joint ministerial decision and test department activities against ministers' collective strategy. A high Treasury official informed us that 'What we are hoping to get out of PAR is an improved collective responsibility among ministers. There's the formal notion of collective responsibility but everyone knows that ministers fight their own corner. A PAR [study] will come to a collective body of ministers in Cabinet or committee and all together will look at one minister's programme.' Assuming that the minister directly concerned will agree to have an important subject studied, and that his colleagues will actually read the study report or the much smaller CPRS gloss on it, ministers should be better able to discuss each other's business. It is possible. Whether they will want to is now being decided.

A second broad purpose of PAR is to undercut the inertia of existing government programmes by undertaking a 'regular spring-cleaning of objectives'. Since PESC tends to narrow the margins of choice, as we have seen, the Treasury 'think that PAR ought to supplement the Public Expenditure Survey by widening the margin of choice for ministers through a more radical analysis of the programmatic objectives and the means used to achieve them.' Departments are obligated to do what they should be doing if their people were not so busy and they had time to take things out of the cupboard and see why they are there. PAR thus constitutes an outside stimulus to do what everyone agrees a good department should be (and some insist already is) doing.

In bold outline the PAR process looks like this. Suggestions for PAR studies can come from almost anywhere – a minister, a department official, a Treasury or CPRS man. They usually originate with departments, are accepted or modified by the Treasury and CPRS, ratified by a Cabinet committee, and wind their way down the departmental apparatus where they are modified again, worked upon, and hopefully emerge at the appointed time. The minister then presents his department's PAR report to a Cabinet committee of his colleagues. The subjects of the studies, their timing, their sensitivity, the analysis that goes into them, the options that are considered or ignored, the talent invested in them – all are subjects for negotiation.

PAR is not a new technique of analysis. It offers no decision rules or shortcuts for thinking about public policy. What is supposedly novel about PAR is the procedure first for guiding and then for deliberating on the analysis that is done. Roughly speaking the new selection process (jointly between department, Treasury and CPRS, with the list of topics approved by ministers) is designed to meet the objective of radically re-examining existing programmes. The deliberation process by ministers as a whole aims at the objective of improved ministerial decision-making.

To appraise PAR in action, we must look in turn at its selection and deliberation process.

This much is clear: PAR can be no better than the topics selected for study. Significant answers depend upon asking significant rather than trivial questions. Yet, precisely because PAR is intended to have practical results, the selection of topics, like any other political activity, becomes a process through which men try to realise their purposes. PAR studies are not only more or less desirable from an analytic point of view, they are also objects of serious strategic concern.

To be considered valuable, PAR studies are supposed to be connected with general strategies of government, the objectives of departments, and large quantities of public expenditure. The first of the criteria would seem to belong to the CPRS, the second to the departments, and the third to the Treasury. (Because PAR studies represent an important mechanism of access to departmental systems for the CPRS, we shall reserve consideration of their participation for the next chapter.) Since there can always be argument about the general objectives of government or of departments, the Treasury criterion tends to be the operative one. 'We do not want studies for five million pounds for minor and peripheral programmes.' The topics chosen should have a 'weighty bulk of public expenditure'. Back in the departments they say that the Treasury might argue that their study was not sufficiently original or fundamental but, in the end, the effective criterion tends to come down to the amount of resources. The fifteen or so topics chosen to be 'PARed' in 1971/2 had only one overall theme; each involved a significant amount of money.

Gamesmanship is inevitable in the selection of particular subjects for PAR analysis. The Treasury knows that some departments try to lighten their housework by warming over an old study which had been salted away in the files. This practice (known in Treasury parlance as a 'Charley-PAR') is difficult to distinguish from one where the department says 'We have been thinking about this for some time and we might as well do it now.' Evangelists have long since learned that it may not matter how a man comes to his decision, so long as he enters the true church. Upon reflection, Treasury people have decided that submitting a study that would otherwise have been done or that, in fact, has already been done is not entirely useless. 'It has meant,' they explained, 'putting the matter into commission. The department can't just write a philosophical essay. This is not entirely a soft option. They have to accept a rather more rigorous analysis and ultimately engage in collective discussion in Cabinet.'

Departments would like to find a topic which, while important, is not sensitive but if this is not possible, they will opt for political convenience. A sensitive policy is one that can or has got you into trouble with ministers, other officials, interest groups, and/or the public. In turning down an alternative offered by the Treasury, for example, a department said 'the policy in question was totally in the melting pot. We tried to analyse it two years ago and got our fingers burned. The management won't let us go any further, not this year.' Certain areas – clinical freedom for doctors, the nuclear deterrants, subsidies for farmers, and many others – are turned down as possible subjects, department officials reported 'because over the years of negotiating you have an idea about what's possible. If it is unthinkable for the analyst to stop these things, there's no point in studying them.' The department might get away with a quiet study on a sacred subject but PAR opens up the whole question for Cabinet decision and that, advised a department official, 'makes it very difficult internally for you'. The mere thought of dealing with the abolition or downgrading of an internal operating unit in this open fashion is enough to send officials away in a cold sweat.

Timing is also vital. A subject that might be just right one year would cause a terrible uproar the next, or vice versa. Ministers and their officials not only want to control the subject of a PAR study, they also insist on having a determining voice in its timing. The minister might think that is something he would rather not discuss just now. 'When a question deemed sensitive comes up,' department officials are likely to admit, 'it would be a great subject for PAR sometime, but as for next year, we make no promises.' Considering that the aim of PAR is to cover the whole of a department's programmes over a number of years, officials can always ask if this year is the right one to look at it.

What happens if a department is dragging its feet on PAR? 'We just hold a discussion anyway', said a PAR overseer in the Treasury. Suppose its proposals do not make much sense? 'We show contempt.' Suppose they keep insisting that the time is not right? 'We say it's all very difficult, of course, but you've got political policy decisions to make and you must deal with them some time and a PAR study is as good a way as any. If we are beaten off, we say, what do you propose to do this year instead?' Looking at the dilemma from a future perspective, Treasury officials hope that a regular programme of reviews will become so firmly entrenched that the question will not be what shall be reviewed but only when, because everything is going in ultimately.

The most pervasive form of PAR gamesmanship is also the major reason that PAR has not gone far toward one of its two original objectives; that is, a radical reappraisal of existing programmes. Talk with administrators in spending departments and they will tell about their abiding interest in choosing PARs that will prove helpful to them. In selecting a topic for analysis, departments usually concentrate on growth areas where they know they can make a good case for the spending totals to go up. Mention the possibility of a PAR to reduce or eliminate a programme and both ministers and civil servants will say that it is 'conceivable' but 'it has rarely happened'. The scope for improvement in government programmes is so great that departments can count on any in-depth study – call it PAR, investigatory committee, or royal commission – to provide a justification for doing more. Precisely this phenonemon was in Gladstone's mind when he cried out a century ago, 'If you intend to have any limit put on expenditure, it is high time that you should be on your guard against efficiency. . . . In the mouth of a Minister who wants to find excuses for a great increase in public burdens, it is a plea that ought not to be admitted without a great deal of carefulness.'[10] Listen now to the typical progression of terms used by a permanent secretary during one of our discussions. 'PAR isn't about what you'd cut out, but about what you'd do differently – what you'd do better – what you'd do more.'

Regardless of the Treasury view of history, PAR is not a logical development of PESC to departments wanting to do more. Quite the opposite. Since PAR to them is usually about increasing not cutting and since PESC is about expenditure ceilings, the two processes are to some extent in conflict, operationally, if not theoretically. 'PAR', to a representative permanent secretary, 'is

10. Quoted in D. H. MacGregor, *Public Aspects of Finance*, (Oxford: Clarendon Press, 1939) p. 48.

something that means you keep bumping up against the PESC constraints on spending through time.' PAR a natural extension of PESC? 'Humbug', replied a spending minister. 'Have you ever heard of PAR taking anything out of PESC? I haven't and I don't think you will as you go around.' And he was right, we did not. The only noticable casuality arising from PAR, at least in its first full year, turned out to be an organisational weakness shown up in one of the smallest and most friendless of the spending authorities in British government. Another PAR suggesting the elimination of a state subsidy was disinherited by its minister.

When PAR is not in a growth area, it is an odds-on bet that this is because political administrators of the department have already decided that they want to switch resources away from this area to another. 'It's conceivable,' said a permanent secretary, 'that we might want to do a PAR in a weak area if we want to get rid of something.' Consider the recent PAR analysis which most people cited to us as one of the truly outstanding studies to date. Everyone agreed that it raised important questions, talked analytically about alternatives, provided a wealth of facts, broadened options. It is also an object lesson in the politics of PAR analysis. The important comments are not those of the outside readers but of the officials in the sponsoring department who created this PAR report.

This is a fundamental area where there has been a good deal of growth and the programme is coming under pressure. The Minister doesn't care to do too much in it and wants to switch resources to [second programme]. This analysis still keeps the overall growth but shows there are some savings. The Treasury will play the line that these should be pooled for other departments, but when it gets to ministers we know that we'll get them back and can put them toward [the second programme].

We learned nothing from this that we didn't know already. In that sense it was a complete waste of time. What use PAR is depends on how you construct it. You know that the big argument is on [say, the number of people to be benefitted]. Now we in this department don't want to [cut the numbers] so we took a great deal of care about laying out the summary, underplaying some things, and overplaying others, particularly the political disadvantages of [cutting numbers]. You know that the only thing ministers will read is the summary. We use the PAR for X to get more for Y.

The objective of a PAR study is not supposed to be gathering collective ministerial support for a pre-determined departmental objective. The Treasury will put its foot down on some subjects which appear trivial or too blatantly loaded in the department's favoured direction, but it would always rather get departments to play along, telling them that they have the initiative if they abide by the rules. Only if the department tries to substitute subversion for gamesmanship will the Treasury insist on different topics and, if necessary, seek ministerial support for its views. The Treasury depends on the desire of their fellow officials to settle matters before they reach exalted and dangerous political heights. When lower officials cannot agree, the permanent secretaries of the Treasury, the CPRS and the department concerned are called in to resolve the matter before it gets to ministers. These family quarrels are not usually carried on in public view of ministers or other departments. They are settled, as one official put it, 'in decent privacy'.

The list of PAR topics agreed by officials and with note of any remaining dissent goes to ministers for approval. At Cabinet level there are two committees that deal with PAR – the Steering Committee, which authorises selection of the issues and a Management Committee (where the Chief Secretary participates), which rides herd over the progress of PAR studies through the various subject-matter committees of the Cabinet.

Discussions in the Steering Committee are rarely contentious, if only because zealous minister-watching will have steered officials away from topics unlikely to be backed by their masters. If other ministers try to suggest a topic, it is likely to be in the form of saying something like, 'Your topic on sugar beet subsidies is too small. How about strategy of agricultural subsidies in the European Economic Community, a much larger question?' 'Hell, no,' the affected minister will reply, 'I've got my own ideas about that; I'm not prepared now to discuss this. I'm damned if I'm having this washing put out on the line. You're right, this is important, that's why I don't want it up now.' Other ministers, fearful of having the tables turned on them one day, are likely to accept this view. And, anyway, who is there to push the recalcitrant around?

The answer, on occasion, appears to be the Prime Minister. We sought out the history of one controversial PAR study where the subject matter was decided, as an official put it, 'over the dead body of our permanent secretary'. The Prime Minister had ultimately ruled in favour of doing the expanded study wanted by the Treasury and CPRS rather than the restricted one favoured by the department. The permanent secretary objected strenuously because he wanted to recommend alternatives to the minister rather than having that done by some outside group. The story, whether you think it is happy or sad, cannot end here, however, because a study still has to be done and this requires continuous departmental co-operation. 'We lost initially,' an official stated, 'but we kept at the specifications. They really can't get very detailed with us because we've got to do the work and not them.' Wary of Pyrrhic victories, the Treasury would rather settle for less with the department and get more in the analysis.

The use of PAR has gone far enough to ensure that there is little payoff on the objective of cutting into the inertia of existing programmes; it has not gone far enough to affect how ministers interact with each other. The second major objective of PAR is to improve collective ministerial decision-making and to do so largely by bringing the results of the PAR on an individual department's programme before ministers as a group. In its idealised form, 'the essence of PAR is that a large number of individuals (Cabinet Ministers and the officials in the centre) must understand the programmes of all departments and relate them to each other and compare them.'[11] Nothing about PAR has even begun approaching this ideal. The selection of topics and deliberation on PAR reports is a distinctly fringe activity for ministers. The actions of one Cabinet committee – which placed a PAR report at the bottom of its agenda for two months and eventually concluded an hour's half-hearted discussion by calling for further studies – is characteristic. Several ministers have tried to use their analyses to gain support for things they already wanted to do. One minister in the first year launched a strenuous attack on another's PAR report, the unanimous suspicion being that he thereby sought to free resources for his own pet projects (a suspicion amply

11. Clarke, *New Trends in Government*, p. 43.

borne out by later events). In either case the result has scarcely been a heightened sense of collective decision-making. Several ministers we talked to were surprised to hear that this had ever been the intention behind PAR.

Part of the problem is that PAR's businessmen founders rather fooled themselves in imagining that there was, even in theory, something distinctly new about the PAR deliberation process. The fact that the reports are to be considered jointly among ministers is not novel. One permanent secretary rightly observed that 'Under the pre-PAR system any analysis which concluded that something should be done would have been considered jointly by ministers.' Likewise, PARs are considered individually and in the same old functional committee structure of the Cabinet (industry, social services, etc.). There is no way of making tradeoffs between one PAR and another.

Yes, some say, but unlike previous presentations, PAR lays out the background facts and arguments; ordinary departmental presentations to ministers resemble a well-polished sales pitch providing only those figures contributing to the thrust of a predetermined case. It is true that PAR reports are less like air-tight, single-minded cases and are capable of being re-analysed to different ends. But that means someone must read the reports and think about the original data. This is not something ministers are likely to do or to set their overworked officials on (unless it is their own PAR report). 'Report?' exclaimed one minister. 'Each one's a book, not a report. No one I know reads them. Maybe you do look at the summary or précis.' These summaries, as we have seen, are scarcely likely to be a disinterested statement unaffected by the way the sponsoring department thinks events should move.

Timing is another constraint on the political effectiveness of PAR. A minister contemplating an important change in priorities in his department may sometimes regard initiating such a study as an opportunity to make this change by broadening his basis of support. It is far more likely, however, that PAR would be the last thing he would think of. PAR is geared to a timetable that is unlikely to coincide with what the minister and his officials deem the strategic moment. They may wish to take advantage of a swing in the climate of opinion or a factional shift within Cabinet. They may deem their chances best by getting an immediate and broad decision by Cabinet, not by waiting for a PAR study (only part of which they can control) to reach its appointed place in the infinite scheme of things. If PAR is supposed to help departments, they will say, they should be allowed to use the results of the studies internally and not be required to launch them into a precarious world earlier or later than they think is proper. They find PAR difficult to link to the usual opportunism.

Whatever the problems of PAR reports' timing, bulk, or sensitivity, the basic fact is that most ministers feel neither qualified nor inclined to deal with other departmental ministers' business. 'Large open-ended questions about whether we should be doing this or that are what the department is for,' bellowed one minister. 'The mind from the outside doesn't have the detailed knowledge for dealing with these things. You'd spend most of your time educating yourself about what the department is doing.' Another minister chimed in, 'Do you think that I can go along to a meeting and say after one afternoon that another department, say DHSS, should be spending less on the elderly and more on day care?' These attitudes may change in time, but they are deeply ingrained; the Treasury is prudent in dampening expectations about any quick payoff from PAR. The coalitions of silence exist throughout the political administration, echoing endlessly that 'I'm not poking holes in their programmes and I certainly hope they're not poking holes in mine.'

Everything depends, then, on whether at least a few important ministers of standing wish to support PAR over a period of time. How much credit do they have with their colleagues and how much of it are they prepared to use up? At a minimal level, PAR is not yet important enough to become a sticking point with ministers. There have only been a few direct fights. It is sufficient, for the time being, that the Prime Minister wants it, though no one yet can say how much of his resources he will devote to it. The Chancellor of the Exchequer is nominally a supporter but he is likely to leave most of the pushing and hauling to the Chief Secretary. How many ministers in the autumn of 1972, the third cycle of PARs, gave political backing? Even with the Prime Minister behind it, most ministers seemed neutral or outright hostile. 'I will have nothing to do with PAR. I'm [minister for X] and will look after my department. Don't come snooping with your PARs and analyses.' Doesn't PAR have any champions? 'Yes,' the consensus of ministers reveals. 'Ted Heath.' No more? 'Perhaps two or three others, though they are not too strong. That's about all.'

Before anyone worries about what other ministers will say, the first requisite of a PAR study that hopes for success is support by the departmental minister. Within the Treasury there have been explicit discussions 'on the whole caper of bringing in ministers at what stages and to what degrees. The minister must present his own paper to the Cabinet committee.' Yet it is not clear whether the sponsoring minister is supposed to be in agreement with everything said in his PAR or not. Certainly if he goes through the formal presentation only to conclude that the PAR is unacceptable to him, no outside minister is likely to rise to its defence (and civil servants in the sponsoring department can expect a hard time the next day if anyone does). That this has happened on at least one occasion and possibly more makes officials even more wary of how they mediate PAR discussions between the central departments and their minister. 'You want to preserve yourself from being crushed between the stone wheels.'

All agree that the few outstanding PARs to date have raised fundamental, mind-stretching questions. The discussion is lively, everyone is sure that it has done a lot of good, and perhaps it has in raising the general level of information. Certain ministers do feel that it did them good to discuss a PAR which began with the question of whether the purpose of education was primarily social, or economic, or an aesthetic good for its own sake. Naturally no conclusion was reached and the cynic can argue that time would have been better spent on the much maligned narrow topics, such as whether or not to create a new university.

In this climate and at least as far as ministers are concerned, PAR threatens to become a recipe for do-nothingism. A PAR report strongly favoured by a sponsoring minister threatens to be no more than the same old departmental advocacy. Disfavoured by the sponsoring minister, PAR may not be taken seriously. If taken seriously, PAR will increase ministerial and interdepartmental argument, and there should be no running away from this fact. Indeed, if PAR does not bring more decisions to the centre, and perforce increases the level (but also the perspicacity) of interdepartmental conflict, it will have failed entirely. Against this, it can always be said that the rows precipitated by PAR are likely to be gratuitous, inasmuch as they arise, not from the felt needs of a department's initiative or political interest from ministers, but from a formal analytic procedure.

Permanent secretaries are another group struggling to find an accommodation to the new PAR procedures. Their first impulse is to defend their own prerogatives as chief advisers on policy. They can readily accept the role of the Treasury, including PESC, in financial control, but they insist that the Treasury is there to look after the global total. If there must be a limit to the total, they will consider making contributions towards the ceiling figure. But PAR goes beyond that, at least in principle, to suggest where cuts should be made and that, they believe, is encroaching on their territory. If outsiders determine how and why and where allocations are made, not too much will be left of the permanent secretary's authority.

More fundamental still is the potential challenge of PAR to ordinary modes of management in the era of the conglomerate department. The larger their departments become, the more permanent secretaries find it difficult to engage in the detailed administration through which they exercise their leadership. If they cannot oversee details, then they must somehow try to reassert themselves on larger grounds of policy. One might think, then, that PAR would be an attractive tool for the policy-oriented permanent secretary. He might think of himself as less of an administrator and more of a policy designer and evaluater. He might ... but a very large change in role would be required. He would always wonder whether, being removed from day-to-day administration, he would ever know what was going on. Something has to give. Whether it is called PAR or by some other name, permanent secretaries will need a mechanism to adapt their style to the new era. Vacillating between a not-too-well disguised hostility and a sneaking suspicion that PAR might offer them a new opportunity, they are more sensitive than ever to the reactions of their ministerial masters.

The Treasury is the one institution which most clearly recognises its own need for PAR. PESC has necessarily involved it in increasing the delegation of authority to the spending departments. The growth of conglomerate departments has necessarily led to the Treasury pushing more details from itself. In 1964 there were nineteen or twenty operating departments and one department in the centre; in 1971 there were nine or ten operating departments and four groups (Treasury, Civil Service Department, Cabinet Office and CPRS) at the centre.[12] This aggregation of departments has further stimulated the Treasury's desire to find better ways of, as one senior Treasury official said, 'putting our fingers on their strategy. The question is: How can you combine greater delegation with more strategic control.' PAR is one major device for doing so, but the Treasury is far from confident that it has found the answer.

Because the success of PAR depends upon departmental co-operation, the Treasury has had to play it straight. It cannot prejudge the matter and say that every PAR must lead to a change. Exactly how the Treasury will use PAR remains to be seen. Potentially, PAR's disaggregated and less hermetic data does offer the opportunity for Treasury expenditure supply divisions to re-analyse and argue about the ongoing momentum of departmental programmes. For the present, Treasury people take great pains to deny that PAR is an underhanded way of finding out where to whittle departments down. 'It is not a question of a curmudgeon cheer "Spend less, spend less!" We have bent over backwards to make it clear that this is not just a cutting exercise. We are hoping to see an option to increase provided there is a balanced reduction elsewhere.' The department that seemingly justifies increased expenditure on one programme will, at the same time, still be under notice that it must find a comparable reduction elsewhere.

Departments are not so sure but that PAR represents, potentially at least, a threat to their spending plans. Long experience has taught them that the Treasury is not half as interested in new ideas costing money as in new ideas that do not. After all, they observe, the Treasury's main interest is improving its grip on public spending, not creating polices costing more money. 'Already', say some, 'we've had the Treasury breathing down our necks suggesting that they hope our PAR this year doesn't come up with anything costing more money.' It is worth remembering that PAR came into existence during an especially favourable spending climate when, with about one million unemployed, no one was under strong pressure to produce economies. This helped get PAR off the ground (analyses could aid departments' spending bids), but continuation of a relaxed climate would undermine both

12. Ibid., p. 42.

PESC and PAR. There is little point in making trade-offs if almost anything goes. The essence of the matter is the ground rules for discussing what goes. Departments feel comfortable and self-satisfied in their complaints that the Treasury is anti-spending. Treasury interference in the content of policy for its own sake, rather than for the sake of economy, is likely to be greeted with a storm of protest about presumptuous interference in departmental business. PAR is a method of trying to ease into such central interference without calling down the thunder around the Treasury's head.

Paradoxically, PAR may offer the greatest immediate opportunity to ministers – but only in their individual capacities as heads of departments rather than as members of a collective government. The background facts and less pre-digested options do offer an enhanced potential for the political heads, and in particular the most underutilized group in Britain, junior ministers, to obtain a better grip on their own department's policy. Major turnarounds in departmental programmes have usually depended upon the appearance of an extremely tough, single-minded minister able and willing to question the fundamentals behind his department's activities. PAR does not eliminate the need for such ministers, but it does make their task a little easier. In the words of one permanent secretary, 'PAR provides the minister with more prompting to undertake these major shifts in programme; it means he needn't be quite such a hero to carry important changes through the department.'

PAR must be looked upon as an instrument of the future. It is less important for what it does issue-by-issue than for its ability to point departments in new directions. Departments and their ministers can always be expected to act in terms of their self-interest; the useful question is whether new procedures such as PAR can provide incentives to view these interests in a different light than before. Assuming it can survive long enough to disseminate its own thought patterns among political administrators, PAR does contain seeds which might help departments move away from self-interest defined in inertial terms of self-defence and towards a conception that prescribes a more active search for better ways of meeting needs and more vigorous checks on the effect of their policies in the real world.

Before policy analysis becomes the counter over which bargains are struck, however, many things would have to happen that have hardly begun to occur. Politicians would have to feel that they were more involved in securing studies of more use to them than has been true until now. A generation of top officials would have to learn how to handle figures without being dominated by them. Departments will have to move further from individual case work toward large-scale resource allocation. And the connection between the seemingly exotic work of the policy analyst and the electoral fortunes of the politician would have to be more apparent to both parties to the transaction. So far, whatever forces there are to press for better ways of dealing with policy and expenditure must circulate and gather the limited strength they can within the narrow confines of the Executive community.

Talking with ministers about PAR suggests that they are far from coming to terms with analysis. Those who oppose it think it humbug; those in the middle conceive it as a necessary nuisance, useful to show the party is being modern; the few who support it most strongly vacillate between believing that it has been too soft – 'PAR has resulted in less analytical questioning of the centre than I wanted' – or that it has been too hard – 'PAR could use a little more finesse in approaching colleagues.' Some want to 'make PAR more acceptable by relating it to the manifesto for the next election'. Making any part of the governmental decision-making apparatus relevant to electoral concerns would not only generate ministerial interest but also civil service suspicion. The question is whether policy analysis would survive in recognisable form as the handmaiden of the next campaign. But why not? The creation of the Central Policy Review Staff was predicated on the notion that the two concerns – better analysis and electoral victories – would reinforce rather than contradict one another.

Ministers may be told that it is in their collective interest to become concerned with the wonders of policy analysis, but a subject that is vaguely in the interest of everyone in general runs the risk of ending up as the concern of no one in particular. What is more, no one can say to what extent problems of British government are due to deficient ways of making decisions or to ministers finding the decisions themselves unpalatable. Civil servants like to claim they want nothing so much and receive nothing so seldom as prompt ministerial decisions. The Central Policy Review Staff was cooked up precisely for the purpose of putting the collective and the unpalatable squarely on the Cabinet table.

7 The Politics of Advice: CPRS and the Government Centre

This Administration has pledged itself to introduce a new style of government.

> The Reorganisation of Central Government, *para. 1*

Style is the half-sister of fashion. Both are cosmetics and neither determines what actually gets done.

> *Permanent secretary*

Heath has always been very adamant that his government would have strategic objectives and that all actions would be weighed against them.

> *Businessman adviser*

The British believe in mobilizing extremely small numbers of people to deal with very large problems.

> *CPRS official*

THE PROBLEMATIC SURVIVAL of the CPRS in its present form and with its existing personnel is not so important as the issues it raises. Whether or not the CPRS endures for any length of time, its initial problems and experiences are invaluable to anyone interested in Her Majesty's government. No post-war reform has more directly highlighted the private relations of those who claim to exercise supreme power. The politics of advice is a permanent feature of the government centre.

It had all seemed so clear at the end of the sixties. The centre needed to be centralised. To the team of businessmen/politicians assisting the Conservative Opposition, as well as to a number of senior civil servants, there was a clear need for arranging independent advice to the Cabinet as a whole. The early idea was that a new central capability in British government could be provided by combining the public expenditure side of the Treasury, the management functions of the Civil Service Department, and the secretarial functions of the Cabinet Office. The complaint was not new. Political administrators have frequently cited the need to improve analytic servicing at the centre. In 1946, Sir John Anderson, the century's one and only example of a man who had served successively as both a senior civil servant and a top political minister, had argued for some sort of central government organisation able to conduct economic studies from a more general perspective than is possible within any department. But who would be the client and how could it be arranged? The essential query was posed more than answered by the usual method of embodying a contradiction in a single sentence : 'While I emphasise the departmental responsibility of ministers as a necessary and vital principle, I at the same time stress the importance as a practical matter, of adequate machinery for making a reality of collective responsibility.'[1]

The precedents were not good for any unit tied directly to the Prime Minister. One notable experiment with a central capability had occurred in the semi-formal group of advisers surrounding Lloyd George at the end of the First World War. The venomous atmosphere – one part superiority, one part envy, two parts malice, inevitably surrounding the men who are closer to the Prime Minister than others think they ought to be – emerges neatly in a letter from Lord Esher to Tom Jones. All the elements are there. Now the P.M. was evidently not a bad sort and might have known 'how to manage 10 Downing Street, *but*, the men around him were a thoroughly bad lot', present company excepted. Then comes the favourite reform, a *Chef de Cabinet* system, followed by an attack on the individual closest to the Prime Minister : 'Hankey ought to fulfil this function, but he does not . . . because

1. Sir John Anderson, 'The Machinery of Government', in *Public Administration* (Autumn, 1946), p. 156.

P.G.P.M.—11*

he funks Warren Fisher [Treasury Permanent Secretary].'[2] From all this one learns that the lot of an adviser, particularly one in the centre of government, is not a happy one. If he is in the Civil Service, someone always wonders why a regular department could not do it; if he is outside of the Civil Service, then he does not know how people around here do business or is guilty of having undue political influence.

Today there is no Prime Minister's Department. The very idea raised hackles everywhere – in the Conservative Opposition, in the new Government, and in the Civil Service. An immediate and sufficient cause for abandoning anything like this approach was that the new Conservative Chancellor of the Exchequer and his successor were adamant. They would not hear of the public expenditure divisions leaving the Treasury, and other leading ministers were antipathetic to these larger ideas.[3] The result was a scaled-down compromise, the creation of a Central Policy Review Staff in the Cabinet Office.

The new organisation came to life with the appointment of Lord Rothschild as its head in October, 1970, and in a short time, there were fifteen full-time employees. It was said that they were there to help ministers collectively. Supervised by the Prime Minister, CPRS would somehow enable ministers to make better policy decisions. Who were these people at the centre of British Government and what were they meant to be doing?

The 'who' is easy enough to answer. The Janus-like nature of

2. Thomas Jones, *Whitehall Diary* (Oxford: Oxford University Press, 1969), vol. 1, p. 276.

3. The considerations have been so well set out by David Howell that they can serve as the summary of a debate that ended up concluding against splitting the Treasury apart:

The practical argument against this is very strong. The machinery for the regular and routine control of public expenditure rests in the Treasury under the Chief Secretary. There is, besides, the consideration that the new analysts would have their work cut out getting departments to think in a new way without at the same time having to fight for the right to a separate existence from the Treasury. The fate of the DEA is too recent to be ignored. It is also very questionable whether much would be gained by weighing down even a strengthened Prime Minister's Office with a mass of routine budgetary duties which the creation of a non-Treasury agency of this kind would place on it.

David Howell, *A New Style of Government* (Conservative Political Centre, 1970), p. 24.

CPRS personnel reflects the desire to plug into sources of information both inside the system, so as not to be surprised, and outside the governmental apparatus, so as to be better able to take the initiative. The mixture of insiders and outsiders epitomises the dual need to use the existing machine and to contribute something novel. Lord Rothschild's seconds in command became Peter Carey from the civil service and Professor C. R. Ross, an outside economist. Seven of the staff (in 1972) came from the career civil service, including two each from the Ministry of Defence, the Department of Trade and Industry, and the Treasury, and one from the Foreign Office. One of these was a professional economist and the others are classified as general administrators with a strong interest in doing analysis. The remaining eight, who did not then belong to the official Whitehall community, included two natural scientists, including Lord Rothschild, who worked in industry, two professional economists, a demographer interested in population policy, and three, who were apparently more difficult to classify, called generalists. The classifications overlap to some degree and in interesting ways. Professor Ross had been a civil servant in the Treasury and the generalist category included another former civil servant. Only Lord Rothschild and Brian Reading, the Prime Minister's personal economic adviser, were direct political appointments; the others, though not then in Whitehall, were hired through civil service procedure. It would be fair to say that only two or three of *all* these gentlemen had such strong party feelings or connections that they could not just as comfortably have served under a different Government that was prepared to use them in a similar capacity.

'What' the CPRS is to do is another matter. The gospel according to the White Paper (*The Reorganization of Central Government*, Cmnd. 4506) laid down four ways CPRS will enable ministers collectively to take better decisions. First, it will assist ministers to 'work out the implications of their basic strategy in terms of policies in specific areas'; second, it will 'establish relative priorities to be given to the different sectors of their programme as a whole'; third, the CPRS will 'identify those areas of policy in which new choices can be exercised'; finally, the central analysts will 'ensure that the underlying implications of alternative courses of action are fully analysed and considered'. The outside layman need not worry that he cannot grasp the practical meaning of these words; neither can anyone else. But this much is clear; it is now a good thing to be concerned with strategy, priorities, alternatives and the long-term; it is definitely not a good thing to be extemporaneous, *ad hoc*, short-term and reactive. Four times in three paragraphs the White Paper invokes an appeal to 'strategic' purpose for the whole government; to anyone unacquainted with the preceding six years of Labour Government, it could seem a little obsessive.

Behind the management jargon is one central thrust. The CPRS is supposed to rock the boat, though to do so as knowledgeably as possible. If it rests too still in the water – squaring everyone, circulating papers, going lightly on departments and officials elsewhere – it will end up with the same lowest-common-denominator views that it was meant to counteract. Political administrators appreciate, at least in the abstract, that the rationale for the existence of CPRS is that it should say and do things ordinary civil servants would not. This support for the theory of being daring is, to be sure, qualified with other words advising caution. It is not surprising that when a bit of the old buccaneer spirit appeared in the formidable bulk of Lord Rothschild, reformers were not quite certain whether he would deliver the goods for Queen and country or sink the ship like any other pirate. Going too far outside the established channels is likely to be risky not only for the captain but for the entire crew of any CPRS-type enterprise.[4]

Men imbued with the mores of the Civil Service are likely to believe that quiet persuasion and good humour amidst carefully selected lunches would have persuaded the right people to do what was necessary. Instead, so this line goes, the CPRS thinks it more fun to create a big splash without getting the desired results. The invariant charge of irresponsibility suggests to us that CPRS has begun to do its job. However bullish Lord R. may appear in a Cabinet Office setting, he is just the kind of person to tackle sacred cows. That creates problems but there would be little point in a man in his position doing otherwise. If he were easily overawed or less courageous, he would miss precisely those qualities that are found lacking in the governmental apparatus.

4. *Cf.* the political furore and apparent prime ministerial displeasure aroused by Lord Rothschild's Wantage speech, which warned of Britain's likelihood of becoming one of Europe's poorest nations by 1985. Reported in *The Times*, 25 September 1973, p. 1.

Lord Rothschild has invested the CPRS with a zest and flair that would otherwise have been missing. He speaks (and occasionally acts) as if he were some night raider making forays for buried treasure. His conversation is light-hearted, irreverent, and self-deprecating, as if to underline the true seriousness of purpose. When you hire a man to do a creative job, you get not only a set of tasks but a personality who fulfils them according to his own lights. Disparaging use of the term 'think-tank' is a nice way of saying that is just what he would like the CPRS to be, if only there was backing enough and time to do it.

The Grit in the Machine

There are some pretty artless fellows in there.

Cabinet Office regular

A large collection of unduly cautious specialists of long standing might be of even less value than a few careless, tactless amateurs. A little irresponsibility is desirable in a section intended partly as an irritant.

G. D. A. MacDougall

I see no reason why our activities shouldn't be in the Treasury.

CPRS official

When the CPRS was set up, the Treasury was scared stiff.

Permanent secretary

Like any new institution in an already crowded government, the Central Policy Review Staff can seem like both a usurper and a Cassandra crying that other people are not doing their jobs properly. Any imaginable description of the purposes to be served by the CPRS must sound like either resource allocation in the Treasury, or substantive departmental advice to a minister, or strategic political analysis by ministers themselves, or a Cabinet

Office briefing for the Prime Minister. Someone can always claim to be doing what the CPRS is supposed to do.

There is the Treasury. Writing about 'A New Style of Government', David Howell declared that 'the centrepiece of the system would be the new body ... concerned with the analysis of programmes, the allocation of resources between them, and efficiency in their implementation.'[5] The sentence could stand as a description of the Treasury. Anyone would be worried about someone whose job description precisely fitted his own, and the Treasury is no exception. The implication that the jobs are the same but that the Treasury might not be doing too well at it has not helped create goodwill.

The relation of CPRS to the Cabinet Office is even more obscure than its Treasury connections. A good book remains to be written about the Cabinet Office. Fully aware that it deserves more detailed consideration than we can provide, we must sketch out its handling of Cabinet business if we are ever to comprehend the obstacles and opportunities facing CPRS. The Rothschild group is in but not 'of' the Cabinet Office. Staff members have been handpicked to operate as a distinctive unit rather than as a regular part of Cabinet Office machinery.

In a 1972 interview, the Prime Minister criticised the common tendency for two departments concerned with a problem to present Cabinet with their own rival papers.

Then there was always an argument about which facts and figures were right, and you sent them away to get all that sorted out. Then there was an argument about the consequences and so on....

So what I've tried with CPRS is to get all this sorted out before it comes to Cabinet.[6]

It sounds all too familiar to Cabinet Office regulars, who are likely to echo the words of one veteran, 'My job is to help settle interdepartmental disputes before they get out of hand.' As a businessman consultant concluded from a study of the Office, 'The

5. Howell, *A New Style of Government*, p. 23.
6. Prime Minister Heath, *Evening Standard*, 1 June 1972, pp. 24–5.

Cabinet Office is the best fire brigade you've ever seen.' Cabinet meetings normally occupy only a few hours each week; they rarely occur more than twice a week or last longer than two or three hours. By convention, the normal agenda includes discussion of foreign affairs and parliamentary business. The remaining space on the agenda quickly fills up with items of urgent political importance. Unless ways were found to expedite Cabinet work, the governmental machine would quickly seize up. Moreover there are always clashes between departments. When a deadlock has been reached, as frequently happens in view of the incessant flow of business, someone has to be found who can resolve it before it gets to Cabinet or, failing that, enable ministers to make an expeditious choice. This someone is pre-eminently the Secretary of the Cabinet and the regular Cabinet Office staff.

Conflict resolution has a logic of its own that does not always prescribe moving from one straight line to another. Delay, for instance, may allow time for things to change, new faces to appear on the scene, or new stances to emerge. Or one side may be brought to say they don't have their facts right, enabling them to recede from a previous position and to come up with a slightly different proposal that would be acceptable. Should the problem be substantial, the Cabinet Office will usually get department officials together to try and work it out. Beneath the Cabinet committees of ministers, in the warren of Cabinet Official committees and working parties, Cabinet Office men find their natural habitat. Some groups will be trying to avoid difficulties among departments before they arise; others will be papering over existing cracks or have had a Cabinet disagreement remitted to them for settlement. In any event, members are expected to contribute something broader and more constructive than their well-known departmental case, though of course not all do.

If all goes well, each official squares the new solution with his minister and prepares a paper with the agreed-upon position for the leading minister. As a face-saving device the Prime Minister might have a paper prepared saying a number of disputed points have been mentioned and it now looks to him as though an acceptable solution would have certain features – a position he can adopt only after knowing that the ministers involved are already agreed.

No one should believe that Cabinet Office officials are pale and pasty men who have no opinions of their own. They come from departments where they have learned how to develop strong views and they do not lose that capacity by moving to another building in Whitehall. But the ideal mediator must have no known opinions. If it were thought that Cabinet Office men supported the Treasury against departments, or one policy position or personality over against another, they would find it difficult to gain co-operation. The Cabinet Office job demands devotion to finding a solution, not necessarily the perfect solution but one that will facilitate, first, a decision and second, a decision that is made on time. Cabinet Office regulars are changed by the office because they must be concerned with moving things along.

Members of the Cabinet Office exert their influence not by taking formal positions but through informal contacts. Their influence is determined not by what they put on paper, but by who talks to whom, where papers get sent and who is invited to meetings. Because Cabinet committees must handle far more business than the Cabinet as a whole, the Cabinet Office can facilitate agreement by varying the composition of official committees that service the ministerial committees. The Cabinet Office determines which paper goes to what subcommittee, when, and in what form. In a system in which time and information are both scarce resources, these are formidable powers. Some Cabinet Office officials may influence a decision by writing a paper slanted in a particular direction; but most can accomplish the same thing by controlling the balance in the study group that will do the actual work. Endless rounds of personal contact and private persuasion within Whitehall make up virtually the whole of the Cabinet Office world.

Each Whitehall network covers part of the other. The Treasury network, the reader may recall, is composed of those hundred or so people in the Treasury and the departments particularly concerned with expenditures. The Cabinet Office network, which almost certainly includes less than 100 individuals, overlaps part of the financial network to include people who are experienced in dealing with each other on issues that regularly cut across departments. A third network, far smaller than the other two, is formed by the nexus between the Cabinet Office and the Prime Minister's Office. The Secretary of the Cabinet is, in effect, the permanent secretary and a chief adviser to the Prime Minister. It was the Cabinet Secretary, Sir Edward Bridges, who went with Churchill to Yalta and Attlee to Potsdam; it was Sir Norman Brook who was a 'tower of strength' to Macmillan at No. 10. While President Nixon brought Henry Kissinger to talks, Wilson and later Heath were accompanied by the Cabinet Secretary, Sir Burke Trend.[7] The Cabinet Secretary manages the Prime Minister's time. He arranges the agenda for Cabinet. His views on what is important carry, therefore, great weight.

The Prime Minister himself is also served by a small communications centre staffed by approximately four private secretaries, all members of the Civil Service. When circumstances permit, these officials sit in the same room and listen in on each other's conversations, a picture that is perhaps the epitome of the British mode of co-ordination. The Prime Minister will also bring with him a personal secretary outside the Civil Service. All together, the Prime Ministerial network, excluding clerical help, involves less than twenty-five people. Its task is to see that the Prime Minister is never surprised, that he gets where he is supposed to go, and that he has as much information about the merits of policy and the desires of the disputants as he can reasonably absorb.

The CPRS has been superimposed on these existing networks. It is a potential threat to all of them. For the departments, the CPRS adds a new element of uncertainty and another hurdle to climb. Must they, after running the gamut of interdepartmental committees at all levels, face yet another protagonist whose reactions, to make things worse, are unpredictable and irresponsible? The CPRS necessarily appears unpredictable because its forays into the departments are sporadic and discontinuous; its irresponsibility emerges from the ability to push bright ideas and ask awkward questions without having the tough executive job of making programmes work. The Treasury is about economic policy and resource allocation, but in both areas the CPRS claims authority. The Cabinet Office, which needs more analytical skill than it has, fears that it will be subordinated to the CPRS. If the Cabinet Office were providing proper analytic assistance, the implication is, there would be no need for the CPRS. Sometimes a sluggish competitive spirit is aroused in the Cabinet Office, but the CPRS can just as easily serve as an alibi for not doing more.

7. Macmillan, *Riding the Storm*, p. 188; Wilson, *The Labour Government 1964–1970*, p. 753.

Anyway, new efforts by the Cabinet Office to expand its scope can now be met with the claim that the CPRS is there to do that. The Secretary of the Cabinet and the Prime Minister's personal staff cannot look too happily on a prospect in which the P.M. seeks a continuous stream of advice from a new organisation that is not geared into any of the old ties that have cemented relationships for so long. Sixteen new men have now to be absorbed into or kept out of the existing networks.

As new boy on the patch, the CPRS must differentiate its contribution. There is obviously little to be gained by trying to become another compromise-creating machine. The litany on strategies, priorities, long-term, etc., must be translated into good works which will be of use to someone and not threaten everyone. CPRS is still struggling to work out this conversion, but we can begin to sketch the general drift of its activity, achieved partly by design and partly by the force of circumstances.

The CPRS can claim two distinctive features: the breadth of its analysis and the political content of its advice. The Cabinet Office cannot deal with people outside of Whitehall. Everything it does has to come from the Whitehall network or be inside the official's head when he gets to the Cabinet Office. No one, in his capacity as a Cabinet Office regular, meets with interest groups or the public. The Cabinet Office is an internal process of government. The rationale for having no outside contact is that it is supposed to be dedicated entirely to serving the Cabinet.

For our purposes, it is important to understand what might be meant by policy analysis in this rarefied atmosphere. Let us suppose that the Treasury and Cabinet Office prepared briefs for the Prime Minister on a disputed policy. The Treasury will be concerned largely with expenditure implications and, if these do not appear to be major, it might do little. The Cabinet Office will try to balance evenly the pros and cons, extracting the main points from the mass of papers provided by the rival departments. All committee members in the Cabinet Office network are encouraged to bring out the broader issues, not merely those sponsored by the departmental protagonists, but that is hard to do. The wider the considerations, the more difficult is agreement. Though the official committee will probably have a chairman and/or secretary from the Cabinet Office, they must deal essentially with what the protagonists put before them. The content of the brief to the minister who is chairman of the Cabinet committee will depend a great deal on the reservoir of experience and quickness of thought that the man who writes it brings with him to the Cabinet Office.

Sometimes the Cabinet Office man can draw on prior departmental experience to write an expanded brief, but if so, it is sheer coincidence. Mostly he is a talented layman trying to relate the issues to a wider context. Perhaps there is a better way of cutting through the conventional PESC classification (e.g., publicity costs in the government as a whole rather than by department) or a wider political context which the department should have caught (e.g., subsidising shipbuilding may create problems for EEC negotiations). Occasionally, the Cabinet Office man will get hold of a friend in a department to do more extensive analysis; more formally, he might try farming out analysis by getting a working party established.

But all of this takes time. Faced with the need for expediting business, the Cabinet Office can only occasionally say that a matter a department wishes to have decided immediately should be subjected to further analysis. For the most part the Cabinet Office has been (and must be) preoccupied with day-to-day pedestrian work – writing briefs, keeping minutes, checking up on progress, getting papers from departments, arranging for legislative proposals to come forward, clearing everything with the main participants. At its base, any man with experience will tell you, 'The Cabinet Office is a high-grade servicing machine.' Only in rare periods, when departments and their ministers are relatively quiescent, as in 1960–4, may the Cabinet Office become a seed-bed of change as officials, thwarted in their usual home-base, seek support for new ideas in the Cabinet committee system. With ministers pushing their own ideas hard, officials tend to lie low and let them bear the burden.

Unlike the Cabinet Office, the CPRS is deliberately empowered to make contact with City financial interests, industry, the academic world and others outside government. Not that these outsiders always have interesting things to say, but it is a chance to broaden a spectrum that otherwise includes only ministers and civil servants. More important, the CPRS is in a central position to offer a competing analysis to those presented from the Treasury's financial lens and the conciliatory presumptions of the Cabinet Office system.

The substance of CPRS analysis can also veer in an overtly political direction as no traditional civil service briefing could. A civil service paper might say that prices are going up by so much and that unemployment is high, but it would not be emphatic about the government's political problem. There is scope here for the CPRS to take a view of the political realities and to present this to ministers with less mincing of words. One of the Chequers strategy sessions held with ministers in 1972 concerned inflation. As one of the ministerial participants reported, 'The facts were borne home to us, what we had promised and what was happening. The statistics had been available to everyone before but no one had wanted to see them. Too unpleasant. We needed reminding about how serious things were getting.' Who else would do this? Another participant observed, 'Officials couldn't say – I don't think most ministers would dare to say to the Prime Minister – look here, we're making an ass out of ourselves on this and that. We're up the creek on inflation, and in another three months we're going to be on the rocks.'

The dangers are clear. Any minister is in a position to cry 'foul' and say that this is the sort of thing ministers themselves are supposed to do. Our job, they say, is to use our own political antennae and not count on government appointees to do it for us. The cost of a broader perspective can be that the CPRS – or anything like it – will be suspected by party activists of being presumptuous or unsympathetic to the party programme, and by civil servants of being too partisan. In the former case, ministers will withdraw support. In the latter, if the CPRS were thought to rush continually to the Conservative Central Office for advice, civil servants might withdraw their co-operation.

An advantage of being new is that you are not committed to the old. In a system where few top positions change, each party thinks the Civil Service has gone stale. During the first year or two, therefore, ministers in a new Government are conscious of the need to impose their way of thinking against that of their predecessors. A new unit that appears to be different can, accordingly, help ministers believe they have had a fair go at instituting change. A quasi-independent unit also helps ministers with the political problem of eating their own words. New governments are prone to exaggerate the difference any group of men can make on policy. If a government must climb down on the whole business of industrial subsidies and 'lame ducks', there is a certain amount of embarrassment involved in overriding officials whose advice was previously taken; a new unit, because it is new, can help overcome this feeling. To make the change on the advice of a committee staffed entirely by former Department of Economic Affairs officials, who had been vindicated by events, would never do.

Which is not to say the CPRS is or should normally emerge victorious from conflicts with departments. The Prime Minister, for instance, has taken a contrary view to that expressed by certain of his colleagues at the prompting of the CPRS on several occasions and at other times he has listened to what the CPRS had to say and given in to the departmental viewpoint. It would be strange if, on balance, the departments and their ministers did not prevail most of the time. The CPRS is justified not as a replacement for government by department, but as an occasional modifier of it. And if, when the CPRS is plainly defeated by departmental protest, officials tunnel away down below to emerge with a similar idea they claim was already in the pipeline, that too is all right. The aim of the CPRS is not usurpation but action.

If the first problem of CPRS is to get its own work to do, its second is not to take on too much or to tackle the wrong thing. Cabinet deals with something like ten issues a week. Attempting to comment on all or most of them would lend a superficial quality to CPRS analyses. Sixteen men cannot constitute a counter-Whitehall, and new boys must worry more about their reputations than those who are already established. Soon enough the word can get out that the CPRS has got its facts and figures wrong or that it has fallen into the same trap that experienced officials have long since learned to avoid. The CPRS must try to produce advice that is relevant to the interest of ministers (so they won't ignore it), timely for the processing of decisions by Cabinet (so it won't be lost in the rush), accurate in its facts (so as to avoid ridicule), original in policy design (so as not to duplicate the work of departments), and brief in compass (so ministers will read it). A large order for less than two dozen men. Nor are all the criteria compatible. Qualities of brevity, timeliness and relevance may conflict with originality, accuracy and profundity.

The general character of the CPRS work-load can readily be

deduced.[8] First are the interdepartmental issues, though these come in a variety of types. If a question is interdepartmental because several departments are having a thundering row, the CPRS is likely to stand clear, certainly until the dust is well settled. Another type of issue more attractive to the CPRS is multi-departmental in that it affects everyone's operations but has no one sponsor (e.g., administration of research and use of computers). If the Treasury did not have proprietary rights over expenditure and the Civil Service Department over personnel, these administrative processes would also be fair game because they are used in the widest range of departments. Another candidate for CPRS interest are what might be called transdepartmental matters, substantive policies dealt with by several departments but which for reasons of long-time horizons, inertia or whatever, tend to become nobody's children (e.g., the general supply and demand for natural resources, manpower, fuel an energy policies, and regional development). Finally, and most troublesome of all, are ex-departmental items, issues which once might have belonged to an individual department or an interdepartmental committee but which has left ministers feeling dissatisfied. The common elements appear to be large cost, lack of confidence in the department or minister concerned, and urgency. Such topics have included the nationalization of Rolls Royce, the Concorde project, and the location of a third London airport. 'When Ministers want someone to hold their hand,' an observer from the Cabinet Office suggests, 'and they find the C.O.'s clammy or the interdepartmental's cold, they say "Let's get Victor Rothschild to hold it".' Should the CPRS, from its own point of view, wish to hold on to every outstretched hand? Not if it wishes to be more than a dustbin for every irreconcilable conflict and unsolveable problem.

The best way of knowing what a minister cares about is to go and ask him, as Lord Rothschild has done. Part of the CPRS work-load originates by design with ministers' immediate concerns. If the CPRS were not careful, however, it would end up working on each and every crisis worrying particular ministers. That may be good for building political support but not for doing in-depth studies and quality analysis. The dilemma, according to a CPRS official, is that 'it's essential to do the necessary thing.

8. Interview with Prime Minister Heath, *Evening Standard*, 1 June 1972, pp. 24–5; *The Observer*, 20 February 1972.

If you're going to be useful to a minister, then you'd better be useful in the short term or you will not be useful at all. But then you risk getting tied up entirely in short-term projects.' The CPRS does not wish to be thought of as usurping the function of television commentators in making off-the-cuff remarks on yesterday's headlines. Nor does it wish to exist in a rarified atmosphere that has no grounding in the expressed needs of politicians. So the CPRS is always engaged in a delicate balancing act between reacting to the ordinary crisis that has already manifested itself and responding to the ones that are not yet visible and which it would like to head off.

Keeping the long-run alive within the CPRS is always an uphill battle. 'You're, in fact, involved,' a harried official mused, 'in an organisation with few people and a perpetual possibility of spreading yourself too thin. We are not always our own master.' Out of the maelstrom of its experience, the CPRS has tried to evolve a series of rules to keep the long-term, by which it means the broader, more time-consuming analyses, from disappearing entirely.

Issues having trivial resource implications, be they public, private, or whatever are not good candidates for the CPRS. The regulations concerning the subject matter may be intricate, requiring substantial investment of manpower, but the consequences are few. 'Sometimes,' an official adds, 'there are issues where the conclusion is foregone and you must ask whether it is so important that you will try to stop it, knowing that you'll probably fail anyway, and that's a reason for keeping out of it. There are times when I say, though not all my colleagues agree, that if you are in doubt, don't do it.' To avoid the trivial or the hopeless, the CPRS must avoid being the receptacle for anything departments do not want to do or do badly. 'This,' they are agreed, 'would be suicide.' The CPRS, like the Treasury, must try to distinguish between the things that departments should be helped to do better rather than those that central organisations should try to do on their own.

Rules on what to avoid are perhaps not as useful as criteria for what to take on. One way around the difficulty is to make some people within the organisation responsible for the broader issues. Now any division of labour in a tiny organisation is bound to break down. But a few CPRS officials are known as 'Mister Short-Run' and others as 'Mister Long-Run', giving them special responsibility to keep from being entirely immersed in the lesser matters. If a topic thought of as short-run must be done, as is often the case, 'the CPRS', said an official who has thought long and hard on the subject, 'tries to pick a well-defined short-term topic. We don't want to become the world's greatest living expert on computers or whatever. We want the job to last three or four months and then finish with it.'

Obtaining a few months in which to do analytical work is not easy. It is not unusual for the CPRS to do an analysis and then discover that 'we never had the opportunity to expound our policies as a whole, or to any particular minister. The Budget was coming up and parts of the package had to be decided then, so the decision was taken piecemeal and there was nothing left to do.' Time may be available on a subject that has not been studied before or that is not presently in the province of a single department. Ordinarily there are analyses competing for presentation within rigid time limits.

The short-term takes on a real meaning when the CPRS, like most ministers, gets the papers on Monday night and the decision is supposed to be taken on Wednesday morning. The CPRS could hardly put in a substantial analysis of its own unless it had been forewarned so as to prepare in the preceding month. That is another reason why it must try to keep good relations with departments. Displays of instant wisdom may not be to the liking of the CPRS but it is destined to be in that business. If it must comment, the CPRS will get on the phone with the Treasury and the departments within the short time available and try hard to have its draft circulated so as to avoid looking foolish. 'Sometimes,' the story goes, 'we run into trouble when commenting on papers at short notice. You can misread the paper and take what is said out of proportion. You can make logically valid comments, but the situation they refer to is not real, which is another reason I believe in sending out drafts. The bush telegraph is fantastically efficient around here.'

All these headaches in the think-tank are predictable enough for an institution trying to carve out living space between ministers and officials, between spending departments, Treasury and Cabinet Office. Like everyone else, CPRS needs the co-operation of the Whitehall community for supplementary manpower, inside information and constructive compliance. The question is, who needs the CPRS? PAR can be jollied along a good while by Treasury interest, but unless ministers know and act as if CPRS is for them, the game is up. Unless the client is also the advocate, the verdict is a foregone conclusion.

Who is Your Client? Who is Your Advocate?

Who is our client? That's easy. We work for the Cabinet. The question is, is the Cabinet working for us?

CPRS official

Now you've probably already discovered that there's always been a phobia about Presidential government here. Anything you suggest must always be for the Cabinet, whether it is so or not.

A businessman consultant

Everyone is embarrassed to say what is true in fact, namely that it's for the Prime Minister. They fear that if they emphasise this fact it will damage his position with his colleagues.

A minister

One has got to be quite clear about that, CPRS is Cabinet Office which serves the Cabinet as well as me.

Prime Minister, Evening Standard, *1 June 1972*

The Prime Minister is not our client, except in so far as he is chairman of a committee and you tend to see the chairman more than the other members. The Cabinet is our client.

CPRS official

The Prime Minister has an office but he does not have a department. The Cabinet Office, many believe, is too closely connected with officialdom. The Treasury has its own minister and its special axe to grind. Why should the Prime Minister be denied access to independent sources of advice from within his own

Government? 'Is it right that, when ministers meet...', Mac-Dougall wrote in 1951, 'the Prime Minister alone should be largely unsupported by expert advice?' [9] The idea of the CPRS, as understood by the businessmen who thought it up, was to give an analytical capability to the Prime Minister. 'We prefer to say Cabinet,' a businessman adds, 'because of the bogey of Presidential government.'

Without prejudging the question of whether CPRS advice might also prove helpful to Cabinet in general, no one doubts that it could not survive unless it had the strong backing of the Prime Minister in particular. 'The Prime Minister is the man behind all this,' an informed observer reports. 'He doesn't like the old seat-of-the-pants politician as well as other ministers do.' Department officials agree that 'no one will listen to the CPRS unless there is a strong likelihood that the Prime Minister will back them, not merely because they are right, but because he is inclined to listen to them'. A party official acknowledges that 'the Prime Minister is evidently their great supporter; he is the one who is interested in resource allocation and in knowing about policy'. A political adviser refers to Prime Minister Heath's desire to be as well informed as any of his ministers on policy problems. 'He has power but not information and he means to get it.'

But political backing has a way of evaporating or becoming diverted. The Prime Minister may provide support on some issues and not on others, in regard to certain personalities but not to different men, a smaller rather than a larger proportion of the time. If the CPRS were forced to rely entirely on backing by the Prime Minister, it would involve him in continual quarrels with his colleagues. It would be unable to gather information through which to create advice that might interest the Prime Minister because departments would not co-operate without a prior word from the man on top. Members of the CPRS are well aware that they need to institutionalise their political backing so that they do not need to refer to the Prime Minister on every issue. Only if departments presume that he is more likely to support than not, and that their ministers will go along, will the CPRS be able to gain the

9. G. D. A. MacDougall, 'The Prime Minister's Statistical Section', in D. N. Chester (ed.) *Lessons of the British War Economy* (Cambridge: Cambridge University Press, 1951), p. 68.

normal and everyday co-operation that is essential for an enterprise that wishes to function on a continuous basis.

To that extent the idea that CPRS is for the Cabinet is not a misleading slogan but a vital political necessity – and a hope. Each minister being, in a pungent British phrase, 'the king of his own dung-hill', the Prime Minister cannot ordinarily issue orders in a field not his own. In an extremity he can remove a minister but he would be loath to push any single disagreement that far. He must, in his person, seek to reconcile collective rule with the individual responsibility of ministers to Parliament. The idea behind CPRS is to get other ministers doing the same, to strengthen the collective over the individual view by somehow joining both together. Perhaps, in asking Lord Rothschild to head the CPRS, the Prime Minister wished to see whether a modern scientist might also perform as an ancient alchemist.

Under the previous structure of advice, only the Prime Minister received a briefing that did not originate completely in a departmental viewpoint. The Cabinet Office did not devote much time to the analysis of policy subject matter and it briefed the chairmen of Cabinet committees rather than the Cabinet as a whole. There may have been fifteen to twenty men around the Cabinet table, of whom three knew something about the subject and about six were interested. If there was a conflict between the Secretary of State for the Environment and the Minister for Trade and Industry no one was there besides the disputants to say what the alternatives were, what their consequences might be, and whether the ones considered constituted the only reasonable options. The CPRS is supposed to give all interested ministers a collective briefing in their capacity as Cabinet members.

By definition, then, the CPRS task is to brief ministers who do not have a direct personal or departmental stake in the issue. The likelihood of pleasing those who are indifferent is considerably less than angering those who care. Mediators in family quarrels are used to being turned on by both sides who suddenly find a focus for their discontent. How much more likely the mediator is to become the injured party when his role consists of telling the combatants that they are all wrong.

While the CPRS would like the Cabinet as a whole to be its client because that would guarantee widespread political backing, experience has made it wonder whether there is such a thing as a collective decision. It is true that every minister does not get what he wants, but these reversals are the product of shifting coalitions within Cabinet, not necessarily of a group spirit that is larger than any of its components. Issues of importance might be expected to concern the Cabinet collectively; unfortunately it always seems as if they concern some ministers more than others. If the CPRS takes on the burden of reminding ministers they have a collective as well as individual role to perform, it could become known as a common scold. The CPRS needs ministerial support, yet its intervention is predicated on the belief that departmental briefs are self-serving. Occasionally it is advantageous to a department to have the CPRS intervene to support them against the Treasury. With its presumed expertise in financial matters, the CPRS might have a better chance of arguing against the Treasury position. But departmental ministers do not like it so well when the CPRS intervenes against them. If the CPRS is successful, some department has lost. Most ministers, therefore, do not seem to like CPRS very well.

It is not difficult to imagine a situation in which a majority of ministers like CPRS participation some of the time, but nevertheless all hate it most of the time. It is possible to make seventeen enemies in Cabinet by doing one thing that each of the ministers disapprove of intensely, even though they approve mildly of the sixteen other actions that do not affect them directly. The CPRS may counter by saying that its main task is to gear policy to the government's political strategy, whose success is in the interest of the Cabinet as a whole. To that the Minister is likely to retort that he – the politician – and not the CPRS is the one to decide what strategy is and whether it is being followed. Politics makes people insecure. Why should a minister, subject to all the other vicissitudes, welcome a new organisation whose purpose is to give advice to fellow ministers so they can criticise how he is doing his job. PAR might suggest that civil servants should be replaced; CPRS cuts closer to home.

These political considerations are not lost on the CPRS, whose members seek to cope with the situation as they find it. There is no law requiring them to intervene everywhere and all at once. They can decide, to use their own jargon, that it is not cost-effective to challenge a particular policy or that it would be better to save their criticisms for another day. They might phrase their comments in such a way as not to take sides between ministers. The sledge-hammer need not be used in every case. It is especially unwise to keep using it on the same member.

One thing the CPRS can do to serve the Cabinet as a whole is to look for situations in which every member feels that he has been badly served. The difficulty is that what a member of Cabinet says in a hypothetical way he may not mean to carry out in a practical manner. In general terms, everyone is against making snap decisions. They all regret that the forty-eight-hour rule (that ministers should have two days' notice of items coming to Cabinet) is observed in the breach. The CPRS may intervene with its own paper not so much offering a different alternative as suggesting that this is not the right time to make the requisite decisions. The desire for quick action is nonetheless universal. The same protesting members often use the very same device they profess to dislike. They will rush in one afternoon asking their colleagues urgently to agree to give fifteen million pounds to X food company because it is in serious trouble, has long been a national and sentimental favourite, and is about to lay off its employees. The CPRS is likely to wonder whether the matter is so urgent or important. It may doubt that the company will collapse overnight. Perhaps the action has implications for governmental policy in which small immediate payments will pre-empt much larger choices in the future. Indeed, the CPRS has prepared a kind of child's guide for ministers containing simple questions to ask whenever someone else says they must act because the moment of crisis is at hand. So far as anyone knows, the document has fallen into the void and suffered an obscure fate. The advice of Thomas Alva Edison (after the American Congress rejected an invention for instantaneously recording every vote) not to devise brilliant schemes to secure objectives that no one wishes achieved is being learned again.

Not taking politics out of the Cabinet, but getting Cabinet politics into the CPRS is its problem. On sensitive issues it does little good trying to interpret the political acceptability of various alternatives from a distance. Advisers need a direct line to what ministers are thinking, but the CPRS has no assured means of doing this on a continuing basis. At the end of 1972, Lord Rothschild reported seeing the Prime Minister only on average of every five to seven weeks.[10] Lord Rothschild and his senior officials

10. 'Thinking about the Think Tank', *The Listener*, 28 December 1972.

cannot appear at Cabinet meetings; that is still *verboten*. But they can and do appear before Cabinet committees. The idea of a non-ministerial advocate at ministerial meetings is strange in the British context and is felt to be so by department officials and their ministers. Yet there is little choice. Otherwise, the CPRS is left in the anomalous position of always being represented by a formal paper that ministers may or may not have read in the car coming to the Cabinet meeting. Departmental ministers have been personally briefed by their civil servants. No one is there to act as advocate for the CPRS position unless Lord Rothschild can get to some minister who, not being directly involved, is willing to risk opprobrium in a cause not his own. For a minister to say that 'what Lord Rothschild's group needs to acquire is more political weight', is the understatement of the year.

Access – The Loneliness of the Long-Distance Thinker

> Because CPRS exists we assume they've got a role. We don't fight a department battle, at least not much. It's not in our tradition. We all know each other in the different departments. One tries to make the machine work.
>
> *Department official*

> I recall the sniggering gossip of Oxbridge graduates in the Cabinet Office in 1965 – 'we were told to give Balogh [economic adviser] all the Cabinet papers, but Trend [Cabinet Secretary] says forget it.'
>
> *Terry Pitt*, The Guardian, *15 May 1972*

> The CPRS is insulated from the public expenditure process and that is not a good idea, because it makes it hard to get into things.
>
> *CPRS official*

If the CPRS wants to get in on what is going on, it needs access to departmental machinery. It could easily be isolated from trends of thinking and opportunities for influencing decisions. Moreover, with a staff of only sixteen people, the CPRS must depend on departments for analytical work beyond the few studies it can manage on its own. In the Whitehall competition for departmental bodies to do the work, the CPRS joins the Treasury and the Cabinet Office. Unless it likes waiting in line, the CPRS must find ways and means of tapping into departmental activities.

Once a year Cabinet decides, with advice from the CPRS, the basic subjects CPRS shall undertake. In the course of an interview largely devoted to the CPRS, Prime Minister Heath added that Lord Rothschild can initiate projects whenever he sees a problem arising, exactly as a department would.[11] Recourse to the Steering Comittee of Cabinet is also available when the CPRS spots a new subject that demands speedy attention. Departments may fight in Cabinet against the choice of a subject but, once it has been authorised, 'we have the right to push our noses in. Even a permanent secretary will not go against that'. Still, getting a formal invitation and receiving helpful assistance are two different things.

Cabinet authorisation for the CPRS is likely to include several omnibus items, such as general oversight of government, 'that would get us in anywhere so that we can legitimately interfere'. As custodians of the overall government strategy, the CPRS can always claim a watch-dog interest. It can say that policy here or there is changing so as to affect the party programme, which makes it proper to ask what the department is doing about it and, possibly, to suggest what might be done to maintain the integrity of the party in power.

The CPRS has an interest in expanding the interdepartmental realm. The wider it is, the more access the CPRS has. The department has an interest in narrowing the range of subjects that allows other people to interfere in what it considers its own business. Experience with the classification of programmes suggests that they may deal with geographic area, the clientele serviced, the process of administration, or major purpose. If a programme is defined by a major purpose like education, defence or health, it would appear to belong in one of the great departments. If the same programme were organised around clientele, such as children or women or shopkeepers, it would evidently cut across a number of departments. The CPRS prefers the principle that allows it to intervene.

11. *Evening Standard*, 1 June 1972, pp. 24–5.

Whether a subject is properly interdepartmental or not, is a subject that medieval scholastics would have enjoyed.

Whether the CPRS is entitled to access on interdepartmental grounds, therefore, depends not necessarily on the intrinsic nature of programmes but on how men choose to define them. Energy policy, for example, might belong to a single department such as Trade and Industry until one argues that there are international implications (sulphur from high chimney stacks in Britain can be found in Sweden) bringing in the Foreign Office, and that the Department of the Environment should be concerned about pollution, and on and on. Conversely, the creation of superdepartments has meant that programmes which some people think ought to be considered together, despite their disparate nature, may not be open to outside scrutiny in that way because they occur within a single organisational entity. Take the Department of the Environment and the question of housing *v.* roads. To some people it does not seem right for the DOE to say it has a total programme and to decide to push roads at the expense of housing without consulting others. They believe these things should come to a central point for decision by the Cabinet as a whole and that CPRS is a proper vehicle for doing that. The minister in charge may have a difficult time seeing the point. And there is no other minister in Cabinet who is likely to take a direct interest precisely because neither roads nor housing are located in his bailiwick.

Analysis takes time and time requires notice and notice depends on departmental political administrators who know better than other people what issues they are likely to bring to Cabinet. Wishing to avoid the *fait accompli*, fearful of chasing after issues at the last moment with weak memoranda, the CPRS sought to create an 'early warning system' [12] whose purpose was to elicit advance information about likely issues for future decision. Departments were asked to tell the CPRS what issues they expected to give to the Cabinet in the next year. To avoid cluttering up its life with lists of trivia, the CPRS would have liked departments to select major issues that concern strategic objectives of government. Instead the CPRS received each department's lists of things too horrible to contemplate that might occur next year. Ask an experienced man what might conceivably happen and he will tell

12. See Mr R. J. East's testimony, H.C. 147 (1971–2), p. 20.

you. There might be civil war in Northern Ireland or scandals in the police forces or crippling national strikes or who knows what. No one says exactly that gazing into the crystal ball is not the business of the CPRS; department officials merely give such a full answer that no one is wiser in the end than they were at the beginning.

It exists; therefore it may get called in. One asset and liability the CPRS does have is that ministers may call on it when no one knows what to do. There are times when policy is fluid and there are substantial disagreements within the departments. Then the expert CPRS adviser may have his moment of glory, provided he has a good idea. Failing that, the CPRS may make a concerted attack on an area of policy by seeking to bring it into commission, thus breaking down the monopoly of information formerly possessed by those who ostensibly are supposed to deal with it. The initial move is to find more than one department involved. The next is to have the newcomer insist that it would be useful to establish an interdepartmental committee to consider the matter. The larger the number of participants, the more likely the CPRS is to be invited, the less any single department can reject its participation, and the more information it may acquire for purposes of inspiring future intervention. The effort to create a committee of top economic advisers from the departments as a counter to the Treasury and to deprive the Treasury of exclusive ownership of the short and medium term forecasts is a move in this direction. Where before, department members who helped the Treasury prepare these forecasts were not even supposed to discuss them with their own permanent secretaries, the Cabinet now has the benefit of comments from a broader group of economists within the government.

Departmental co-operation may be reluctant, but it is not entirely absent. Department officials would rarely deny information outright; they would always give some assistance. Asked in a shrewd way, department officials, after all, can never tell when they might find it advantageous to persuade the CPRS people of their view. So long as the CPRS has political sanction, departments will go along with it without creating too much fuss. It may not be a love feast but departments have not tried to sabotage CPRS.

CPRS would like to have automatic ways of getting into the act

P.G.P.M.—12

so that it doesn't have to make special arrangements every time. The Treasury is assured access on anything that costs money, which means virtually everything, but the CPRS has no such ready-made formula to justify its interventions. Having drilled many a dry hole, the prospectors are likely to cast covetous eyes on the gushers that can produce a constant flow of privileged access. PAR is one such stream. Under the concordat that brought PAR to the Treasury, the CPRS is entitled to be involved at every point – the selection of studies, the work on analysis, the discussion of results. It alone is allowed to brief the Prime Minister on each PAR study. The Treasury is interested in getting better analysis through PAR and in gearing its results into the PESC cycle. CPRS wants to introduce an order of priorities outside of the PESC cycle in the form of a governmental strategy. It also wants to use PAR to widen the scope of its influence.

Ever mindful of the need to answer the question of why they are there when the Treasury is supposed to do that job, CPRS tries to distinguish its own outlook. People who control expenditures must be interested in controlling it. They may be interested in whether the policy makes sense, but under stringent conditions they must treat all customers on the basis of distributing misery equally. Whereas the Treasury 'would think of the stones it could squeeze the best,' CPRS officials will say, 'we can say that expenditures should be increased.' While the Treasury is concerned with large expenditure programmes, the CPRS might be more interested in the quality of life or in objectives that did not immediately implicate substantial sums. Concern with the desirability of objectives, as well as the money spent on them, would presumably be an important CPRS interest.

Yet the fact is that the CPRS too must be concerned about resource constraints; that is a large part of what analysis is about. If resources were unlimited, there would be no need for analysis at all. Maybe there are real differences in approach between the Treasury and CPRS, and perhaps thrashing about would turn up more of them, but we are doubtful. The Treasury is concerned with getting value for money as well as overall totals; it does take an interest in programmes that affect expenditures outside of government. If the Treasury cares about totals, so must the CPRS or anyone else who shapes responsibility at the centre.

An important difference in emphasis between the Treasury and

CPRS does lie in the scope of the studies they seek to encourage. The Treasury is likely to be satisfied if an area of importance is handled in a better way; the CPRS will extend coverage in line with its interdepartmental emphasis. The Department of Education and Science, for instance, might think it was involved in education and not in social services, but the CPRS will say otherwise. Where programmes are not organised around specific clientele, the CPRS will try to get studies going on how citizens of certain ages are treated under different services. It can always say that the individuals must be treated as a whole and not fragmented. Were circumstances reversed, and departments organised around age groups, the CPRS could maintain the opposite point of view with equal conviction. Nor is this necessarily devious. It is desirable to have someone looking at problems from a point of view other than the one enshrined in the organisation charts.

Broadening the scope of PAR studies brings in more departments; lengthening the time horizons gives the CPRS more time to do research itself, to evaluate research done by departments, and to come up with a position of its own in time for ministers to act. The tendency of departments to concentrate on tiny slices of their activities runs counter to CPRS interests because the policies considered are neither large enough to justify its attention nor do they continue far enough into the future to suggest points of critical decision. The larger the scope of a PAR study, the more it is worthwhile looking at different ways of doing things. The point is not so much to ask how, say, the existing educational system would look in an imaginary and ideal world, but whether modifications are possible. No one is interested in making such decisions fifteen years from now; the CPRS would like to know what decisions with large future implications it should get in on during the term of the present government.

In addition to trying to make PAR studies wider and longer at the outset, the CPRS tries to shape them while they are under way. It will argue that only half of the relevant options have been considered and that others, mentioning a few, should be taken into account. At this juncture the CPRS needs to make a strategic decision: should it 'pick on bad eggs now and get a reputation for needling the department by saying "there's a bloody awful system that needs to be torn down"' or should it suggest more modest changes. The mild view stems from the conviction that 'it is absolutely essential to convince the departments they will get benefits out of this'. The sharp view arises from the conviction that CPRS exists 'to deal hammer blows now and again'. The predictable reaction to the hammer blow is pain. The department screams; the CPRS retreats, replying that it will be happy if one or two more options are considered and agreeing that the entire edifice need not be torn down just now.

Radical reappraisal depends on political guidance. CPRS officials would like to ask ministers whether they think an existing programme will be viable in the years ahead and, if not, whether they have backing to proceed with a more critical analysis. They know that 'if the minister does not give support, there's no point whatsoever in going ahead'.

Retaining the possibility of ministerial backing depends heavily in turn on maintaining decent relations with the Treasury. Having the Chancellor of the Exchequer, in addition to a spending minister, come down on the CPRS would nearly always prove fatal. It would involve the Prime Minister in a conflict with two of his important departmental colleagues which, even if won, would bode ill for the future. Access to information also depends heavily on being kept informed by the Treasury, the one organisation which knows, if anyone does, what is going on. CPRS officials may not always want to live cosily with the Treasury but they certainly have not figured out how to live without it.

As usual in village society, both sides have people who know one another. Half of the CPRS staff come from the Civil Service directly and most of the other half have had governmental experience, including two ex-Treasury men. Like the professionals they are, these people have worked out the usual accommodation. The CPRS man, knowing he cannot write an effective brief unless he has sufficient time, would hope to be kept informed about the progress of any proposals involving major expenditures. Unless time was very short, he would, in turn, expect to show a draft of his commentary to the Treasury and wait for its reaction until sending it on further. The Treasury and CPRS officials would not accept all of each other's suggestions, but they would definitely try to show each other what they thought. That is the way the machine works. For the most part CPRS and Treasury officials are correct when they say their relations are agreeable and they do not normally quarrel. Only at the edges, when they disagree about whether the CPRS should be legitimately involved in a particular policy, are there ripples in the surface calm.

The Treasury could easily live without the CPRS, but not vice versa. When the Rolls Royce and the Mini face a collision, one may have more to lose than the other, but is also likely to inflict far more damage. CPRS does not 'want to disagree with the Treasury by accident. If we must disagree, then we want it to be by design about something we consider important.' Treasury men can afford to wait and see whether the CPRS is around long enough to be worth worrying about. CPRS men have to worry here and now, which is not entirely inappropriate for an organisation that is supposed to act as a political conscience.

The Uneasy Conscience

CPRS man: If we do this our stock will fall lower than ever.

Minister: It's at zero now.

Even if it's a balls-aching business, politics is in such low esteem with the people that it's not bad to keep forcing us to confront what we were supposed to achieve when we came in.

A minister

The CPRS is warmed-over Whitehall.

A permanent secretary

It is too political.

A permanent secretary

I'd like to know how independent that body is, I really would.

Ex-Labour minister

The CPRS is an uneasy conscience. Its purpose is to remind political administrators of things they would rather forget. Today's evil is never sufficient; the CPRS must make tomorrow's problems part of today's considerations. It must remind the Government of its failure to carry out past promises. The accomplishments of yesteryear are other people's meat : the CPRS must feed upon the half-digested portions of current errors, lest they become future failures.

The CPRS is supposed to deal with the translation of party objectives into governmental policy. Of national objectives, it can always be said that they are vague, multiple and conflicting. Because governments must appeal to different groups at various places and times, they satisfy a broader constituency by emphasizing opposing values. This is true of all governments in a democratic society. The Heath Government, for instance, was caught between general rhetoric espousing freedom of choice at the local government level and its specific will on such things as housing rent and free school milk. The dilemma was nicely summed up by the Principal Finance Officer in Health : 'all governments want to give local authorities more independence provided that the local authorities do what the Government wants them to do'.[13] In the confrontation between substantive policy and local freedom of choice, which pronouncement of the Conservatives or which party principle should prevail? Merely to point out the contradiction would leave ministers dissatisfied and the CPRS more unpopular than ever. It must try to establish a preference ordering among candidate policies and sell these to the political men.

Before the CPRS can give advice to ministers on how to carry out their objectives, therefore, it must first discover what these are supposed to be. Its members pore over party documents, election manifestoes, and campaign speeches, trying vainly to impose a sense of order out of the disparate collection of sounds and happenings. Then they try to compare what ministers said during the election they were going to do with what has been done, emphasizing the distance between where they are and where they said they were going, suggesting what might be done to close the gap. The strongest line for the CPRS to take is that among an array of options made available to ministers, Proposal A rather than Proposal B is more consistent with announced party policy. Yet the minister who disagrees can always find another party statement that appears to justify his position. By getting in early, before lines have had a chance to harden, the CPRS may on occasion circumvent this difficulty. A weaker position for the CPRS is to say that departmental options are too narrow, that the

13. H.C. 323 (1970–1), p. 86.

time scale is too short, that no real effort has been made to estimate costs. To attack a departmental position without having a better alternative to suggest is at best a delaying tactic to provide more time for analysis, and at worst a way of making enemies without offsetting the loss by making new friends.

The Conservative Party is keen to show it has kept faith with the voters. Higher up, it may be viewed as strengthening citizen confidence in government, thus enhancing authority and legitimacy. Lower down it may be viewed as a good election tactic. Either way, the Conservative Research Department issues periodic reports with titles such as 'Conservatives Keep Their Promises'.[14]

Interpreting the party programme is by no means the special preserve of the CPRS. Every minister can claim that is his task and he is doing it well. Any civil servant can say, as many did to us, 'my function is to help my minister get his policies approved. Now these purposes are found in the Party manifesto and so my purpose is to help him realize the Party's programme.' Civil servants traditionally prepare policies for incoming ministers based on careful perusal of party documents and his own speeches. The Conservative Party might be excused if it wished to have a small voice in monitoring the implementation of Party programmes. There is no lack of willing helpers. Given that the here and now is so heavily populated with talented spokesmen, the CPRS seeks to become still more distinctive by emphasising its proprietary interest in something called long-run strategy.

'I don't expect this within my working lifetime,' a CPRS man confesses, 'but I would like to have the government considering its objectives as a totality, not each individual department separately and then horse-trading. At least there should be a set of people who look at the situation as a whole.' Neither he nor anyone else, of course, can say what it means to look at the situation as a whole. The situation reflects the characteristic distaste of analysts for the messy ways in which policy invariably emerges through a political process. One way of conceptualising the whole would be to say that there should be an interest separate and apart from those of the individual departments, though putting it that way would suggest that the CPRS view is also limited and partial. Another way is to suggest that there is something more virtuous about the long- and something seamy about the short-run.

14. Conservative Research Department, 14 June 1971, no. 12.

The CPRS deliberately attracts people who say that 'I am temperamentally a long-run man. There is not enough concentration on the long-term in the British machine.' He wants to have an idea of where he is trying to go 'even if you know that you are not likely to get there and even if the idea's wrong.' The long-run, to this man, means not better knowledge of how to secure future effects but a willful choice of which ones are desirable.

Talking to departments about the next ten or twenty years leads them to engage in defensive behaviour. Since their first duty is to protect what they have, they will tell you they plan to do everything they are now doing and to do more of the same in the next decade. Should a department actually come up with something new, the CPRS would bring in the question of priorities. Does the department have objectives and how can these be realised within the existing financial constraints? That type of interaction makes the CPRS look like the Treasury, an appearance that cannot be mitigated by saying that the CPRS is interested in more than cuts. Resources are limited for everybody, except those who disappear into the mists of long-term strategy.

By and large, CPRS officials believe that 'most Cabinet members are temperamentally, by training and by experience, extremely disinclined to pay attention to the long-term. We are asking them to think longer term, that is, toward what objectives are they working. Then they can take their short term actions with the longer term in mind.' The only example anyone could think of was the Prime Minister's well-known insistence upon joining the European Economic Community. The desire to get it all over with, if not once and for all, then possibly on a yearly basis, is so appealing that political administrators begin to wonder why it hasn't been done. Perhaps, they reason, they are so preoccupied with daily crises they do not have time to sit down in peace and quiet to figure out how far they have come and where they would like to go. That is what Prime Minister Heath meant when he told a reporter that 'I had seen Cabinets which all the time seemed to be dealing with the day-to-day problems and there was never a real opportunity to deal with strategy....'[15]

Enter the semi-annual one-day think-fest of the Cabinet at Chequers, the country residence of the Prime Minister. The site is well chosen to suggest that this is an unusual occasion at which

15. *Evening Standard*, 1 June 1972, pp. 24–5.

ordinary routine is not to be followed. Permanent secretaries and junior ministers may come separately later; they can use a little inspiration like the rest of us. The Civil Service is not present. This is the time for the CPRS to link the short- and the long-term outside of the usual adversary context of Cabinet meetings. Cabinet members are not in executive session; it is not a time for taking decisions. But what exactly are they supposed to do besides peek in the historic Cheqeurs' guestbook?

The CPRS cannot just cry out 'Remember the long term!' as if it were Dunkirk. Is it a seminar on the future, to be forgotten as soon as the present intervenes? No, it is supposed to be about strategic thinking. But what is that? Is it strategic to have discussed inflation and holding down wage settlements, as was widely reported in the press in May of 1972, or is that just the type of crisis issue they are supposed to be getting away from? Affairs of the moment could not be entirely absent because the Secretary of State for Northern Ireland, Mr Whitelaw, the Minister for Industry, Mr Davies, and the Leader of the House, Mr Carr, were absent from Chequers; their presence was required in the House of Commons. Joining the Cabinet for that session were the Chief Whip, Mr Pym, who is in charge of the European Community Bill, the Chief Secretary of the Treasury, Mr Jenkin, who was there for discussion of government spending, and the Parliamentary Secretary for the Civil Service Department, Mr Baker, who was concerned with machinery of government. In a session lasting five-and-a-half hours, the ministers apparently discussed their record in social policies 'with some satisfaction', though the Treasury's reaction to larger expenditures in the field of social services was not recorded.[16] But what future guidelines could they set down if there were no decisions taken?

Discussions with ministers about the meetings at Chequers show a remarkably uniform pattern: they all think the idea is wonderful but they hate to do it. 'Most ministers', a fairly disinterested observer revealed, 'go to Chequers feeling very, very grim.' They believe that long-term strategies are superior to short-term muddles. They think it is good to get out of the ordinary rut onto extraordinary headlands. Once they arrive, however, they have trouble figuring out where they are and why they are there.

16. *The Guardian*, 23 May 1972.

In the beginning, most of the people had scarcely been together as a group since forming the Government and the meetings, needless to say, have started off cold. But they have soon warmed up into the kind of discussions which could never occur at a Cabinet meeting. 'In the Cabinet,' observed one participant, 'you tend to represent your department and if you're in charge of schools and pipe in with the idea that our inflation policy is all wet – well that is just not on. At Chequers everyone is there as a party politician; your role is different.' It is, of course, a debatable question whether better policy gets made by party politicians or departmental representatives.

The trouble with politicians it seems is that they act like politicians. 'The problem,' lamented one 'is not so much to get ministers interested in the longer term, but in those questions that will not have an immediate impact on them personally in the next year or two.' A more direct man stated that 'After two years we lost our girlish laughter and started thinking about our getting ourselves re-elected.' To CPRS officials 'the political problem is that ministers are interested in winning the next election. They want attractive issues for next time and not necessarily those that might go on at a later date.' It may be, as a third minister suggested, that 'the next general election is a great clarifier of minds,' but it would not appear to offer enlightenment on what is usually termed the long-run.

In so far as the CPRS is supposed to deal with broad strategy and not narrow details, its critics say, it has failed. Where, they ask, is the strategy? There is no strategy; instead of working on that, as it was supposed to, the CPRS has allegedly involved itself in everyone else's business. Why do its enemies vehemently insist that the CPRS return to the catch-words by which it advertises itself instead of the activities in which it engages? Because if the CPRS confines itself to general objectives and long time frames it will keep out of their way. It will also be useless.

The most frequently-voiced criticism of CPRS is also the most revealing: it unhinges delicate interdepartmental compromises or brings well-conceived policies to a halt without having created anything to take their place. If everyone were doing their job properly, this type of criticism continues, there would be no need for the CPRS. We agree. That the private ties of kinship and culture inside the government community are not working as well as they should is precisely the point. The challenge is not to define problems out of existence but to find procedures and machinery so that governors do their jobs better. It is what earlier political writers, men sometimes considered fuddyduddies nowadays, used to call a problem of the British Constitution.

8 Idylls of the Constitution

CONTINUITY AND CHANGE have been our themes. But which is which and is either improvement? And, more important, can there be improvement? There has been no shortage of brave new styles, white-hot technological revolutions, and new looks in British government. We began our research against the soot-caked façade of Whitehall; as we finish, the black smudgy face has been sand-blasted into its original, pristine appearance. Even the Treasury building in Great George Street looks brighter. Fresh bodies – or a whited sepulchre? Inside the 'with it' post-Fulton Civil Service Department, the ancient varnished panelling of the old Admiralty Building has been overlaid with plum and white trim. Beyond the brilliant, plastic reception area and its crimson furniture lie ministers' offices straight out of *Habitat*'s catalogue, magenta chairs like quicksand and tables which defy anyone to sit around them. It is change of a sort, but what does it signify? Is PAR just a new bit of plum and white trim on the old ways, CPRS another piece of mod administrative furniture which no one can figure out how to use? For show or for real can the constitution accommodate these and other strange growths on the body politic?

Constitutional interpretation tends to be used as the great apologia for British government. It does not help people find ways out of the inevitable political dilemmas, only confirms them. At the hands of its interpreters, the British constitution is an oracle which can only tell you why any and every particular change contemplated will not work. Whereas in some nations the existence of a written constitution means that almost anything can be done (or at least justified), in Britain the unwritten constitution is read to mean that almost nothing can be done. Its principles are ethereal bodies unable to offer any positive guidance but always ready to descend on any change as a violation of their spirit. To summon these Harpies, you need only suggest something different.[1]

The constitution of a nation is an important matter, particularly in an era when most of the nations in the world lack even a semblance of the order with which Great Britain is favoured. It is far too important to be allowed to become a caricature which operates so as to exclude reform. The British constitution has always been said to consist of the organic tissue of practices that underlie the effective government of Her Majesty's realm. We agree with that view. What these practices are, why they exist, where they go wrong – to begin to answer these questions it is necessary to study government. What tends to develop instead is a tacit conspiracy of silence. That political administrators find secrecy useful is understandable; that citizens and social scientists should acquiesce is less so. Academic reservations are clearly marked out – voting, parties, interest groups, parliament – but the Executive fortress itself is proclaimed sacrosanct. Those inside who do not wish to be seen make common cause with those outside who could try to see but do not. THE Constitution is their common pretense.

Chestnuts We Have Known

If with nothing else, every interpreter of the British constitution comes armed with a bag of well-tried conundrums for debating the subject. A list of the major topics would look something as follows:

Policy versus expenditure
Ministerial versus civil service power
Treasury intervention versus departmental responsibility
Prime Ministerial versus Cabinet government
Departmental sectionalism versus collective government
Expert versus amateur civil servants
Centralisation versus local freedom of choice
Long term strategy versus short term expedients

The most interesting thing about this list is that each entry is usually discussed as if it were hermetically sealed against the

1. See, for example, the four column leader in *The Times* (24 August 1972, p. 13) on the Spectre of a Prime Minister's Department.

others. Mix up the choices and the inconsistencies become over-whelming. Departmental sectionalism, according to the current line, is holding sway over collective deliberation; yet attempts by the centre – be it Treasury, CPRS, or whoever – to increase collective capabilities of government will necessarily be a slur on the grand tradition of departmental and ministerial responsibility. The Civil Service, we are told, is too amateurish and behind the times; it requires increased ability to anticipate problems, plan responses, and break out of the reactive mould in which decisions are based on the lowest common denominator of possible agreement. A moment later we will be told that bureaucratic power has already taken over far too much responsibility from political ministers. The growth of Prime Ministerial government threatens Cabinet government; it apparently does not have much to do with combating departmental sectionalism. Is it not a pity that Prime Ministers choose their governments to balance off a parliamentary position rather than choosing those who will make the best ministers in the departments concerned; or is it such a pity for the advocate of improved Executive responsiveness to Parliament? Imagine you were a Prime Minister trying to decide in the abstract about how frequently to switch ministers around departments. 'Long tenures,' cry some, 'else you politicians will never be able to master the Civil Service and departmental policy.' 'Short tenures,' say others, 'or collective government will be wrecked by ministers going native.' 'Medium-term tenures,' advise the compromisers, 'because collective government requires a minister to be master of his own department.'

Arrangements for governing in Britain demonstrate with a particular perversity the more general proposition that there is no one best way to organise men for every purpose. Whichever way you move you are bound necessarily to alleviate one difficulty and aggravate another. You cannot create conglomerate departments in order to increase the amount of business Cabinet must handle and then complain that critical policy questions have been withdrawn from the purview of Cabinet. Or, to put it more precisely, you can and do complain, but not in a way that adds to anyone's enlightenment. It is difficult to accept the idea that there are no perfect solutions.

All this suggests the obvious: new arrangements can offer up improvement along one line only at the expense of possibly affecting other desiderata adversely. It is a question of which way one wants to shift various proportions and balances. And since one never quite knows how the various strings on this particular cat's cradle interact, a healthy dose of circumspection would repay any would-be reformers. No amount of caution will, however, provide the right answers to the wrong questions.

Much of our task, as we have conceived it, has been either to abandon or reformulate many of the traditional queries so that they are, at least in principle, capable of receiving reasoned study. It will be obvious to anyone who has read this far, that we do not find many of the usual riddles particularly useful in understanding the expenditure process. Although no one can juggle all these chestnuts at once, we can conclude by addressing constitutional practices and deficiencies in three of the most important areas (recalling that our evidence is drawn from spending rather than any other type of government decision).

How are expenditure and policy linked: does policy determine expenditure rather than the other way around or is this a distinction without a difference? Are governments ignorant because they can't find a grand strategy or does the search for a strategy indicate that something is wrong with their intelligence? Who is on top: is power complex or is it just that we have a complex about power?

So What? Expenditure Decisions and Policy Choices

> I have so often maintained it in this House that I am almost ashamed to repeat it, but unfortunately it is not a principle which has yet sufficiently entered into public opinion – expenditure depends on policy.
>
> *Benjamin Disraeli, 1862*

> This great, rapid and menacing expenditure. If those in office do not mend their ways, a financial crisis will take place in this House, which will render it impossible for the public business to be carried on.
>
> *William Gladstone, 1868*

If the government as a whole should be rationed, as was suggested by politicians in the days of retrenchment, or the departments rationed, as has been suggested later, policy was being made to depend on expenditure.

D. H. MacGregor, Public Aspects of Finance, *1939*

If the system is to be viable, Cabinet decisions should, in my opinion, commit the departments to do their best, both in their own spending and in influencing that of local authorities, to keep the expenditure within the allocation; and to plan their forward policy on this basis. This is the basis upon which the department's work should be founded; and not, as it were, the automatic consequences of policies already laid down. This whole PAR/PESC system implies this.

Sir Richard Clarke, New Trends in Government, *1971*

It seemed as if the hon. Gentleman believed that the level of policy was determined by a choice of how much a programme was to be increased in terms of cash[,] when it is the other way. It is the policy decisions that are made and the White Paper projects, in expenditure terms, the effect of those policy decisions.

Maurice Macmillan, Chief Secretary to the Treasury, Parliamentary Debates, *9 December 1971*

What difference does it all make? Does expenditure depend on policy, as Disraeli said and Macmillan reasserted? Or does what we do depend on how much we have to do it with, as Gladstone and Sir Richard would have it? The direction of dependence between policy and expenditure is one of those grand, old debating issues embedded in British politics. Every time someone complains about the growing burden of public spending without also looking at what is done with the money, they are affiliating with the Gladstonian school. Every time someone complains that the party programme is being wrecked by economic preoccupations – from balance of payments' crises to traditional Treasury stinginess

– they are summoning up the ghost of Disraeli. Which way is it? Which way should it be? Too many people have tried to answer the 'should' question without looking to see what is done.

Those who have followed our account of the British expenditure process this far should be in no doubt about our answer to the great debate. Politicians may dispute, but experienced officials know that expenditure is policy; policy is expenditure. Or at least they are so intermeshed in the vast preponderance of public business that any either/or answer about causation is foolish. Nor should this be surprising. We have seen how machinery of British central government is deliberately designed to promote this mixture. The role of Principal Finance Officers linking Treasury and spending departments, the establishment of the Permanent Secretary as department accounting officer, the conventions of advance consultation with the Treasury – these and many other features are aimed to ensure that questions of policy and expenditure are inextricably tied to each other. In this fundamental sense, the Treasury has finally won. After fifty years of hard-fought, though publicly inaudible battles, the Treasury of the 1970s can be said to have gained that high ground for which its most brilliant official heads have struggled. The words of one of its greatest, Lord Bridges, describing the work of another, Warren Fisher, can stand as fitting monument to the design and the victory :

> ... he said that economy was not something to be imposed on departments by a Treasury acting as the 'single-handed champions of solvency keeping ceaseless vigil on the buccaneering proclivities of Permanent Heads of Departments'. He encouraged the Heads of all Departments to come and bring their troubles to him and to discuss them semi-officially. ... They learned that it was a nonsense to try to formulate policies and ignore their financial consequences, but that the two, policy and finance, went hand in hand.[2]

Since the establishment of PESC, it is a lesson successfully borne home not only upon permanent secretaries but upon all political administrators, whether they know it or not. PESC begins with the most elemental expenditure/policy link by raising the question, what is existing policy? Our discussion has shown how

2. Sir Edward Bridges, 'The Treasury as the Most Political of Departments', Pollak Lecture, Harvard University, 1961.

even this commonsensical question quickly becomes overlaid with legitimate doubts concerning what the government is supposed to be doing. The search for existing policy inevitably becomes entangled in questions of interpreting money sums. An existing policy presumably does not mean to spend the same £X no matter what happens (though grants to the Royal household do take on this character); if that were accepted, spending could acquire an entirely different policy meaning and effect as circumstances changed. When policy puts on the garb of expenditures, there is a great deal of room for reasoned argument. 'Our policy is to accomplish this objective', someone may say. Yet every political administrator knows that there is almost no limit to the sum of money which might be spent for any one of the great purposes of government. Policy may, therefore, be taken to mean maintaining a certain rate of expenditure and a certain rate of improvement in order to move toward the social/political objective. But any improvement factor has to be laid down at some point in time, which is to say that it too becomes a residue from the past. Others may react by arguing that our policy is to meet the emerging expectations and needs of people, thus requiring a larger rate of improvement. If only one could tell just when the policy has changed, he would be better able to tell what it is (and vice versa) but there are seldom any clear milestones or markers. An increase in demand occurs, expenditures shoot up, but has policy changed? If policy means that something deliberate is done, no one can say for sure where spontaneous change ends and where responses to deliberately contrived incentives begin. Operating through time, spending policy includes both political administrators' intentions and their reactions to the consequences of past intentions which were acted upon. Typically, therefore, policy and its economic wherewithal is not something sitting out in the world and waiting only to be discovered. Experience has to be interrogated by men and the results interpreted by their judgements. Policy is a series of ongoing understandings built up by political administrators over time, understandings left to run when practicable, repaired where necessary, and overturned when they are desperate.[3]

In the fullness of time these understandings may, under the

3. One of the most philosophically inclined ex-civil servants defines policy, not as goal setting or goal seeking, but in terms of norms and standards accepted 'as the best realistic governors of their efforts within the

PESC/PAR procedure, be more systematically bargained over than before; some policy activities may be formally recognised to be controllable and subject to rations of money, others to be settled *ad hoc*, others uncontrolled but subject to indirect influences, others legally unalterable. But the subject matter and the use of the categories themselves will still be questions for political bargaining between Treasury and departments, not of intellectual discovery or technical invention.

Financial effects hide. In the everyday working relationships inside government, as well as in the creation of major new programme departures, the link between expenditure and policy is complex and (largely) covert. Policy effects of the expenditure process are not usually expressed through spending departments and Treasury bombarding each other from a distance about X million pounds versus one-half X million pounds for policy Y. The expression of policy effects is in terms of competing people rather than competing money sums.

A large turnaround in policy, as with the Nation's first road programme of the fifties, is likely to be the result of several years' detailed preliminary work among senior Treasury and relevant departmental officials. With the final result likely to be somewhere between the most and least ambitious proposals, the amount of money is obviously not a *post hoc* issue, but neither will the Treasury be so disinterested in the policy content as to merely offer the department a set sum and then wash its hands of the affair. The same is true on less grand policy departures. Almost any paper concerning an emerging policy choice and going to the minister will say at the bottom that the department officials are consulting on the matter with the Treasury. This consultation will be carried on with ministerial knowledge in general but without specific ministerial approval of the, as yet, undetermined policy. The entire process, as we have continually emphasised, will be based on trust, meaning in any such cases that consulting department and Treasury officials can rely on each other not to be briefing their ministers on the negotiations in advance. The formulative analyses will be hewed out through a series of drafts, and the out-

time-span for which they plan, having regard to the total expected resources and the total expected claims upon them'. Sir Geoffrey Vickers, *The Art of Judgement* (London: Chapman and Hall, 1965), p. 98.

come of this collaboration is then presented to the minister. 'All previous drafts are forgotten,' a negotiator observed. 'It's as if they never existed when it comes time to go to the minister.'

At later stages, when an existing policy is battling for more money, the interrelationships will be almost as well-hidden from insiders as from outsiders. Rarely does a government department as a whole do anything. When a bid comes from one area of a department, other divisions will be checked for savings. The Principal Finance Officer knows that to reveal that one division has had to be constrained at the expense of another can only create resentment. 'Keep people as sweet as you can,' is the finance officer's motto. 'You have to find an excuse to squeeze money out of the other division so they won't know they're suffering for another's benefit.' Few people can see the whole picture, although some outside the centre of the department are bound to ask questions when they see others growing and their plans coninuing to be held up.

In all these consultations within departments, and between departments and Treasury, it is much more than total figures that are controlled. Any experienced policy analyst will confirm the dictates of reason; the same alternative that proved attractive at a higher sum may make little sense at a lower figure. It may be desirable to build new houses, for instance, when the total amount available permits the cost per unit to fall below a certain figure. When the expenditure ceiling is much lower renovation and rental might provide more units of comparable size. The result is a change, not merely in money sums but in the content of housing policy. Indeed, it might prove attractive to shift the funds to another purpose altogether where the fit between programmatic desires and available means is closer.

Hence it follows that there is considerable nonsense in the notion that the Treasury's concern can and/or should lie only in financial questions, not substantive policy. Finances are an integral part of the substance and any political administrator who does not understand this will never understand why his fine paper plans remain just that. Let us assume the minimalist's position : that (as Ely Devons summarised from the 1957/8 public testimony to the Select Committee on Procedure) the effect of the Treasury on departmental policy is negligible 'apart from control over the total amount of expenditure'.[4] For anyone tempted to underrate the far-reaching policy effects of expenditure totals, there is no better corrective than to read through the Cabinet discussions of defence and foreign policy during the 1930s. By 1937, the rapidly growing defence expenditure was distinctly worrisome to the Chancellor and Treasury. The Prime Minister willingly concurred both with the sound view that economic stability was an essential element of Britain's defensive strength and with the not-so-sound view that more would be added to this strength by expenditure restraint than by buying more arms. At the end of 1937, the financial problem was judged to be so important that a precursor of PESC was used 'to bring the total Defence Expenditure over the five years 1937–41 within the total of £1500 millions'. The defence and foreign policy implications which were considered to flow from this constraint were far from trivial. Priorities became the order of the day. Top rank would have to be given to home defence, then the protection of trade routes, then defence of the Imperial territories; co-operation with the allies would be a fourth-rank priority. Any aid or expeditionary force eventually going to France was thereby guaranteed to be improvised and uncertain. The Air Force bomber and overseas capability would have to be held back to give scope for improvements in fighter defence (a fortunate choice, as it proved in the Battle of Britain less than three years later). The possibility of doing more for the Air Force would be considered 'if it should prove that there was any margin out of the £1500 million. . .'. Most important of all in these early days of appeasement, the Cabinet agreed 'That the limitations which finance imposes on National Defence place a heavy burden on diplomacy which renders it desirable as soon as may be to follow up the conversations between the Lord President of the Council [Vt Halifax] and Herr Hitler.'[5] Setting spending totals is not neutral for policy contents.

The exceptional presence of projected total expenditure ceilings in the Thirties has become commonplace in the 1970s. The implication of the entire PESC/PAR apparatus is that all department planning (and its influence on local authority policies) should be based on keeping within particular money allocations. Local

4. Ely Devons, 'Treasury Control', *Essays in Economics* (London: Allen and Unwin, 1961), p. 96.

5. Cab. 23/90 (1937).

authorities' experience demonstrates how even their large formal freedom in current expenditure can be effectively shaped by the expenditure process. Local authorities may not be controlled by central government but they are successfully influenced by the policies urged upon them and by keeping Rate Support Grants at such a level that the pain of having to turn to local taxation will help keep the spending totals within the bounds defined by Treasury and Cabinet. Ministers, pressure groups, reformers of all kinds, and government departments themselves are constantly urging local authorities to do more for this or that pet policy. Local representatives are likely to feel a just frustration, as some parts of government urge extension of policies and another part, in the form of the Department of Environment (in close contact with the Treasury), sets the basic expenditure parameters which constrain these policies. '[Local authority representatives] come to me and complain about this,' stated a government negotiator, 'but you can't stop ministers talking. My answer is to tell the local authorities that they can do what they want. But they've got their Rate Support Grant and any more spending they want to do has to fall entirely on local rates. It's cold comfort to them but it does help control total spending.'

Movement toward expenditure ceilings is certainly not complete in the spending departments of central government. Some categories of expenditure have been found to be totally unsuited to one yearly ration of money and no more. Some ministers have felt little compunction at going outside the PESC cycle for a pre-emptive strike on resources. Some in the Treasury, including the most senior levels, have not maintained what one called the 'schematic purity' that Treasury control would be limited to the totals and projections of large expenditure blocs, rather than policy details. PESC has not worked out quite as intended. Yet even if the original PESC purity had been maintained, it has always been misleading to think that control over expenditure totals meant decreased Treasury involvement in policy. Quite the opposite. PAR, like other attempts to integrate policy analysis into the expenditure process, aims at a more effective rather than a decreased Treasury role in policy. Consider the concordant between Treasury and Ministry of Technology when Sir Richard Clarke was the latter's permanent secretary at the end of the sixties.[6]

6. Described in Clarke, *New Trends in Government.*

Policy which was amenable to an expenditure ration was to be reviewed each year with the Treasury when the total was negotiated; the Treasury would receive quarterly reports on commitments being undertaken, reconciling these to the ration and sampling two or three cases in detail. Major expenditures which could not be programmed ahead were handled as always on an *ad hoc* basis. Policy involving expenditure not directly subject to department control would be discussed with the Treasury to determine whether spending might best be contained within the allocation by indirect means or by changes in the law. In short the 'logical' extension of PAR from PESC, which Treasury men like to cite, means that the Treasury can undertake a much more far-reaching conception of control, a conception aimed at discussing what departmental objectives are, how expenditure relates to them, and whether such objectives are in fact being achieved. The chickens are beginning to come home to roost for all those who used to complain of the Treasury's picayune questioning of detail; the successor of a Treasury interested only in details is a Treasury becoming much more interested in the worth of the department's own policies. How far PAR will be allowed, or able, to go in this direction remains to be seen. PESC has at least prepared the way.

What PESC has also done, though unintentionally, is to introduce a *sub rosa* 'fair shares' approach in thinking about the five-year rates of increase for various policy blocs. Whereas before PESC, department officials could never be quite sure who was doing well or what deals had been made with the Treasury, by the end of the sixties the annual PESC report gave a comprehensive score card on which everyone could and did measure their expenditure standing. Those lagging try to bring their growth line up to the others; those in the lead make their case for special treatment as strongly as ever, but know that they are vulnerable to being pulled back into the rest of the pack. Departmental presumptions are, of course, more than matched by Treasury efforts to maintain the established shares, at least until the next PESC cycle. Departments have their allocation and will be expected to stay within it. Treasury ministers now have a ready-made line of defence and standard of measurement in judging department appeals for new money. To this extent at least, PESC has reduced some of the scope for surprise intervention of ministerial tastes.[7] Inertia is at least predictable.

Much more than facilitating a fair shares approach, PESC has given heavier weight to the always-present incrementalism of existing policy. The Public Expenditure Survey displays the vast panoply of implicit decisions in government, i.e., decisions to leave things as they are. In its backhand way, PESC expresses not only what is but also what ought to be. Unless a participant proposes that something different should be done, the presumption is that the existing situation will prevail, advancing only by marginal increases. In almost any social situation the burden of proof is on the proposer, not those preserving the past, but PESC systematises this tendency into the standard way of doing business. Overcoming the vast momentum of ongoing policy is like fighting a scabies epidemic : success depends upon someone scratching vigorously enough to break the transmission chain. PAR has not yet led to much effective itching.

Although PESC enshrines small steps forward from the preceding base, this is not to say that the changes involved are unimportant to policy. Political administrators know that the margins they value and fight for can significantly affect government programmes. A small change up or down can yield more than a proportionate difference to a host of government activities. Not least important are the attitudes which are affected far down the line. Just a tinge of generosity rather than meanness can change people's outlook. It can mean, for example, that an authority wishing to be innovative can do so without having to cut something else; this is not a minor matter since every new idea faces enough enemies without also having to fight someone who has paid the offsetting price for its trial. At stake may be a new re-

7. In the current era of PESC allocations and projections, it would be unlikely that anything could happen comparable to the experience in settling war pensions after the Second World War. The story is that both Treasury and Ministry of Pension officials agreed that an increase in war pensions wasn't on and the Chancellor would not have it. The Minister of Pensions was not even briefed for a second line of defence, and came back from the Cabinet meeting amazed. The Chancellor, former pacifist Stafford Cripps, had urged that disabled ex-servicemen deserved better and agreed to raise war pensions, not merely to the existing 26 shillings for general pensions, but to 30 shillings. A difference in war pensions over general pension rates has remained ever since.

search capability, an experiment with language training, a few more floating teachers to relieve others, all small changes but perhaps enough to help policy adapt to a changing world or to affect the spirit of interaction between government services and their clients.

Whatever happens to PESC the Treasury still has a few of its own substantive policy feuds to fight. To set down many of these norms is difficult because they often depend on this or that personality at the Treasury. Every department has had experience with sudden bursts of sniper fire. Someone in the Treasury will be bothered about something, say a subsidised accommodation in some education programme, and the department will find itself suddenly thrown into a running argument. How many places are falling free, why aren't there more, when will the remaining subsidies be ended? The argument may go on for years and then, just as suddenly, Treasury interest disappears; the bothered official has moved on. Once convinced, the Treasury man can be a powerful ally in advancing certain policies, although not all concur in this way of doing business. One reason why PAR moved to the Treasury was that its expenditure division officials had the wide-ranging policy expertise to handle the flow of business. They are expected to take a view on whether a proposal is 'a sensible and valuable way of spending money on an objective'.[8]

Certain Treasury views are institutionally ingrained. A proposal cutting down the general tax base, such as a plan involving new fees for a social service, will usually be *persona non grata*. The Treasury believes that serious inroads into the scope of general public revenue will restrict its own freedom of manoeuver in managing the economy, as well as reduce the programme's reliance on general Treasury expenditure control. The Treasury as an institution also has a general aversion to subsidising private industry. Most there would share the view of the Second Permanent Secretary that 'generally it is desirable that industry and international competition should be conducted without the need for subsidies'. The battle for subsidy is likely to be long and hard. An undersecretary in charge of this expenditure division testified that 'in principle if we have to put money in at all, the terms on which it is put should be as tough as possible. The advantage of saying our terms should be tough is to reinforce the point that the

8. D. O. Henley, H.C. 323 (1970–1), p. 24.

Government is the lender of last resort and not to give people the idea that the Government is a soft touch. ... Certainly one does not want to get bogged down in endless doles.'[9] With this, of course, has to be balanced the judgement on special need; anyone able to meet extremely tough terms presumably would not have needed a subsidy in the first place. There are also definite views on the means of subsidy. When the Treasury does finally agree, it likes subsidies out in the open. Hidden subsidies in the form of artificially low interest rates run contrary to Treasury doctrine, although there are numerous examples of where the Treasury has lost the battle. 'The basic principle is that the Government lends at approximately the rate at which it borrows after allowing for expenses of borrowing. ... The lending should contain no element of subsidy in the normal sense,' said the Second Permanent Secretary.[10]

The one outstanding blind spot in most Treasury doctrine is taxation. The existing regulations of national taxation tend not to be regarded as an element of subsidy when policies are being weighed up. Since the Treasury sees taxation largely in terms of its job of economic management, policy costs are treated as the amount of money spent (or economic resources absorbed) and not as the amount of revenue lost because of special provisions in tax regulations. The idea sometimes discussed in the House of Commons Expenditure Committee of compiling a 'tax expenditure budget' to show the lost-revenue cost of various policies has met with a cool reception from the Treasury. The response to the idea that some of the Board of Inland Revenue's activities should be subjected to PARs is positively chilly. Yet viewing tax advantages and expenditures as interchangeable ways of allocating public resources is so sensible that we believe it will prevail over time.

Does the hostility to public subsidies extend to social policy as well as industrial policy? We have no reason for thinking that the Treasury is deliberately harder on social policy than on any other spending proposals (for what it is worth, our impression is that Treasury officials are more likely to be mildly left than right of centre and more critical of expenditure on defence than on most

9. H.C. 546 (1970–1), p. 67.

10. Sir Samuel Goldman, Second Permanent Secretary of the Treasury, H.C. 28 (1971–2), p. 545.

other areas of policy.) Whenever the Treasury is attacked for being Tory, we should recall that it is convenient for many department officials and ministers to have the Treasury play the bogeyman in resisting social spending. The effects of expenditure practices on social policy tend to be indirect; they arise from subtle gaps in analysis rather than conscious ideological subversion. The villain of the piece turns out to be, not this or that institution, but the presumptions of the expenditure process itself.

In the first place, there is little incentive to review the major cash benefit programmes. Spending on cash transfers is treated as one of the most inflexible elements in the entire system of expenditure control. PESC uses the convention of projecting forward the existing level of benefits and demographic changes affecting the number of beneficiaries. More hypothetical cost projections are, of course, used in unpublished form, but these typically concentrate on linking the rates of existing benefits to changes in prices and industrial earnings. For political reasons, if nothing else, the existing programmes are also immune from variations for purposes of economic management; Treasury officials know that once a social benefit is put up to stimulate demand, there would be little chance of getting it back down when the economy had responded.[11] Since new cash benefit schemes are likely to be equally inflexible and costly, any period of stringency (which is to say most of the time) is likely to be accompanied by a strong reluctance to enter into new commitments. Historically, Treasury memoranda have proceeded by juxtaposing the vast size and growth of cash benefit programmes with the current economic maladies and gone on to argue that proposals for new liabilities in this area should be treated with caution.[12] The result of a high fixed cost for new programmes, and the adaptation of old programmes largely in terms of conventional price adjustments, is to create a form of inertial guidance in the income maintenance side of social policy. Apart from creeping adjustments of benefit rates, the expenditure process strongly reinforces the natural tendency to leave things pretty much as they are.

The expenditure process exhibits a second over-arching social policy influence by deemphasising redistributive questions. Political judgements on the distribution of costs and benefits are,

11. See Treasury testimony, H.C. 450 (1971–2), p. 5.
12. T. 172/1684 (1929); T. 175/114 (1939).

to be sure, registered throughout the political bargaining surrounding expenditure decisions. But taking the path of least resistance suggests paying most attention to criteria which have the strongest numerical backing and most systematic exposition. In the last ten years, expenditure calculations in economic resource terms have far outpaced other important ways of expressing the implications of spending money for this or that programme. A recent Treasury memorandum has stated that 'a major consideration in planning public expenditure is the extent to which spending by the public sector involves claims on the supply of resources becoming available either from domestic output ... or from imports.'[13] In everyday English, this means that the Treasury is trying to sort out the various effects on the balance of payments and domestic demand arising from different public expenditure programmes. A £100 change in public spending is seen to make more or less than a £100 difference in both foreign exchange and economic resource terms, depending on whether the money is spent on pensions, student grants, wages and salaries, or capital investment. But public policy is about distribution and redistribution as well as about economic management. As the department responsible for economic stability and balance of payments, it is understandable that the Treasury should develop its measures of the resource demand and import substitution effects of expenditures. What is less justifiable is that these economic arrays of expenditure implications do not coexist with and compete against evaluative formats from departments other than the Treasury. One of our themes in considering PESC and PAR has been the leverage gained by some political administrators in getting others to think about problems in their terms. Since no one is in a position to refer to the distributive or other social effects of various forms of public expenditure, economic perspectives are likely to be most predominant. Those interested in social policy need to be reminded that they cannot win a game in which they do not compete.

Financial controllers in all nations go through the motions of requiring offsetting savings from would-be spenders with a new idea. The development of PESC in Britain has given special

13. Memorandum presented to the Public Expenditure Committee General Subcommittee, H.C. 450 (1971–2), p. 17. See also Treasury discussion of the significance of social security increases, H.C. 149 (1972–3), pp. 5 ff.

emphasis to compensatory reductions to make room for a new programme in a department's projected expenditure allocation. The obvious result is that there is considerable difficulty in getting any all-round improvement across the broad range of a department's activities. Expenditure bargaining is about give and take. Those wanting to take usually have to admit that something, even a little something, can be given up.

The counterpart of this dialectical process is a random savageness in those policies which the departments deem to lie outside their central expenditure blocs. Almost any department can call upon a number of outlying programmees to make the sacrifice for the greater good of its central programmes. Like the weakling in a herd of antelope, the small isolated programme is vulnerable, if not to being devoured, at least to having chunks periodically taken out of its rump. There is for example, no obvious reason why museum charges, welfare milk and grants for free school meals should fall under the Department of Education, but when the Department has been called upon to offer up savings, it is from these runts that they have often come, rather than the giant blocs of teaching and curricular costs. Similarly the obvious reason why adult education has been ravaged for paltry sums of money is its isolation from other programmes. A Finance Officer will tell you that 'you had to pay the price somewhere. Pruning is the price you pay for maintaining and advancing other things more worthwhile.' The division man of these eternally lean programmes will reply 'Why us? Why not those great overgrown programmes?'

If the expenditure system makes it difficult to get all-round improvements, it makes it equally difficult to get particular programmes terminated. Even with its tangential programmes a department is much more likely to prefer nibbling away a bit here and there, rather than see an entire programme swallowed up to produce the savings. PAR was ostensibly designed to aid fundamental questioning about whether an activity should be performed at all, but this intention has not yet worked out in practice. Even in the most severe cutting operations, the departments have a relatively free hand to distribute the pain as long as the total adds up to the amount agreed with the Treasury. Possibly, with the next deflationary period, someone will feel bold enough to pull PAR data out of the files and start attacking sacred cows. But it seems unlikely that those with access to the data will be the kind of people inclined to make trouble for others and themselves. Would-be butchers still need a government licence.

Do the various cutting exercises and savings offsets endemic to the expenditure process actually distort the meaning and effect of government policies? Emergency cuts are, of course, likely to hit spending on capital equipment far more severely than current expenditures on wages and salaries. 'Current expenditure,' observed a prescient finance officer, 'is chaps.' Hordes of teachers, hospital technicians, not to mention civil servants themselves, cannot be laid off at will. 'Capital expenditure,' on the other hand, as the Principal Finance Officer of the Home Office said, 'rather tends to be in the front line when economies are being considered.' [14]

The honest answer to the question of whether spending cuts, offsetting savings, etc., impose dislocations on substantive policy is that no one knows. A minister, given the norms of departmental advocacy, finds it difficult to stand up and say 'I have made these savings and cuts in my department's valuable work.' Any cuts actually achieved are likely to be burrowed away in the form of a diminished rate of growth, the deferring of needed capital expenditures, a shadow cut in money that could not be spent – anything that can be disguised rather than the explicit evaluation of a given activity. In a dozen different ways, British political administration is admirably suited to papering over important trade-offs between this or that policy expenditure. Policy defects are likely to be denied until the last moment on the grounds of embarrassment which might result to the minister (and, as his silent partners, the civil servants). Except in rare crisis situations, the Cabinet and its committee system chugs along quite happily considering social and industrial aid expenditures compartmentally rather than against each other. Every insider directly concerned with a new initiative, everyone conventionally considered to have an interest in a subject will be put in the picture and squared. Anyone not within the convention pattern of those concerned will have little scope or inclination to argue about the indirect effects being created or the distributional consequences. In the social departments, there is the lingering suspicion that their industrial colleagues are unduly prone to spending emergencies outside the PESC cycle which pre-empt much of the

14. G. H. McConnell, H.C. 321 (1970–1), p. 76.

possible resources, but it remains only a suspicion and not grounds for argument inside government.

Above all, no one knows the policy effects after savings, cuts, and other expenditure manipulations because no one knows the policy effects before savings, cuts, etc. The impact of spending on public policy is largely an uncharted realm. The natural advantage of the Treasury is that it can talk about the financial effects of expenditure on economic stability and the balance of payments, views which most other people can neither dispute nor counterattack with other expenditure effects. Those output measures which exist, e.g., so many hospital beds occupied, students per teacher, crimes solved per police constable, and so on, constitute fairly easily quantifiable performance measures. They do not say anything about the effects on hospital patients' well-being, young people's education, or urban crime. Of all the departments, Education has gone farthest in the development of 'output budgets' and programme structures. But the Department is ignorant about how a different rate of expenditure increases in one programme affects other programmes: does more spent on ancillary staff and audio-visual aids lead to a decreased need for regular teaching staff? Does it lead to improvement in the quality of education itself?

In the last analysis, the expenditure process affects policy by offering an obstacle course and ground rules for those claiming to act on society's behalf. The folkways of making spending decisions provide a crucial context for natural selection among our presumptive rulers and their ideas. Their successes and failures affect everyone. Talking around in British central government leaves one in no doubt that various political administrators (civil servants at least as much as ministers) have had an important say in the kind of prisons, roads, universities, housing, hospitals, pensions, in short almost every conceivable public good with which the polity provides itself. Those who know how to use the politics of public spending are able to claim the all-important expenditure margins available for policy. They advance their policies more effectively than others; they avoid the effects of cutting exercises and off-setting savings better than others. Those less skillful, strong, persistent and lucky will have to grudgingly accede, as did one official, that '[say, health] is running away with it right now. [Their minister] resists pressures and ours doesn't... [A permanent secretary] got the papers approved ... pre-empted resources ... stole a march on us. ... Now we'll have a harder time.' Of him who cannot make his way in this league, it will be said with a sneer that 'he gets nothing without having to give his right arm for it'. For all the kinship and community, it is still a tough world.

Political administrators have to possess abundant personal resources to make it in their society. Beneath their hard shells, however, often lies a soft underbelly of idealism. Seemingly inured to disappointment, cynical about the devious ways of men, distrusting all argument as potentially self-serving, they still desire to rise above it all to some higher realm of collective good.

Thought and Action: The Philosopher's Stone

Avowed empiricists by profession, British political administrators are at times secret idealists. They lust after a philosopher's stone, the welfare function that would enable them to determine the relative worth of expenditures on one purpose versus others – highways versus hospitals versus schools versus houses. They love politics, but they are secretly disappointed at their inability to substitute a rational formula for political conflict. Perhaps 'There remains,' as Peter Berger suggests, 'something in all of us of the childish belief that there is a world of grownups *who know*. There *must* be – because we, evidently, *don't know*.' [15] Perhaps men could know if they thought properly. Maybe the contaminating elements lie in the oft-repeated accusation that politicians are addicted to short-run expedients instead of long-run strategies and to individual rather than collective interests.

'Long-run', 'strategy', and 'objectives' have become the honorific catchwords of the day. While mouthing them engenders a sense of purpose and wellbeing, attempts at application generate enormous confusion. Neither policy analysis nor the politics of advice will be much improved while political administrators remain divided by this common vocabulary of loose talk.

To say that the present is clear but the future is cloudy is misleading. Retrodiction is no mean art. An immense amount of

15. Peter Berger, *The Precarious Vision* (New York: Doubleday, 1961), p. 83.

governmental time is spent trying to understand, not what will happen in the future, but what has already happened in the recent past.[16] It is hard to go from here to there when we do not know the 'here' as well as the 'there'. When men speak of the 'long-run', they evidently refer to a time-span longer than the next year or two. How much longer depends on their estimates of the period during which actions now contemplated will have their most significant effects. The concern of decision makers should be with the things they can do at the time they can do them, not with future possibilities that will be the responsibility of other men. The long-run can only come in as part of current considerations; it is a way of trying to extend vision into the future from the only standpoint anyone ever has, that is, the present. Injunctions to political administrators to consider a time horizon of ten, fifteen, or even twenty-five years should not be, though they often are, interpreted to mean that they should spend their time worrying about what their successors will be doing two to five governments from now.

Action can only be taken in the present. The question is whether one can disentangle the effects of alternative policies – including inaction – in the next few years from those they will have in the more distant future. Assuming that difficult task can be done, the next question becomes one of the weight to be given to the immediate as opposed to the more distant consequences. Complaints that politicians favour the short over the long-run should be interpreted to mean either that their estimates of consequences are different from their accusers' or that they favour the people who will be helped earlier rather than those harmed later. The time perspective one chooses, then, depends upon more or less educated guesses about the extent and value placed on different outcomes when they occur along the stream of time. Policy analysis is supposed to provide better information to make these choices.

The word 'strategy' is another way of blurring the issue by presuming that the person who applies it to his preferred policy can distinguish larger from smaller future effects. Strategies are presumably distinguished from tactics. Field Marshals like to call themselves strategists and talk about lieutenants as tacticians. The

16. Sir Alec Cairncross is particularly illuminating on this point. See his collected *Essays in Economic Management* (London: George Allen and Unwin, 1971).

P.G.P.M.—13

endless history of error in war should be sufficient to convince any-one that knowing which moves will have the largest desired effects is already the better part of winning the battle. Developing a strategy means placing a bet that current actions will prove right because they move the future in the larger directions intended rather than the smaller ones that are not.

When strategy is taken as a shorthand expression for 'general ideas and predispositions to keep in mind while making decisions' there is probably not much harm in the term. The folly arises when a spurious air of precision is created as indefinite and definite articles become attached; normally level-headed men then begin to hear the Siren call of the jargonists. They begin to think there might be something in the world called 'a' or 'the' strategy which can serve as their foolproof guide in making difficult choices on public policy.

The call for a strategy is, in reality, a plea for a preference ordering among conflicting policies and objectives. Finding ex-amples of strategy is difficult because the purpose of the govern-ment process is to arrive at the hierarchy of values that is implied in meshing a series of long-term objectives so that short-term actions can be taken to help achieve them. If a Government were to set out at the beginning a consistent order of priorities under which future choices would be decided, there would be little left for anyone to do. Strategy, in that sense, is not the beginning of politics but its end.

Because it has been made willy-nilly the guardian of party programme in government, the CPRS is especially vulnerable to attack on the grounds that it has not provided a strategy of govern-ment. Failure to come up with the strategy would not surprise anyone who realised what that elusive term meant. Few should expect a central advisory body to render consistent what nature had pulled apart or to provide a single direction for the Govern-ment when it must have many. If the Government said that it would not intervene in the economy, at least not nearly so much as before, the best the CPRS or anything like it can do is to give the resulting contradictions a respectable running, not make them disappear. For such an organisation to do more, it would stand justly accused not, as has been alleged, of strengthening Prime Ministerial government but of becoming a super-government itself. Strategies are simple-minded notions with which parties occasionally come into office and historians sometimes attach as convenient labels for disparate happenings but which never characterise the actual operations of any Government.

The accusation that ministers do not care about long-run strategies is misplaced. Ministers are no less interested in what is good for their country at any point in time than are other people. They are quite as capable of thinking ahead. But what are they to think about? What they are interested in is how bloody awful it was in the past, how much better they are making it and what they shall do next. They are also specialists in public opinion and they tend to reflect their perception of that opinion. They cannot speak for public opinion in the future any more than a policy analyst could tell them what would be desirable in the next century.

If it were true that politicians resist the long-term because they are always worried about elections, (thereby restricting their time horizon to five years at most) the behaviour of civil servants, who can expect a quarter century or more on the job, should differ markedly. But it does not. Departments as well as ministers have policies. Drift, as it is called, is usually the continuation of a departmental policy that other people do not like.

The departments are, or should be, fair game for anyone with a better policy idea. But they are also responsible for keeping things on an even keel until that glorious day arrives. Having operating responsibilities, they are less willing than outsiders to answer every conceivable question before bestowing a certificate of analytical approval. Anyone finds it easier to think up questions for others – how does housing affect schools, welfare, incentives to work? – than to devise a serious alternative policy. If ministers 'worry about being reactive but do not act', as a puzzled minister put it, it may be that it is not only easier to be reactive but that it is difficult to find an attractive alternative. Creativity is in short supply; that is the problem. If policy advisers wish to interest ministers in taking a different view of the nation's problems, they must have something specific to offer. The time to create new policy, whose implications have been thought through as far as anyone knows how, is not in a conversation among nineteen garrulous men in the Cabinet room, but in someone's head long before. Expanding the supply and demand for advice in central government is, therefore, a subject of prime importance.

No intelligent person wishes to spend time providing information for people who are not even potential users. Before we worry about supplying advice we might pay attention to the likely demand among political consumers. There is economic theory to the effect that demand creates its own supply. Is there a collective interest in paying the costs of getting better advice? Is there, indeed, a collective interest at all or is this just another touching search for the philosopher's stone?

If collective interest is taken to be anything produced by joint interaction, we need worry no further; it is only another word for result. Searchers after the philosopher's stone, however, are likely to use collective interest to designate some standard external to the political process against which to judge individual actions. The trouble is that men are unlikely to agree on how to apply this standard in practice. If all men agree, it exists but is not needed; if they do not agree, positing its existence does not bring men closer together. The collective interest, as we see it in the expenditure process, is not an independent touchstone against which particular claims can be made to ring true or false. What constitutes the collective interest is the appreciation of interdependence among each other's efforts; it is one consideration among others against which claims should be weighed in open competition. Invariably giving way to the claims of mutual interdependence is no more a guarantee for good policy than fighting your own corner is a surety of disaster. When ministers are asked, for example, to make spending sacrifices on behalf of their fellows they will be asked to reject one line and adopt another to help win the next election or to maintain the unity of Cabinet. It is not self-evident whether the public will be better served if the minister insists, thus risking a Cabinet crisis, or if the policy his department prefers is cut back.

The least 'selfish' minister can easily turn out to be the most damaging. A precipitous decline in spending plans or in a minister's reputation may cripple a desirable policy for years to come and decrease the future good that could have been done, all in the name of a collective interest that was scarcely threatened or not worth preserving anyway. Invoking the idea of collective interest does not provide an operational guide to better decisions; it alerts us to the fact that it is the mix of considerations which must be evaluated in any reform.

The same principle applies when we broaden our focus from the individual minister and his department to the collective realm in which higher civil servants and politicians attempt to govern the nation. If the interest we are discussing is governmental, then political administrators will naturally place their concerns above others. The political administrative community is, as we know, extraordinarily sensitive to its own operations. It is less sensitive to outsiders, i.e., the people in whose name the community is acting. Determining the collective interest becomes especially problematical when the needs of citizens are being balanced against those of political administrators. The collective interest becomes, as its name implies, a collection of interests.

Where are we? Back again to the concepts of community and policy first identified in Chapter One. The dichotomy between departmental and collective intrests, between internal governmental and wider public interests, are manifestations of the need to balance cohesion and effective action. Consider the relationships outlined in this four-fold table:

| | Policy | |
	Good	Bad
Weak	1	4
Strong	2	3

Community

It is evidently in everyone's interest (Case 2) to adopt good policies that are highly effective in serving the public and which enhance community among political-administrators. Few would advocate

(Case 4) bad policies that disrupt the community relationships of government. No, the difficulties arise when community and policy appear to conflict so that more of one must be traded for less of the other. It is at such times that a prime minister will argue (Case 1) that his government must not solve its internal problems at the expense of public dissatisfaction or (Case 3) that it is more important for them to stick together than to seek perfection in policy. Neither course is an unambiguous expression of a collectivity or its interest.

It is the way of the world for men to prefer the known and the certain to the opposite. Most participants in the expenditure process are professionals in community, amateurs in all else. The future effects of policy must seem far more uncertain to them than the present deterioration of their relationships. That is why, as we have seen, it takes a major financial crisis to get ministers to take their collective medicine. Left to its existing inclinations the Government will, for the most part, put community above policy.[17]

In the abstract, the collective interest refers to little more than altruistic as opposed to selfish motives and is either a tautology or a chimera. If all it says is that the majority is larger than the minority, we already know that. If it suggests that political administrators should be more altruistic and less selfish, that advice is applicable to all of us. We, too, have our beliefs about what structures and procedures would be in the long-run interest of the Nation. Like everyone else, we think our individual preferences are in the interests of the whole group. Our task is to explicate and defend them. Those inside the government should have to do the same thing among themselves and to outsiders.

It is in the collective interest, as we perceive it, to shift the balance of emphasis from preserving community to improving policy, from the interests of political administrators to the interests of citizens. There is no need to encourage ministers to pursue departmental interests. Nor does anyone have to inculcate the will to survive in politicians or maintain cohesion among civil servants.

---

17. This is not to say strategically inclined ministers shun an opportunity to interest public opinion in their needs. A recent example was a speech by the Secretary of State for Social Services, who lamented that 'for the moment community services for handicapped and elderly people would have to be compromised in favour of more residential places, because of the limited money available for day care'. *The Times*, 19 May 1972.

Information on community is plentiful but analysis of policy is scarce. Cabinet members rarely get to choose between rival positions, each well-analysed; take it or leave it is the more common approach. But injunctions to be good will get us nowhere. What incentive might there be to make it worthwhile for ministers, in their own interests, to relax community in order to improve policy?

One possible device, out of favour since the demise of the Department of Economic Affairs, is to create overlapping departmental duties as a spur to each other's efforts. The larger the number of departments, the more likely their concerns will overlap and rival analyses be presented to Cabinet. From this perspective it is clear that community has triumphed over policy in the form of a smaller number of conglomerate departments. The needs of Cabinet for intimacy, collegiality, and dispatch won out over more and better information on policy. All the more reason, then, to seek other incentives for accomplishing similar purposes.

A different approach is to make someone or some institution the repository of a collective interest in generating better information and advice on policy. The Treasury, in a manner of speaking, has served this purpose by requiring justification before approving expenditure. But the Treasury does no substantial analysis of its own except on taxation and economic management, which means that other policies are most expertly appraised in terms of how they contribute to these (possibly conflicting) purposes. The creation of the CPRS to serve ministers suggests that at least one minister must champion the cause if any are to promote interests not directly their own. Yet a minister for Cabinet Advice would, by himself, carry little weight. Advice is cheap. Departmental ministers are not likely to listen unless there is someone to whom they must pay attention. We believe there is much to commend a more activist role by the Prime Minister. Far from threatening collective government this is one good way of spurring other ministers to work at turning the chimera into a more operational reality. What it does (and should) threaten is departmentalism by default.

The first requisite is to lay to rest the fashionable and arid debate on whether Cabinet government is giving way to a Prime Ministerial (read Presidential) form of government. Our evidence concerns only the spending of public money, but it is enough to alert us that the prior question ought to be 'what difference does it make whichever way the question is answered?' Presumably Cabinet government denotes an arrangement of joint authority which is greater than that of any individual minister, including the Prime Minister; the Prime Minister does not decide in his own right but leads under the mantle of Cabinet consensus. Yet the U.S. President hardly rules by hierarchical command even within his own executive branch, much less outside in Congress. He, too, must be careful to take account of other powerful figures, dismiss individuals with only the greatest discretion, and find the politic way to express the government's will. He, too, risks being overwhelmed if he invades the prerogatives of others who act as his shields as well as his surrogates.

What, then, might Prime Ministerial government look like in the expenditure process? In the first place, the motor of government initiates would rest inside 10 Downing Street. Bright ideas might, of course, come from anyplace, but the major and essential requirement for turning ideas into reality would have to be the push from the Prime Minister's office. Similarly all participants would accept the Prime Minister's right to veto proposals at odds with his conception of the government's will. Not least important, the vital personnel for controlling, vetting, maintaining relationships with departments using public money would be in the Prime Minister's office. They would definitely not be under a powerful man like the Chancellor of the Exchequer. And, of course, any Cabinet member dissatisfied with the way things were going would be ultimately expendable without directly threatening the Prime Minister's position at the top. Members of the Government would need each other but they would need the Prime Minister more than they needed each other as members of the Government. From what we have seen about expenditures there is clearly still a long way to go before we talk about Downing Street even faintly resembling the White House, let alone government by Prime Minister.

If one-man government were looming, the organisation of advice to prime ministers would hardly be so troublesome. Presidents have no difficulty obtaining as much (and more) than they can use, but as exemplars of collective rule, British prime ministers find it difficult to arrange for heavy doses of advice from outside the civil service. On the vast bulk of spending issues, prime ministers, while retaining the title of First Lord of the Treasury, must still work through a powerful fellow-minister, the Chancellor of the Exchequer. There is an underlying truth in calling the Prime Minister 'first among equals'. Other Cabinet members need the Prime Minister, but scarcely less than he needs them or than they all need each other. A child unable to feel pain can hardly survive; a person who cannot be sued becomes a pariah because no one can afford to deal with him. A Prime Minister who cannot afford to lose openly must, by the same token, be selective and circumspect in exercising the leadership necessary to win. A U.S. President, by contrast, knows he can be defeated on a dozen fronts so long as he is victorious on others. As long as his defeats are not inevitable and his 'batting average' is not too low, the President remains strong and may actually increase his strength by daring to fight the good fight. Because he can afford to lose, he can afford to lead.

At heart, British Cabinet government retains, with a devilish twist or two, all the characteristics of government by committee. The major twist in British Cabinet government arises from the fact that most committeemen are also the chief executives of their departmental empires, empires where their individual reputations are made and/or unmade. They are on their own, but they are not alone. They may not always stand but they do fall together. Cabinets are composed of people who know each other only too well, and any insight they lack into each other's mode of behaviour is easily made up after the first intensive round of discussions. Everyone knows they serve themselves by serving their departments. The ardour of each in performing his assigned role is (or is supposed to be) checked by the others doing the same.

Prime Ministers have always been in a position to inject their political judgements into the expenditure process, particularly on the communal issues of holding the Cabinet and Party together. The usual consultations between P.M. and Chancellor in advance of Cabinet sessions on expenditures are conducted for precisely this purpose. In the daily round of business the Prime Minister can hardly fail to notice who fights hard and who is disposed to defer to him and to the Chancellor. The P.M. can make his preferences felt by placing the most aggressive ministers in departments whose programmes he wishes to further or surrounding ministers who push forward with other ministers in committee who push back. By choosing a strong Chancellor or by varying his support for him, the Prime Minister has already gone far in shaping the final allocation.

What is needed now is that the Prime Minister's resources for policy advice should be made as good as his resources for political manipulation. The more he can contribute toward substantive improvement the more his cabinet colleagues (and hence their departments) will be motivated to compete in similar terms. He would have to pick his spots, but a little unpredictability would lead everyone to keep their analyses handy. It might seem as if the Prime Minister could play the role of monitor, insisting that others do their work before receiving his assent. Presumably the Cabinet Office now sees to that. Without having alternative sources of analysis and advice, however, the Prime Minister (through his staff) can only observe whether the departments have gone through the motions, not whether they have done the job. He needs to have more analyses on his own to draw upon.

The costs to the Prime Minister of playing the analytic game would be considerable. His private office would have to be expanded with an infusion of 'irregulars' who would hardly be welcome in Whitehall. He would necessarily be thrown own frequent dispute with his departmental colleagues. Conflict might rise while accomplishment remained the same because no outside adversary staff can do the actual work for the departments. Nevertheless the potential gains are commensurate with the risks. Because he knows more, the Prime Minister would be able to undertake a few more initiatives. Since he is likely to be blamed when things go wrong, he might as well have an initial say in putting them right. But his time, energy and resources are sufficiently limited to keep his direct interventions selective. We believe the Prime Minister increasingly will be impelled to take a more activist course in policy formulation by the growing public realisation that his government is responsible for disposing of so much of the national income each year. Competence in policy will become, if nothing else, a necessary defensive measure for Prime Ministers. And as the effects of joining the Common Market become more pronounced, the Prime Minister's and Cabinet's ability to make British interests felt there will increasingly depend on better use of domestic resources for public policy. The cliche will be given new meaning; influence abroad will indeed depend on strength at home. Participating effectively in the European Community is likely to require trading a little community inside British government for more effective policy in the country.

Consideration of collective government and prime ministers has, by no mere coincidence, led us to the same point. The problem is not that one or the other is 'too strong' but that both are too weak. Apprehensions concerning Prime Ministerial government would be more accurate and productive if they were directed away from the illusion of personal government, power grabs, and jobs too well done, and towards the opportunities missed and tasks poorly fulfilled. It does no good to rub the philosopher's stone and call for a long-run strategy or transcendent collective interest; no genie (or genius) will emerge to show the true path and protect us on the way.

The weakness at the centre of British government is struggled against manfully by the Treasury, CSD, Cabinet Office, and CPRS. But it is a debility all the same. How might it be overcome? Before we push further into this thicket it seems wise to try to learn from experience. We have, in the course of discussing the expenditure process, come across efforts to change the machinery of government. That most intended reforms fail is by now no news; the governmental landscape is littered with their debris. We are fortunate in being able to draw for instruction, however, on the major modern reform in the machinery of resource allocation, the Public Expenditure Survey Committee. Nowhere in the world, to our knowledge, has the annual budget been replaced with an effective mechanism for controlling the level of expenditure several years into the future. What can we learn from this success about the requisites of reform?

The founders of PESC were lucky. Their innovation might have died in its infancy had it not been rescued by times calling for severe financial stringency. But it was more than luck. The men behind PESC had an idea that could be put into practice. They could instruct others on how to do it and they could check to see whether it had been done. This operational quality is lacking in programme budgeting, which fails around the world when the political currents run against it and does not succeed when times are favourable because no one knows how to implement it.[18]

PESC could work with men and machinery as they are. It did

18. See Aaron Wildavsky, 'Rescuing Policy Analysis from PPBS', *Public*

not need to postulate a new type of administrative animal, or create a wholly new institution to breathe life into an otherwise moribund body. Readily grafted onto the existing Public Spending Group in the Treasury, PESC could place its small apparatus in a well-established home.

Not that PESC was easy to establish. It required years of patient effort to improve procedures and gain co-operation. Treasury men never lost sight of the consideration that PESC had to serve the purposes of departments besides their own if it were to last. So they set out to create a nexus of common interest. All was not sweetness and light and many a detour was allowed, many bits of nonsense tolerated, so as to create a feeling of mutual responsibility for a joint enterprise. Yet, in the end, PESC had to have an ultimate client whose interests were vitally connected with its survival. It proved useful to Chancellors of the Exchequer, Chief Secretaries, and the Public Spending Group as a whole. It helped them, so they protected it.

PAR is, as our account reveals, one of the prices to be paid for PESC. The cost of acquiescence to expenditure limitations was enhanced protection for items already safely ensconced. 'Harder to get in' also meant 'more difficult to throw out'. Each reform not only compensates for the defects of the old, but creates new faults to be resolved by future efforts. That is why the work of perfecting social arrangements, which cannot wait for history to unfold all its secrets, is never finished.

The collapse of the committees of non-spending ministers shows what happens when a reform is so much for the good of all that it is in the interest of none. Spending ministers want either more money or to put up a jolly good show if not getting it. Non-spending ministers want less work and more friends; instead, they were asked to work harder to make enemies. If making cuts *in camera* had genuinely been in the collective interest, it would not have been necessary to choose a committee loaded against spending. Spending departments span the entire range of state activity outside of economic affairs and internal management. Virtually anything that is done must be in the interest of one of them. 'The'

Administration Review, vol. XXIX, no. 2, March/April 1969. Also see Naomi Caiden and Aaron Wildavsky, *Planning and Budgeting in Poor Countries* (New York: John Wiley and Sons, 1973).

collective interest is too flimsy a foundation on which to build improvements. If advances are to be made, power must be mobilised to improve advice at the centre.

Government and Action: The Power Complex

Who has the power? Who has too much power?

These traditional questions require one to weigh up ministers against officials, Executive against Parliament, Treasury against departments, departments against collective Cabinet. Making sense of British government in terms of relative power would require two conditions, neither of which we have found to exist. First there would have to be a fairly distinct, independent 'thing' over which to have power and contend. But policy, as we have seen, is not that kind of thing. Brought down to earth into spending decisions, policy turns out to be not only what is being done (in so far as that can be imperfectly ascertained) but a confluence of partial understandings among interested participants that change with the unfolding of events. Instead of being a constant which conveniently lies still as combatants argue about how to carve up the body, policy is a variable that is likely to get up and leave the scene before the inquest.

Second, looking at British government in terms of who has 'the' power or 'too much' power is productive only if more for one side means less for the other. This is manifestly not true in most of British government. In examining the process of deciding how to spend public money, we find that the primary fact of life is reciprocity. Virtually every point of potential conflict is also a point of unavoidable mutual dependence. Self-restraint for self-interest is present on almost every side. Treasury *v.* spending departments; officials *v.* ministers; finance officers *v.* Treasury *v.* departmental divisions; Chancellor *v.* spending ministers – each has plenty to fight about but each also desperately needs the other. The Treasury is hopelessly lost if it must redo the departments' work, dig out all of its own information, and fight every inch of the way for everything it wants. Every senior official in a spending department prefers a strong minister to a cipher, for at the end of the day only ministers can fight it out for the departmental view. A Chancellor who cannot bring most spending ministers to co-operate without constant rounds of resignation threats cannot hope to survive.

Spending ministers who cannot count on the Chancellor to carry most of the economic arguments know, or learn, that their collective appetite for money can soon ensure that no one gets anything, including re-elected in the midst of economic crisis. The arrangements civil servants arrive at to facilitate their own continued life together must always be balanced against the risk of personal embarrassment and departmental setbacks arising from not knowing their ministers' minds well enough.

In sum, the power process in the British Executive resembles a slightly leaky terrarium, with each growth dependent on the by-products of the other. Given this close interdependence it quickly becomes misleading and/or trivial to ask who has the power, the supplier of CO_2 and consumer of oxygen, or the supplier of oxygen and consumer of CO_2? The unhelpful answer is everyone and no one has ultimate power. What matters is the balance among inhabitants, for they must all live together and cope with occasional, sharp climatic blasts from the outside. The solution for any imbalance is not to cut back, much less tear up, the strongest but to cultivate and strengthen the weaker members of the community. Since all are interdependent, all can lose. None may control policy as a recalcitrant world frustrates their best efforts and the weakest drag down the rest with them. While the constitutional chestnuts on relative power draw their inspiration, at least unconsciously, from classic doctrines of separated powers, our account has harkened back to Hume and Blackstone to examine not only the value but contemporary reality of the mixture of shared powers.[19] Consider, first, the most traditional query, the relations between ministers and civil servants.

British people want the best Civil Service going and are worried that they may now have it. Ministers and other participants reject as utter nonsense the idea that there is a civil service conspiracy to prevent politicians in office from carrying out their policies. No one doubts that civil servants will do their best once the policy line has been laid down. Conformity to command, however, does not end the problem so much as begin it. 'The danger of the Civil Service lies in its excellence,' an ex-minister tells us. 'The problem is that they are all too good. They are confident of

19. '. . . herein consists the true excellence of the British government, that all parts form a mutual check upon each other.' William Blackstone, *Commentaries on the Laws of England* (1775), I, 154.

their own excellence and, what is worse, of their permanence. They weave you in a cocoon of ability.' The fear is that civil servants will put the case for their policies so well that ministers will find them too plausible. No doubt a bunch of bumblers would not create this forceful impression, but no one really wants dolts. So we must reject the most evident way of dealing with the problem, i.e., making the best civil servants less talented. The same applies to their co-ordination. If the term is anything more than a disguise for coercion – 'if you two do not behave I will co-ordinate you' – co-ordination means that everyone who counts knows what his fellows are doing. In that restricted sense the higher Civil Service is superbly co-ordinated. Yet the idea rankles. 'One of the first shocks I had as a new minister. I fought a fierce battle in Cabinet. "We won," I said, bursting into my department office where I had sped by cab. "Yes, I know, Minister, congratulations!" said the civil servant.' Everybody knows what everybody else is doing. If they did not, of course, they would not be doing their job.

The civil servant's job is not simply to co-ordinate but also to mitigate conflict or, put another way, to enable disputes to be carried on within reasonable bounds. His personal ties and exchange of information makes this possible. Relationships that smooth the way are naturally welcomed by the minister. But when he wants an extra hard or novel push he will find that the ties do indeed bind and exclaims, 'The Civil Service is the tightest club there is. Your civil servant has been in six other departments before he came to you. The elaborate promotional network assures he'll not want to make enemies elsewhere.' Few stop to think that the civil servant who is ordinarily prepared to ride roughshod over his colleagues might not be in the best position to help his minister on other matters.

Rare in any system will be the policy which results from a minister's bright idea never thought of before, carried on his shoulders over the bodies of his officials, through the dark valley of Treasury review and upward to final Cabinet triumph. (This pilgrim's progress like John Bunyan's, more properly belongs in the realm of homiletics.) Top civil servants are few, but ministers are even fewer. 'Ministers,' the senior Treasury man said, 'are only 50 chaps with a lot of things to do.' The bureaucracy, which exists to compress, suppress and shape information, must perforce do most of what there is to be done. The surest way of incapacitating a minister is to tie him up in detail so that he cannot get loose to deal with other matters. Some decisions today are not so much caused by anyone, whether he be official or civil servant, as derived from sequences of past actions. Other decisions are based on complex patterns of mutual interaction; the official anticipates the minister, who is responding to a signal from the official, who in turn was reacting to the minister, who ... that hall of mirrors is entered only at the price of losing all perspective. The answer to the great question of ministerial versus civil service power turns out to be so prosaic that no one is really interested in hearing it. Sometimes ministers are more powerful than officials in regard to certain areas of decisions; sometimes the reverse is true; and sometimes neither is in charge, however much they may pretend to the contrary.

The power relations between minister and officials over departmental policy will always pose a chicken and egg problem. It is a nonsense to ask who has the power when a brief is being edited for the minister : the official because he edits or the minister who creates the image for the editing. It is not worth anyone's time to try and determine who 'really' decides when each proposal is based on an assessment of the other's desires, modified by raised eyebrows and significant glances. What does matter is that most of the time on most issues, ministers, sitting alone at the top of their departmental empire, can exercise their political leadership only through civil servants' second-, third-, or fourth-hand anticipations of ministers' likely reactions. Trained minister-watchers though they may be, officials are not mindreaders and cannot know what could be teased out of ministers with more prolonged attention, argument and monitoring at the ministers' right hand. The machine is responsive, but what it is responsive to is largely its mental construct of ministerial leadership.

Ministers could take a more objective view of the uses and abuses of civil servants if they were not required to depend on them so completely. Even if they do not suspect their civil servants of sabotage, indeed, even if they have every reason to believe civil servants are doing everything to help them, the nagging doubt remains that a more sympathetic adviser would have done better by them. It is less a question of officials refusing to follow the dictates of a given policy and more of excluding from debate the kinds of ideas and follow-through that the minister might have favoured if only he had known about it.

Ministers need more outside advisers inside government with them.[20] In reaching this judgement we are not at all disregarding the fact that outsiders threaten the advantages of the civil service community. It is foolish to act as if other values were not involved. The question is which way to move the balance, not how to get something for nothing. There are no free lunches. A panel of consultants outside the government has access to few of the important papers and in the press of day-to-day decisions is likely to be of little use to the minister. The comments of a former Cabinet secretary (and Treasury Permanent Secretary) are exactly to the point :

> If full benefit is to be derived from economic (or indeed other) advisers, it is no use putting them in a separate compartment from those who are engaged in the day-to-day work of administration in those fields in which advice is needed. Advisers must be given access to the same sources of material as those on which the administrators are working. They must live cheek-by-jowl with them and share their anxieties and aspirations. Only so can advisers make their influence felt at the early stages when facts are being sorted out, theories are beginning to emerge and the first pointers to future policy are being formulated.[21]

Obviously, not all ministers are the same – some actually like detailed administration or revel in representing their department to outside constituencies – and the kinds of advice they want will necessarily vary with the type of person they are and the departmental situation they inherit. Fortunate indeed is the department

20. Adoption of the French *'Chef de cabinet'* system has been advocated as a means of reducing ministerial dependence on the Civil Service and giving them eyes and ears they can trust. If the French experience is any guide, however, ministerial cabinets would be a means of enhancing rather than reducing civil service influence. A preponderance of advisors come from higher civil servants on the rise. The *grands corps de l'Etat* are not kept away from ministers by this device but given privileged access to them. Nor would a British version serve precisely the same purpose, for French departments are collections of bureaus, where the purpose of ministerial cabinets is to settle internal conflicts, while British departments are constituent elements of central government. See A. D. deLamothe, 'Ministerial Cabinets', *Public Administration*, vol. 43, 1965.

21. Bridges, *Treasury Control*, p. 14.

whose needs for policy guidance, internal administration, and outside representation coincide with the desires and abilities of its minister. But then neither are all permanent secretaries and other civil servants the same. British Government is not Minister Silly confronting Civil Servant Sharp. All political administrators puzzle about what to do in a complex world. The difference is that the officials' puzzlement is usually kept under house wraps, while the ministers remain unmobilised and unnurtured by any group of fellow advisers/colleagues in the department.

No one should underestimate the difficulty of bringing non-civil service advisers into government. Unless their reputations make them unassailable, they are likely to be regarded as amateurs who interfere with the workings of the machine without being able to improve it. They are the kind of people who create trouble without staying around to pick up the pieces. Ask any minister about his experience with outside advisers, and you are likely to hear a biological analogy in which a self-contained system rejects foreign elements. 'Alien bodies', 'expelled like white corpuscles', 'considered bulls in the civil service's china shop', 'they castrate you', – these are expressions used by four ministers. Tensions and rivalries are inevitable at this level. Even the most successful outside advisors can be expected to survive little more than two years before being enveloped, rejected, or worn down by the established Civil Service. Yet the very difficulty of the task suggests how important it is that it should be done. In time, senior civil servants may realise the protection afforded to them by an improved articulation of ministerial leadership.[22] The real question is whether ministers will take the risks, for they cannot improve their capacity for choice without sharing more of the political credit.

The problem is not that the Civil Service is too strong and creative in devising public policy, but that politicians are too weak and not creative enough. Much of the argument for increased ministerial power vis-à-vis the Civil Service in the departments is

22. In February 1972, for example, the James Tribunal of Inquiry into the collapse of the V & G Insurance Company cleared ministers of responsibility but criticised by name the undersecretary and two assistant secretaries responsible for the insurance branch of the Department of Trade and Industry. The wrath of the Society of Civil Servants was aroused, particularly by the fact that none of the ministers supposedly responsible for the insurance branch over the years were criticised. *The Times*, 17 February 1972 and 13 March 1972.

from this perspective merely a misplaced criticism of political opposition in Britain. There is something insidious in the extent to which reformers have tried to tool and retool the political administrative machine into a mechanism for throwing up and working through all possible alternatives and policy options. Consideration of alternatives is not an agenda item for some grand strategy session of civilian generals; it is part of the evolving societal process by which dissatisfied people try to respond to felt needs at any time. Preoccupation with the administrative machine's comprehensive examination of alternatives (a preoccupation which inevitably ends in stultification since no one knows how to consider all alternatives) easily comes to serve as an excuse for superficial policy analysis by the political party in opposition. False hopes, disillusionment, and equivocations are the likely line of development when mere good intentions come up against the tough business of governing with workable ideas. Any new minister coming into office will find on his desk the fluff of party manifestoes moulded into something like workable propositions, as far as his civil servants are able to do so. Bureaucracy would only be frustrating party government if there were something there to frustrate first. The evidence suggests to us that not only is there little danger of civil service conspiracy but that officials will initially go along with an astonishing range of nonsense. The worst bits will not be helped along very much – and officials in other departments are adept at sensing this – but neither will they be sabotaged. The minister will be left to carry the can. Officials will be content to sit back and let the fish run, knowing that in the end schools of dogma will flow in their direction when they rise up against the bait of real life problems. And they can do so largely because of the abysmal preparation by politicians out of office.

The same untapped potential extends from the opposition party to Parliament as a whole. Feeble ministers are a natural outgrowth of feeble Parliaments. The aim of increased parliamentary participation in policy analysis should be, not the remote and vain hope of wresting a bit of power from the Executive, but the more sensible preparation of men who can make the Executive work better once they get there. A major reason governments do not do better is that knowledge of how to make some people better off without making others worse off is lacking. No government of the day has a monopoly on what little wisdom is going on the subject. On the contrary, the growth of such knowledge is a social process to which contributions from many sides are required. Parliamentary expenditure committees may not be foci of power directly able to influence resource allocation, but they could perform important educational functions. They could use and encourage centres of outside analysis, whether these are groups loosely attached to government departments, universities, or essentially private endeavours. The tough, day-to-day work of the parliamentary expenditure committees could offer a uniquely down-to-earth training for policy-oriented M.P.s. A Member often spends a decade or more in Parliament before having a chance to occupy a ministerial position. Part of that time could be used to inform himself on major areas of policy, to question and get to know officials, to learn ways of making bureaucracy justify itself to a layman's scepticism, and to share experience with his fellows. The man with this kind of training in his kitbag will be in a better position for eventually supplying political leadership to a department than one who knows nothing more than outwitting an opponent in the cut and thrust of public debate. As things stand, service on these committees does not fit into the career aspirations or life-styles of M.P.s. The question of whether they wish to change is as important, or more important, than the usual conundrum about whether ministers and civil servants will allow them to operate.

The need in British Government is to cultivate new potencies, not to cut back old powers. This applies as fully to traditional criticism of Treasury power as it does to the issues of collective government, Prime Ministerial rule and ministerial versus civil service power. Is the Treasury too powerful? More to the point is the fact that other departments and offices are insufficiently sensitive, knowledgeable and adaptable. Treasury influence rests not on a hard-nosed interpretation of formal powers but in personal networks, sensitive bargaining, and up-to-date information that operate to create habits of mind leading to anticipation of Treasury reaction. PESC has taken it a good way, though by no means all the way, toward controlling money sums; PAR may be beginning to take it further towards analysis of substantive policy. What is needed is not somehow to hold the Treasury back, but to enhance the ability of operating departments and the Cabinet to compete with its judgement.

The opportunity for Treasury control still rests largely on a department coming forward to ask for more money in the most justifiable way it knows how. The Cabinet may always dispense with Treasury advice; if it does so by being able to weigh competing analyses, there is a chance that better decisions will emerge out of a more intelligent debate at the centre; if it can only do so by force of numbers or flights of fancy, Treasury predominance is not necessarily a bad thing. But things could also be much better. Treasury men should be made to face up to the implications of their own rationalisations. Their view on public expenditures, they will say, is only one among many; against the Treasury's economic perspective Cabinet ministers are bringing to bear other political, social and historical judgements. Those who do not recognise they are doing this are said to be 'sloppy thinkers', 'don't know what game they're playing', 'expressing a silly and incompetent idea'. Very well then, there should be no room for Treasury objections to improving others' capacity to formulate these rival judgements. As things stand at present the advice coming to ministers in the department, to Cabinet members in Downing Street, or to any new Government may be rejected, procrastinated about, distorted or maimed; the one thing it is not likely to be is counter-analysed.

There is a kind of rough justice in the fact that both ministers and Members of Parliament are separately responsible for sustaining the devices that could, if used, make their participation more effective. The two exceptions to the mixture of powers pervasive throughout British political administration are Parliament and the CPRS. Both need the co-operation, information and goodwill of others, but it is not clear how or why others should need them. The Government needs only the disciplined tolerance of its backbenchers and certainly not the goodwill of the Expenditure Committee. Ministers need CPRS in the abstract, but whether they know so in practice is still being decided. If M.P.s and ministers will not risk a little to make use of the Expenditure Committee and CPRS, then perhaps it is just as well that the existing balance of information and influence stays as it is. But such counsel is too despairing. Improvements are possible.

A Last Word

Given the political administrative community described in this volume, it seems rather much to expect large returns from giving a new procedure to a new institution. A new procedure to an established institution or an established procedure to a new institution seems more likely to succeed. Thus we believe that there is more to be gained by clinching the development of PESC and PAR in the Treasury, and only later breaking these procedures and personnel off to a new central body, rather than giving some bright new Cabinet Department the task of getting PAR going. Reformations should at least await conversion and establishment of the faith. But what should be our objective?

Returning to first principles, the rise of the Civil Service was predicted in part on a desire to assure neutral competence and continuity, a byproduct of the attempt to reduce the corruption of Parliament by patronage. The Civil Service which has resulted is one part occupational classification and three parts state of mind.[23] Partisan neutrality, competence and continuity have been achieved superbly, but this has necessarily been at the expense of other values. Proposals for change in the machinery of advice for Cabinet and Prime Minister now come as the culmination of movements for economic rationality and for political responsiveness. One movement has led to increased emphasis on calculating costs and benefits of alternative policies over longer periods of time; the other has led to proposals for closer congruence between the advice received and the political values of the governing party. The two movements intersect at the level of policy analysis. Partisans at the centre cannot provide neutrality or continuity comparable to the Cabinet Office but in small number they can supply analysis and responsiveness. Civil servants could provide as good analysis as anyone but they can never create a sufficient appearance of responsiveness, which is not only a matter of objective performance but of subjective belief. If it is a question of using partisans as analysts or civil servants as partisans, the former is preferable.

23. There is no statutory definition of either the Civil Service or a civil servant, apart from statements of qualification for pension rights. When necessary, the civil servant is defined in the terms used by the Tomlin Commission at the end of the 1920s, 'Servants of the Crown, other than holders of political or judicial offices, who are employed in a civil capacity and whose remuneration is paid wholly and directly out of moneys voted by Parliament.' An excellent discussion is in Sir Edward Bridges, 'Portrait of a Profession', pp. 3–6.

From this perspective strengthening PAR and the CPRS is far from a radical or anti-constitutional move.

The space we devoted earlier to PAR and CPRS is justified neither by their current eminence nor their guaranteed chances for survival. But the felt needs to which they respond – the needs for better and more responsive policies – should, we believe, become an increasing crucial part of British central government. The Keynesian revolution in economic thought has carried the day; economic management is 'in', it has been in for a generation, and above all, it has been in at the Treasury. The rules on when to spend and when to save are few and manageable. Ministers feel comfortable with them; they believe that using the guidelines of economic management expresses the Cabinet's contribution to macro-policies of economic stability, growth, and full employment. The same cannot be said for micro-policy dealing with decisions directed more narrowly toward health, transportation, and so on.

The present and growing danger is that macro-analysis of the economy is tending to overwhelm micro-analysis of policies, if only because so many political administrators feel more confident with the former than the latter. A nation spending so much of its total income on government endeavours cannot afford to have this situation continue. All net cash outflows are most assuredly not the same, not even when adjusted for resource impact, import substitution, and other refinements (incantations, if you prefer) of macro-economies. Few people today believe in the Gladstonian idea that 'all public expenditure is bad' and especially no one should believe it when the rider is added, 'except when the Treasury says it is good'. Up till now, the macro tail has wagged the micro dog; it is time that both acquired a place up front where the barking and gnashing of teeth take place.

With so much of the nation's labour and treasure disbursed by government, there is a persistent need to improve the quality and structure of advice on which substantive policies are based. And nowhere is this need greater than regarding advice to ministers as a group. The 'collective capability' of British government is not weak in the sense that individual ministers are deliberately sacrificing a view of the best general interest to their own departmental or personal interests. The collective interest is at a discount, not because it is deliberately disregarded, but because there is little chance for appreciating what it might be. The advisory servicing to ministers as a group – that is, the Government – is infinitely weaker than their servicing as department heads. Their collective interest need not be considered synonymous with a grand strategy or cosmic solutions unanimously agreed upon; indeed, we have argued that it should not be. A collective view can also arise from the competition rather than the harmony of ideas. Our objection to the existing structure of advice at the centre is that it is monopolistic rather than competitive, defaulted rather than disputed. Bringing out and settling disagreements among ministers is generally a more healthy way of finding a collective view than glossing over or neglecting the important issues at stake. Conflict is inevitable; badly supported positions less so. The need is not for unanimous agreement but for better argument.

The CPRS is supposed to help ministers do just that. At present it is a compromise between a partisan and civil service organisation, between a Prime Ministerial and departmental organisation, and between a civil service and a ministerial advisory group. The CPRS fudges all these issues. In doing so it is a typically British creation, but it is also an unduly weak growth. To be effective, it must have a political client. If it is not to be the Prime Minister alone, it must be the Cabinet.

On the assumption that the Cabinet is its client, strengthening the CPRS, or something like it, requires a larger organisation of analysts entirely outside the civil service, at the beck and call not merely of the Prime Minister but of each departmental minister as well. The CPRS might begin building a political clientele among ministers if it could brief them in private without their civil servants. Ministers might value a different opinion not only on issues outside, but also inside their department. This is not now done. Civil servants can be found co-ordinating their briefs to different ministers, but departmental ministers getting together to settle an issue between themselves before officials have tried to sort it out can expect strenuous objections from their officials. A CPRS-like advisory unit which briefs ministers in private can expect to be blasted as partisan, presumptuous, disrespectful and dangerous. But if they do not do it, the CPRS or its successors will revert to being simply more of the same.

Alternatively a unit like the CPRS might serve as partisan advisers to the Prime Minister. It could be argued that the unit would provide analyses on domestic issues that the Cabinet Office does not. But that rationale would not apply to the Treasury, which is supposed to give advice on the desirability of proposed expenditure to the Prime Minister. Constitutional lore has it that the Prime Minister is First Lord of the Treasury for whom all advice is meant, though he may not always choose to exercise that prerogative. Why is other advice necessary if the Treasury is already supplying it?

Yes, what about the Treasury's role? In the midst of a lecture on the Civil Service Department, its Permanent Secretary, Sir William Armstrong, drew attenion to the anomalous position of the Treasury (as whose Permanent Secretary he had recently served). 'It is noteworthy,' he wrote, 'that whereas the Cabinet secretariat are responsible to the Cabinet as a whole, and in particular to the Prime Minister, the people in the Treasury concerned with the control of expenditure function are brigaded with their other colleagues under the Chancellor of the Exchequer. Thereby hangs a tale which is of considerable interest, but which is so long that it would have to form the subject of a quite separate lecture.' [24] Regrettably, though understandably, that other lecture has never been given.

The essence of policy analysis in British government has always been financial administration. And the essence of financial administration has been to force taxation (economic management has subsumed taxation in the post-war era) and expenditure to compete with one another by making the same minister responsible for both. No doubt that was once true. No doubt it is still true if relating expenditure totals to perceived economic requirements is all we care about. But the proposition is misleading if it suggests that Chancellor and Treasury place equal weight on their dual functions. They do not by at least four to one. If a man's heart lies where he spends his time, Chancellors care far more about taxes and employment than they do about the content of most public policies. Their rewards and sanctions lie in how well the economy does and not in the effectiveness of governmental programmes. And what is true for the Chancellor must also obtain for the Permanent Secretary who wishes to serve him. The growth

24. Sir William Armstrong, 'The Civil Service Department and Its Tasks', in *Style in Administration*, ed. Richard A. Chapman and A. Dunsire (London: George Allen and Unwin for the Royal Institute of Public Administration, 1971), p. 323.

of the conglomerate departments only makes this macro-economic preoccupation all the more alluring in the Treasury. Instead of trying to get separate departments and their various heads competing against each other, the modern Treasury can now expect any one department to have a much wider range of expenditure to manipulate in order to get its money sums right. The relative ease of expecting offsetting savings from within huge department budgets only adds to the tendency to worry about economic trade-offs rather than policy analysis.

Now we can see what is at stake. It is so difficult to arrange an advisory apparatus for the Prime Minister and Cabinet because there is one that isn't quite one. Those who stand and wait on the Chancellor of the Exchequer may also serve the Prime Minister but they do not exactly work with him. Those who purport to give advice but do not constrain, by their very presence, those who would but cannot. The fact that the Treasury is ever so decent about it all just makes it more difficult to realise something is wrong.

The CPRS may not be much, but unless it or something like it succeeds in performing an analytic role at the centre of government, the Treasury will not long survive in its present form. Informed scepticism is not a substitute for sustained analysis. A policy of rule or ruin is dangerous but feasible; ruining others without ruling will not, in our opinion, prove a viable option. The Treasury must take its chances by becoming an analytic body in its own right; it cannot ultimately succeed by inhibiting others from offering advice, or by claiming that departmental efforts are a substitute for its own, or that its inspired guesswork, while it may be good enough for a Chancellor of the Exchequer who cares about other things, is really policy advice for the Prime Minister. The half-truth of the past – we in the Treasury manage the economy and hold down spending, you in the departments run your own affairs but recognise our indispensable part – will become less serviceable with the passage of time.

The other side of the situation is the way in which the Treasury has, in typical fits of indeliberation, been sidling into substantive policy analysis. Cabinet ministers and the Prime Minister are entitled to have more and better (or at least, responsive) advice. If they cannot or do not want to obtain it from outside government, it must come from inside the machine. The Treasury has recognised the need by trying to implement PAR. By what right is the economic manager/taxer/expenditure controller getting involved in the vital internal analyses of what a department ought to be doing and how? It is by right of conquest – conquest expressed not in terms of brute power but information and competence. The Treasury network reaches into all departments in a more thorough way than any other competitor. It takes a responsibility for the government as a whole and acts as if it were more than the repository of a single minister's domain, though he be as important a person as the Chancellor of the Exchequer normally is in the Government. Its Public Spending Group has, or could prepare if suitably reinforced, policy advice on the widest range of issues.

The conduct of substantive evaluation by the Treasury is fraught with difficulty. The creation of analytical staff would, of course, increase the size of the Spending Group. Easy contact among its members would perforce decrease. Far more significant would be the change in the fundamental rationale of the Treasury's control of expenditure. Relations with departments would grow more distant as the Treasury necessarily assumed more of an adversary role. In the end, we believe, the Treasury might end up knowing fewer secrets but more truths.

In time, people are likely to get used to the idea of the Chief Secretary, as in the last few years, carrying the view of Treasury/ PAR policy analysis in the Cabinet. Ordinarily the Chief Secretary has been too junior a man to carry the burden but a functional division of labour has grown up between his office and the more economic-management-minded Chancellors of the Exchequer. The line of duties extends from total economic policy, to public spending totals, to expenditure ceilings for departments, to allowances for individual programmes. We think it will be beneficial if the practice of breaking this continuum in about the middle continues to develop, with the Chancellor responsible for operating the Keynesian levers, a Chief Secretary in charge of substantive policy analysis and expenditure vetting, and ministers in the middle using analyses from Treasury, CPRS, and their own departments to fight for their allocations.

By this time the Treasury would become even more of an anomaly among departments than it is now. No other department would have two senior ministers. Once the status of the Chief

Secretary becomes elevated, there is less reason for him to defer to the Chancellor. Hence the idea is likely to grow of adding the Cabinet Office and Civil Service Department to the Chief Secretary's group to make, not a Prime Minister's Department, but a central Cabinet Department. This 'permanent' analytical staff would be joined by an outside advisory unit that changed with each Government and/or Prime Minister.

But all of this, or whatever happens, is a tale to be told by future intruders into the Executive community. In the meantime, the competition between the Treasury and the departments is good for both. So is Programme Analysis and Review. Departments should be encouraged to stretch their analytic reach. They will have more incentive to do so if they must compete with a strengthened Central Policy Review Staff and outside ministerial advisers. The enhanced respect for government that could come from motivating the major actors to perform better, and to be seen as responsive, is well worth the costs in terms of increased friction. Our contention is that a fair bit of civil service community can be afforded in return for an increased capacity for ministers to get independent advice.

The government of public money in Britain is not a game played out for its own sake, for one-upmanship or personal advancement, although all of this occurs. Political administrators are keenly aware that beyond any gamesmanship is the serious business of determining the amount and allocation of resources devoted to public purposes. They are worried about subject matter. Given varying departmental responsibilities, personalities, and circumstances, political administrators seek the best results in the lives of people. They are concerned men and women. But there is a connection between the games they play on the inside and the welfare of their clients on the outside. Political administrators are not supposed to care about everyone in general and no one in particular. Specific interests – the education of the young, the livelihood of farmers, the housing of the aged – are entrusted to them. If they do not articulate these interests within government, the faint voices from outside may get muffled or carried away by the din of daily business. Then the corridors of power will echo only to the official shuffling of feet and paper. If ministers and officials do not learn how to score in Whitehall, where the championship games are played, the people who depend on them will be shut out. To help others, British political administrators must also learn to help themselves.

Britain's governors care but they are not all-knowing. Hard work, conscientiousness and good intentions are not enough. Criss-crossing networks in the Executive community have produced some of that benign overlap and duplication in information necessary to reduce errors and avoid irreversible mistakes. With its fairly sharp boundaries in kinship and culture, however, theirs is a community more reliable about people inside than about policies linking insiders and outsiders.

No one knows the answers. Organisational form is a gross variable; there are always so many intervening factors in any situation that it is rarely possible to connect the effectiveness of a particular policy with a defect or virtue in the processing of information or juxtaposition of personnel. All the more reason that people should be freer to dispute the issues. The government community needs to be opened up so that outsiders and insiders have more in common – including an understanding of each other's problems. Making governors more responsive to those in whose name they govern is no once-and-for-all operation achieved by some bright new institutional structure or a one-shot importation of businessmen into the Whitehall village. Nor is much improvement likely to result from proclamations on the abstract desirability of altering general habits of mind or working relationships. Reforms depend not only on a bright idea, but on hard digging to find out what is going on and even harder insistence that these results be interpreted through the give and take of frank discussion. British political administration can hardly be said to be over-burdened with conflict. If a line has to be drawn at this point in time, it should move in the direction of more rather than less analysis, advice, and conflict.

Bibliography of Official Documents Cited in the Text

UNPUBLISHED CABINET AND TREASURY PAPERS

P.C.E.	37(10)	Cab.	23/90, 1937
C.P.	165(37)	Cab.	23/99, 1938
C.P.	256(37)	T.	172/1684, 1929
C.P.	7(38)	T.	171/287, 1931
C.P.	118(39)	T.	172/1790, 1932
Cab.	23/77, 1933	T.	171/315, 1934
Cab.	23/78, 1934	T.	171/317, 1934
Cab.	23/88, 1937	T.	175/114, 1939

PUBLIC EXPENDITURE COMMAND PAPERS

Cmnd.1432, *The Control of Public Expenditure*, 1961.

Cmnd.2235, *Public Expenditure in 1963–4 and 1967–8*, 1963.

Cmnd.2915, *Public Expenditure: Planning and Control*, 1966.

Cmnd.3515, *Public Expenditure in 1968–9 and 1969–70*, 1968.

Cmnd.3936, *Public Expenditure 1968–9 to 1970–1*, 1969.

Cmnd.4017, *Public Expenditure. A New Presentation*, 1969.

Cmnd.4234, *Public Expenditure 1968–9 to 1973–4*, 1969.

Cmnd.4515, *New Policies for Public Expenditure*, 1970.

Cmnd.4578, *Public Expenditure 1969–70 to 1974–5*, 1971.

Cmnd.4829, *Public Expenditure to 1975–6*, 1971.

Cmnd.5178, *Public Expendiuture to 1976–7*, 1972.

HOUSE OF COMMONS PAPERS

Select Committee on Income and Expenditure Report, vol. 5, 1828.

Sixth Report from the Select Committee on Estimates; together with the Minutes of Evidence taken before the Committee. (H.C. 254), 1957–8 session.

Fourth Report from the Select Committee on Procedure; (H.C.303), 1964–5 session.

First Report from the Select Committee on Procedure; together with proceedings and Minutes of Evidence. (H.C.410), 1968–9 session.

Expenditure Committee; (As is obvious from the text, we have found the evidence to the subcommittees an invaluable source of information. This is particularly true of all the work of the Public Expenditure (General) Sub-Committee and of other Sub-Committee hearings during the 1970–1 session. Subsequent work of the subject matter subcommittees during the 1971–2 session tended to drift into narrow byways almost indistinguishable from those followed by the old Estimates committees)

Second Report from the Expenditure Committee; together with the Minutes of Evidence taken before the Education and Arts Sub-Committee. (H.C.545), 1970–1 session.

Third Report from the Expenditure Committee; together with the Minutes of Evidence taken before the Public Expenditure (General) Sub-Committee. (H.C.549), 1970–1 session.

First Report from the Expenditure Committee; together with the Minutes of Evidence taken before the Environment and Home Office Sub-Committee. (H.C.47), 1971–2 session.

Third Report from the Expenditure Committee; together with the Minutes of Evidence taken before the Public Expenditure (General) Sub-Committee on 13 December 1971. (H.C.62), 1971–2 session.

Sixth Report from the Expenditure Committee; together with the Minutes of Evidence taken before the Trade and Industry Sub-Committee in sessions 1970–1 and 1971–2. (H.C.347), 1971–2 session.

Seventh Report from the Expenditure Committee; together with Minutes of Evidence taken before the Public Expenditure (General) Sub-Committee, 31 January–1 May 1972. (H.C.450), 1971–2 session.

Fifth Report from the Expenditure Committee; together with Minutes of Evidence taken before the Public Expenditure

(General) Sub-Committee, 24 January 1973. (H.C.149), 1972–3 session.

Eleventh Report from the Expenditure Committee; together with the Minutes of Evidence taken before the Public Expenditure (General) Sub-Committee, 13 June 1973. (H.C.398), 1972–3 session.

The following Minutes of Evidence were published but not yet assembled into single volumes while we were working:

Education and Arts, 29 November 1971–19 June 1972. (H.C.-39) 1971–2 session.

Employment and Social Services Sub-Committee, 17 March–26 October 1971. (H.C.323), 1970–1 session. (H.C.154), 1971–2 session.

Environment and Home Office Sub-Committee, 9 March–27 April 1971. (H.C.321), 1970–1 session. (H.C.107), 1971–2 session.

Public Expenditure (General) Sub-Committee, 23 May–27 June 1972. (H.C.281). 1971–2 session.

Steering Sub-Committee, 16 December 1971 and 27 January 1972. (H.C.147), 1971–2 session.

Trade and Industry Sub-Committee, 16 March–21 July 1971. (H.C.546), 1970–1 session; October 20–6 1971. (H.C.320), 1970–1 session; 17 November 1971–15 March 1972. (H.C.28), 1971–2 session.

Index

Anderson, Sir John, 305
Andrew, Sir Herbert, 140-1
Armstrong, Sir William, xiv-xv, 24, 203, 385

Baldwin, Peter, 229, 283
Balbour, Arthur (later Lord), 242
Baring, Sir Francis, 263
Barnes, Sir Denis, 224n.
Berger, Peter, 360
Blackstone, Sir William, 374
'Bounce', theory of, 93-4
Bridges, Sir Edward (later Lord), xiii, 39, 44, 55n., 81, 112, 112n., 118, 313, 345, 377
Brittan, Samuel, xiii, 160, 173
Brook, Sir Norman, 313
Businessmen: as advisers in government, 271-9, 297

Cabinet: meetings, 22, 188-97 passim, 311; minutes circulated, 133; composition, 134; bargaining in, 146, 148, 192-4; referral of issues from committees, 165; problem of understanding, 169-70; expenditure timetable, 171; scope for decision-making, 174-6, 381; uninterested in departmental detail, 184; ministerial appeals to, 187; deliberation on PAR, 295ff.; as CPRS client, 322-4; weakness of advice to, 383-4. See also Cabinet Government; Collective interest.
Cabinet committees, 85-6, 181-7, 209, 295, 297

Cabinet government: as federation of departments, xiv-xv; and Cabinet committees, 183; ministers' lack of time for, 186; and ministerial voting, 195; advice in, 268-71, 310-15, 381-9; number of departments, 300-1; and CPRS, 323-6; versus departmentalism, 341-2; and collective interest, 364-6; versus Prime Ministerial government, 367-9; future organisation of, 386-9
Cabinet Office, 6, 86-7, 272, 310-15, 383
Cabinet Secretary, 312-13
Calculations, 21-9, 61-8, 189, 351-2
Central capability unit, 272-3, 305-6, 383, 386-9. See also Central Policy Review Staff.
Central Policy Review Staff: mentioned, x, xvi, xvii, xix; relation to PAR and PESC, 197, 279, 285, 291, 330, 331; significance of, 265, 304-5; origins and rationale, 267-76 passim, 305, 306; staff characteristics, 306-7; difficulty of defining role, 307ff.; concern with strategy, 307-8, 334-5, 337-8, 362-3; and regular civil service, 308, 309-16, 332-3, 338-9; relations with Treasury, 310, 330-1, 332-3; dependence on ministers, 316, 321-6, 381, 384; Chequers meetings, 316, 336-8; topics for study, 317-20, 327-31; timing of

work, 320; and collective briefing, 323–4, 367, 386, 388; relations with departments, 326–33; early warning system, 328–9; and party programmes, 334–5; long-run thinking, 336; view of ministers, 336; constitutional status, 382; future prospects, 384–5

Chamberlain, Neville, 207n.

Chancellor of the Exchequer: use of economic crises, 31; and taxation, 77, 161; relations with Chief Secretary, 153–4, 191; general, 159ff.; as manager of the economy, 160, 176, 385; and Prime Minister, 161–2, 181–2; party differences in, 162–3; bargaining with spending ministers, 163ff., 177, 185; preparation for Cabinet, 171–81 *passim*

Chef de Cabinet system, 305, 377n.

Chesterfield, Lord, 242

Chief Secretary: origins of office, 151–2; relation to Chancellor, 153, 191; skills necessary for office, 155ff.; relation to officials, 158; and incrementalism, 158; bargaining in Cabinet, 191; participation in PAR, 295; possible future role, 387

Churchill, Sir Winston, 134, 159, 268, 269

Clarke, Sir Richard, 3, 22, 76, 96, 178–9, 203, 209, 240, 258–9, 344, 350–1

Civil servants: and minister-watching, 51–2, 131–2; mobility within civil service, 80–4, graph 81; in Cabinet Official committees, 85–6; policy role illustrated, 101; view of ministers, 130–1, 132–3, 226; briefing of minister, 138–41, 240; co-ordination among, 190, 375; relied on by businessmen advisers

in government, 273, 278; criticism of capabilities at government centre, 274; as policy analysts, 286–7, 382; and Central Policy Review Staff, 308, 309–16, 332–3, 338–9; ambiguous feelings toward their ability, 374–5; and James Tribunal of Inquiry, 378n. *See also* Community.

Civil Service Department: control of PAR, 277

Collective interest: meaning discussed, 323–4, 335, 364–6, 384

Committee of non-spending ministers, 184–7, 209, 372

Community, in British government: defined in relation to policy, xv–xvi, 365–6; size, 3, 4n., 7; formal organisation, 4; networks in, 6, 16–20, 85–7, 278, 312–13; physical location, 7–8; characteristics summarised, 36, 78, 373–4; in civil servants' relations with ministers, 131–2, 138–9; in relations among ministers, 164–5; as part of PESC process, 229–30, 241–2; in PAR analyses, 285–6; and CPRS needs, 320, 332–3; need to de-emphasise in favour of increased competition, 358–60, 365–6, 373ff., 388–9; and outside advisers, 370, 376–7

Competition, lack of: between departments, general, 95–7; from ministers' briefings, 138–9, 141; between ministers, 167, 186–7; with Treasury macro-economic views, 171, 355–6, 358–9; in Cabinet committees, 183–4; through PESC, 190, 227–9; in PAR process, 298, 299–300; aim of CPRS to counteract, 308; need to redress, 367, 373ff., 384, 388–9

Confidence, 14–21 *passim*. *See also* Trust.

Conglomerate departments, 97–8, 117, 126, 300, 342, 385–6

Constitution, British, 339–42

Contingency reserve, 72, 225–6

Co-ordination, 9, 18–20, 69–74, 375, 384

Costed options, 92, 259

CPRS, *see* Central Policy Review Staff

Crosland, Anthony, 133, 145

Crossman, Richard, 133, 242

Culture, political administrative: defined, 1. *See also* Community.

Deals: between Treasury and spending departments, 98–101, 347; between spending ministers and Chancellor, 136–7, 191–2; among spending ministers, 146–8, 167–9; illuminated in PESC, 239

Delegation from Treasury to spending departments, 104, 111–18, 301

Department of Economic Affairs, 209–10

Departments, spending: government as a federation of, xiv–xv; reputations, 17, 21, 64; alliances among, 96–7, 146–8; opposition to Treasury delegation, 115; internal financial arrangements, 119–20, 122, 232, 357; Cabinet lack of attention to, 184; and PAR, 284, 301; number of, 300–1; relation to CPRS, 326ff.; lack of competitive analysis vis-à-vis Treasury, 380–1. *See also* Treasury/department relations.

Devons, Ely, 348–9

Diamond, Jack (later Lord), 45, 151, 154, 213–14, 216

Disraeli, Benjamin (later Lord Beaconsfield), 182n., 343–4

Economic crisis, and expenditure cuts: general, 30, 30n., 162; in 1931, 192n.; in 1967, 194, 211–12, 254; in 1950s, 206–7

Economic management, and expenditure control: 31–2, 73–4, 77, 172–80, 204–5, 259–60, 383, 385

Embarrassment, importance of avoiding: 10, 15–16, 51–8 *passim*, 256

Esher, Lord, 305–6

Estimates, 108–9, 205–8, 226, 249–50

Expenditure process: schematised, 4–6; figure, 5; Cabinet timetable for, 171; PESC timetable, 200; as simplifier of calculations, 192

Expenditures: total, xi; functional distribution, figure, 24; margins for change in, 24–5, 226; annual percentage changes by programme, table, 28; general climate favouring, 29ff., 135; capital, 113, 358; and taxation, 77, 177–80, 245–6, 354; relation to GNP and productive potential, 173–5, 210–11, figure, 211; difficulty of interpreting percentage changes, 260

Farm Price Review, 183, 224

Finance officer, *see* Principal Finance Officer

Fisher, Sir Warren, 83, 118, 306, 345

Focal year, 213–14

Foot, Michael, 261

Forecasting: general, 173; GNP, 210–11; in PESC, 221–5, 240; and the long-run, 360–1

Fulton Report, 81n., 82, 266

Gladstone, William Ewart, 103, 161n., 293, 343

Goldman, Sir Samuel, xi, 21, 24, 43, 179, 202, 216, 256, 353–4

Hamilton, Sir George, 37

Heath, Edward: develops reform

proposals while in opposition, 270–1; quoted, 276–7, 310–11, 321, 336; support for PAR, 296, 298; support for CPRS, 322

Heath Government: 1970 cuts, 25; effect on expenditure climate, 31; composition, 134; and productive potential, 175; accepts PESC, 214; use of defence projections, 236; reforms in the machinery of central government, 271–340; contradictions in party programme, 334

Henley, Douglas, 189, 216, 226n.

House of Commons, *see* Parliament

Howell, David, 273, 306, 310

Hunt, John, 79, 284n., 356

Improvement factor, 99, 183, 219

Incrementalism: identified, 23–5; historical continuity, 26; unequal marginal changes, 27, table, 28; and expenditure climate, 34; in Chief Secretary's job, 158; as existing policy, 220; encouraged by PESC, 238–41, 352–3; importance to policy content, 352–3

James Tribunal of Inquiry, 378n.

Jay, Peter, 198, 251

Jenkins, Roy, 168–9

Jennings, Sir Ivor, xiiin., 26, 44, 78

Jones, Thomas, 269

Kinship, in political administration: defined, 1. *See also* Community; Civil servants, mobility.

Kogan, Maurice, 82

Lloyd George, 269, 305

Local authorities, 232–3, 334, 349–50

Long-run: ambiguity of term, 360–4

McConnell, G. H., 358

MacDougall, G. D. A., 310, 321

MacGregor, D. H., 344

Macmillan, Harold, 167–8

Macmillan, Maurice, 344

Meyjes, R. J., 276

Ministers, general: relations with civil servants, xiv, 20, 33, 130–1, 132, 341, 375–6; working hours, 22; as source of expenditure climate, 33; tenure, 130; private office, 132; sources of standing, 143; need for improving advice to, 270, 370, 376–7, 383–4; businessmen's views of, 273; and use of PAR, 289–90, 296–9, 302, 303; and CPRS, 316, 324, 335, 336–8; long-run calculations, 363; training in Parliament, 379–80. *See also* Cabinet, meetings.

Ministers, Spending: role as advocates, 20, 134–42 *passim*; relations with Principal Finance Officer, 119, 125; briefing, 138–42, 240; skills necessary for success, 142–50, 195–6; alliances among, 46–8, 167, 190, 239; use of Prime Minister, 149–51; appeals from Chief Secretary, 153–4; relations with Chancellor, 164–5; insist on right of appeal to Cabinet, 187; fighting as communication, 195; second thoughts on expenditure process, 197

Nationalised industries, 108, 231

Nigel, Richard Fitz, 37

Overspending, 107, 222

Padding expenditure requests, 44n., 89

PAR, *see* Programme Analysis and Review

Parties, 334, 335, 378–9. *See also* Heath Government, Wilson Government.

Parliament: as example of government community, 10–11; and ministerial embarrassment, 16, 51; Select Committee on Estimates of 1957–8, 208–9; indirect role in expenditure process, 244–5; historic role, 245–50; debate on PESC White Paper, 251, 254, 255; specialist committees, 252ff.; Select Committee on Expenditure, 253, 262, 354, 379–81; Executive withholding information from, 254–7; role dependent on Members' interest, 260–3, 381

Permanent secretaries: relations with Principal Finance Officers, 120, 124–5; views on reforming central government, 275–6; and use of PAR, 300

PESC, *see* Public Expenditure Survey

PFO, *see* Principal Finance Officer

Pitt, Terry, 326

Playfair, Sir Edward, 136

Pliatzky, Leo, 40, 76

Plowden Committee, 184–5, 198, 208–9

Policy: viewed in relation to government community, xv–xvi, 365–6, 383, 388; explanation of treatment in text, xx–xxi; effect on expenditure climate, 32–5; relation to expenditure, 87–8, 101, 102, 194, 264–5, 343–60 *passim*; and delegation, 114; lack of comparison in Cabinet, 188; definition in practice, 217–20, 345–6; M.P.s' view of relation to expenditure, 261–2; implications of meaning for interpretations of relative power, 373

Political administration: meaning, 2, 3; characteristics summarised, 36

Powell, Enoch, 261

Prime Minister: as spending ministers' ally, 149–51; and Chancellor of the Exchequer, 161–2, 181–2; historic role of advisers to, 268–70, 305–6; private office of, 312–13; as CPRS client, 322–4; power not a threat to Cabinet government, 341–2, 367–9; need for more active role in policy analysis, 367, 369–70

Principal Finance Officer: role in creating trust, 18–19; and deals with Treasury, 98; general, 118–29; and spending minister, 119, 125; relations with permanent secretary, 120, 124–5; skills necessary for success, 121–5; internal relations with spending divisions, 123, 232, 348, 357; corporate spirit emerges, 127; and PESC, 200, 232. *See also* Treasury/Spending department relations.

Private government: meaning, 2

Productive potential, 173–5

Programme Analysis and Review: introduced, xvii, xix, 197, 265; relation to PESC, 197, 242, 290–4, 351, 372; and Parliament, 255–6; origins of, 267–76 *passim*; struggle to control implementation, 276–7, 353; departures from founders' intentions, 280; PAR Committee of officials, 280; nature of analysis, 281–3, 288–9; clients for, 283–5; bargaining on, illustrated, 285–6; objectives of, 289–300 *passim*; deliberation process, 290, 297–300; topic selection, 290–6; and ministers, 296–9, 302, 303; and permanent secretaries, 300; use in Treasury, 301–2, 382, 386–7; CPRS participation, 330, 331; lack of fundamental questioning, 357; constitutional status, 382; need to develop further, 388

Programme structures, 272, 279, 359

Public Accounts Committee, 243, 249, 250, 263

Public Expenditure Survey: general significance, xvii, xix, 198; role as spending ceiling, 63–4, 107, 199–200, 230–5, 350–1; as part of governmental community, 79, 230, 241–2; effect on Treasury/ spending department relations, 79, 106, 109–10, 112; in Cabinet bargaining, 172–81, 188; relation to PAR, 197, 280, 290, 293–4; objectives of, 199–200, 207; official Committee, 199, 201; timetable, 200; White Papers, 200–1, 210, 215, 228; historical origins, 203, 207n., 349–50; changes from 'forward planning' to planning the path, 211, 213; and meaning of existing policy, 217–21; price basis for costing, 221–2; nature of projections, 222–5; failure to evoke competition, 227–9; and strategy of future savings, 235–8; and incrementalism, 238–42, 352–3; reasons for successful reform, 240, 371–2; and local authority spending, 349–50; and Parliament, 250–1; businessmen's views on, 272; relation to policy content, 345–58 *passim*; need to keep in Treasury, 382

Public Spending Group, section in the Treasury: size, 23; figure of organisation, 38; composition, 39; tenure of members, 65–6; meetings, 71–2; mobility of members, 82–4, table, 83; operation of PESC, 201ff., 372; proposals to split from Treasury, 273, 275–6, 306; gains control of PAR, 278, 279, 353; as central adviser, 386–7

Rate Support Grants, 350

Relative Price Effect, 96–7, 215

Resource Impact Effect, 215, 356

Revenues, *see* Taxation

Riddelsdell, Miss M., 224

Rothschild, Lord, 276, 279, 306, 308–9, 318, 325–6

Running tally, 72, 213

Salter, H. C., 225

Serpell, Sir David, 203

Sharpe, Baroness, 133

Shortfall, *see* underspending

Simon, Sir John, 198

Stevenson, Matthew, 203

Strategy: in expenditure bargaining, 88–98; in PESC, 235–42; as CPRS concern, 307–8; ambiguity of term, 361–3, 372; as society-wide process, 379

Suez crisis, 32

Supply debate, 243–4, 250

Targetry, 49, 91, 224–5

Taxation: relation to expenditure, 77, 177–80; and role of Parliament, 245–6; Treasury doctrine on, 354; and policy analysis, 385

Thatcher, Mrs M., 136, 237

Thorneycroft, Peter: resignation as Chancellor of the Exchequer, 31, 143n., 167–8

Transfers of authorised expenditure, 104, 108–11

Treasury: distinguished by sensitivity rather than power, xiv, 37; organisational chart, 38; political role, 39, 51–4, 113; norms, 40–61 *passim*; non-technical orientation, 44, 60, 100; views on economic growth, 48–9; internal communication and referral of issues, 54n., 55–6, 68–75; drafting ability, 58–60; use of sampling, 63; substantive policy views, 65, 67, 102–3, 353–5; unpopularity of, 77,

78n.; 'rationing approach', 77–8, 181, 189; concern for details, 79, 104–5, 111–17, 229–30; exchange of personnel with other departments, 82–4; role as 'longstop' for others, 115–17, 354–5; appointment of PFO, 120; officials' relation to Chief Secretary, 158; expenditure judgement in Cabinet, 171–81, 200; won over to PESC, 208; and Department of Economic Affairs, 209–10; view of PESC totals, 228–9; co-operation with Parliament, 247–9, 253, 254–5, 258; businessmen's views of, 272; need to reform role in policy analysis, 274, 350–1, 367, 385–8; and implementation of PAR, 277–84, 291, 300–2; relation to CPRS, 310, 330–1, 332–3; success in making policy relate to expenditure, 345; not too powerful, 380–1. *See also* Public Spending Group; Treasury/ Spending department relations.

Treasury/Spending department relations: networks of trust, 16–20; co-ordination of briefs to ministers, 19–20, 347–8; bargaining, general, 46, 88–103, 191; mutual needs, 75; during 1950s, 79; co-operation, 79–87; interchanges of personnel, 81–4; conflict inevitable, 87, 89; norms for, 94; deals, 98–101; centralisation of, 119–20; economic guidelines, 175–6; in PESC, 201, 229–30; negotiation

on PAR, 285–6, 301–2; example of concordant, 350–1; departments as weak partner, 380–1. *See also* Community.

Trend, Sir Burke, 313

Trust, in government community: meaning, 15; methods of creating between officials, 17–20; between officials and ministers, 20; as aid to calculation, 23, 61–3; role in arranging transfers, 110; in Principal Finance Officer's job, 121; between Treasury and M.P.s, 258; in PAR analysis, 285

Underspending 104, 105–8, 222

United States, comparison with Britain: size, 7; political processes, 8–12 *passim*; programme budgeting, 272, 274; Presidential and Prime Ministerial government, 368–9

Vickers, Sir Geoffrey, 347

Walker, Patrick Gordon, 190n.

Wigg, George (Lord), 267

Wilson, Harold, 21

Wilson Government: and productive potential, 175; economic crisis of 1967, 176, 194–5, 211–12, 254; concern for higher taxes, 178; establishes Department of Economic Affairs, 210; growth of expenditures during, 211; expected expenditure after 1970 election, 235; consultation with departments, 267